Like a Brother, Like a Lover

Georges-Michel Sarotte currently teaches English and American literature at the University of Paris, and has been a visiting professor at the University of Massachusetts at Boston.

Like a Brother, Like a Lover

Male Homosexuality in the American
Novel and Theater from Herman Melville to
James Baldwin by

Georges-Michel Sarotte

Translated from the French by Richard Miller

Anchor Press/Doubleday
Garden City, New York
1978

Like a Brother, Like a Lover was originally published in French as *Comme un frère, comme un amant* by Flammarion, © Flammarion, 1976.
The Anchor Press edition is the first publication in the English language.
Anchor Press edition: 1978

ISBN 0-385-12765-0
Library of Congress Catalog Card Number 77-80912
Copyright © 1978 by Doubleday & Company, Inc.
All Rights Reserved
Printed in the United States of America
First Edition

For Cyrille Arnavon with deep gratitude and affection

"I am in town for a few weeks but I return to Rye April 1st, and sooner or later to have you there . . . to put my arms around you and *make* you lean on me as on a brother and a lover. . . ."

(Letter from Henry James
to the sculptor Hendrik
Andersen)

Contents

Preface to the American Edition   ix

Introduction   xiii

Part I: A History

Chapter One–The Evolution of the American Sexual
       "Establishment"   3

Chapter Two–The Evolution of the Homosexual in the
       American Novel—Melville to Baldwin   12

Chapter Three–The Homosexual Character on the
       Stage   30

Part II: Four Archetypes of the Homosexual Couple

Chapter Four–Adolescents   37

Chapter Five–Teacher and Pupil   61

Chapter Six–The Captain and the Soldier   70

Chapter Seven–The White and the Black   92

Part III: Homosexuality and the Theater

Chapter Eight–Tennessee Williams: Theater as
       Psychotherapy   107

Chapter Nine–William Inge: "Homosexual Spite" in
    Action   121

Chapter Ten–Edward Albee: Homosexual Playwright
    in Spite of Himself   134

*Part IV: The Circumstances of the Homosexual as
    Reflected in the Novel and Theater*

Chapter Eleven–Small Town and Big City   153

Chapter Twelve–Three Categories of Homosexual   164

Chapter Thirteen–Between the American Woman
    and the American Virile Ideal   185

*Part V: Latent Homosexuality: Short of and Beyond True
    Heterosexuality*

Chapter Fourteen–Henry James: The Feminine
    Masochist Syndrome   197

Chapter Fifteen–Francis Scott Fitzgerald: Self-
    virilization and Its Failure   212

Chapter Sixteen–The Feminine-Masochist Tempera-
    ment in Certain Jewish Characters   229

Chapter Seventeen–Jack London: The Hypervirile
    Syndrome   240

Chapter Eighteen–Ernest Hemingway: The (Almost)
    Total Sublimation of the Homo-
    sexual Instinct   262

Chapter Nineteen–Norman Mailer: The Overt Latent
    Homosexual   279

Conclusion: Another Country   293

Bibliography   306

Index   328

Preface to the American Edition

It will perhaps seem strange that the first comprehensive, systematic analysis of male homosexuality in American theater and fiction has been written by a Frenchman. The present volume began as a doctoral dissertation (Doctorat d'Etat, Sorbonne, 1974); it was ruthlessly condensed and thoroughly revised for publication in France (1976), and is now being offered to the American public in English translation.

My long residence in the United States, my love for American literature, and a personal interest in depth psychology will explain this psychological investigation into the literature of another country. I am aware that some of my statements will perforce give rise to objections among certain "gay" and "straight" readers. The former will reproach me for not having supported their just demands with sufficient aggressiveness; the latter for having unduly tarnished the reputations of some of the immortal names in American letters. Some will tax me with defeatism and collaboration with the enemy; others will accuse me of annexationism when they read my sections on Jack London, Henry James, F. Scott Fitzgerald, and others.

To the former, I reply that, on the one hand, the present study aims at scientific objectivity and that, on the other hand, the homosexual condition in American society, until very recently—like that of blacks and, to a lesser degree, of women—could not help but give rise to frustration, despair, and *neurosis*. Could anyone be a well-adjusted homosexual in the United States of the 1950s?

How could one *become* homosexual in a country where the very word could not be pronounced,* where society as a whole, with its dictatorial and totalitarian policies, bent all its energies toward thwarting, from early childhood, the *natural* homosexual desire?

In order to grow and strengthen, this fundamental instinct had necessarily to make use of a fault in the family nucleus (the microcosm of society as a whole), to avail itself of a disturbed parental pattern. The homosexual adolescent's awareness of his peculiar nature, which placed him so clearly in opposition to the American virile ideal—of which heterosexuality was part and parcel—could only throw him into obsessive neurosis, fostered by his guilt complex, his fear of "exposure," and the feeling that he was monstrous. If the American black, considered as an outcast charged with every crime, as a stupid or a vicious animal, could take refuge in his family; if women, seen as castrating, socially inferior creatures, felt that they were nevertheless adored, desired, and indispensable to men's happiness, the homosexual had no such moral or social consolation. A masked, invisible man, he knew that he was a criminal *by nature,* the one who brings scandal upon his own family, who, although the very cause of his distress, would turn upon him as the most ruthless prosecutor.

Until very recently, the Western—and particularly the American—homosexual was cast as a neurotic in literature, assumed to be a reflection of society. Not even Daniel Curzon's *Something You Do in the Dark* (1971), a well-written, lucid, intelligent *and* militant novel, "whitewashes" the gay male. Curzon's "hero," Cole, described without complacency or self-pity, caught as he is between self-hatred and the unashamed affirmation of his identity, seems to me the faithful image of the American—the Western—homosexual of the 1970s. He is a creature in transition: still a prisoner of social taboos and fears, he resolutely looks toward the future, a future where bisexuality (more hetero or homo according to the individual) will be the rule. It is quite likely that the generations to come will possess a greater mental

* In *Sex and Personality,* Lewis M. Terman and Catharine Cox Miles noted, in 1936, that "homosexuality" was the most "electric" word in the English language, and "hardly mentionable."

equilibrium than homosexuals (or heterosexuals, for that matter) today enjoy, for homosexuality will no longer be synonymous with warped personality, with all the consequences for the ego that such warping entails.

It could be argued that the *bêtes noires* of militant homosexuals, Edmund Bergler and Irving Bieber, were right, until the late 1960s—as opposed to the stance Peter Fisher or Wainwright Churchill. For though Bergler's and Bieber's inquiries and surveys suggest disdain and hatred for homosexuals, they perfectly mirror the contemptible reality of the homosexual condition before the great years of the liberation of minorities in the United States. Yet it does not take much audacity to predict that young Americans under twenty years of age (or more safely still, the next generation), *informed* as they are of the diversity of human possibilities, will be able to choose knowingly, willingly, deliberately, and calmly the road they wish to follow. Kinsey was making a sweeping statement when he declared in 1948,

> Whatever factors are considered, it must not be forgotten that the basic phenomenon to be explained is an individual's preference for a partner of one sex, or for a partner of the other sex, or his acceptance of a partner of either sex. This problem is, after all, part of the broader problem of choices in general: the choice of the road that one takes, of the clothes that one wears, of the food that one eats, of the place in which one sleeps, and of the endless other things that one is constantly choosing. A choice of a partner in a sexual relation becomes more significant only because society demands that there be a particular choice in this matter, and does not so often dictate one's choice of food and of clothing.

Those were bold and comforting words, but partly wrong. It was not, in those days, a matter of conscious choice, but rather of mental *conditioning*, either by society or by the deviation of the parental pattern from the ideal model set up by society. The homosexual novelists and playwrights have felt this, in depicting characters and situations illustrating the conclusions of the "homoerotophobic" psychiatrists and psychoanalysts. But it is only fair to say that the homosexual militants were right to attack blindly, to "whiten" their world and "blacken" that of the enemy, since the forces were too unequal and the vicious circle had to be broken. In order to enlist all the support required, it was necessary for them to proclaim that their cause was the noblest, the purest, ever, that those who were not with them were against them. There was no room for the irresolute, the scrupulous, the supporters of scientific objectivity. It was held that homosexuals were *not* neurotic, despite American society's hairraising homophobia. To that society's thesis that homosexuality was evil was opposed the antithesis that "gay is good." The synthesis is in the making before our very eyes. Soon "gay" will be morally neutral, like "straight."

To those who will take me to task for drawing into my study a large number of major American writers (because of their latent or not-so-latent homosexuality), from Melville to Bellow, from London to Mailer, I reply that illustrious critics have preceded me in this interpretation of some aspects of these writers' personalities and works: D. H. Lawrence and Maxwell Geismar (to whom Leslie Fiedler is greatly indebted), Leslie Fiedler himself, Richard O'Connor, Leon Edel, Jean-Jacques Mayoux, Roger Asselineau, and many others. The homosexual motif that runs through Melville's or James's stories is no longer questioned by any serious critic. My objective has simply been to go deeper into these authors' lives and minds, and to do so in a systematic way, before drawing general conclusions.

Introduction

We can understand the term "homosexuality" in either a broad or a narrow sense. Broadly, it signifies an unconscious erotic attraction to a person of the same sex; taken narrowly, it means that sexual *contact* is *consciously* desired. Let us resist the temptation to include in this study all of the affectionate feelings two men can have for each other. Leslie Fiedler is mistaken, in my view, to employ the word "homosexuality" with regard to Nigger Jim and Huck Finn: friendship, companionship, affection, and tenderness are all present, but not sexual desire. The relationship between the protagonists of *Of Mice and Men*, affectionate as it is, is not homosexual, whereas the feelings between Bo Decker and Virgil in *Bus Stop* clearly seem sexual (as all of William Inge's dramatic work seems to demonstrate). Nor have we considered Oliver Wendell Holmes's *A Mortal Antipathy*, since the fear of women is not of necessity a "sexual deviation."

The list of books written about male homosexuality is enormous; from Sandor Ferenczi to C. A. Tripp, "homosexual desire" has been the subject of essays and psychoanalytical studies that attempt to define it. When the subject is examined closely enough to distinguish nuances and variations, however, we are forced to distinguish three varieties of homosexual desire, according to the varying degree to which it is repressed. Following the terminology of Ferenczi, I will employ the terms "homoeroticism," "homosexuality," and "homogenitalism." However, visible behind these three terms is the male *body*. Thus, for our purposes here, there can be neither homoeroticism, homosexuality, nor, a fortiori, homogenitalism, unless there is also a desire for *contact* with the *body* of another male. This desire may be unconscious on the author's part, or the character's, in which case we will use the term "homoeroticism." The typical Hemingway hero, overtly heterosexual as he may appear, is homoerotic, not homosexual: the hero's actions appear to reveal a desire for bodily contact, but behind this façade the male body itself is completely expurgated. In the work of London, on the other hand, his obsession with the male body indicates a clear *homosexuality*, which is never consummated, which never turns into *homogenitalism*. In his work, the "manifestation of repression"—to use Freudian terminology—is much more obvious than in Hemingway's, but never becomes open, never becomes "overt" homosexuality. Thus, the term "homogenitalism" will be employed when there is actual sexual contact, or coitus.

Briefly, then, when distinctions are necessary, I will reserve the term "homoeroticism" for that diffuse feeling in which are mingled the barely realized desire to make contact with the body of another male; "homosexuality" will signify that this desire is overt—either where, despite the author's interior censorship or that imposed by the morality of the period, everything indicates that it is an actual fact, or where the author himself clearly suggests it. For example, we can say that Jim, the protagonist of Gore Vidal's *The City and the Pillar*, has both homosexual and homogenital feelings and relations, whereas Brick Pollitt, the protagonist of *Cat on a Hot Tin Roof*, has had a clearly homoerotic relationship with Skipper, who, for his part, was an overt homosexual. Captain Vere and Claggart, in *Billy Budd*, are homosexually attracted to the handsome sailor, just as Captain Penderton is attracted to the soldier Williams. Similarly, Leon Edel believes that Henry James had homosexual feelings for Hendrik Andersen, the young, handsome Danish sculptor, but he cannot prove that their relationship was ever homogenital.

The following study will have a threefold purpose: psychoanalytic, sociological, and literary. It will call upon psychoanalysis in drawing conclusions about American society, but we will be viewing this through the perspective of the American novel and theater. It is to be hoped that this overall view—the first to be devoted to this subject—will throw a special, but revealing, light on the American novel and theater from Herman Melville to James Baldwin.

Like a Brother, Like a Lover

PART I

A History

No longer abash'd (for in this secluded spot I can respond as I
    would not dare elsewhere),
Strong upon me the life that does not exhibit itself, yet contains
    all the rest,
Resolv'd to sing no songs to-day but those of manly attachment,
Projecting them along that substantial life,
Bequeathing hence types of athletic love,
Afternoon this delicious Ninth-month in my forty-first year,
I proceed for all who are or have been young men,
To tell the secret of my nights and days,
To celebrate the need of comrades.

Walt Whitman, *Calamus*

Chapter One

The Evolution of the American Sexual "Establishment"

In 1890, the year in which his brother Henry wrote "The Pupil," William James, in his masterly work *The Principles of Psychology*, wrote that most men "very likely . . . possess the germinal possibility" of "unnatural vice." Of course, according to James, it was the inhibition of "the instinct of physical aversion toward a certain class of objects [those of our own sex]" in the "ancients" and in "modern Orientals" that accounts for the difference between them and modern Western man, not the inhibition of a homosexual instinct in the latter. However, preceding as it did Havelock Ellis and Freud, William James's affirmation of basic human bisexuality revealed exemplary courage and clear thinking. But the effect of such statements on the public as a whole was minimal; few were reading psychological works in 1890.

In 1897 the Englishman Havelock Ellis published the first volume of his *Studies in the Psychology of Sex* in London. One of the volumes in the series, *Sexual Inversion*, created a scandal in Great Britain which forced the publishers to cancel the press run of the book. This objective, scientific work was published in the United States beginning in 1901, but Ellis's influence was confined to medical and scientific audiences.

Freud was not invited to the United States for a series of lectures until 1909. In 1910 A. A. Brill translated *Three Contributions to a Theory of Sex*, a work in which Freud affirmed basic human bisexuality and—like James—stressed the influence of society and civilization on the unilateral development of sexuality.

However, according to H. M. Ruitenbeek, the author of *Freud and America*, Freud's lectures "aroused no widespread popular attention," and "at first, only a few physicians and psychologists were interested" in the translation of *Three Contributions*.* Only after World War I did psychoanalysis become available to the American mind, but there was still no thought—far from it—of questioning sexual dichotomy.

In 1936 Lewis M. Terman and Catharine Cox Miles, notwithstanding their professed desire for objectivity and tolerance, lent their scientific support to American prejudices in their book *Sex and Personality: Studies in Masculinity and Femininity*. According to them, the most masculine men in America are engineers and architects, the most feminine are artists. Professors fall somewhere in the middle. The biggest surprise, and one which the authors were hard put to explain, was the discovery that policemen and firemen were at the bottom of the virility scale.

Terman and Miles, for the purpose of questioning them, cited Margaret Mead's statements concerning the malleability of sexual behavior. In 1949 the American anthropologist published *Male and Female*, in which she set forth her theories again and applied them to American society. Mead explained that American culture had fixed once and for all the physical appearance and desirable character traits of males. The boy who finds that he is not meeting the requisite conditions "may give up altogether"; that is, he may renounce virility and take refuge in sexual inversion. "The little rabbity man who would have been so gently fierce and definitively masculine in a culture that recognized him as fully male" thus attaches himself to a male who "possesses the magnificent qualities" he himself lacks. According to Mead, the American male must avoid an interest in music, painting, poetry—professionally, at any rate. He must earn a great deal of money, advance in his work, have a wife and children.

In 1942 Philip Wylie produced a widely read book, *A Generation of Vipers*, in which he made some intelligent comments about homosexuality. He condemned "male ignoramuses" "who

---

* Freud's influence on the public at large, and on American literature, has been traced by F. J. Hoffman in *Freudianism and the Literary Mind* (1945).

stand ready to slug nances on sight," noted that "discreet surveys" had revealed a considerable number of homosexual relationships in the American upper and middle classes, and went on
to say that the other social classes were beginning to follow suit.
He regarded the homosexuality latent in every man as a basis for
making psychological projections which could lead to an understanding of the opposite sex.

Chapter 21 of Kinsey's *Sexual Behavior in the Human Male*
(1948) is wholly devoted to homosexuality. Kinsey and his col-
laborators remind us that the Jewish and Christian religions
consider homosexuality an abnormality, and that in 1948 Anglo-
American laws were extremely strict with regard to this facet of
human sexuality. Yet, they continue: "37 per cent of the total
male population has at least some overt homosexual experience
to the point of orgasm between adolescence and old age." They
reveal that "in certain of the most remote rural areas there is
considerable homosexual activity among lumbermen, cattlemen,
prospectors, miners, hunters, and others engaged in out-of-door
occupations." These men are very virile and *also* homosexual: "It
is the type of homosexual experience which the explorer and pioneer may have had in their histories." Kinsey and his group
adopt the "continuum" theory and refute the prevailing masculine-feminine, homo-heterosexual dichotomy. Their impressive
documentation leads them to conclude that "only 50 per cent of
the population is exclusively heterosexual throughout its adult
life."

Edmund Bergler was the leader of the attack on the Kinsey
Report. In 1948 he published an article in *Psychiatric Quarterly*,
entitled "The Myth of a New National Disease." He returned to
the arguments of this article in 1957, and set them out in a famous book, *Homosexuality: Disease or Way of Life?* Bergler's article and book are written in so violent and passionate a tone,
and they reflect such contempt and hatred toward homosexuals,
that it is almost impossible to imagine him "curing" any of his so-
called patients. According to him, "Homosexuals are essentially
disagreeable people, regardless of their pleasant or unpleasant
outward manner. . . . they are subservient when confronted
with a stronger person, merciless when in power, unscrupulous
upon trampling on a weaker person." Obviously, Bergler is

anathema to militant homosexuals, a distinction he shares with Irving Bieber.

Against the backdrop of American reality, it is not hard to imagine the problems of the American homosexual. If the musician, the painter, the sensitive person, is constantly required to fight against public opinion, what must life be like for the overt homosexual?

Donald Webster Cory attempted to explore this question in *The Homosexual in America: A Subjective Approach,* published in 1951. In his view, the American homosexual is continually being forced to wear a mask, to conceal himself from his family, from those whom he most loves—and who love him, without recognizing his real personality. The author gives a list of rights of which (in 1951) homosexuals were deprived, notably, "all government benefits under the G.I. Bill of Rights." Yet in no state does the penal code contain the word "homosexuality." The word is replaced by such terms as "crime against nature," "sodomy," "sex perversions," "buggery," and so on. In New Hampshire and Vermont the law speaks of "lewdness." In Georgia, one risks life imprisonment for committing sodomy. Cory ends by urging the homosexual of 1951 to revolt, calling upon him to stand forth and claim his rights. Yet he is aware of the vicious circle in which the 1950s American homosexual is caught: if he does not come out into the open, he will never bring about a change in his legal status, but if he does, he is certain to become a martyr to the cause. As Gide wrote in *Corydon:* "Oh, victims! Victims as many as you please. But not a single martyr. They all deny it; they always will deny it." The homosexual liberation movement of the late 1960s, assisted by the liberation movements of blacks and of women, has broken down this barrier.

Wilhelm Reich, whose theories shook the foundations of the Establishment, considered homosexuality to be a neurosis society must tolerate, since a repressive society has created it: "It can be reduced only by establishing all necessary prerequisites for a natural love life among the masses." (Cf. *The Sexual Revolution: Toward a Self-Governing Character Structure* [1930].)

However, Reich's impact was less positive than that of Herbert Marcuse, also German born, and, like Reich, strongly influenced by Marxism. Marcuse's influence on American youth in the 1960s was considerable: he is said to be in part responsible for the student unrest in the latter part of that decade. Where the liberation of instincts and the breakdown of sexual categories is concerned, he attempts to set up the bases for a society free from taboos with regard to "perversions," one in which the Reality Principle will cease to be the all-powerful despot ruling over and reining in our instincts. "Beyond the Reality Principle" there is room for a leisure society in which the distinction drawn between Agape and Eros will, as Plato predicted, become nugatory. The author of *The One-Dimensional Man* refutes the Freudian theses according to which every civilization worthy of the name is, by its very nature, against the "Id."

In his book *Life Against Death*, Norman O. Brown joined Marcuse in stating that "as long as the structure of the ego is Apollonian, Dionysian experience can only be bought at the price of ego breakdown. Nor can the issue be resolved by a 'synthesis' of the Apollonian and the Dionysian; the problem is the construction of a Dionysian ego." Citing in support of his argument Thoreau and his search for "a purely sensuous life," Brown states that the human body will become polymorphous perverse and that it will delight "in that full life of all the body which it now fears." In his attempt to reconcile the life of the body with that of the spirit, he evokes Oriental and Occidental mysticism, psychoanalysis, and modern poetry. Everything tends to prove the "fundamentally bisexual character of human nature."

For some twenty years the novelist Gore Vidal has fought a campaign for sexual tolerance. His two principal arguments are, on the one hand, that law, which has ceased to be the secular arm of the church, ought no longer to be based on the Bible, and, on the other, that man is basically bisexual. In his novels and essays, on the radio and on television, and in various magazines, the author of *The City and the Pillar* has set himself up as the poet of sexual tolerance and, above all, of homosexuality, in an already overpopulated world. His efforts—joined with those of some philosophers, psychologists, psychiatrists, churchmen, and legal figures—have succeeded in shaking the foundations of the heterosexual establishment. Vance Packard, for example, investigating the youth of the 1960s, emphasizes the fragility of traditional sexual categories. The author of *The Sexual Wilderness* does not believe that this encourages homosexuality; homosexuality is merely more visible than it formerly was. Paul Goodman was another prophet of the new sexual identity. However, this Reichian disciple, a self-proclaimed bisexual, was extravagant to the point that his iconoclastic statements missed their intended audience. The poet Allen Ginsberg has also haunted the outskirts of sexual liberation for many years, and openly practices what he preaches.

Thanks to the wide rifts opened in the American heterosexual Establishment, homosexuals, beginning in the 1950s, have become organized, and have made their voices heard. Impetus was given to the homophile movement by the Kinsey Report, Donald W. Cory's book, and reaction to the McCarthy witch hunts. The role played by homosexual societies in the 1950s (the Mattachine Society, among others) consisted mainly in counseling homosexuals and providing them with lawyers, doctors, psychiatrists, or ministers; these groups were careful not to confront American society head on. By 1968 there were more than forty such "homophile" societies scattered across the United States.

In 1961, however, the Mattachine Society of Washington was founded and began to take the offensive, organizing demonstrations and "picketings," giving press conferences, and rendering ineffective the argument that homosexuals are peculiarly subject to blackmail, by becoming open and overt. This sort of activism was helped by the attitude and positions adopted by some well-known sociologists, including Evelyn Hooker, who in 1968 was the chairman of the Committee on Homosexuality of the National Institute of Mental Health. The conclusion of the committee's report stated that homosexuality was neither a disease nor a behavioral anomaly. In 1974 the American Psychiatric Association, under heavy pressure from militant homosexual organizations, removed homosexuality from its list of mental illnesses. In the 1970s the aim of homosexual organizations has been to obtain equal rights for homosexuals. Their slogan, "Gay Is Good," is also the theme of many books dealing with the history of the homophile movement (cf., among others, *The Gay Mystique,* by Peter Fisher, and *Introduction to the Homophile Movement,* by Foster Gunnison). But despite these advances, homophile literature gives one the impression that the American sexual Establishment has barely changed since the appearance of Cory's book, or since the "Stonewall Rebellion," when the police who had arrived to close a Greenwich Village bar were greeted with a hail of stones and other missiles. (Since then, New York's homosexual population has commemorated the event with a huge annual parade along the main streets of Manhattan, ending in a mass rally in Central Park. Similar demonstrations are held in every large American city.) Today, the Gay Activists Alliance employs the tactics of direct confrontation, attempting to play a direct part in the country's politics by putting pressure on candidates for public office. During the 1972 Democratic Convention, and again in 1976, homophile groups were highly visible.

Both Catholic and Protestant churches have traditionally been the sworn enemies of the homosexual. They have succeeded in enforcing their condemnation of "unnatural" practices by quoting the Bible, both the New and the Old Testaments. Derrick S. Bailey refutes many of these arguments in *Homosexuality and the Western Christian Tradition;* and D. J. West, in *Homosexuality,* traces the development of the biblical attitude toward homosexuality. The law and the church are intimately joined at their base. Brought to the United States and incorporated into the civil code, this Christian morality has been translated into a whole series of penalties ranging—according to the state—from a fine up to life imprisonment.

For several years now, however, the church and the law have both been changing. Many churchmen, (Helmut Thielicke, Neal Secor, Ralph W. Weltge, etc.) now tolerate or defend homosexuality. In the New York *Times* of November 19, 1967, ninety Episcopal priests published a statement in which they affirmed, among other things, that "a homosexual relationship between two consenting adults should be judged by the same criteria as a heterosexual marriage; that is, whether it is intended to foster a permanent relationship of love." In every large American city there are today churches whose parishioners are for the most part homosexual. In San Francisco, for example, the Reverend Troy Perry, author of *The Lord Is My Shepherd and He Knows I'm Gay,* blesses homosexual unions. Although all of this activity is still only sporadic and timid, the press, the radio, and television are giving increasing coverage to this new attitude prevalent in some sectors of the church.

In 1951 Judge Morris Ploscowe, in *Sex and the Law*, demonstrated why "sodomy laws" were ridiculous and unenforceable. Many members of the legal profession have since joined him (Lewis I. Maddocks, Gilbert M. Cantor, etc.), and have shown the extent to which such laws do more harm than good. In 1961 Illinois became the first state to repeal its "sodomy laws." Since 1969 a number of other states have followed suit.

Two special cases that reveal better than any other American intolerance toward homosexuality are the Army and the federal government. The Armed Forces exclude homosexuals from their ranks. Until 1973, when President Nixon put an end to the draft, the homosexual who openly admitted his sexual preference when drafted was rejected for the service and risked having considerable difficulty afterward in finding a job. Likewise the government would not employ homosexuals on the grounds that they were vulnerable to blackmail; they were deemed to be "security risks." (Homosexual organizations have for years demonstrated that blackmail is the result of "sodomy laws.") It is well-known that Senator Joseph McCarthy had hundreds of homosexuals or purported homosexuals fired from federal jobs; in most instances the fear of scandal kept such persons from appealing their cases.

In the summer of 1975 American newspapers, radio, and television were reporting the case of Sergeant Leonard Matlovitch, a decorated Viet Nam veteran, who was expelled from the Air Force for announcing publicly that he was homosexual. When he decided to appeal his case to the Supreme Court, a *Time* magazine cover story (September 8, 1975) reported on the situation. The article noted that no one any longer believes that homosexuality exists only among interior decorators, dress-designers, actors, and ballet dancers. Everyone knows that it is present among bankers, lawyers, architects, and businessmen, some of whom are married men with children. *Time* noted that some fifty universities are offering courses in homosexual psychology, sociology, and literature, and that eight hundred homosexual groups are spread across the United States; the biweekly homosexual newspaper *The Advocate* has a 60,000-copy circulation, and the National Gay Task Force has some 2,200 members.

In addition, some large businesses, such as AT&T, the Bank of America, IBM, Honeywell, and NBC Television, now recruit personnel without distinction as to sexual preference. However, although one or two politicians are declared homosexuals, in nearly all states homosexuals still find themselves refused apartments or jobs. Even *Time* concluded its article somewhat ambiguously by quoting a psychoanalyst's negative viewpoint: "This is a society that is increasingly denying its impotence by calling it tolerance, preaching resignation and naming all this progress."

Thus, the American homosexual moves within a very small area, but is a continual threat to the American virile ideal. The prototypical nonconformist—since all of American society holds to this virile ideal that shuts out the sensitive, artistic, "feminine" man—he continues to confront the supporters of the status quo, and to suffer from the prejudices that are anchored in the American mind, upheld by the country's legal and moral underpinnings, which, although somewhat weakened by the younger generation, are still far from crumbling.

Chapter Two

The Evolution of the Homosexual in the American Novel—Melville to Baldwin

The Nineteenth Century

Melville, whose work—as we shall see in a later chapter—is in many ways homosexual, is essential to any discussion of the homosexual in the American novel before the 1940s. In *White-Jacket* (1850), he writes of the relationship of a young midshipman and his older partner: "The story itself cannot here be related," writes Melville; "it would not well bear recital." The sailor is a "forlorn, broken-down, miserable object, truly." The midshipman has the sailor flogged sadistically after having divulged in "undignified familiarities" with him. It is not the first time this has happened: other sailors have already had to put up with his "capricious preferences." The sailor and the midshipman are both faceless, nameless characters; they remain abstractions, principles of evil that must be muffled in a special vocabulary, an alembicated syntax, full of distancing negations.

The work of Henry James, to whom we will devote a later chapter, contains many "homosexual" figures. We can find them in "A Light Man" (1869), in "Collaboration" (1892), and in "The Pupil" (1890), to which we will return. In all these stories, however, "homosexuality" is always camouflaged as paternal, fraternal, or friendly affection. In *The Turn of the Screw* (1898), however, it is clear that James wishes us to understand that the valet, Peter Quint, has initiated the pretty little Miles, who, in his turn, initiates his comrades, those he "likes," since he "wants his own sort." Recalling Melville in his use of veiled, quickly stifled revelations, which are then returned to, and in his use of *double entendres* clearly indicating sexual brutality, James plays throughout the story with the reader's imagination. Although he has a name, Peter Quint, the adult homosexual is only a ghost (does the governess truly see him, even though he is dead before her arrival at the house?), a spirit of evil attacking an attractive child. And little Miles's homosexuality perishes in the arms of the governess. Homosexuality, therefore, can be concealed within an "innocent paradise full of furtive pleasures," as Baudelaire wrote of childhood. Miles will never become Peter Quint.

Allan Dale (the pseudonym of Alfred Cohen) published a novel entitled *A Marriage Below Zero* in New York in 1889. It is almost unbelievable that such a novel could have been published there, and at that time. The narrator is a young English girl of high social standing, naïve and shy. She marries Arthur, a very handsome—too handsome—young man, who is always in the company of a man older than himself, Captain Dillington. Everyone gossips about the two "friends," but the girl (who reports everything objectively) remains ignorant of their relationship for more than three hundred pages (despite an astonishing number of revealing incidents, obvious situations, hints)! Arthur, who is detested by "real men," who is very gentle—too gentle—with his wife (whom he treats like a sister: their marriage is never consummated), moves inexorably toward suicide after his lover's arrest. This novel, which is set in England, the United States, and France, is a masterpiece of restraint, of "behaviorist" technique, of dramatic irony; the narrator's naïveté serves as impetus for the plot. However, and this was a *sine qua non* for the publication of such a work in the nineteenth century, the two homosexuals are stereotypes: the handsome, effeminate young man, timid and passive, on the one hand, and the adult man, diabolically ugly, a "salon" Mephistopheles, on the other.

In 1906 the American writer Xavier Mayne (the pseudonym of Edward Irenaeus Prime Stevenson) published *Imre: a Memorandum*, in Naples. The tone of this novel is entirely different from Dale's: it is a blatant, overt glorification of the English narrator's homosexual love affair with a Hungarian lieutenant, the mag-

nificent Imre, an incarnate dream who is possessed of every
physical and moral virtue. Here we have a defense and an illustration of virile homosexuality, inspired both by antiquity and
by the philosophy of Edward Carpenter: the ideal of purity, of
complete virility, of loyalty toward the beloved, etc. The narrative traces the inner sufferings of the two men before their ultimate acceptance of amorous ecstasy: they live happily ever
after! However, note should be taken of all the protective devices adopted by the author: private European publication, European protagonists, a contempt for effeminacy, long suffering
before acknowledging one's true nature, a union that is primarily
sentimental. And even hidden behind his pseudonym, the American author claims to be merely the "editor" of these memoirs.

World War I

"Hands," the first story in *Winesburg, Ohio* (1919), by Sherwood Anderson, has as its theme the physical contact between a
young teacher and his students. This physical contact—hands
caressing children's shoulders and hair—occurs between a man/
woman, a kind of poignant androgyne, and very young boys.
Homoerotic relations between men and men were not offered the
reader at the turn of the century; however, in light of the other
stories in the collection, it is evident that Anderson is demanding
a liberation from accepted morality, a relaxing of repressive society.

In the same year Henry Blake Fuller, in *Bertram Cope's Year*,
described three homosexual types. Basil Randolph is a repressed homosexual who sublimates his love for young men in a
generalized love for youth itself; Arthur Lemoyne is the prototype of the effeminate homosexual, mannered, selfish, liking to
dress as a woman; but Bertram Cope himself, a young university
professor, is the first likable homosexual in American literature.
He is charming, and attractive with a typical Anglo-Saxon handsomeness. Fuller describes the life of the Arthur-Bertram couple
by means of a "behaviorist" technique that suggests without
being explicit. It is up to the reader alone to draw conclusions by
reading between the lines to detect the revelatory objects, gestures, and words. In *The Devils and Canon Barham* Edmund

Wilson reports that the author's friends were greatly shocked and that poor Fuller "disparaged his own courage by saying that he wished he had never written it, and he burned up his manuscripts and proofs. It was ten years before he ventured to publish another novel."

A parable related in the first part of Waldo Frank's novel *The Dark Mother* (1920) appears to be a parable of homosexual acceptance, seen as a perfect fusion of friendship with a man and love for a woman. In order that the parable's hero understand this, a vision of an otherworldly being is necessary, an angel seen in a dream, and a cry from this creature "half known to himself": "Make one my friend and my lover!" The dream had already been used by Sherwood Anderson, whose young teacher's caresses in "Hands" made his pupils "dream" of a future society in which the American male would enjoy a less rigid personality. Between the American parable and American reality, however, there was a yawning abyss in 1920: David, the mother-fixated adolescent, and Tom, the evil and sadomasochistic lawyer, mutually destroy one another and separate after a homoerotic relationship that never becomes homosexual. In Frank's next novel, *The Death and Birth of David Markand,* David is little more than a walking corpse without any purpose in his life, and Tom, the prototype for a whole series of satanic homosexuals— even more so than Captain Dillington in *A Marriage Below Zero* —continues to be the incarnation of irresistible—yet resisted— temptation.

The Great American Novelists (1925–38)

In the work of Ernest Hemingway, the first homoerotic figures appear in "The Battler" (1925), which offers us a physically and mentally broken character (like Melville's sailor and black servant (as in James), a subhuman, who is a foil to the healthy youth of the vigorous Nick Adams. In 1927 the short story "A Simple Enquiry" presents an Italian officer, effeminate, timid, and ashamed of his inclinations, who attempts to seduce a young soldier. *To Have and Have Not* (1937) devotes several pages to two rich outcasts, the Harvard-trained composer Wallace John-

ston and his "heterosexual" gigolo, Henry Carpenter, whose later
suicide is inevitable. Homosexuality is the final stage in his
downfall, occurring just before his death. The relationship between the two men is marked by a barely concealed hatred and
by the insults they continually exchange. Other homosexual
figures in Hemingway's work include the effeminate cook in "The
Light of the World" (1938) and the Mexican bullfighter in "The
Mother of a Queen" (1933). The cook makes veiled advances to
the narrator and his friend Tom—adolescents who are healthy
in both mind and body and who reject him contemptuously.
As in "The Battler," the homosexual is one of the unpleasant facts
of life. As for the bullfighter, he is a hateful and heartless creature. It should also be noted that Hemingway, the great admirer
of Spanish *machismo*, the bullfighting expert, makes his bullfighter a Mexican.

The *Notebooks* of F. Scott Fitzgerald contain many comments
to indicate that Hemingway's friend had nothing but contempt
for overt homosexuals. In *Tender Is the Night* (1934) homosexuals are men/women, "pansies," "fairies": Dumphry and Campion are, of course, members of a socially outcast group that sur-
rounds the McKiscos. They are cowardly, outlandish; they are
subhumans to be ridiculed, since laughter dehumanizes and
creates the required distance. In the last third of the novel a
young Chilean noble named Francisco makes an episodic appearance. He is handsome, lively, and charming. Through the eyes of
the psychiatrist Dick Diver, we no longer see a "pansy" but a
"homosexual." (The word occurs in the context of a medical con-
sultation.) However, his diagnosis prefigures that of Edmund
Bergler: homosexuality, an obsessional neurosis, saps the energy
that should be turned to social activities. Preceding the definitive
version of *Tender Is the Night* by some years, "The World's
Fair" and the *Notebooks* contain a description of a homosexual
bar that was not incorporated into the 1934 version. The "boys"
are pitiful, horrible creatures; some are handsome but stupid;
others seem to have a kind of nobility, but this suddenly dis-
solves into "girlish fatuity." Their confrontation with such a degenerate milieu fills the novel's characters—as in Hemingway—
with an irresistible desire to escape.

In "A Casual Incident" (1931) James T. Farrell describes the advances made by a "masculine" Pole, a deep-voiced giant of a man, to a twenty-year-old boy. The Pole's lisp and his habit of pursing his lips quickly destroy our initial impression of masculine strength. Farrell's young man, like those of Hemingway, shuns this incarnation of evil. In his introduction to the 1938 Modern Library edition of *Studs Lonigan*, Farrell reminds us that in his early stories his characters were "boys' gangs, drunkards, Negroes . . . homosexuals, immigrants . . ."—in short, social outcasts.

To the young Irish hero of the trilogy *Studs Lonigan* (1932–34) the homosexual appears as a gross, fat adult. Leon, a music teacher, has the pendulous breasts of a woman, oily smooth skin, and the thick, sensual lips of a lascivious gypsy. A final touch that irrevocably casts Leon out of Studs' narrow world: "His nose [was] Jewish." When Leon places his hand on the boy's shoulder, Studs "felt as if he needed a bath." In the second volume of the trilogy, Studs allows himself to be accosted by three vulgar, mincing queens; for a second, he is tempted to try it, "out of curiosity," but a rush of "self-disgust rose, changing his mind." In *Studs Lonigan* the portrait of the homosexual is colored by the obsessive desire of Studs, an anti-hero, to be a hero.

In *Of Time and the River* (1935) Thomas Wolfe creates in Francis Starwick a charming homosexual, but with the maleficent charm of a living corpse. Although Starwick, a young and brilliant drama professor at Harvard, helps Eugene Gant, the provincial, innocent student, to discover friendship, the joy of living, and the beauty in the world, the author alerts us: a "tragic fatality" hangs over Eugene's "friend, his brother—and his mortal enemy." Over six hundred pages later, having become debauched and dissolute, the brilliant professor moves to be a "fairy." Far from America, in Paris, sexual debauchery has turned him into a "living corpse." Now the poison that was once taken with such pleasure must be got rid of: having unmasked the imposter, Eugene, in a "lust to kill," beats up his former idol. The language of this scene clearly reveals the orgasm of hatred that seizes Eugene, and that it is also an orgasm of love. The embrace has occurred, but the spirit and morality have triumphed.

In *Main Street* (1920) Sinclair Lewis defends the effeminate

young Erik Valborg, but in Raymond Wutherspoon, an intran-
sigent Puritan and probably a repressed homosexual, he allows
us to glimpse the yearnings for revenge that weakness can conceal. In *It Can't Happen Here* (1935) Clarence's softness, his
yellow undergarments, are in no way prejudicial to his sexual
preferences, whereas the villains in the novel are horrible, sadomasochistic, homosexual brutes. Homosexuality is regarded as
one of the vices inherent in fascism—a ridiculous vice, a dangerous vice.

The Big Money (1936), by John Dos Passos, contains several
homosexual characters: Tony Garrido, the young and handsome
Cuban who is a lazy, syphilitic thief; his mentor, a fat, baby-
faced Cuban; his lover, a "greasy looking, blackhaired" hotel
bellhop; Max Hirsch, the sadistic Austrian count who kills Tony
in the course of a wild night on the town with some sailors;
O'Donnel, the Irish archimandrite; Gloria Swanson, the black
"fairy"; and Florence, a tall, husky black.

As for minor novelists, back in 1931, a woman, Blair Niles,
published a sympathetic story, more a psychosociological investigation than a novel, on the condition of the homosexual in the
United States. *Strange Brother* explores a whole gamut of the
American homosexual life styles, from transvestite to well-
adjusted male, white and black. Niles analyzes the homosexual's
relationship with his society (courts, prison, small towns and big
cities), his psychological history from childhood to adulthood.
She paints a complete picture of homosexual life: the public
search for a partner, reading material (Whitman, Carpenter,
scientific studies), solitude, sadness, the guilt complex that leads
to the suicide of the protagonist, Mark, when he falls victim to a
blackmail attempt. Finally, preceding Charles Jackson, Carson
McCullers, John Horne Burns, and Alfred Kinsey, Blair Niles
speaks of the *continuum* of human sexuality and preaches tolerance and compassion.

A minor novel by James Cain, *Serenade* (1937), depicts a
"straight" male who has a homosexual experience with composer
Winston Hawes, the novel's evil and effeminate villain. Jack
Sharp admits to his illiterate Mexican mistress his five per cent
homosexuality, which exists in every man! In Elliott Paul's novel
Concert Pitch, published the following year, the novelist charac-

terizes Robert Maura, a pianist, as narcissistic and cruel—a repressed homosexual arrested at the Oedipal stage. In contrast, Piot, the overrefined critic, is described with a sympathy which increases as the narrator comes to know this overtly homosexual character.

In 1939 Hester Pine, in *Beer for the Kitten,* depicted the life of a group of professors in a provincial university including a homosexual professor of literature (unlike other characters, he is described from the outside only), affected, delicate, a gourmet, despised by his colleagues. Nelson de Graff (note the foreign-sounding name!) strikes us from the beginning—even before we come to know of his homosexuality—by his physical appearance, which makes us uncomfortable; he is repugnant. Having failed to seduce the handsome, all-American student Peter, a nice, honest, and serious boy, De Graff takes revenge by grading him unfairly. Despite his girl friend's repeated urging, Peter refuses to denounce the dishonest professor, who at the novel's end leaves the campus (of his own free will) to take a better position elsewhere.

Toward Tolerance (1940–47)

Henry Bellaman has the honor of having been the first writer to have expressed in a popular, best-selling novel (*Kings Row,* 1940) what psychoanalysis had known for fifty years: that an adolescent can be sexually attracted to another adolescent. Temptation is no longer visited solely upon despicable subhumans, on alien souls, on disturbing "enchanters," but takes on the features of an adolescent boy in a small American town at the turn of the century. Because Jamie Wakefield is a "sissy," "girlish," "too pretty for a boy" (in his teacher's words), he is attractive to his comrades, the young European Parris and Drake, the all-American boy, with whom he strolls hand in hand. These friends think that Jamie is different but that he is "all right." However, the "delicate plant" of this special friendship withers: Jamie voluntarily abandons such things and dries up, while his comrades turn their interest toward women. In *Kings Row,* however, there is a spirit of tolerance new to the American novel, although foreshadowed by Sherwood Anderson, Sinclair Lewis, and Blair Niles.

Love is indivisible in Carson McCullers's novels, thus homoeroticism is merely one aspect of eroticism. Still, in *The Heart Is a Lonely Hunter* (1940) homoeroticism joins two outsiders who live only on the fringes of the American dream—Singer, an angelic deaf-mute, and Antonapoulos, a feeble-minded Greek. But Captain Penderton, the protagonist of *Reflections in a Golden Eye* (1941), is an *American* officer in love with an American soldier. His feelings are never consummated, but assuaged in an orgasm of hatred when he murders the soldier. In addition, beneath his rough exterior, Penderton turns out to be a coward, a sadist, a kleptomaniac; and the soldier is more like an animal than a man. However, Carson McCullers does make the sexual attraction of one American military man for another the subject of her short novel; that she is a woman enables her to carry this off.

In *The Lost Weekend* (1944) Charles Jackson writes of a delayed adolescent, a man unsuccessful in repressing and sublimating his homosexual tendencies, which he shares with all adolescents. He attempts to drown them in alcohol. Don, the protagonist, has occasional lucid moments with regard to his sexual leanings, but in order to make him palatable, the author—a husband and father—covers his tracks, refuses to reveal anything of his past, and gives his hero a mistress. It is as if Jackson were dreaming of a society in which homosexual love will no longer be shameful, in which it will no longer appear in the form of Bim, the lisping and grotesque male nurse, but that of Cliff Hauman, the young marine officer in Jackson's next novel, *The Fall of Valor* (1946): "The face looked typically American, the very personification of the American boy—the contemporary hero; so much so that he ceased almost to be an individual: he was the epitome of a type." By way of contrast, Arne Eklund is an effeminate man, "the daydream turned inside-out." When Professor John Grandin, a latent homosexual, suddenly seeing himself as he truly is, makes the fatal gesture of drawing Cliff toward him, the latter, in horror and disgust, knocks him out. Like Don in the preceding novel, John Grandin comes to the realization that the ideal, virile homosexual relationship is not viable in American reality. On the other hand, in Cliff Hauman, Jackson depicts a latent homosexual who is obsessed with the memory of his pal Walt, with whom he made love "through a woman" in threesomes. Cliff overreacts to Grandin's advances. The homosexual American dream can only be a mirage. If Cliff had acceded to John's advances—or Don's, or Charles's—he would have fallen apart, would have found himself disfigured, hideous, down among the grotesques, the caricatures, with Bim and Arne Eklund. To be homosexual and not to be homosexual: to be and not to be—that is the question! The author murders his dream in order to save it.

This is also the dilemma facing John Horne Burns, the author of *The Gallery* (1947). In this collection of short stories, we encounter the sexual continuum earlier sketched by Charles Jackson. Because of the war and their expatriation, certain men have defied the narrow sexual categories. However, all the relations among the men in the Gallery are confined to the homoerotic. Having poked fun at "Esther" and "Magda," two British sergeants, Burns describes the love-friendship between the magnificent Captain Joe and the handsome Florentine Orlando. The blond American and the brunet Italian remind us of the pioneer-Indian couple in James Fenimore Cooper, and prefigure the couple in James Baldwin's *Giovanni's Room*. Walt and Cliff had a homosexual relationship through a common female partner, but in one of the stories in *The Gallery*, Captain Motes reads the love poetry his wife has written to him to his friend Lieutenant Stuki, who lies naked on the bed, trembling and writhing with pleasure. Here again, woman is an alibi, an instrument. Physical contact between them occurs only during a massage (as in a scene in *The Fall of Valor*, or in D. H. Lawrence's *Aaron's Rod*).

The End of My Life (1947), by Vance Bourjaily—another war novel—takes place in the Middle East. It depicts a group of young men, several of whom are homosexual. Billy is a corrected and edited replica of Jamie (*Kings Row*): pretty as a girl, he no longer lisps, but does his job efficiently and takes pleasure in it. His pals, Freak and Skinner (who remind us of Drake and Parris, respectively), are touched by his charm: "He really looks like a girl. . . ."(In one of the stories in *The Gallery*, a sergeant uses this same excuse with regard to a male nurse.) Rod, the neurotic homosexual who is trying to repress his tendencies, yields to temptation. Freak and Skinner try to understand him, but with mixed success.

Knock on Any Door (1947), by Willard Motley, takes us into the Chicago underworld, where Nick, the stud, prostitutes himself to older men. The novel also describes his sexual relationship with Owen, a lonely and melancholy man who is somewhat feminine, but not effeminate. Their physical relationship is masked by timely "lapses of memory," a device that is also employed in *Big Money* and *Serenade*. The steady homosexual becomes the friend of the virile young stud. What progress over *Studs Lonigan!*

Two novels written in 1947 by homosexual authors depict the overt homosexual as a grotesque and effeminate creature. Merle Miller allows one of the protagonists of *That Winter* to be "picked up by a fairy," and he describes another's disgusted and contemptuous reaction to the discreet advances of an overelegant client in a bar; yet the passionate and devoted friendship of "normal" young people is highly praised. Gore Vidal, in *In a Yellow Wood*, introduces George Robert Lewis, a mannered, effeminate aesthete, and also a pale and bejeweled waiter who walks like a woman afraid of being attacked.

Liberation: 1948 to the 1970s

Not every author dealing more or less directly with homosexuality relied upon the Kinsey Report, once it appeared in 1948; but after such a scientifically sound challenge to sexual morality, it became difficult to stereotype the invert without the risk of being regarded as backward, ill-informed, or ignorant. Popular literature or literature aimed at any group—high-brow, middle-brow, or low-brow—was thereafter obliged to deal with the subject of homosexuality with at least some semblance of objectivity.

In 1948 Gore Vidal courageously published *The City and the Pillar*, which was a defense and an illustration of homosexuality —even though he felt obliged to terminate his novel with a melodramatic murder in which the protagonist avenges John Grandin for the punishment Cliff inflicted on him. (In the revised edition of 1965 the vengeance of the homosexual takes an even more appropriate form: Jim wins out in the final struggle and rapes the heterosexual Bob.) The book, which was a best-seller in America, opened the door for the overtly homosexual novel. After it, the only thing to be increased was the degree of salaciousness. The trial of Burroughs in Boston in 1965 was concerned with pornography, not homosexuality. After Vidal, there is no longer any need for us to trace the evolution of the homosexual character, to probe an author's devices and stratagems to force the reader to accept such a character. The mask had been removed. The misty, shadowy character of *White-Jacket*, who had been spoken of only with many rhetorical precautions and circuitous turns of phrase, was now able to take center stage in a best-selling novel. Today, Vidal's novel seems fairly mild, but in 1948 it was such a shocker that the New York *Times* refused to print advertisements for it.

1. The Predominantly Heterosexual Novel

Reading *The Homosexual in America*, by Donald W. Cory, in the aftermath of the Kinsey bombshell, Norman Mailer reworked the character of homosexual Teddy Pope in his novel *The Deer Park* (1955). In Mailer's first novel, *The Naked and the Dead* (1948), General Cummings is an affected, feminine figure hiding real cruelty beneath a frozen mask. Hollingsworth, a bisexual character in *Barbary Shore* (1951), is a strange young man, a liar who is both sly and sadistic. Teddy Pope, however, is a nice young actor; and—a sign of the times—a very "masculine" character, Marion Faye, admits his deep homosexual tendencies.

Another war novel—like *The Naked and the Dead*, *The End of My Life*, and *The Gallery*—is James Jones's *From Here to Eternity* (1951), in which soldiers go "queer hunting" for money, as did Nick in *Knock on Any Door*. Some, such as Angelo Maggio, think that queers are "all right, they just peculiar is all." Others, such as the hero, Prewitt, are slow to see them as human. And Bloom is the hypervirile prototype who cannot survive self-revelation: laden with athletic trophies, a real he-man, he believes or knows that he is homosexual and commits suicide. Out-and-out inverts (Hal, Tommy) are depicted with relative objectivity. In this world without respectable women (in wartime Honolulu), the inverts replace them to some extent.

As instances of the predominantly homosexual novel were on the rise, the heterosexual novel was becoming more liberal, yet the homosexual character continued to be refused total and complete humanity. If the character remains on the periphery of the plot, he is treated "normally" (Teddy Pope, Hal, Tommy), but he is made ridiculous when he approaches the core of the novel (Hollingsworth). In most cases, if the character is more than a sketchy outline, he will also be a heterosexual.

2. Bisexuality

Philip Wylie's *Opus 21* (1949) was published just after the Kinsey Report and attempted to apply the conclusions reached in Kinsey's work. Wylie's narrator, Philip, urges Yvonne to accept uncomplicated bisexuality. He brings her to an understanding of her husband, Rol, whose bisexuality has plunged her into despair. The narrator takes pains, however, not to practice the principles he enunciates. In *The Disappearance* (1951), also by Wylie, the world of men is suddenly cut off from the world of women. Without women, certain minor figures in the book turn to homosexuality with transvestites, who are delighted at this unexpected opportunity. None of the protagonists, however, cross the threshold, despite their tolerant opinions.

Not until J. P. Donleavy's "beat" novel *The Ginger Man* (1958) do we encounter a heterosexual who, deprived of women, openly seeks a homosexual adventure. This novel attempts to be morally free. In line with Kinsey's view of homosexuality as a more or less deliberate choice, *The Ginger Man* presents a protagonist who varies his sexual diet according to his circumstances. The two protagonists of this perceptive, amusing, and rakish novel are Sebastian Dangerfield, the narrator, and Kenneth O'Keefe. The novel is set in Ireland—outside the American milieu, in other words—and O'Keefe, not the narrator, is the one who yields to temptation. Unsuccessful at seducing girls, he similarly fails in his attempts with boys. O'Keefe finally abandons homosexuality and returns to masturbation, since his experience as a pederast only serves to complicate his life further.

Whereas O'Keefe turns to homosexuality after thought and calculation, the characters in Robert Phelps's *Heroes and Orators* (1958) indulge their tendencies without neuroses, without any liberal pretense, simply and naturally. Taken both individually and as a group, they are a living example of the continuum of which Kinsey, Jackson, and Burns have written. However, though the characters are fully aware of their homoerotic longings and even though they recognize them without any moral opprobrium, Roger, Mark, and Gib, the male protagonists, replace the men they desire with tomboys or prostitutes whom they share between them. Gib is a hero, a whole, complete human being; and the narrator, Roger, is the eternal admirer, the poet in love with the hero, his "better Nature." A quotation by Johannes de Silentio stands as epigraph to the novel: "As God created man and woman, so too He fashioned the hero and the poet, or orator."

The narrator-protagonist of Alexander Trocchi's "hip" novel *Cain's Book* (1960) is a gentle addict who is completely bisexual. He is totally liberated, both sexually and emotionally, and lives in perfect harmony with his instincts. He is a creature apart, on the fringes of American society (his background is European; he lives on a houseboat), and he foments and engages in a revolt against all sexual taboos.

3. *Three Primarily Homosexual Novels: Is the American Homosexual Couple a Viable Entity?*

Gore Vidal wrote *The City and the Pillar* in 1946. As mentioned, it was uniquely homosexual in subject matter, and marked a turning point in the American novel when it finally appeared in 1948 after a delay by the publisher. In his Afterword to the revised edition, Vidal revealed his motives for writing the novel: "I was twenty-one when I wrote *The City and the Pillar*. . . . I wanted to take risks, to try something no American had done before. I decided to examine the homosexual underworld . . . and in the process show the 'naturalness' of homosexual relations. . . . All human beings are bisexual. Conditioning, opportunity

and habit account finally (and mysteriously) for sexual preference."

The book was in fact a *succès de scandale*. Vidal tells us that
his novel was greeted with "shock and disbelief," that, as noted,
the New York *Times* refused to accept advertisements for it, and
that most of the critics were hostile. In 1948 strong stands were
taken for and against the novel. On the one side were the pioneers of sexual tolerance, Gide and Kinsey, who were enthusiastic about the book (Kinsey wrote to Vidal, complimenting him
on "your work in the field," and Gide sent him a copy of his book
Corydon, which was not to be published in the United States
until 1950). In opposition, the New York *Times*, John Aldridge,
and many others considered the novel devoid of any literary
quality. Some critics (Richard McLaughlin, for one) noted the
novel's "pioneer" value, its "realism," and its "honesty." In any
event, since it became a best-seller in 1948, the book has continued to be read (Vidal revised it in 1965), and it was the first
wholly homosexual novel to reach a wide public. Yet it was un-
compromising: as Ray Lewis has written—and Vidal has
confirmed it—the character of Jim Willard represents "the author's attempt to shatter the American stereotype of the homosexual as an effeminate, socially undesirable interior decorator."

The story is linear: Jim Willard, handsome, tall, an accomplished tennis player, has a sexual experience with Bob when
they are seventeen and eighteen years of age respectively; Bob is
also handsome, shorter than Jim, but equally well built. Bob
feels somewhat ill at ease after they have had sex. As planned, he
joins the Navy and goes on to lead a perfectly "normal" life,
whereas Jim, through a series of sexual or sentimental adventures, attempts to recapture the same feeling of "completion" he
had once experienced with Bob. These attempts continue until
the day when he meets his old friend (now married and a father) again, makes advances to him, and meets with a horrified
response. In the face of this reaction, Jim kills Bob (in the revised version, as we have noted, he rapes him).

In the context of postwar American society, Jim is certainly
the most normal homosexual *imaginable*—as, according to Leib-
niz—our world is the best of all *possible* worlds. Yet, though
close to normal, with his good looks and his lack of effeminacy,

this outwardly healthy and clean-cut young man has nevertheless experienced an abnormal childhood: a domineering mother, and a harsh father whom his son hates. The flaw has been present since childhood, and all of Vidal's persuasion and Jim's blind innocence cannot conceal this emotional imbalance.

Conformity, the desperate attempt to adhere to the American virile ideal, forms the basis of the neurosis from which David, the protagonist of James Baldwin's novel *Giovanni's Room* (1956), suffers—as it was at the basis of Jim Willard's emotional flaw. By refusing to face the conjunction of love and homosexuality *in their lives*, both young men achieve an *appearance of normality*, a precarious balance that is based not on their acceptance of their true identity, but on a split in personality: homosexual instincts are satisfied anonymously, shamefully, and the emotions find release in schizophrenic reverie.

The homosexual couple in American literature is not a happy couple. In *Bertram Cope's Year* (1919), Bertram felt contempt for Arthur; and not again until *Giovanni's Room* are two men who "love each other" described as sharing a room. However, it should be noted that, from the time they begin living together, their ephemeral happiness begins to deteriorate. David's anxiety, his neurosis, infects his relations with the young Italian. Both males have had experiences with women (Giovanni has even been married), and are unable to free themselves completely from their pasts. And, at every street corner, awaits that "male prison" of which Baldwin writes in his essay on Gide: "The really horrible thing about the phenomenon of present-day homosexuality . . . is that today's unlucky deviate can only save himself by the most tremendous exertion of all his forces from falling into an underworld in which he never meets either men or women, where it is impossible to have either a lover or a friend, where the possibility of genuine human involvement has altogether ceased. When this possibility has ceased, so has the possibility of growth."

The ending of *Giovanni's Room*—like that of *The City and the Pillar*—is brutal and fatal. Since Giovanni is Italian and since the characters are in Europe, the reader thinks for a moment that they may make a go of it, that their union will be more lasting than Jim and Bob's brief experience. However, David's puritanism, as *Homo americanus*, is enough to upset the precarious balance. In Giovanni's voice, Baldwin informs us that homosexuality will not be viable in the United States until the American has freed himself of sexual prejudices.

In describing the white characters in his novel *Another Country* (1962), James Baldwin revealed the problem at the heart of the homosexual couple's relationship. Eric (American) and Yves (French) temporarily re-create the schema of a heterosexual couple: Eric is the male, older, more experienced, breadwinner; Yves, whose prettiness is frequently referred to, represents the couple's female element with his charm and grace. The contrast between them, accentuated by the difference in nationality, is maintained throughout the novel. What will happen, however, when Yves becomes a "man" like Eric? "On the day that Yves no longer needed him, Eric would drop back into chaos."

The beginning of their liaison, the growth of their feeling for each other, and their perfect happiness, are related by the author with a sympathy full of admiration, and there is an attempt to communicate this to the reader that he may share in it. Vidal had tried to overturn the myth of the effeminate homosexual as the sole representative of the "brotherhood" by making Jim, his hero, a handsome and athletic young man; yet he took care not to describe affection, kisses, tender caresses. In *Giovanni's Room* Baldwin put his hymn to homosexual love into the mouth of a secondary and foreign character, the Belgian Jacques. In *Another Country* he steps across the threshold and describes the intoxicating caresses of Eric and Yves. This highly romanticized tale, beginning to the tune of a Beethoven piece at Saint-Germain-des-Prés, remains chaste and pure until the men visit Chartres, where they make love for the first time in a hotel in the very shadow of the cathedral. This is truely a love story; its atmosphere is one of purity, peace, and mystic union.

However, both the protagonists are set apart from the mass of homosexuals, from the furtive and ashamed figures they have known in the past. Upon his return to the United States, Eric turns to Cass, an American girl, whereas Yves, before his encounter with Eric, had been neither homosexual nor heterosexual! Baldwin exalts the love between two characters who are nearly "men," just as Vidal had depicted Jim as being on the border of normality. Baldwin's purpose is to make their love acceptable to the reader, to make the reader feel sympathy for this male couple by creating situations that are traditionally associated with love between men and women. He seems to be saying, "They're just like you: they do as you do, therefore they are you."

To Vivaldo, a "heterosexual" with whom he will make love later on, Eric announces that he is in love with Yves. Immediately they sit down to talk together about their respective lovers, confiding in each other. On Eric's bed, they sit "like two soldiers, resting from battle, about to go into battle again." We are thus made to understand that when Vivaldo and Eric have sexual relations later on in the book, they are two "soldiers," two virile men, embracing each other and making love. Vivaldo, the handsome, normal man who is heterosexual but still open on occasion to homosexual adventures, and Eric—who is now Cass's lover (since Yves is still in France)—make love together as men. However, they do not form a "stable" couple. An encounter between two men, marvelous as it can be, is nonetheless ephemeral of necessity—since real men primarily love women.

However Baldwin, describing this love scene with a certain tenderness, is unable to resist comparing one of the men (Vivaldo) to a woman: so long as penetration had not taken place, the virile, soldierly friendship remained viable; later, we return to sexual dichotomy, in other words to heterosexuality. *There can be no virile homosexual.* Neither Vidal nor Baldwin really believes it possible. It can appear true only at special moments, brief as they are vivid, at times of adolescent ambivalence, or in pederastic situations à la Greek, playing on the sexual ambiguity of the sex object and on the pseudo virility—a relative virility, maturity, rather—of the sexual protagonist.

The book, however, ends on a note of hope. The last scene depicts Yves's arrival in New York and Eric awaiting him at the airport: "Yves looked up joyously, and waved, unable to say anything. *Eric.* And all his fear left him, he was certain, now, that everything would be all right."

But we know—Yves and Eric have told us so themselves—that "it cannot go on forever," for when Yves becomes a *man*, the difference between them will vanish, and "chaos is come again." We must nevertheless salute this attempt—unconvincing as it is —to end a "bisexual" novel on a note of homosexual hope.

Chapter Three

The Homosexual Character on the Stage

Different fields of artistic endeavor tend to advance toward tolerance at different rates of speed. In the "literary" arts, the order of liberalization is descendingly: novel, theater, cinema, and television. Of the four, the novel is the most intimate means of communication: it whispers secrets to the reader, permitting the reader's reactions to remain private. The theater, on the contrary, is a public place (albeit restricted to a ticket-buying elite); therefore the dramatist does not feel himself to be as free as his novelist colleague. He hesitates to provoke the audience, since, sensing they can be observed, they will not dare to conceal shock at his iconoclasm, his flouting of taboos. The homosexual dramatist has had to wait longer than the novelist to be able to speak about his experience. In fact, twenty years separates the novel from the theater in the sphere with which we are dealing. And the cinema, which is aimed at an even larger public, follows the theater fairly closely. Not until the 1970s, when the young in America began to question the moral values of their civilization, did television first deal with homosexuality. Debates, films, news stories, plays, all presented characters who had hitherto—even more than blacks—been invisible men. The liberalization of television, a medium which intrudes into the very heart of the familial group—the group which is perceived as homosexuality's prime enemy—has consecrated homosexual liberation.

This liberalization, this liberation, did not result without a certain amount of protest. It is revealing that the theater became the prime object of recriminations: more "visible" than the novel as a medium, its liberalization was therefore more shocking. Interestingly, by the time homosexuality reached the cinema and television, morals had already changed to such a degree that complaints were muted and went virtually unnoticed.

From Tea and Sympathy to The Boys in the Band

In 1953 a minor American playwright dared to make the theme of his play the problems encountered by an adolescent boy attempting to conform to the American virile ideal. In *Tea and Sympathy* Robert Anderson confronted the myth of American-style virility. He gave us a timid and somewhat feminine young man, Tom Lee, who was, however, apparently *heterosexual*, and contrasted him with a hypervirile athlete. Bill, an insensitive and brutal man was, *from all the evidence*, a latent homosexual. Laura, Bill's wife, would appear to be the author's spokesman: "Manliness is not all swagger and swearing and mountain climbing. Manliness is also tenderness, gentleness, consideration," she tells her husband.

Two years later, in *A View from the Bridge* (1955), Arthur Miller dealt with a very similar theme. Eddie Carbone, a first-generation Italian-American, has acquired all the prejudices of the Anglo-American toward the more gentle, artistic European, in this case his nephew Rodolpho, who sings like a nightingale, sews, and cooks. However, when Eddie kisses him publicly on the mouth in an attempt to humiliate him, doubt arises in the spectator's mind with regard to his true, unconscious motives.

James Barr's play *Game of Fools* (published in 1955 by One, Inc., a homosexual organization in Los Angeles) is more a part of the history of the American novel than of the theater. Its virulence and its propagandistic elements, which would make it acceptable to the most extreme homophile liberation movements, made the play impossible to stage in 1955; it could only be performed in private before invited audiences, or read by the public. Written in the midst of the McCarthy era, the play is a denunciation of the state, the police, the law, the army, the church, etc. In addition, the author has tried to cover all psychosociological bases by describing several types of homosexuals, and by depicting the varied reactions of their families.

In *The Best Man* (1960) Gore Vidal—who is an insider in both the worlds of politics and inversion—showed the ease with which a politician is ruined by the discovery of a homosexual relationship in his past. Vidal takes advantage of the opportunity offered him by the stage to reiterate his familiar message of the separation that exists especially for homosexuals between public and private life.

Two plays by LeRoi Jones which were produced in New York in 1964 offer homosexual characters. In *The Baptism* the homosexual is a pompous black, who is nonetheless fairly amusing and much less a hypocrite than the Methodist minister or the bigoted old woman. In *The Toilet*, set in the lavatories of a public school, LeRoi Jones seems to denounce violence in adolescent relationships, and to sympathize with the love of a tender-hearted black tough for a courageous young homosexual white.

A similarly violent climate tempered by homosexual tenderness is found in *Fortune and Men's Eyes*, a study of homosexuality in prison. Written by a Canadian, John Herbert, the play was presented for the first time in the United States off-Broadway in 1967, and later was made into a film. Its restricted prison setting enables the author to examine closely the personalities of various types of homosexuals: Mona, "almost more feminine than effeminate"; Queenie, "coarse, cruel, tough and voluptuously pretty"; Rocky, the hypervirile queer-basher, who rapes Smitty, the one character who is not gay, and whose arrival in the cell triggers the drama. Smitty is "a good looking, clean-cut youth of clear intelligence and aged seventeen years. He has the look of a collegiate athlete." He ultimately falls in love with Mona, but their love scene is cut short by the play's denouement. Interestingly, in the original production of the play Mona, the most feminine character, was portrayed by a black. (By 1970 Sal Mineo could stage the rape scene using naked actors.)

Following the immense success of *Hair* in 1968, *the theater caught up with the novel*. It became possible to say anything and to show anything on the American stage. A whole series of plays containing nudity, a proliferation of scabrous situations hitherto seen only in the American pornographic novel (whether hetero- or homosexual), succeeded in immunizing the audience against the horror they had always had of the one person defined solely by his sexuality—the homosexual. Thus, Mart Crowley was able to speak openly and frankly, and to bring onto the stage homosexuals who dared "speak their names." *The Boys in the Band* was original only in that its characters appeared on stage and not in a novel, *where chances are they would have gone unnoticed,* lost in the vast crowd of their own kind. It is a fact, however, that seen in flesh and blood in the theater, they produced in the spectator an unsettling impression. The sight of men congregating, loving, laughing, crying like everyone else— whereas before they had existed only in novels or as members of a secret, infamous society—suddenly forced the audience to recognize that they were human beings like everyone else. For the first time on an American stage, a dramatist offered the general public a slice of homosexual life—a digest of everything the novel had been saying for decades—that had never before been staged without being heavily veiled, deformed, or altered often out of almost all recognition. In short, *The Boys in the Band* was the crossroads at which the homosexual American novel and the theater met. In this sense the play is a key for decoding plays with a homosexual tinge. In addition, it parodies the genre: there are mocking references to Tennessee Williams, William Inge, and Edward Albee; the character of Alan is straight out of *Cat on a Hot Tin Roof,* and the stud is a caricature of all of Inge's "he-men." (See Part III.)

PART II

Four Archetypes of the Homosexual Couple

Ah, lover, and perfect equal,
I meant that you should discover me so by faint indirections,
And I when I meet you mean to discover them by the like in
  you.

Walt Whitman, Calamus

Chapter Four

Adolescents

Hero-Worship (The "Crush")

In *Les Enfants Terribles* Jean Cocteau speaks of the hero-worship of a boy for a young man who is bigger, stronger, more handsome, or simply more adventurous than himself. Paul, pale and sad-eyed, "loves" Dargelos, the school bully, who is brutal and arrogant: "He looked for Dargelos. He loved him. This love gnawed at him even more viciously because as yet he knew nothing of love. It was a vague, intense sickness, one without remedy, a chaste desire, without sex, without goal." This love, which is in fact an idealized, narcissistic projection, helps the adolescent to grow to manhood by means of a process of identification. By admiring another boy who seems to him the essence of virility, by adoring him and desiring to absorb him, to interiorize him in some manner, the younger boy allows himself to be penetrated by him, allows him to mold his gestures, to form his attitudes. The adolescent who walks like a "he-man," who assumes the pose of a "tough guy," will gradually acquire the habit of doing so *naturally*.

Freud has stated that such identification marks a normal stage in the development of a boy's personality. When for some reason or other it fails to occur, the younger admirer, unsuccessful at introjecting the virile essence of the object of his admiration, remains fixed at this stage. Having failed to become a man by imitation and interiorization, he will love as a woman. His admiration and his desire to emulate the other becomes erotic in nature, and throughout his life he will form attachments to these stronger types, the handsome boys he will continue to idolize in the vain hope of captivating them by sexual means. Indeed, Freudians say that in every case the homosexual repeats throughout his life the aborted adolescent process of attempting to become a man by identification, either with his father—who ought to be his son's "hero"—or with an older comrade, and often with both simultaneously.

American literature teems with descriptions of such adolescent emotions. Hero-worship and idealization can be found in the works of Fitzgerald, Faulkner, Charles Jackson, Tennessee Williams, and Carson McCullers, to cite but a few. Only in Fitzgerald's writings does this introjection *apparently* succeed; in the works of others, adolescents fail this challenge.

The Hero and the Adolescent in the Work of F. Scott Fitzgerald

Fitzgerald's biographer, Arthur Mizener, has dealt with the tendency of the author of the Basil stories to idealize certain men, mainly college athletes. He examines the development of such hero-worship and traces it to the author's own adolescence. He quotes Fitzgerald: "The captain of the losing side was a dark, slender youth of perhaps fourteen, who played with a fierce but facile abandon that . . . sent him everywhere about the floor pushing, dribbling, and shooting impossible baskets from all angles. . . . Oh, he was fine, really one of the finest things I ever saw. . . . after I saw him all athletes were dark and devilish and despairing and enthusiastic."

In the Basil stories, which are more or less autobiographical, we find this obsession with an athletic and virile "hero" who fills the younger boy with admiration and emotion. In "Basil: The Scandal Detectives," Basil, "hanging back in a shadow," fixes his eyes "not on Imogene but on Hubert Blair." Like the homosexual Genet with the tough Stilitano, Basil desires to imitate Hubert's gestures, his poses: "In tribute to Hubert's passing, he practised leaning against a tree and missing it and rolling a skate down his arm, and he wore a cap in Hubert's manner, set jauntily on the side of his head."

In the short story "Basil: The Freshest Boy," Ted Fay's arrival in the theater recalls Saint-Loup's entrance into the dining room of the Grand-Hotel, as well as Chad's arrival in Strether's box at the theater in *The Ambassadors*. The theater is described as a "feminine," "powdery" place in which Basil feels at ease, but the appearance of Ted Fay, captain of the Yale football team and the symbol of virility, leaves him thunderstruck: "Basil felt a sort of exquisite pain." The author's personal mythology turns Ted Fay into a young man with blond hair and green eyes, well-built, close yet distant, so inaccessible that Basil is haunted by him throughout the performance. The physical aspect—moral qualities are regarded as being somehow feminine—is always at the basis of an urge to identify oneself with the hero: from the very beginning Basil is struck by physical beauty. "Basil: The Captured Shadow" introduces Andy Lockheart: "at eighteen, captain of his freshman baseball team, handsome . . . a living symbol of the splendid, glamorous world of Yale." Throughout the year, Basil apes his walk and attempts to imitate him in all things.

In Fitzgerald's work this stunned fascination with athletic virility always remains on just that level; it is never "consummated." His entire personality, his desire to be admired and accepted socially, would have prevented Fitzgerald from turning to homosexuality, even had he consciously wanted it. Yet his ardent love for virility, however ambiguous it may have been, was nothing compared to his horror of the effeminate man—the only "visible," and therefore "real," homosexual he knew of. Remaining something of an adolescent throughout his life, Fitzgerald embodied Basil's sexual immaturity and never resolved the confused emotions of his young alter ego.

Hero and Adolescent in the Works of Faulkner and Tennessee Williams: The Role of the Sister

In William Faulkner's *Absalom, Absalom!* both Judith and her brother Henry are fascinated by Charles Bon. He represents for Henry what Hubert Blair, Ted Fay, or Andy Lockheart represented for Basil. Physically, however, Bon is the opposite of Basil's heroes. He is a Frenchified dandy with almost feminine characteristics. But to young Henry, who has been harshly brought up by his father under Spartan conditions, Bon's elegance and maturity are admirable indeed: "Yes, he loved Bon, who seduced him as surely as he seduced Judith."

In Faulkner, hero-worship is clearly sexual in nature: Henry desires to be his sister so that he may be possessed by his hero. This character of Faulkner's, denser and more complex than any of Fitzgerald's, experiences desire and attempts to assuage it in a socially acceptable way by encouraging Bon to marry Judith. (The marriage will collapse when Henry discovers that Charles Bon not only is his half-brother but also has Negro blood.) Faulkner describes Henry's feelings for Bon in language that sounds almost like Cocteau: "that complete and abnegant devotion which only a youth, never a woman, gives to another youth or a man."

Bon responds to the love his admirer feels. "Perhaps in his fatalism he loved Henry the better of the two, seeing perhaps in the sister merely the shadow, the woman vessel with which to consummate the love whose actual object was the youth."

The admirer-sister-hero triangle recurs in a semiautobiographical story by Tennessee Williams entitled "The Resemblance Between a Violin Case and a Coffin." Henry wanted to become his sister in order to be possessed by Bon; Williams's character is in love with Richard, the "hero," because he has always identified with his sister: "She had fallen in love. As always I followed suit."

Faulkner and Williams, more concerned as they are with sexuality than was Fitzgerald, recognize the homosexual ramifications in hero-worship that are brought to the surface by the sister's presence; she is the admirer in female guise. Henry, and Williams's narrator, fail to identify with the "hero," and they come to realize that they are identifying with the sister. Henry's life is ruined; he kills Bon and later dies in the flames of the Sutpen estate. The narrator of Williams's story—who is Williams himself—takes refuge in daydreaming, but becomes unwaveringly homosexual.

Hero and Adolescent in the Works of Charles Jackson and Carson McCullers: The Role of Sexuality

Even when it remains at the level of asexual adulation, hero-worship is a favorite theme of American novels dealing with homosexuality, since the homosexual writer correctly regards hero-worship as the perilous passage of a boy in his development into a man. During the bisexual (latent) period of preadolescence and puberty, such a feeling is always on the verge of turning into physical desire. It is the vulnerability of this emotion that has long fascinated authors of homosexually oriented novels.

Charles Jackson in *The Lost Weekend* describes the past of his protagonist, Don: "All the woeful errors of childhood and adolescence came to their crashing climax at seventeen. They gathered themselves for a real workout in the passionate hero-worship of an upperclassman during his very first month at college, a worship that led, like a fatal infatuation, to scandal and public disgrace, because no one had understood . . . least of all the upperclassman." Although Don sincerely believes in the nonsensual nature of his admiration for the other student, the reader knows otherwise, and is aware of the character's hidden tendencies.

In *Clock Without Hands*, Carson McCullers introduces young Jester, who experiences the gamut of passionate emotions for the athletic boys in his school, and above all for Ted Hopkins, "the best all-around athlete" in the school. With discretion and delicacy, McCullers depicts Jester's troubled emotions as he seeks out Ted's glance in the school corridors, his heart in his mouth, never receiving more than a word or two from his admired. Jester eventually falls in love with Sherman, a black boy with blue eyes. Here again, what passed for hero-worship was actually sexual in nature, since in the whorehouse where he goes to prove he isn't "like men in the Kinsey Report," Jester is able to carry out the heterosexual act only by thinking about Sherman.

Affectionate Friendships

Some writers are less concerned with describing this usually one-sided admiration—an admiration which is more intense, passionate and dangerous for the younger character in search of a virile model—and have dealt instead with affectionate school friendships, the sentimental relationships that prefigure love between a man and a woman. What makes these relationships different from the other is that here the emphasis is less on the fascination felt by the younger boy who wants to *be* the older than on the feelings both of them experience, feelings that run from ambiguous friendship to a repressed desire for sexual contact.

In the Romantic Mode

In *Pierre; or, The Ambiguities* (1852) Melville describes such friendships as "short, by one degree, of the sweetest sentiment entertained between the sexes. Nor is this boy-love without the occasional fillips and spiciness, which at times, by an apparent abatement, enhance the permanent delights of those more advanced lovers who love beneath the cestus of Venus. Jealousies are felt. The sight of another lad too much consorting with the boy's beloved object, shall fill him with emotions akin to those of Othello's." Pierre and his cousin, Glen, write passionate notes to each other, "love-friendship missives." In Glen's letters to Pierre, "the unfaltering stream of *Beloved Pierres* . . . not only flowed along the top margin of all his earlier letters, but here and there, from their subterranean channel, flashed out in bright intervals, through all the succeeding lines."

There is something soft, tender, in such a feeling; something that does not conform to—it actually flouts—the American virile ideal. This sentiment does not involve idolizing the captain of a football team who inspires admiration and a desire for identification, but rather it means abandoning oneself to the charms of romantic love with another adolescent. Melville emphasizes that this is only a "stage," a moment of refuge before crossing the threshold into the heterosexual, i.e., the adult, world: "But as the advancing fruit itself extrudes the beautiful blossom, so in many cases, does the eventual love for the other sex forever dismiss the preliminary love-friendship of boys. The mere outer friendship may in some degree—greater or less—survive; but the singular love in it has perishingly dropped away." Psychiatrist Henry A. Murray, in his introduction to *Pierre*, speculates that this transformation of adolescent love into heterosexual desire does not appear to have been totally successful in the case of Melville himself.

Intense Friendships: The Acceptable Relationship

Almost a century after Melville, the American writer William Maxwell made love-friendship the subject of his novel *The Folded Leaf* (1945). It is not unlikely that he found his subject in Melville's works. The quotation from Tennyson he uses as an epigraph employs a similar metaphor, that of a folded leaf slowly opening.

The friends in Maxwell's novel are Lymie Peters—dark, skinny, poor at sport—and Spud, the prototype of the virile American: handsome, strong, an accomplished athlete. Lymie's feelings for Spud are "partly pride (he had never had a friend before) and partly envy . . . the wish closest to Lymie's heart, if he could have had it for the asking, would have been to have a well-built body, a body as strong and as beautifully proportioned as Spud's."

Once their friendship is recognized as sensual love, it changes, becomes sublimated, that it may "survive," to use Melville's term. It had been a friendship replete with ambiguity, with intimate albeit chaste physical contact, and with jealousy which sought pretexts for misunderstandings; it was based on the relationship between protector and protégé which conceals emotions between lover and beloved. Having reached its apogee in a searing moment, in a chaste kiss, the love-friendship between the two adolescents—suddenly aware of their feelings—subsides.

Spud and Lymie experience what psychiatrist Erich Fromm has called "symbiotic union." Lymie, the masochistic element of the pair, "escapes from the unbearable feeling of isolation and separateness by making himself part and parcel of another person who directs him, guides him, protects him; who is his life, his oxygen, as it were." Becoming part of him, Lymie is thus "part of his greatness . . . power . . . certainty." The masochistic relationship, Fromm maintains, "can be blended with physical, sexual desire; in this case it is not only a submission in which one's mind participates, but also one's whole body" (*The Art of Loving*).

Lymie is the prototype of the moral masochistic homosexual,

the "rabbity man" of whom Margaret Mead speaks in *Male and Female,* whose tendency toward self-abuse is alleviated by his attachment to the muscular splendor of another.

Intense Friendships: The Importance of Physical Attraction

Notwithstanding his emphasis on the chastity and purity of Lymie and Spud's relationship in *The Folded Leaf,* William Maxwell emphasized the preponderant part played by the body, by bodily admiration and bodily desire, in their friendship. Louis Bromfield in his novel *Mr. Smith* (1951) went a step further to battle against the puritanical hypocrisy of small-town America. In his attempt to liberate the emotions, he depicts the physical component of adolescent friendships. A section of his novel is set in the masculine world of the college fraternity, where physical appearance is as important as physical, athletic ability. *Mr. Smith's* narrator informs us: "I 'made' one of the better fraternities for a variety of reasons. I was not bad looking. I had clean expensive clothes. . . . I showed some prowess in athletics and I had money to spend."

"Mr. Smith's" looks are typically American: "The face was perhaps a better-looking than average face, with a straight nose, a rather full mouth, blondish, slightly curling hair, a rather stubborn chin." Here we have the face of *Homo americanus,* the incarnate dream that haunts the American homosexual imagination. We find it set on the shoulders of David, Baldwin's protagonist, and it recurs in each of Gore Vidal's novels.

At college, Smith is attracted to the handsome Frank: "As I have grown older and experienced more it has occurred to me that there existed between Frank and myself a kind of physical attraction. . . . It was, of course, something which neither of us could or would recognize and something which most people never quite understand or realize—the attraction of two pleasant, good-looking people of the same sex for each other."

Intense Friendships: Relationship Rejected

A Separate Peace (1959), by John Knowles, takes place in a private boys' school known as Devon (since identified as Exeter), where English public-school traditions have been upheld amidst

Gothic architecture, parks, and playing fields. The first pages of the book introduce Phineas (Finny), the school athletic star, twin brother or first cousin to the heroes in Fitzgerald, Maxwell, Bromfield, et al. Gene Forrester, the narrator, returning to the school several years later in search of the past—like Tennyson in *In Memoriam*—remembers Finny, his partner in a tormenting and tormented relationship. With Finny, Gene had experienced the conflicting feeling that Lymie felt for Spud: envy, mixed with pride at being the friend of such a strong, handsome boy.

In the totally masculine universe of Devon School, their friendship changes into hatred out of fear of its changing into love. Gene recalls that the envy which then seemed to him perfectly normal was in reality hatred for Finny's physical superiority. His awareness of his own physical inferiority had engendered his fear of becoming—as Lymie did—the passive element in their union. Gene's fear is of wanting to be the other not simply by taking him for a model to rival and to emulate; his worry is that in attaching himself to Finny he would come to love him. Gene's hatred of Finny reveals his refusal to eroticize the desire for identification with him. This frantic refusal to become Finny's masochistic partner is translated into a fatal act: Gene shakes the branch from which they are diving hand in hand into the river. In attempting to kill or maim Finny by means of the tree which ironically is the symbol of their friendship (they had become "best friends" after daring each other to jump from the topmost branch), Gene would destroy the virile ideal to which he cannot conform, and in so doing become himself, without complexes and neurosis. His act takes on far-reaching social implications. Gene mutilates the American Dream, the cause of so much sexual maladjustment.

Finny, the dream incarnate, dies during an operation following another fall: a bit of bone marrow escapes and, with symbolic import, blocks his heart. Gene subsequently joins the Navy, that "virile" branch of the service whose homosexual bent is considerable. Here he must keep pace with the other recruits: "I fell into step as well as my nature, Phineas-filled, would allow."

His identification with Finny has been achieved at the cost of the idol's mutilation and death: Gene, sober and dull, has destroyed Finny's "harmonious and natural unity." We can imagine that Phineas's presence within the narrator will form the basis for a powerful neurosis. Gene's return to Devon School years later in search of his past is the expression of an insurmountable frustration for having missed out on happiness, for having mislaid his own identity, his life.

Initiation

Homosexual Initiation as Defiance

In *The Folded Leaf* the "sissy"—long a peripheral type in American literature—became a character of central importance. In Truman Capote's *Other Voices, Other Rooms* the character Joel is a new version of Lymie, or of Jamie in *Kings Row*, but his emotional development is so meticulously described that he takes on an allegorical quality. Capote's novel treats the renunciation of virility and the conditions that favor it.

From the novel's first pages, we can discern the figure of the rejected masculine prototype in structured southern society: Sam Radcliff, the rough truck driver who brings Joel to Noon City, heightens by contrast the incongruity of the boy's presence in such surroundings, just as there is something somehow wrong with Jamie's presence in Kings Row, or Lymie's in Chicago. Radcliff has his own notions about what a "real boy" ought to be, and he is shocked by Joel: "He was too pretty, too delicate and fair-skinned; each of his features was shaped with a sensitive accuracy and a girlish tenderness softened his eyes, which were brown and very large. His brown hair, cut short, was streaked with pure yellow strands." From the beginning—as in the novels of Maxwell or Bellaman—the dissonance between the effeminate boy and his surroundings is physical, and the authors have quite naturally expressed this difference in the same words.

Joel's sexual fantasies arise in the course of a search for his father. They take the image of a window opening onto a completely different world into which one cannot go, a window that allows a glimpse into intimacy. Looking in a window one day, Joel sees, "most puzzling of all, two grown men standing in an ugly little room kissing each other." This furtive, horrible vision serves to introduce him to homosexuality. More subtle, and hence more dangerous, is the vision at another window of the "queer lady." This vision is superimposed in Joel's mind on the previous one: "She was holding aside the curtains of the left corner window, and smiling and nodding at him, as if in greeting or approval." Like Miles in *The Turn of the Screw,* Joel sees creatures who are mysterious, almost supernatural, and troubling. They are in fact projections of an inclination which is gathering force and seeking an outlet. Joel "debarks" into the haunted domains of his own inner demons.

The only model at hand to satisfy his search both for his father and his own identity is his uncle Randolph, with the plump little feet, varnished toenails, and a woman's ring. In the letters Joel writes to a chum, he lies: his father is young, tall, athletic. Ironically, the only person who comes close to this virile ideal is Idabel, the tomboy. "He wished he were as brave as Idabel." Far from helping Joel achieve virility, she rejects him, casting him into the world of the effeminate, the girlish. The only child of his own age with whom he might have been close, Idabel becomes instead a reproach to him: more of a boy than he is, she makes him constantly ashamed of himself.

The only virile presence is—paradoxically—the memory of Pepe Alvarez, the handsome boxer whose brute strength represents animal violence in this feminine world. For Joel, Pepe is at first only a name on envelopes in a mail box. It is a name that reeks of *machismo* to a young and delicate boy. It soon becomes apparent that uncle Randolph is passionately in love with Alvarez, his opposite. Just as Joel seeks his father in order to become him, Randolph is bound to this embodiment of virility and sensuality.

Randolph recounts the story of his life with Alvarez after Joel discovers that his father is an idiot, confined to his bed, and also after losing a quarrel with Idabel—thus losing a bit more of his virility. These incidents start Joel on the path to accepting a different sexual role. Without a strong father-image whose virility he might emulate, with no hope of dominating a woman, he can now enter Randolph's room full of silks and baroque mirrors, a world that will one day be his own. Despite his revulsion for such bad taste, for effeminacy which like Nirvana entraps one, the room is a foretaste for Joel of the homosexual life he will lead once he has given in to his uncle. The "queer lady" of his "heterosexual" fantasy was in fact none other than Randolph himself, reliving a scene at a costume ball where, dressed as an eighteenth-century countess, he had danced with Alvarez without the latter knowing who he was. Randolph's supreme joy: to be mistaken for a woman! "Ah, if I were really me!"

Capote's novel deals with the perilous moment of passage from childhood to adolescence when everything can be lost or won. Yet the chances of Joel's becoming heterosexual are slim indeed.

By the end of the book Joel has recognized his inner personality, and the joy he shows seems to indicate that he hopes to make his life a paradise, not a homosexual hell. This will obviously be difficult, to judge by the neurasthenic solitude of his teacher, Randolph, shut away in his room, living with memories and dreams, and confessing—like Starwick, the professor in *Of Time and the River*—that he is more dead than alive, a creature whose only moments of inner peace are when he can be "himself," dressed as a French countess. When Joel again sees the queer lady in the window, he recognizes his own inner demon whom he must face in order to exorcise it and live in peace with himself: "unafraid, not hesitating, he paused only at the garden's edge where, as though he'd forgotten something, he stopped and looked back at the bloomless, descending blue, at the boy he had left behind."

Other Voices, Other Rooms is a novel of self-recognition, particularly homosexual recognition. From an allegorical viewpoint, its moral is to follow one's basic nature against the ideals of a hostile society. Joel's refuge in homosexuality is the only solution to the anxiety plaguing anyone who adopts against his nature the sexual mores of society.

Truman Capote ended his novel at the threshold of "initiation," the moment Joel gives up wanting to be a "boy"—that is, a copy of what a male ought to be within American society. William Goyen's novel *The House of Breath* (1950) is wholly devoted to the *sexual initiation* of its characters—the narrator, Christy, and Follie. This initiation occurs during adolescence in an atmosphere of poetry, out of doors, in celebration of sexuality in a natural, pantheistic ceremony. Capote's style, rich in overtones and metaphors, masterfully captured the foreboding atmosphere of a small southern town drained by the sun, where the only reality seemed to be the strange, the mysterious. In Goyen's novel, the sole reality is memory, the memory of a disturbing and poetic childhood that is recalled by the narrator, who has left Charity, a Texas town. Here, as in Capote, the sexual longings of adolescence are embodied in an atmosphere of extraordinary mystery and strangeness. Instead of a "queer" lady, there is a "strange" river which speaks, young people run away to join circuses (like Idabel and Joel), or become sailors (as Idabel wanted to do).

The narrator's first orgasm occurs during a swimming party. It is a homosexual orgasm, since Christy, the narrator's uncle, knows that he has been its cause. Indirectly, therefore, Christy initiates the narrator. He himself had been initiated in the poetic atmosphere of a ship. (In this novel, water is a masculine symbol; it is the sailor's element, the symbol of men living with men, far from the feminizing conventions of landbound society.) On the ship where he was a sailor, Christy was attracted to a face that reminded him of his brother Follie. It is a scene of overt incestuous desire from which the female element is totally absent: it is the desire for a man who resembles one's brother.

Christy had raised his brother Follie, who is less than fond of him because he considers Christy effeminate: "I was Follie's mother all those years, makes me part woman and I know it and I'll never get over it. . . . Began to wear Mama's kimono and highheeled shoes and play show." In Christy's remembered world, everything has dissolved into femininity. Initiation is truly the passage from one sex to another. In Goyen's novel, as in *Other Voices, Other Rooms,* homosexual initiation means becoming the "queer lady," wearing high heels or powdered wigs. In the hypervirile atmosphere of a small southern town, there is no place for ambivalence, or for the "normality" of feelings that go "against nature." One is either white or black, male or female.

The love that exists between Christy and the narrator becomes the experience which reveals the narrator to himself, makes him part of life, of the world and its beauty. It marks the end of his adolescence and the beginning of adulthood. After it, the narrator can leave Christy, leave the "house of breath," and set out for freedom—or for slavery. Initiation, as the violation of innocence, is a rite of passage, and it can lead either to hell or to heaven. Like Capote, Goyen stresses this dual possibility, although the outcome, whether happy or unhappy, means little. Most important is the discovery of one's identity, which, both for Joel and the narrator of *The House of Breath*, turns out to be a sexual identity that is rejected by society. The narrator, however, like Randolph, employs all the poetry of metaphor to transform the wound, the rape, the abandonment, into a magic rite that gives him knowledge of the world and of himself.

Homosexual Initiation Outside American Reality

Follie and Randolph rebel against the meanness of their surroundings, but their rebellion reveals the extent to which those surroundings have marked them, since it is manifested by flight: Randolph's escape into his timeless room, into memory and sexual fantasies, and Follie's running away to a circus—a carnival atmosphere which is a parody of joy—and lastly the narrator's flight from the house of breath.

In his famous short story "Pages from Cold Point" Paul Bowles treated, at this same period (1949), the theme of homosexual initiation with a moral detachment that was capable of being sustained only for the brief space of a short story. As in *Other Voices, Other Rooms* and *The House of Breath*, initiation is tinged with male incest, that is, with "concentrated" homosexuality. Joel yielded to his uncle, Christy saw his brother in the person of his first lover, and Goyen's narrator was seduced by two uncles, Christy and Follie. In "Pages from Cold Point" Bowles casts a father and his adored, handsome son, Racky, onto a tropical island following the mother's death. There is something equivocal in the father's adoration of his son, given his jealousy of Racky's black friends, with whom the young man spends all his time, and particularly of Peter, the seventeen-year-old gardener.

This beautifully written story is of a liberated neutrality that is found in no other literary work of this period. Free from finan-

cial problems and without any social prejudices, the two protagonists are removed from society. The story's truly amoral and
revolutionary element is the American father's complete and
complicitous acceptance of his son's homosexuality. Generally
the father is the virile role-model with which the son attempts to
identify; here, however, the father is depicted as liberal and tolerant. The revelation that Racky has been "initiating" his black
comrades, far from dividing father and son, brings them closer
together, literally into the same bed. Yet even here beneath this
story of a well-balanced adolescent's free choice of an amoral
way of life is the common theme of flight from American society.
And it is important to remember that the moral detachment and
"normal" attitude toward homosexuality were at this time viable
only within the brief span of a short story, and within the paren-
thesis of life outside America.

Homosexual Initiation Within American Reality

GORE VIDAL'S ADOLESCENTS

The adolescents of Melville and Faulkner, on the one hand,
and of Capote, Goyen, and Bowles, on the other, are in some degree un-American in their behavior, their longings, their way of
life. Melville's Pierre, who has a European first name, lives
among refined, New England society and writes sentimental letters full of Beloved's and Dearest's. Henry Sutpen idolizes a pre-
tentiously French, effeminate dandy. And the protagonists of
Capote, Goyen, and Bowles, who cross the threshold into homosexuality—in contrast to the unfilled longings of Pierre and
Henry—take refuge in a separate world that is poetic and
strange. The heroes worshiped by Basil, Jester, Don, and "Mr.
Smith"—magnificent athletes, perfectly integrated into school
life and into the small town, the microcosm of America—are
elevated on pillars of purity, inaccessible to contact with their
admirers, and are not in any way involved in sexual initiation.
Bowles's Racky initiated young comrades who were black and
Cuban—not Americans.

In 1948 Gore Vidal brought together two American adolescents, white, athletic and virile, "idols," "heroes," in mutual ini-

tiation. The effort amounted to making Spud into Ted Fay's lover.

Vidal's overt attempt to break the stereotype of the effeminate, contemptible homosexual in *The City and the Pillar* is a partial failure, since the one "normal" partner becomes a completely heterosexual American male—it is the very definition of his normality.

Vidal's obsessions are revealed in book after book. In his next novel, *The Season of Comfort* (1949), he deals with the ambiguous world of adolescence where sex between virile, healthy boys is "normal," part of the accepted morality, and thus does not produce in them incapacitating neuroses or lead them to take refuge in a special reassuring but sordid milieu. Bill is the protagonist; his name is a typically American name, a real boy's name, which, like Jim or Bob, seems to be a concentration of virile energy—unlike Pierre, Basil, Lymie, Jamie, Joel, etc., which have something vaguely European about them, something different, something feminine.

Bill shares the attitude typical of Vidal's young men, who are continually on the verge of homosexuality—fearing it while at the same time wanting to taste its pleasures. Jess, the class leader who adopts Bill as his protégé, "does things," and Jimmy Wesson, who is handsome, virile, and equally popular, becomes Bill's first sexual partner. "They did things with one another at night," and after initial feelings of remorse (which protect their virility and normality), they repeat the experiment many times. However, like good American heroes—and following what psychology and sociology have taught us—they abandon these practices when they have their first heterosexual experience. But before this "conversion" (the unfolding of the leaf, as William Maxwell expressed it, or the appearance of the fruit, in Melville's words), Jimmy and Bill are "in love" with each other, although Bill, who is aware of the nature of the emotion he is experiencing, never pronounces the word.

Bill experiences only a passing interest in girls. When he happens to make love to a girl, it is only in the company of other athletes, including Jim: "He found the act unsatisfying, but the circumstances were exciting, strange." The "act" is the heterosexual act, and the "circumstances" the basically homosexual atmosphere of those orgies in which one girl is the shared partner of a group of men.

Vidal is attempting, as usual, to preserve his adolescents' normality, at the same time he has them commit "abnormal" acts, as if protecting by magic the purity and innocence of sexual relations between handsome, athletic boys. Jimmy's memory will remain fresh and pure, enhaloed by his wartime death in the Marines—a virile death indeed. Bill's character is later reincarnated in the narrator of "Pages from an Abandoned Journal." We meet him in Paris frequenting homosexual hangouts while (theoretically) a heterosexual. Five years later, we meet Bill again. Gradually we discover that he has become homosexual and that Helen, his fiancée, has married someone else. In Vidal's books (and Baldwin's)—as in Proust's—all the male characters sooner or later become homosexuals.

In "The Zenner Trophy," a story in the collection *A Thirsty Evil* (1956), Vidal pushes his obsession with "normal" adolescent homosexuality to its limits. Flynn and Sawyer are caught in the act by two members of the faculty. Flynn is the school's most outstanding athlete. He is the epitome, or archetype, of the adolescent hero.

He is easily recognizable as the "All-American Boy": well-scrubbed, young, healthy, virile but not tough, with his crew-cut hair, young men like him were summed up in the phrase "clean-cut." However, the symbolism of short hair that curls as soon as it is allowed to grow (which makes Flynn resemble Dionysus) is obvious: underneath the accepted exterior, under the shell society imposes—and which the "normal" boy adopts without difficulty—there lies concealed a love for sensuality, ready to blossom (Flynn reads Keats, the most sensual of English poets). Dionysus, the god of wine and nature, is the counterpart to Apollo, god of classical beauty and restraint.

Thus we have a boy who loves another, no less athletic, no less well-integrated boy: "He's on the track team. He's the best sprinter we've got," Flynn says of his friend. And in contrast to the shy Mr. Beckman, to whom is assigned the task of expelling him, Flynn appears well-balanced and the personification of contentment. Faced with this well-developed and contented young man, so calmly but so firmly flouting the most solid American institutions, Mr. Beckman reaches an awareness of the wreck of his own life, and of his own solitude.

It is no accident, however, that moral detachment—particularly Flynn's flouting of established morality—is depicted in a short story rather than in a novel. The short story takes as its subject a searing, unique *instant*, a brief moment out of a life, cut off from past and future, whereas the novel sets such moments in the context of reality, where life—that is, the Freudian antagonism between the pleasure principle (the particular sensual moment) and the reality principle (antihomosexual society) —sees to it that undesirables are ghettoed in sordid places where people like Flynn and Sawyer would find it extremely difficult to experience happiness. Within the confines of a short story, however, this utopia is possible. It recalls, completes, and carries forward the utopia envisioned in "Pages from Cold Point," but it is even more daring, since it describes amorality in an American school in the 1950s, the training ground of "he-men." And ironically, the school hero, the winner of the envied and symbolic athletic trophy of a vast, virile mythology, becomes the happy homosexual rebel.

ADOLESCENTS IN THE WORK OF JAMES BALDWIN

The early pages of *Go Tell It on the Mountain* (1953) make plain the importance of seventeen-year-old Elisha in the emotional life of John, a slightly younger Harlem black: "He . . . was a preacher. John stared at Elisha all during the lesson, admiring the timbre of Elisha's voice, much deeper and manlier than his own, admiring the leanness, and grace, and strength, and darkness of Elisha."

Baldwin, like Vidal, catches his adolescent boys at the moment of sexual uncertainty. On his fourteenth birthday, John masturbates while fantasizing a woman, but the author immediately adds that his fantasies (like those of Jim or Bill) are not exclusively heterosexual: "In the school lavatory, alone, thinking of the boys, older, bigger, braver, who made bets with each other as to whose urine could arch higher, he had watched in himself a transformation of which he would never dare to speak."

Joel was too pretty to be an authentic American boy, as was

Jamie in *Kings Row*. John's problem is his ugliness. This physical complex is combined with hatred for his stepfather, who is violently hateful toward John, the living reminder of his wife's sin: "In [his fantasy] world John, who was, his father said, ugly, who was always the smallest boy in his class, and who had no friends, became immediately beautiful, tall, and popular. People fell all over themselves to meet John Grimes."

This is almost identically the dream of Lymie, puny, clumsy, and introverted, who adapted to the virile ideal by an erotic attachment to the handsome and virile Spud. As in Maxwell, the adolescent's introversion, his existential *malaise*, is accentuated by his rejected identification with his father. Lymie's father was a man who had ruined his life; John Grimes's stepfather—his true father had committed suicide when very young, before marrying John's mother—is too forbidding. Identification requires admiration, love, and, of course, desire to be like the other. Now, "he lived for the day when his father would be dying and he, John, would curse him on his deathbed."

His stepfather forces John to cut himself off from the world, forbids him to play with the other boys who normally assist a child in assuming his sexual role. Boys playing ball in the street become the embodiment of a dream. They are the epitome of grace, virility, freedom from care, of adjustment and zest for living. John observes them through the window while sitting in his father's chair, consumed with the desire to be with them, *to have a body like theirs*. He realizes that intellectually he is superior to them, but he also knows that in the boys' world intellectual ability means nothing.

Elisha is the handsome, athletic boy, pure and heterosexual, whom we have already encountered in so many white American novels. John admires and loves him, and he manages to have physical contact with him in the guise of friendly scuffling. In church, while they are supposed to be cleaning, they engage in such a struggle, and the body-to-body contact, filling John with "strength that was almost hatred" and "wild delight," takes on highly equivocal characteristics in the context of his admiration. The hatred John comes close to feeling recalls Lymie's emotions when struggling with Spud, a contest which leads to orgasm in

Maxwell's novel. In such a contest, which like most has a sado-masochistic component, hatred is an emotion very like love—or, more precisely, eroticism. The body's presence is intensely felt, each muscle becomes visible: hands touch shoulders and biceps, knees struggle to make contact with the enemy's belly. When Elisha's hands are clasped around John's waist, his breathing takes on a quickened rhythm as though he were making love. John, who does not want to be conquered, experiences pleasure at seeing his idol's face show cruelty—cruelty which changes to tenderness once the struggle is over: "I didn't hurt you none, did I?" Elisha asks.

Symbolically, John's "conversion" occurs "in the dusty space before the altar which he and Elisha had cleaned." It is a transformation prompted both by hatred for his father and love for Elisha. As part of the ritual, Elisha submits to the power of the Lord and speaks in tongues; seeing him, John too goes into a trance. For John the trance becomes the most intimate means—much more so than struggle—of entering into contact with Elisha and, simultaneously, of denying his father. "As he cursed his father, so he loved Elisha."

Just before John leaves Elisha, he places his trembling hand on the older boy's arm and asks him to love him in advance as he is, as he will be: "No matter what happens to me, where I go, what folks say about me, no matter what *anybody* says, you remember—please remember—I was saved. I was *there*." Elisha then kisses John on the forehead, "a holy kiss." The sunlight "fell over Elisha like a golden robe, and struck John's forehead, where Elisha had kissed him, like a seal ineffaceable forever." This kiss is John's true initiation. Chaste and holy, yet its immutable and permanent character makes it like a deflowering to mark the passage from innocence to knowledge. Henceforth, John can face the hostility of the world and of his father—like the narrator of *The House of Breath* once Christy has broken his "seal of secrets," or like Joel when he comes to accept his fundamental personality. The final words of *Go Tell It on the Mountain* echo those of *Other Voices, Other Rooms:* " 'I'm ready,' John said, 'I'm coming. I'm on my way.' "

Baldwin's short story "The Outing," written in 1951 at the

same period as *Go Tell It on the Mountain*, focuses on the same Grimes family, Elisha, and the community of "saints." In this story, John is still Gabriel's despised son. From the first, we are aware that John has transferred his affection to David, an older boy who in turn dreams of Sylvia, a pretty teenager who seems to prefer Elisha's company. In the course of the church outing, the characters of both John and David are revealed.

David is one of the boys playing in the street to the full admiration of John behind the window in *Go Tell It on the Mountain*. In the short story, however, John is intimate with one of these semidelinquent youths, which is far more exciting than being chastely kissed on the forehead by a "saved" adolescent, a Sunday-school teacher, a self-controlled prude like Brother Elisha! Being the intimate friend of one of these street boys—against whom his father has warned him as one warns a girl against an overexperienced boy—is tantamount to breaking free at last from the family shackles, from the strict, puritanical, effeminate upbringing which prohibited him from going out, forced him to stay home with his mother, and precluded his contact with virility. However, his father's harmful and castrating hatred, which has destroyed John's desire for identification, has already taken its toll, and John cannot take the same attitude toward David as a "normal" boy would toward his idol; John's is the attitude of a homosexual toward the man he loves.

He is jealous when he sees the extent to which David is preoccupied with Sylvia, and he realizes that although he had thought he was interested in her too, he was mistaken. Eventually David returns to him, having spent most of the day with Sylvia, yet the outing ends badly for John. All at once he realizes that David will develop "normally" and will one day leave him. "But now where there had been peace there was only panic and where there had been safety, danger, like a flower, opened."

Woman is present, waiting—involuntarily—to come between boys who are in love, because in Baldwin's work the one who is loved must always retain a certain degree of heterosexuality if he is to remain the Beloved. Elisha and David are both *primarily* heterosexual. And woman will always be a rival for the homosexual. Here we have, in embryonic form, the schema of *Giovanni's*

Room, in which Hella is the rival—the momentarily successful rival—of Giovanni; his love, which is without any sense of guilt, recalls that of John. (Giovanni is Italian for John, and Giovanni's beloved is also named David.)

David of *Giovanni's Room* recalls his first homosexual experience with Joey, another adolescent. This occurred one summer at Coney Island where they had spent the day swimming and flirting with girls (of whom they are actually afraid). They return to Joey's house and take showers: "And I think it began in the shower." These are also Vidal's settings: the sun and water and showers are pivotal in *The City and the Pillar* and *The Season of Comfort,* where sexual awakening similarly occurs under the aegis of bodily cleanliness. In David's case, the usual wrestling develops into a carnal embrace on Joey's bed. Trembling, hearts pounding, they kiss, inwardly terrified of what they are doing.

This fear, mixed as it is with the irresistible attraction for another boy's virile body, is experienced *ad nauseam* by David when he is with Giovanni, or with the soldier and sailors that haunt his life. Again like Vidal's protagonists, David is trapped between his horror of homosexuality and his frantic desire for masculine embraces. This reaction of fear and guilt reveals a desperate attempt to preserve mental health. It is a conflict which both Vidal and Baldwin confront, and in book after book they attempt to resolve it. Commonly for both, the sexually confused stage of adolescence is the chosen ground on which homosexuality—linked with heterosexual desire for the girls on the beach (in *Giovanni's Room*) or in dreams (in Vidal's novels) —can briefly flourish and appear to be accepted as healthy, virile, and normal.

In *Giovanni's Room* the boys are white; in *Go Tell It on the Mountain* and "The Outing" they are black. *Another Country* (1962) is a crucible in which the races and sexes are combined, and for the first time in Baldwin's work we have a black boy loved by a white, a schema that reminds us of Carson McCullers's *Clock Without Hands.* (Both novels are set in the hostile South.)

Eric is a feminine child who likes to dress up, to put on his mother's clothes and perform in front of a mirror—he wants to be an actor. Baldwin, in a flashback, examines the genesis of sexuality in the boy and his acceptance of it.

Eric's first love is LeRoy, a young black of seventeen, one year older than himself. Gradually, in spite of social pressure—created by both whites and blacks—the boys' friendship increases and becomes erotic, despite Eric's own ignorance; he is not yet aware of his true nature, notwithstanding his vague, intense feelings and his obsession with LeRoy's body, which is "hideously desired." Eric is a version of John, while LeRoy is the embodiment of David ("The Outing") and, to a lesser degree, of Elisha. However, *Another Country* does not end after the act of initiation, and Eric's desires in time become reality. LeRoy becomes his first lover.

The homosexual's—Eric's—adolescence ends with the difficult but complete acceptance of his identity. Homosexual initiation—as with Joel (*The House of Breath*) and John Grimes—opens the door to the adult world, a hostile world in which one must nonetheless live, while attempting at all times to be oneself, sincere and whole, preserving in oneself all the innocence and richness of that marvelous moment of initiation.

Baldwin's novels follow a graph drawn in black and white. The homosexual theme changes according to the color arrangement. John Grimes was initiated by a black; David, the white protagonist of *Giovanni's Room*, by a white; Eric, white, by a black (this heteroracial and homosexual initiation foreshadows the mixing of races and sexual preferences in the novel), and lastly, in *Tell Me How Long the Train's Been Gone*, Baldwin returns to intraracial homosexual initiation. Leo Proudhammer experiences his first orgasm in the arms of his older brother Caleb, a handsome, independent young man, virile and militant, a modern version of David and LeRoy. Here again, initiation is combined with incest, which is a reflection of the basic narcissism attributed to the homosexual personality.

Leo's initiation occurs midway through the book, and it foreshadows the ending, which is Leo's discovery of true love within his own sex and race in Christopher, a young black revolutionary, yet another avatar of the many young, virile, black rebels haunting Baldwin's imagination. As in the other novels, the initiation is in no way accidental; it is predetermined by the adolescent's deepest unconscious tendencies and serves to reveal to him his true nature, the nature he comes to accept at a relatively late stage. In this novel, as in the others, the theme is self-acceptance. Between initiation and his acceptance, Leo Proudhammer lives a lie. The novel's circular structure (aside from the many flashbacks it contains) is an attempt to unite the ecstatic moment of initiation with the more lucid, less tumultuous, but also enduring moment of the discovery of love, which is, for Baldwin, homosexual happiness.

Chapter Five

Teacher and Pupil

During their school years, Lymie and Spud, Pierre and Glen, Finny and Gene, Vidal's and Baldwin's adolescents loved each other roughly but with tenderness, had passionate homosexual experiences with each other, or acted out their relationships in an atmosphere of sadomasochistic interdependence that was not consciously sexual. Teachers were a world apart, and they rarely intervened to disturb these relationships of which for the most part they were totally unaware.

The schema of these "liaisons," however, was shaped by a link between an older and a younger character. In Fitzgerald's stories, Basil's "heroes" were as distant from him as adults: the hero's qualities served as an ideal for Basil, but there could develop no intimate relationship between them. Don, in *The Lost Weekend,* idolized an older boy during his adolescence, and similarly in *Clock Without Hands,* Jester felt love and admiration for Ted. The theme of love-admiration of a younger boy for one older than he was made overtly sexual in *Absalom, Absalom!,* in Williams's story "The Resemblance Between a Violin Case and a Coffin," and in Bromfield's lucid analysis. Adolescents who consider the Other an equal are rare. Lymie, Gene, and the other boys admired their comrades Spud, Finny, et al., and the older boys were attracted by the natural contrast they saw in the younger boys. Adolescents themselves and uncertain of their own virility, they treated the love-friendship relationship with varying degrees of condescension according to an active-passive (sadomasochist) schema, for the purpose of assuring or reassuring themselves of their own masculinity.

We recognize here the same relationship that was prevalent in ancient Greece between master and disciple. In an article in *Playboy* Paul Goodman, an overtly homosexual writer, declared that the taboo against homosexuality weakens the educational system and depersonalizes it. He contended that the teacher-pupil relationship is almost always an erotic one. If we fear this intrinsic erotic feeling's becoming overtly sexual, the teacher-pupil relationship degenerates or, worse, becomes cold and harsh. Our culture is wanting in sexual pedagogical friendships —both heterosexual and homosexual—which have been characteristic of other cultures.

In *The History of Education in Antiquity,* H. I. Marrou deals with these friendships, or "dreadful aberrations," and the role they played in the teacher-pupil relationship. According to him they derive from an "antifeminine ideal of complete manliness," common to so many American authors, from Cooper to Hemingway, by way of Jack London. This ideal cannot help but fascinate the homosexual imagination, whose conflict lies in the apparently irreconcilable natures of virility and homosexuality. Marrou contends that the homosexual attempts to resolve the frustration of his inability to reproduce by means of pedagogic pederasty. He explains that for the Greeks, education (*paideia*) was based on deep and intimate relationships that personally linked a young mind—the *eromenos,* or Beloved—to an older mind—the *erastes,* or Lover—which acted as a model, guide, and initiator of relationships that were disturbed and heated by the spark of passion.

The teacher's attraction for his pupil appears in many stories with homosexual overtones. In addition to those mentioned below, there is Charles Jackson's *The Fall of Valor,* in which Cliff Hauman reacts to a teacher's surreptitious advances; Vance Bourjaily's *The End of My Life,* in which the character Ron believes he has discovered a homosexual among his teachers; J. D. Salinger's *The Catcher in the Rye,* in which Holden Caulfield is certain that Mr. Antolini is making advances to him; Paul Goodman's *Parents' Day;* John Horne Burns's *Lucifer with a Book;* and J. P. Donleavy's *The Ginger Man,* in which O'Keefe has a relationship with one of his young French students.

The Teacher, a Gentle Father-Figure

In his biography of Henry James, Leon Edel tells us that "The Pupil" (1891) is based on a true story, and he emphasizes the fact that "the friendship and affection between tutors and their charges were regarded as normal in the Victorian age," and that "there was among readers or editors" no "awareness of or alertness to deviation." However, he notes that in this case the editor-in-chief of *The Atlantic Monthly* rejected James's story: "Scudder may have been worried by the possible hint of unconscious homosexuality in the attachment of tutor and boy."

Morgan's parents, Americans living in Europe beyond their means and experiencing periods of relative prosperity followed by sudden collapses into near indigence, travel, neglecting to pay their bills, including the salary of their son's tutor. Such a way of life is sure to have a profound effect on a boy's character, caught between a domineering mother and a father who prefers his elder son. Morgan's parents appear to want to be rid of him; they are pleased at the affection that develops between tutor and pupil and encourage it. James delineates the emotions of a future homosexual: a feeling of parental rejection and, an inability to identify with the father (here an ineffectual man who is always absent and prefers the older brother).

Events are precipitated by the parents' sudden financial collapse. They regard this as an opportunity to rid themselves of their adolescent son "temporarily" (they do not get rid of the elder Ulick, nor of their two daughters), and hand him over to his tutor for good. Morgan, overcome with joy at this maneuver, cries out, "Do you mean that he may take me to live with him— for ever and ever? . . . Away, away, anywhere he likes?"

Morgan symbolically turns "away from his father . . . with a light in his face," and looks at the tutor, Pemberton. The overwheming emotion causes the boy's heart literally to stop, evidencing the personality breakdown of a being from whom the basis for the "ego" has been suddenly withdrawn. His escape from neurosis, his hope of living in another world, the world of someone he loves and who loves him in return, brings on the breakdown of his emotional equilibrium by undermining the bases of his ego.

A superb psychologist, James intuited with great genius one of the generative patterns of homosexual neurosis: mismatched parents, a domineering, overprotective mother concealing her lack of love for her child, an "absent" father both in a real and figurative sense, unable to communicate with his son, who eventually "turns away" from him once and for all to identify himself with another—but too late, since the introjection does not occur before puberty, and the attempt at identification inevitably leads to eroticism—and a weak, lonely, introverted child, rightly resenting his parents' "rejection," despite appearances.

The appearance of the young tutor, an erastes whose mission it is to shape his pupil's mind, and personality, in other words to replace the father allows James to complete the pattern which results in homosexuality. That spiritual intimacy borders on sexual intimacy, as Paul Goodman has stated, is implicit in this story by James.

At the story's symbolic ending, mother and "lover" tug at the body of the child whose heart has stopped: "He half tore him from his mother's arms and, for an instant, while they were both holding him, they looked all their dismay into each other's eyes."

James's story was first published in *Longman's Magazine* (1891); it was later reprinted in *The Lesson of the Master* (1892). For this second appearance, James altered the original text to moderate the tenderness and love between tutor and pupil. In the separation scene (when Pemberton must leave for England), the phrase "he had never loved him so," was deleted. In another passage, the word "tenderly" to describe the manner in which the tutor holds his pupil in his arms, was also omitted. In addition, the incongruity of Morgan's temperament is blunted in the second version: "The humor that made his queer delicacies manly" is replaced by "The humor that made his sensitiveness manly." The link between the "lover" and the boy's mother is more obvious in the original closing: "they looked all their dismay into each other's eyes" becomes "they looked, in their dismay, into each other's eyes."

The Virtues of "Pedagogic" Teaching

In "Hands," Sherwood Anderson dealt with the pedagogical virtues of physical contact between teacher and pupil, a contact that occurs in "The Pupil" but which Henry James was careful not to comment upon, for his moral rebellion against a puritan and narrow-minded America never took the form of strong, open denunciation. But Anderson, more iconoclastic than James and taking advantage of the prevailing interest in Freudian psycho-analysis, went much further and extolled the pedagogic virtues of homoerotic contact between teacher and pupil: "Under the caress of his hands, doubt and disbelief went out of the minds of the boys and they began also to dream."

For Anderson, as for Paul Goodman, an atmosphere of love and erotic tenderness can assist in the development of person-ality for both teacher and disciple. This is the Platonic ideal of eroticizing the pedagogic relationship, the erastes and the ero-menos. In "Hands" the children say nothing *until a scandal oc-curs:* childhood and adolescence easily tolerate love on many levels as long as society does not violently interfere; society is what transforms the polymorphous-perverse being into a het-erosexual. Scandal is the manifestation of a clash between the id and the superego. As soon as some "evil" is discerned in the teacher, homosexuality looms up, the smile becomes a hideous grimace. Already conditioned by his society, the pupil sees his overattentive teacher as the ultimate incarnation of evil.

In *Of Time and the River,* Thomas Wolfe describes Eugene Gant, a small-town boy, similar in his naïveté to the children in "Hands" before the outbreak of scandal. Like them, Eugene gives way to his professor's charms and profits from his compan-ionship, despite the man's bestial grimaces, his often strange way of speaking, the overrefinement and undue elegance of his apartment. As with master and disciple in ancient Greece, the pupil learns nothing very concrete from Professor Starwick, but he is made aware of life, of the beauty of nature and of culture, through his contact with the admired older man.

In describing the erastes-eromenos relationship, H. I. Marrou mentions "the lover's desire to gain the boy's affection and shine before him [that arouses] feelings of ardent and active admiration in the latter." Complementing this expenditure of loving effort by an elder concerned to promote the growth of a younger man is the latter's desire "to respond to this love and show himself worthy of it." In Wolfe's novel, the elegant setting of Harvard—an all-male school at the time—is the perfect counterpart to the type of place in Greece in which this kind of ambiguous and rewarding relationship flourished.

It may be that in Sparta Eugene and Starwick would have been lovers, and that both men would have benefited from this love. Instead the younger man reacts violently when he finally understands the elder's morals, an indication of Western socialization. Eugene's recognition of the devil's face beneath the professor's pleasant appearance corresponds to the explosion of the scandal in "Hands," and to Morgan's death in "The Pupil." The abscess must be lanced, or one of the lovers must die, in order that morality—Christian morality—may be upheld.

In the company of the older man, the master, the boy glimpses the possibility of one day knowing "the enchanted city of the great comrades and the glorious women," in which everything will be joyful, poetic, beautiful and fine, happy. However, Starwick's *presence* alone is not what magically changes everything for Eugene, but their discussions, which also have a pedagogic value, as Eugene later recalls: "Ah, but I was *good* there! I could see how he admired me, how high a place I had in his affection." Eugene is thus a prime example of Marrou's "ennobling power of emulation."

Furthermore, despite his horror and disgust, Eugene is fully open to and grateful for his master's decisive and ineradicable influence, so long as his true nature is forgotten. However, the beauty and rewards of this Harvard friendship are destroyed by Starwick's self-loathing and by Eugene's outburst of hatred when he realizes that he has been in danger of flouting society's taboos.

While in *Of Time and the River* society does not intrude upon the "suspicious" teacher-pupil relationship as it did in "Hands," it is interiorized by the characters and the author, which only makes it more cruel.

The Corrupter of Healthy Youth

Paul Steitler, the young faculty assistant in Frederick Buechner's *A Long Day's Dying* (1949), forms a friendship with Leander Poor, a student, in the setting of an all-male campus.

Paul informs Lee's mother that because of his work he is "a kind of professional corrupter of the young. Lee can tell you." He is talking, of course, about the deleterious influence of literature, which teaches "something fairly unnerving about life," but the irony in the statement alludes to Socrates's pederastic pedagogy. Paul's interest in the bodies of his students can be glimpsed in another statement: "What really gets me is the sense that I'm instructing a lot of beautiful, healthy children in the use of crutches, which at this point in their career is a morbid and rather pointless lesson." The youthful body—particularly the male body—can exert all its erotic power in the campus atmosphere, where adults are subjugated and moved by the grace and charm they themselves no longer possess. Paul is Lymie turned professor, trying to find another Spud to whom he can attach himself. He is Basil, in *Bertram Cope's Year*, who tries to become intimate with a young man—Bertram in particular; and he is the adult Fitzgerald attempting to identify with a man he runs into on the Champs-Elysées.

An arrested adolescent, Paul is trying to be one with confident youth—a mad undertaking, because too late—or to extract from it and incorporate into himself the elixir of that youth, or rather, the elixir of virility. Paul realizes this is "a fervent insane hope," however, when he speaks of his true reason for preferring certain of his students. Men who have not accepted the conditioning of American society can hardly expect to be models to students without certain consequences. Sooner or later scandal will result, a public disgrace in "Hands," and personal shame in *Of*

Time and the River. In *A Long Day's Dying* scandal is avoided by the teacher's self-punishment and his defensive coldness and distance.

The Inverse Relationship: Teacher in Search of a Father

In Christopher Isherwood's novel *A Single Man* (1964) the pedagogical setting is merely a pretext. The novel deals with the life of a lonely homosexual—he *happens to be* a professor—who cannot get over the loss of his friend. However, Isherwood, who has himself taught at several universities, is fully aware that in our day teacher-student relationships are no longer as intimate and rewarding as in ancient Greece. George, the homosexual professor, can't help admiring lustfully the young athletes playing tennis near his classroom; and he attempts, with simultaneous boldness and reticence, to make advances to Kenny, one of his students. The aging homosexual—professor or otherwise—is an isolated creature, and his condition is the more unhappy because he is in constant contact with the young, who are seen as healthy and content. Throughout *A Single Man* the tone is one of nostalgia, sorrow, solitude, and death.

George's contact with Kenny occurs during a midnight swim. The swim, a prelude to so many great love scenes, here leads to no more than a father-son contact, but the "son" is the professor, whereas Kenny assumes the adult role:

> And now Kenny is dragging him out, groggy-legged. Kenny's hands are under George's armpits and he is laughing and saying like a nanny, "That's enough for now!" And George, still water-drunk, gasps, "I'm all right," and wants to go straight back into the water. But Kenny says, "Well, *I'm* not—I'm cold," and nannylike he towels George, with his own shirt, not George's, until George stops him because his back is sore.

Abandoning himself to this maternal tenderness, George all but renounces his role in the Greek Ideal of educator-guide, an example for his student. Instead he is content to be guided by the student. Often in modern American literature, the homosexual teacher uses his position to approach a student who he believes embodies the virile youth he no longer possesses and that he probably never had. Although George may harbor the traditional Greek desire to transform his relations with Kenny into a sexual union, brutal, fruitful, and profound—not mere flirting, not merely a professor-student relationship—he will be bitterly disappointed. For the moment, however, masturbation enables him to "conjure up" two tennis players he has seen on the campus courts, and to have intimate relations with them in his imagination.

Chapter Six

The Captain and the Soldier

Sexual Attraction

In *Giovanni's Room* James Baldwin directs the reader's attention to a soldier and two sailors who invade his protagonist's sexual thoughts. David tells us that once, while drunk, he created "a minor sensation by flirting with a soldier." Refusing to admit his true nature, David reasons that he is in danger of losing his balance, of descending into the depths of homosexuality when he catches himself staring at a handsome sailor: "And . . . had our contact lasted, I was certain that there would erupt into speech, out of all that light and beauty, some brutal variation of *Look, baby. I know you.*" Later, fleeing from Hella, his fiancée, he spends three debauched days with a sailor he picks up on the Côte d'Azur. Similarly, in *The Fall of Valor* it is a marine, Cliff Hauman, who arouses homosexual longings in John Grandin. Author Charles Jackson depicts Grandin as hiding, like a treasure, the photograph of the battle-exhausted marine, fast asleep with his rifle in his arms, under the blotter on his desk. And in *The Season of Comfort* Jimmy, the object of the hero's only homosexual experience, dies in the Marines during the war.

There are innumerable examples: the figure of the sailor or soldier—or better still the marine, the sailor-soldier in one—haunts the homosexual imagination. Its fascination obviously lies in barracks or shipboard life, where men live only with men, without women, "shoulder to shoulder, drinking together, fighting together, giving themselves up for one another," in Peter Nathan's words. Perhaps, too, this absence of women on the floating island of the ship or in the military camp, satisfies a primitive need for purity and innocence,* both of which are constantly threatened by woman's sanguinary menstruations. Primarily, however, the sailor embodies the obsession of the homosexual (or of the heterosexual unsure of his masculinity) for the virile ideal. A ferocious fighter, the sailor becomes misogynist in his quest for total virility, a descendant of the ideal Spartan by way of the Prussian officer.

Jean Genet, in *Querelle de Brest*, has explained the sailor's mysterious and sensual charm as the essence of sadomasochistic virility:

> The notion of love or lust appears as a natural corollary to the notion of sea and murder—as it is, moreover, the notion of *love against nature*. No doubt the sailors who are transported by . . . the desire and need to murder belong first of all to the Merchant Navy, thus are veterans of long voyages, nourished on ships' biscuit and the cat-o'-nine-tails, used to leg irons for any little mistake. . . . yet, it is difficult, in a city of fogs and granite, to brush past the huskies of the Fighting Navy, trained and trimmed by and for deeds we like to think of as daring, those shoulders, profiles, mouths, those sinuous, turbulent rumps, those strong and supple boys, without imagining them capable of murders that seem entirely justified by their deigning to commit them with their noble bodies.

And, as W. H. Auden remarked in *The Enchafèd Flood:*

> It is not an accident that many homosexuals should show a special preference for sailors, for the sailor on shore is symbolically the innocent god from the sea who is not bound by the law of the land and can therefore do anything without guilt. Indeed, in a book like Genet's *Querelle de Brest*, the hero is at once god and devil. He is adored because, though he is a murderer

---

* Ironically, antihomosexual Christianity has inherited the same need from Greek civilization.

and a police informer and sexually promiscuous in every sense, though, that is, he loves no one but himself, is in fact Judas, yet he remains Billy Budd, the beautiful god who feels neither guilt nor remorse, and whose very crimes, therefore, are a proof of his divinity.

This attraction the invert feels toward the sailor can further be explained by the fact of homosexual relations on the forecastle, where promiscuity—the lack of personal intimacy—facilitates the discovery of another man's body. H. I. Marrou notes the military origins of Spartan homosexuality, and Melville was aware of this too, when he wrote *White-Jacket* in 1850:

> What too many seamen are when ashore is very well known; but what some of them become when completely cut off from shore indulgences can hardly be imagined by landsmen. The sins for which the cities of the plain were overthrown still linger in some of these wooden-walled Gomorrahs of the deep. More than once complaints were made at the mast in the *Neversink*, from which the deck officer would turn away with loathing, refuse to hear them, and command the complainant out of his sight. There are evils in men-of-war, which . . . will neither bear representing, nor reading, and will hardly bear thinking of."

Joseph Noel, in *Footloose in Arcadia*, reports a conversation between Jack London, Michael Monahan, and himself:

> "They were soldiers that perverted Rimbaud?" Jack asked.
> "Yes."
> "Sailors are that way too. Prisoners in cells are also that way. Wherever you herd men together and deny them women their latent sex perversions come to the surface. It's a perfectly natural result of a natural cause."
> Then he told us of what he called the fo'castle lovers he had encountered on his early trip to the Far East.

Life on Board, Life on Land

Dana, Melville, and London have described this universe of "men together." Beneath the hypermasculinity is the fear of becoming feminine, of re-creating in this world-within-a-world the sexual dichotomy of the human species. As Dana observed in *Two Years Before the Mast:* "An overstrained sense of manliness is the characteristic of seafaring men. . . . if a man comes within an ace of breaking his neck, and escapes, it is made a joke of; and no notice must be taken of a bruise or a cut; and any expression of pity, or any show of attention, would look sisterly and unbecoming a man who has to face the rough and tumble of such a life . . . everything near and dear was made the common stock for rude jokes and unfeeling coarseness."

Frequently in his work Melville reminds us that on board ship effeminacy was treated with contempt. In *White-Jacket* an overrefined officer is nicknamed "Selvagee," the term for an extremely supple, fine rope; in *Omoo* Miss Guy is the nonvirile captain of *The Julia;* in *Redburn* Harry Bolton is persecuted by the crew not only because he is ignorant of shipboard tasks but because he is pretty as a girl. London, who had been a sailor and had read and loved Melville, wrote in *The Sea-Wolf* of the sailors: "There is no balance in their lives. Their masculinity, which in itself is of the brute, has been over-developed. The other and spiritual side of their natures has been dwarfed—atrophied, in fact."

Dana describes the corporal punishments that Captain Frank Thompson took voluptuous pleasure in inflicting: "As he went on his passion increased, and he danced about the deck, calling out as he swung the rope, 'If you want to know what I flog you for, I'll tell you. It's because I like to do it! Because I like to do it! It suits me! That's what I do it for!'"* Melville links sadism and homosexuality more directly still when he has the young, perverse midshipman in *White-Jacket* flog an experienced sailor after hav-

---

* In his *Studies in Classic American Literature,* D. H. Lawrence admired this "natural form of human coition, interchange."

ing granted him his favors. Further attesting to this sadistic behavior, London describes Captain Wolf Larsen as inflicting all
kinds of corporal punishment on his sailors and on the protagonist of *The Sea-Wolf*, Humphrey, the intellectual.

On distant lands, however, freed from discipline and prejudice, sailors form liaisons with the natives that are clearly
homoerotic, if not homosexual. The Kanaka appears in *Two Years
Before the Mast*, as the character Hope, and in Melville, along
with several other handsome natives. Again in London's books
we meet the Kanaka or the handsome half-breed, virile and yet
feminine enough not to constitute a threat to the hero, as in *The
Sea-Wolf:* Oofty "was a beautiful creature, almost feminine . . .
and there was a softness and dreaminess in his large eyes which
seemed to contradict his well-earned reputation for strife and action."

There are as well certain tender feelings evident on board, despite the authors' assertions and the brutality they depict. Dana,
Melville, and London stress the refusal of sailors to display any
"feeling," but Melville, in *White-Jacket*, writes that "we main-
top-men were brothers one and all, and we loaned ourselves to
each other with all the freedom in the world." In *The Sea-Wolf*,
London describes the friendship between Leach, handsome,
brave, calm, and virile, and Johnson, for whom he cares after
horrible brutalization. They will die together like romantic
lovers, drowned by the captain.

Oddly, all these sailors, depicted as unfeeling and brutal, are
nearly bewitched by the arrival of a beautiful boy, soft yet virile
and courageous. In his presence the sailors become tender; they
treat him adoringly and often pamper him. The narrator—a
sailor, but more literate, more sensitive than the rest—becomes
the spokesman for the crew's adulation. Descriptions of the
beautiful sailor are often painstakingly precise. Thus, in *Two
Years Before the Mast* Bill Jackson has the arms of a Hercules,
tanned cheeks, teeth of a sparkling white, "and his hair, of a
raven black, waved in loose curls over all his head and fine open
forehead; and his eyes he might have sold to a duchess at the
price of diamonds. . . . he was a fine specimen of manly
beauty." Melville uses precisely the same words and tone in
describing Jack Chase, who has such power over the crew that

none of them speak against him when he cries at the cruelty of corporal punishments.

Yet only in *Billy Budd* does the handsome sailor find his perfect incarnation. Billy Budd is the sailor's *essence*, the embodiment of vigorous, almost superhuman, beauty, all muscle and soft abandon. Every man aspires to be Billy Budd, eternally young and beautiful, without either past or future, adored, innocent and pure, passive yet dominating and subjugating his fellows. His is also the perfect androgyne, cast into a world of men without women. Isolated on ship, Billy Budd is demigod of the Beautiful, the Good—what each man wants to be or dreams of being.

Model for Reference: "The Prussian Officer"

The tropisms of homosexual sadomasochism were given classic form in D. H. Lawrence's story "The Prussian Officer." It is an allegory of the denial of passions that are "against nature," or, to use Gide's term, "against custom."

The Prussian officer is characterized as harsh, rigid and cold: "bristly" moustache, "stiff" hair, "rugged" face, "brutal" mouth, a "cold fire" in his eyes. He seems to have turned away from all human contact: "He had never married," and after having sex with his mistress, he is "still more tense," his eyes "still more hostile and irritable." Toward his soldiers, he is "impersonal," but "roused," he is a devil.

And yet the captain's vulnerability is apparent from the outset: his lips are "brutal," but "full," suggesting sensuality; those "cold fire" eyes are light blue, the color of tenderness, innocence, repose; that his mother was a Polish countess evokes his romanticism and refinement.

In contrast, the soldier, Schöner, embodies instinctual, human animalism. His eyes are "expressionless," and in fact he seems never to have thought, but to have received life directly through his senses, for he acts "straight from instinct." Schöner's presence is "like a warm flame upon the older man's tense, rigid body, that had become almost unliving, fixed."

Lawrence meticulously describes the development of their

relationship: the captain's irritation when he is "becoming aware" of the young soldier's presence, his sense that the bond between them is growing more and more intimate. Their conjunction is truly physical: Schöner feels "something sink deeper, deeper into his soul, where nothing had ever gone before," and likewise "the influence of the young soldier's being had penetrated through the officer's stiffened discipline, and perturbed the man in him." Each man is thus violated by the other. Neither can again be totally self-possessed. The captain's sadism is as much due to his desire for innocence and purity—nonlife—as are the orderly's attempts to efface himself. Their sadomasochistic relationship is described as a series of physical contacts: obsessed by the soldier's thumb ("He wanted to get hold of it and— A hot flame ran in his blood"), the officer touches it with a pencil. Later, he kicks the soldier: "As [the soldier] was crouching to set down the dishes, he was pitched forward by a kick from behind. The pots went in a stream down the stairs. . . . And as he was rising he was kicked heavily again, and again." This is actually rape.

On maneuvers, the soldier decides to fight back, to oppose sadism with sadism. Later, the captain is served by the soldier: the soldier holds a bottle of beer against his thigh, uncorks it, and pours it into a mug for the captain. The phallic symbolism and voluntary coitus are plain.

Communication between them could have been based on love, but the soldier rejects it: his fists are clenched, that is, his sensuality can no longer be expressed to the captain other than sadistically. It is sadism he reacts against: "a strong torment came into his wrists." Seconds later, the officer symbolically stops "beneath him." A few moments later the soldier throws himself upon him: "And the instinct which had been jerking at the young man's wrists suddenly jerked free. He jumped, feeling as if it were rent in two by a strong flame." The captain's sadism is a defense against his desire to be penetrated by the soldier, by life, by homosexual love. The convulsions of his body under Schöner's hands recall the convulsions of coitus. Since Krafft-Ebing, we have known that sadism is inseparable from masochism.

They will be united in death: "The bodies of the two men lay together, side by side, in the mortuary, the one white and slender, but laid rigidly at rest; the other looking as if every moment it must rouse into life again, so young and unused, from a slumber."

The soldier dies of sunstroke. The image of fire has become overwhelming. The "hot flash" traversing their bodies is symbolic of the pangs of conscience, of passion—anger, hatred, or desire. The officer, by expressing his homosexual love sadistically, the soldier, answering sadism with sadism, turn the soft flame of love into a devastating blaze.

Lawrence had a panic fear of homosexuality. G. H. Ford recalls, in *Double Measure,* that Lawrence, despite his fundamental androgyny and his ardent interest in the male body, wrote the following words in a letter (two years after publication of "The Prussian Officer"): "These horrible frowsty people, men lovers of men, they give me such a sense of corruption, almost putrescence, that I dream of beetles." Elsewhere, he contrasts insects, which are contemptible and repugnant, with animals: "I like men to be beasts—but insects—one insect mounted on another—oh God!" Yet it would be easy to demonstrate that his work is replete with scenes in which homosexuality is both overt and glorified.

Lawrence had a horror, like André Gide, of the overt homosexual, the effeminate man, the "invert." Both of them, however, dreamed of a strong, virile, sensual friendship, yet Lawrence wished that it never be *homosexual.* This is like attempting to square the circle. Thus the only acceptable outlet was, according to Moore's commentary on "The Prussian Officer," the "homosexual-sadistic frenzy," in which the relationship develops from an "awareness of the other," to consummation and reconciliation, *without contact,* in death. Such is the price men must pay if they love each other yet are unable to admit it.

Norman Mailer, who has always been interested in the subject of homosexuality, gives an explanation for Lawrence's attitude: "He had become a man by an act of will, he was bone and blood of the classic family stuff out of which homosexuals are made, he had lifted himself out of his natural destiny which was probably to have the sexual life of a woman. . . ." "But homosexuality would have been the abdication of Lawrence as a philosopher-king. Conceive how he must have struggled against it!"

Lawrence did not succeed in reconciling his intellect, his will, his desire for domination, and his overwhelming need for another man's body, save by identifying with the heroines in his novels (with Lady Chatterley, for example, who is possessed by the rough, virile Mellors), or by having Rupert Birkin and Gerald Crich make love to each other during a wrestling match, or by allowing the Prussian officer and the soldier to consume each other in a brutal, orgiastic struggle. Homosexuality is not virile—is "inverted"—unless it is evoked by struggle, by combat ending in death—the proof of its nonviability.

Schöner, therefore, is Lawrence's homosexual temptation, the "perverse" sensuality that assails him, while the captain is his superego fighting against basic homosexuality. For Lawrence, sadomasochism is the sole "solution," as it was in the flogging of the sailor in *Two Years Before the Mast*. Brute force is often glorified for just this reason that it means resistance of homosexual tendencies.

The American Prototype: Billy Budd, Sailor (An Inside Narrative)

Written near the end of his life and published after his death, Melville's *Billy Budd* is a spiritual allegory—as E. L. Grant Watson says, a "testament of acceptance," but also a "testament of resistance," in Phil Withim's words. *Billy Budd* is a masterful expression of inner conflict.

Watson has indicated the narrative's sexual aspect. He speaks of the "bitter perversion of love which finds its only solace in destruction" (sadism as a defense mechanism), and he sees the novel as Melville's daydream of a sexual paradise wherein man would have "rights," in which there would be no "ban" and the martial law of the *Indomitable* would not prevail.

Billy Budd, the Handsome Sailor, is a type that appears to have obsessed Melville from *Typee* to *Billy Budd*, as his *homosexual temptation*. He is forced to disguise and sublimate this temptation in aesthetic admiration (mythological references, the relationship between a gentlemanly soul and an attractive appearance, the Platonic theory of a handsome body reflecting a noble inner man, a celestial gaze denoting innocence and purity, etc.). Billy is the essence of masculine beauty (strength), animated by feminine tenderness. This devirilization and dehumanization is a stratagem: Billy cannot be a "real man," for he must be liked and coddled by the sailors on the *Rights-of-Man* (who court him as though he were a girl) and on the *Indomitable* (whose crew is also somehow feminized). Throughout, Billy symbolizes the Good, and at the novel's end he becomes an angel, a Christ figure.

For Melville, the *Rights-of-Man* is a sort of democratic society à la Whitman—or Marcuse—where the instincts are not shackled by the ego and the superego, where love and concord reign freely. This is a homoerotic paradise that is predominantly virile: Billy, who is immensely strong, freely admits that he was found in a pretty silk basket. Aboard the *Rights* there is no need to "sublimate" love into rude friendship or to pervert it into sadism; there are no taboos. When he is forced to let Billy go, Captain Graveling finds difficulty in repressing his sobs in the presence of Lieutenant Ratcliffe, the envoy from the warship.

Since Billy symbolizes "instinct," the Freudian id, as Schöner symbolizes happy sensuality, it is necessary that he—like Lawrence's soldier—have no past life. He has neither family, parents, or a real name, and appropriately, his surname symbolizes the bud about to flower. "Baby," a nickname, suggests "childish innocence" or, in Freudian terms, the "polymorphousperverse," the "pleasure principle," which has not yet been exposed to the repressive "reality principle" and which, as a result, is still "amoral," though not "immoral."

Neither does Claggart have a past; no one knows who he is or where he comes from. On board the *Indomitable*, a highly civilized ship (the sailors are like "dames of the court," and Billy is a "rustic beauty"), the crew is under martial law, and Claggart serves as the chief of police against any possible mutiny, because Claggart is the very symbol of repression, always inspiring terror. His pale countenance evokes the pallor of the law, and as such he is an admired pillar of society, thus the symbolic beauty of his forehead, mouth, and body. While the "objective" eye of the narrator sees him as the symbol of harmony in organized society, the sailors hate him because he dominates and represses them. It should be remembered that some sailors have been "pressed into service" "impressed" against their will, i.e., "repressed."

Claggart shares with the ship's captain, Vere, the trait of self-control. However, of the three protagonists, Vere alone has a past which is related in any detail. Set between the Edenic id, that is, Billy, and Claggart, or the social conscience of the superego, is Vere—the name suggests virtue, virility, and also change, "veer"—who represents the ego of the *Indomitable,* its personality. As an existential unit, the ship thus symbolizes the human being and—we imagine—the author himself.

Billy is singled out "at first sight." His arrival threatens to destroy the *Indomitable's* perfect organization, for Claggart, Vere, and the crew are charmed by Billy's *beauty.* Their intuition of the lost Eden he represents threatens to upset the established order. The superego itself comes close to giving way: Claggart's "bitter smile" is the symptom of his inner struggle; his desire for the innocence he feels he is unable to experience represents the yearning of repressive society for the vanished Eden or for a less repressive society in which the instincts—homosexuality among them—were given free rein. But Claggart's defense mechanism turns him toward sadism, and overt, vehement denunciation. He warns Vere of danger.

Attention should be paid to the symbolism of this scene in which Vere "becomes sensible" of Claggart's presence: the Prussian officer similarly "became aware" of Schöner's presence. In their choice of language, both Melville and Lawrence discreetly stress that changes occur *inside* their characters. Vere, the ego, becomes suddenly aware that his superego desires to speak to him, just as the Prussian officer felt that within himself his instincts, the id, were beginning to gain control and were about to overthrow the ego and the superego, which had hitherto acted together as a unit. Claggart is the *inner* part of Vere's personality, and after his warning, the ego's first reaction is to doubt that danger truly exists: Vere's feelings toward Billy are in no way harmful; they are pure and innocent.

Here is the onset of a neurosis, a conflict between the three elements of the personality. The id wins out: Billy kills Claggart. Once the id has dethroned the superego, the ego is about to cede, to "veer." However, in order to maintain the balance of the personality—shipboard discipline—an unparalleled effort of will is required to rely on custom, on tradition, whence the hasty convening of the court.

Vere feels panic, just as without the superego the ego goes insane. He silences within himself all feelings of objectivity, sympathy, "conscience," which are the opposite of law. In assuming Claggart's role, he demands Billy's death and orders the court to consider solely the act of murder.

Later, alone with Billy, Vere attempts to sublimate his love into paternal affection. The narrator, with great delicacy, abandons his usual omniscience; he does not follow the captain into Billy's cell as he is loathe to probe the feelings of the two men too deeply. Melville tells us only that "the austere devotee of military duty, letting himself melt back into what remains primeval in our formalized humanity, may in the end have caught Billy to his heart, even as Abraham may have caught young Isaac on the brink of resolutely offering him up in obedience to the exacting behest." As the *Rights-of-Man* and Melville's imagery have already indicated, in earlier times paternal love was hardly distinguishable from Love.

Billy, instinct released from some immemorial past, has no place in our society. He agrees—he must agree—to his own sentence: "God bless Captain Vere," he announces, and the crew repeats it after him. Vere, too, will die murmuring Billy's name:* he will never forget the beautiful blond man he was forced to sacrifice.

The authorized naval chronicle gives a different version of events, "doubtless for the most part written in good faith," according to which Claggart was "vindictively stabbed to the heart" by William Budd, whose "extreme depravity" is roundly condemned.

* ". . . while lying under the influence of that magical drug which soothing the physical frame, mysteriously operates on the subtler element in man." It is obvious that Melville is saying that the drug has liberated his unconscious.

Billy Budd illustrates Melville's acceptance of Christian morality—American style. Like Vere, like D. H. Lawrence, Melville
relied upon tradition, custom, and martial law to control his
deepest sexual tendencies, which so many critics of his work
have discerned. *Billy Budd* is his testament of resigned acceptance, since in 1891 the author was unable to conceive of a society without repressive moral and social laws. In the course of his
voyages to Polynesia, Melville actually glimpsed another sort of
society in which male friendship "at first sight" had all the characteristics of heterosexual love. This is the lost paradise experienced by Ishmael (*Moby Dick*), who exhorts his fellow crew
members not to "cherish any social acerbities" and to "squeeze
ourselves universally into the very milk and sperm of kindness."
Although Ishmael's gazes are eloquent, their message is not
transformed into action. When Queequeg embraces him as a
man embraces a woman, his first "civilized" reaction is to escape
from his arms and to denounce the indecency of their "conjugal"
embrace. He soon realizes, however, that this "marriage" is not
really shocking, since "in a countryman this sudden flame of
friendship would have seemed far too premature, a thing to be
much distrusted; but in the simple savage those old rules would
not apply." In this context, Melville's strategy was to use a complex symbolism that enabled him to write about his insoluble dilemma: how to love a young man purely and innocently in the
America of the nineteenth century. The only acceptable solution
was to imagine a utopia in which love could be unfettered. However, the Beloved, when conceived by a civilized writer for a
civilized audience, must become a principle, a symbol, an
allegory, a man who is devirilized at best, disincarnate at worst.
In spite of his inner rebellion against the repressions of society,
Melville had too much respect for his own culture to make Billy
Budd, the embodiment of his obsessive homosexual temptations,
into a man of flesh and blood.

Melville's parallels with D. H. Lawrence are important. As we
have noted, Lawrence had a panic fear of homosexuality, and he
burned the captain and the soldier at the stake of sadomasochism. The Prussian officer cannot face life, since it would
entail his acceptance of and abandonment to homosexuality. Sadism is a method of satisfying his "passion" while preserving his

virility. As soon as he symbolically abandons sadism and speaks to Schöner "as if amiably," the latter kills him. Lawrence could not permit any tender relationship to exist between them. Melville reacts in a somewhat similar fashion. He too was unable to resolve the conflict between his three protagonists save through death. But there is no manifest sadism in his work; Claggart does not overtly mistreat Billy. (There is, though, an element of masochism in Billy's passive acceptance of Vere's death sentence.) As in "The Prussian Officer," the instinct murders the intellect, because neither Lawrence nor Melville was able to reconcile homosexual temptation and morality with their notion of the virile idea. In both cases, sadomasochism represents the struggle of the ego, which destroys the id on the orders of the superego. This is the classic of neurosis.

The Degeneration of the Archetype

The Caricature

Any apparent parallels between *Billy Budd* and "The Prussian Officer" are a coincidence, springing from the profound similarity in temperament of their authors; "The Prussian Officer" was written in 1914, while *Billy Budd* was not published until 1924. There can be no doubt, however, that Carson McCullers's *Reflections in a Golden Eye* (1941) derives its inspiration from "The Prussian Officer." By then it was possible to speak more frankly than before about certain human tendencies; Carson McCullers, a married woman, neither feared arousing suspicions about herself nor had to play tricks with her unconscious. As a result, what had been imprecisely stated before could now be made clear, what had been merely alluded to was now made explicit almost to the point of caricature.

Of the two protagonists in *Reflections in a Golden Eye*, the soldier is the closest to Lawrence's original. He has the same innocence, purity, animal grace, strong hands, silence, and expressionless eyes as Schöner. Like the Prussian officer, McCullers's Captain Penderton is violently attracted to this young soldier.

"The captain was overcome by a feeling that both repelled and fascinated him—it was as though he and the young soldier were wrestling together naked, body to body." And, "The thought of the young man's face—the dumb eyes, the heavy sensual lips that were often wet, the childish pageboy bangs—this image was intolerable to him."

Yet Captain Penderton is a caricature of the Prussian officer. Whereas Lawrence subtly delineated his character's withdrawn personality (clear blue eyes, Polish descent, full lips), McCullers makes direct statements to avoid mystification. She informs us that Penderton "obtained within himself a delicate balance between the male and the female elements, with the susceptibilities of both the sexes and the active powers of neither." We learn that he "had a sad penchant for becoming enamoured of his wife's lovers." Like Lawrence's officer, or the captain of the *Indomitable*, however, he affects indifference and rigidity.

The evolution of the relationship between captain and soldier follows a familiar curve. Their first meeting might have been taken directly from "The Prussian Officer" or *Billy Budd*. McCullers, obviously aware of the incident of the soup (which Billy spills at Claggart's feet) and the wine (in Lawrence's story), begins this relationship with a cup of coffee which Williams overturns on the captain's new trousers.

Here, we encounter the same symbolic elements as in "The Prussian Officer": the sun, the horse as a sex symbol—the Prussian officer had assuaged his sexual desires on horseback or with prostitutes—and a wood clearing symbolizing nature, in which a man can regain a certain balance by means of pansexuality. For all these similarities, however, the captain is no fine cavalier mounted on his horse, but a grotesque effeminate who desperately tries to appear a virile horseman.

Independent of her influences, McCullers makes explicit the mysterious relationship. In this novel, indifference is replaced with a love-hate relationship, with frantic desire for the forbidden physical contact other than by means of sadomasochism. Because of his rank, the officer must be the sadistic element, despite his inner femininity. The soldier is taken aback at the captain's attitude toward him. However, since, like Schöner or Billy Budd, he is a kind of semianimal, he accepts his lot fatalistically.

Williams is a virgin: because his father warned him that women carry a mortal disease, he derives sexual pleasure merely from gazing upon the beautiful, stupid Leonora, and touching her while she is asleep. But, like Billy and Schöner, an innocent appearance is joined with violent, instinctive strength: Williams has killed a black, and his fist is as murderous as that of the former two. Just like them, the soldier will die. Williams is shot by Penderton, a murder that results from sadomasochism. Surprising Williams during one of his peeping-Tom sessions (obviously masturbatory), the captain kills him, thus ridding himself of the involuntary cause of his own torment.

Social Satire

The captain-soldier relationship in Norman Mailer's *The Naked and the Dead* has been elevated in rank. Set against the background of the war in the Pacific, the sadomasochistic relationship between General Cummings and Lieutenant Hearn is described in detail. Mailer is precise, and like McCullers he employs banality to make his social satire more virulent.

The lieutenant is an intellectual, and therefore, unlike Billy and Schöner, he quickly recognizes his superior officer's true nature: "He had known men who were casually like him, the same probable capacity for extreme ruthlessness." Hearn is not a personification of instinct: he sees and understands, and he plays warily. His game of chess with the general is symbolic.

In this chess game between the officers the sensuality of Lawrence or McCullers is purified, intellectualized. Mailer does not dwell on his characters' bodies. Here, the important thing is not that the general is disturbed by the young man's animal grace—which he shares with all his predecessors—but that this champion of fascism is ready to abandon himself to the first intellectual, liberal lieutenant who happens to come along! We are told that the general had once wanted to sew and paint "like a girl," before being sent off to military academy by his father—where he developed a crush on his cadet colonel, a tall, dark-haired young man. In addition, General Cummings thinks of his military successes as successful flirtations. Having repelled a force penetrating his front lines, he explains to Hearn, "This kind of thing is what I call my dinner-table tactics. I'm the little lady who allows the lecher beside me to get his hand way up under my dress before I cut off his wrist."

Again, we have the basic schema of "The Prussian Officer": the general wants to dominate, to enslave his subordinate, to possess him. In each case, and logically in light of their respective rank, the elder appears to win before the final dénouement. Here, as in *Billy Budd*, the superior officer sends his subordinate to his death.

Contact is frustrated—as it is in every love-hate novel—because one of the two partners (or both) draws back or fails to understand what is going on. Sadism grows out of this kind of frustration: "Cummings surveyed Hearn with loathing. Hearn was an embodiment of one mistake, the one *indulgence* he had ever permitted himself, and it had been intolerable to be with him since then." Once again, the "warm flame" of love fails. The cigarette that Hearn stamps out in his rage on the floor of the general's tent is a symbol of his refusal to burn with love, and the general humiliates his lieutenant by ordering him to pick up the butt he has thrown down.

Set in this military context, General Cummings's homosexuality becomes part of the author's social commentary and accentuates the novel's irony. The tyrant who derives pleasure from maintaining a brutal sway over his men is a sadistic effeminate who orders them on a dangerous mission out of motives that are personal as well as strategic. Here the homosexual theme is not the central one: it serves merely to indicate the absurdity of war and of the military and social system, to demonstrate the profound weakness of a rigid and seemingly impenetrable militarism that treats men as pawns at best, and as women at its worst.

The entire novel is replete with a deliberate misogyny. Diana Trilling has remarked that *The Naked and the Dead* depicts women "only as offstage noises, the distant rumble of remembered sexual excitement." For example, the supreme insult Sergeant Croft can find to hurl at his exhausted troops when they refuse to continue their march is "Bunch of goddam women!" Croft, the savage, the brute, the ideal lover, treats his men like women, as if he were the only man among these weak hens. In his view—and he is following the American ideal—virility knows neither fear nor friendship, which is a feeling that can quickly become suspect, emasculating: "Croft always despised a platoon leader who made efforts to have his men like him; he considered it womanish and impractical." This fear of the feminine, this contempt for woman, is rooted in a fanatical narcissism that is clearly a variation of homosexuality. After a sexual adventure, Croft thinks, "You're all fugging whores," and he ends, *I hate everything which is not myself.*"

Thus, the relationship between Hearn and General Cummings is set against a background of brutality and misogyny similar to the shipboard life described by Dana, Melville, and London. This sadism is the result of the merciless struggle their characters wage within themselves, a struggle between their instincts and their social conscience. They might well say, like Genet's Lieutenant Seblon in *Querelle de Brest:*

> "God grant that I may envelop myself in my chilly gestures, in a chilly fashion, like some very languid Englishman in his traveling rug, an eccentric lady in her shawl. To confront men with, you have given me a gilded rapier, chevrons, medals, gestures of command: these accessories are my salvation. They allow me to weave about me some invisible lace, of intentionally coarse design. That coarseness exhausts me, even though I find it comforting."

The Extreme Case: The Acceptance of Sadomasochism

In *Eustace Chisholm and the Works* (1967) the captain-soldier relationship reaches its nadir. James Purdy, who was more than likely familiar with the novels here discussed, evidently believed that the archetype of McCullers and Mailer had yet to reach its ultimate point and he set out to develop the theme to its limits. The last part of the novel treats of the sadomasochistic relationship between Captain Stadger and the enlisted man Daniel Haws. Seen in the perspective of the entire evolution of this genre, Purdy's novel is the extreme model, the opposite of "The

Prussian Officer," and thus helps us to define the tropisms of such a liaison's development.

Purdy concretizes the metaphors contained in "The Prussian Officer." Schöner felt himself to be "connected" to the officer; Purdy writes, "Once Daniel looked down at his wrist as if to check whether there was a fetter resting there." Lawrence's soldier felt he had been "disemboweled" by the Prussian officer's physical mistreatment; Purdy describes Haws "carrying his bowels in his hands like provisions." The episode of the spilled liquid in Melville, Lawrence, and McCullers here becomes: "Suddenly nauseated, he vomited near Captain Stadger's brilliantly shined shoes." Et cetera.

Free from both the guardians of inner censorship and the restrictions of social censorship during the period he was writing, Purdy magnifies his characters' features to such an extent that they seem to be reflected in a distorting mirror. Metaphor and image become an actual scene, actually being lived: the soldier's body, whose carnal presence we once felt so vividly upon being shown only his strong, sensual hand, is stripped naked—"including his shoes and socks." However, it has lost its erotic charge; the disturbed, obsessive relationship between Stadger and Haws is made so murderously explicit that it becomes suddenly ridiculous. The Prussian officer's clear-blue, though glacial, gaze indicated a repressed feminine softness; here, although the American officer's blue gaze is also glacial, it is his T-shirt, "an almost feminine blue," which designates his latent feminine masochism. In this way, Purdy debases the theme from the heights where everything *appears* to be pure by reducing it to the nauseating depths where everything is crudely literal.

In 1958 a minor novel was published that examined and crystallized the officer-soldier archetype. *The Sergeant* describes the relationship between the young, handsome soldier Tom Swanson and Sergeant Callan. By making the superior officer a mere sergeant, Dennis Murphy has deintellectualized the prototypical officer, who becomes a creature of mere flesh and blood. On the other hand, the soldier is more aware and can analyze the nature of his relationship with his superior. All the components of the archetype are present: physiques, actions, sadomasochism, etc. However, in this novel the scenes are explicit and the final struggle clearly reveals the sergeant's sexual desires. The interesting thing about this novel, within the context of the evolution of the archetype, is that Tom survives the homoerotic experience and finally turns to women. The narrative can be seen as an allegory of the passage from adolescent homosexuality—harshly repressed after an inner struggle—to adult heterosexuality. The sergeant, a virile prototype, is a career soldier with a magnificent service record who has taken refuge in self-discipline. He commits suicide at the end of the novel, and his death "frees" Tom. Their cathartic struggle recalls the situation of Eugene Gant, who was freed from Starwick in an "orgasm of hatred."

The Barracks, an Ideal Setting for Virile Homosexual Love?

In Hemingway's short story "A Simple Enquiry" a major attempts, with immense precaution, to initiate his orderly into homosexuality. Hemingway characterizes the major as a feminine creature with delicate gestures who, while stretched out on his bunk, hesitatingly asks the young soldier if he is really in love with his girl friend. Although allusions to the soldier's girl friend give rise to jealousy—as was also the case in "The Prussian Officer"—they do not lead to sadistic rage on the major's part, since the basic difference between the two men resides in their ideal. The Prussian officer is harshly rigid and intellectual; the Italian officer is delicate, shy and reserved, effeminate. He does not wholly accept the role of virile authority his uniform provides him. His homosexual desires need not be transformed into sadism so that he can preserve his self-image.

We have already mentioned the couple formed by Captain Motes and Lieutenant Stuki in one of the stories in The Gallery (1947) entitled "The Leaf." They are a perfect couple, in which the higher ranking officer and his inferior easily complement each other, Lieutenant Stuki playing the womanly role of orderly —he does the housework—while the captain upholds both his marriage and the authority of his higher rank. They come together through the convenient intermediary of the love poetry the captain reads to the lieutenant, who lies naked under his mosquito netting, writhing with pleasure. Their unawareness keeps their mutal attraction from being transformed into overt homosexuality, or from being perverted into sadomasochistic cruelty.

Two minor authors have dealt with this theme of military love and have *attempted to free it from brutality*. James Barr and Loren Wahl chose the barracks as the "ideal" setting for virile love affairs. Having two warriors experience tender or physical love is a truly revolutionary act. In *Quatrefoil* (1950) Barr presents the archetypical captain and soldier, officer and subordinate, in the characters of Lieutenant Commander Timothy Danelaw and Ensign Phillip Froelich. Here the Navy provides a completely virile setting. We again have the pedagogic schema of older/younger, lover/beloved: Tim teaches Phillip to be happy, to accept himself as he is. He plays the role of teacher and protector.

However, the virile, normal homosexual couple will not live happily. Once his pederastic mission is completed, there is nothing left for Tim but to die. His death is symbolic of the voluntary withdrawal of the Greek erastes when the eromenos becomes a man. However, the newly created man will preserve as a part of himself the lessons of his master, the ideal of total, happy virility he has inculcated. Barr describes no sadomasochistic perversion such as we have found in Lawrence, Melville, London, Murphy, or Purdy; there is no concealment, as in Burns's stories; there is no hesitant, allusive modesty, à la Hemingway: what we have instead is a frank glorification of a fruitful and enriching love affair between a superior officer and an ensign. This novel seems "modern" because it expresses an ideal that is thousands of years old but long perverted by Judeo-Christian civilization—the Spartan ideal. However, Tim's death demonstrates the extent to which the author remains a prisoner of the taboos of the society he condemns.

During this same year (1950) Barr's publisher—Greenberg—also published *The Invisible Glass* by Loren Wahl (Lawrence Madalena), which is also set in the female-free world of the barracks. It describes the love affair between Lieutenant Steve La Cava (like the author, he is Italian-American) and Chick Johnson, a black soldier. The officer desires the soldier, but his feel-ings are not reciprocated. The novel takes place in Italy shortly before the end of the war. The white officer, who has no racist feelings, has already had a series of homosexual adventures be-fore falling in love with Chick. After an evening drinking to-gether, they make love. However, during the night Chick—now sober—leaves the bed they have shared; this begins the separa-tion that will lead to the lieutenant's suicide.

Here, as in *Quatrefoil,* the relationship between the two men becomes increasingly intimate. In Wahl's novel, the scene is mi-nutely described: the stretched-out leg, the arm embracing the other's body, legs intertwined, faces that touch, mutual caresses. This is the most tenderly erotic of all the novels that deal with captain and soldier. And this tenderness, which changes to coldness but not to hatred on Chick's part while remaining ten-derly passionate on Steve's, prevents their relationship from turn-ing into hatred or to sadomasochism. Steve's moral misgivings are not sufficiently strong or conscious for him to transform them into a saving cruelty. When—suddenly in a homosexual bar—he becomes aware that he is really "like that," irremediably homo-sexual, and that he is also desperately in love with Chick, it is himself he punishes, killing himself while evoking God. He might be said to have directed his sadomasochism against him-self. The novel ends with the death of one partner, as did "The Prussian Officer," *Billy Budd, The Naked and the Dead, Reflec-tions in a Golden Eye, Eustace Chisholm and the Works,* and *Quatrefoil.* Only the lovers in "A Simple Enquiry" and "The Leaf" are spared, because they are characters in short stories, mere "moments."

Chapter Seven

The White and the Black

Theory

The White Viewpoint

Among the racially mixed homoerotic or homosexual couples in American literature are Hope and the narrator in Dana, several sailors in Melville who are intimate with Kanaka friends (the archetype is the "marriage" of Ishmael and Queequeg), the characters of Jack London, Hemingway's boxer and his friend,* and Loren Wahl's lieutenant who is united with a black in such a way that the color of Chick's skin is almost gratuitous.

D. H. Lawrence was the first to note this archetype. In his essays on nineteenth-century American literature, Lawrence remarks that James Fenimore Cooper "loved" "the aboriginal American" even more than had Longfellow or Prescott: "He yearned mystically to the soul of his Red brother. . . . All futurity for him lay latent, not in the white woman, but in the dark, magnificent presence of American Warriors, with whom he would be at one in the ultimate atonement between races." Lawrence takes note of Cooper's emphasis on the Indians' physiques, with their agile, soft, sensual beauty, "utterly dependent on horses": "They have beautiful limbs, that cleave close to their horses, almost as one flesh. . . ." Analyzing *The Last of the Mohicans*, he remarks that the "love" between Natty Bumppo

---

* It should be noted that Hemingway denied that the two men had a homosexual relationship.

and Chingachgook creates a bridge between the "opposite shores" of the beings they represent. Their love is so "profound" that they do without words or gestures. It is a perfect communion, "invisible, intangible, unknowable"; and, "From this communion is procreated a new race-soul, which henceforth gestates within the living humanity of the West." Lawrence uses the term "polarity" to describe their relationship, a word he usually reserves for carnal union between men and women.

In his examination of *Two Years Before the Mast*, he finds a similar love relationship between the narrator and Hope, although here it is less mystical but more ephemeral than was the case with Natty and Chingachgook. Lawrence was also the first to demystify Melville's symbolism: with regard to Ishmael and Queequeg and their idolatrous act, he writes, "The sophistry with which he justifies this act of idolatry is amusing, and very characteristic of Melville. . . . Plainly, he cared nothing about worship, and he loved Queequeg. Elsewhere he says he loved the savage's 'large, deep eyes, fiery black and bold.'"

In *Love and Death in the American Novel*, Leslie Fiedler expands on Lawrence's remarks. "To be sure, there is a substitute for wife or mother presumably waiting in the green heart of nature: the natural man, the good companion, pagan and unashamed—Queequeg or Chingachgook or Nigger Jim." He further states, "Natty Bumppo, the hunter and enemy of cities . . . and Chingachgook, nature's nobleman . . . postulate a . . . myth, an archetypal relationship which also haunts the American psyche: two lonely men, one dark-skinned, one white, bend together over a carefully guarded fire in the virgin heart of the American wilderness. They have forsaken all others for the sake of the austere, almost inarticulate, but unquestioned love which binds them to each other and to the world of nature which they have preferred to civilization." "Yet," Fiedler continues, "the passion that joins male to male in Cooper is not in its implications as innocent as he wants to think." Fiedler regards these pure "marriages" between two men as "homoerotic" relationships that dare not speak their name, as seemed the case when Fiedler's own formulation of this theory in 'Come Back to the Raft Ag'in, Huck Honey,' "met with a shocked and, I suspect, partly willful incomprehension."

The Black Viewpoint

In *Black Skin, White Masks* psychiatrist Frantz Fanon naïvely declares that Caribbean men never experience the Oedipus complex, and therefore on the islands there is no homosexuality, which is, rather, an attribute of the white race, the result of Western civilization. Needless to say, homosexuality exists in every civilization, even the most primitive, and the Antilles, like Africa and the black ghettoes of the large American cities, have homosexual populations. Yet, Fanon's superiority complex is shared by the black American writer LeRoi Jones, whose plays, for that matter, introduce homosexual characters with a regularity that borders on obsession.

In a 1965 essay entitled "American Sexual Reference, The Black Male" Jones states:

> Most American white men are trained to be fags. For this reason it is no wonder their faces are weak and blank, left without the hurt that reality makes—anytime. That red flush, those silk blue faggot eyes. . . . the most extreme form of alienation acknowledged within white society is homosexuality. . . . a people who lose their self-sufficiency because they depend on their "subjects" to do the world's work become effeminate and perverted. . . . (And over the years even the hero image of the white American has changed to where most of the heroes, leading men, etc., on television or in the movies, at least look like out-and-out fairies.)

A forthright heterosexual, Eldridge Cleaver, offers an explanation for this latter phenomenon. In *Soul on Ice*, he connects the systematic devirilization of the black by the white man to cultural oppression. He is more explicit, however, with regard to the black American's homosexuality. Having noted, à la Fanon, that the brainwashing to which blacks are subjected fixes in them the desire—actually "death-wish"—to be white, Cleaver continues:

It seems that many Negro homosexuals, acquiescing in this racial death-wish, are outraged and frustrated because in their sickness they are unable to have a baby by a white man. The cross they have to bear is that, already bending over and touching their toes for the white man, the white man, the fruit of their miscegenation is not the little half-white offspring of their dreams, but an increase in the unwinding of their nerves—though they redouble their efforts and intake of the white man's sperm.

The young black thus becomes homosexual because he is devirilized by identifying with the white man, the very sham of virility, according to Jones and Cleaver, who feel the black is the essence of masculinity. The homosexual black has given in to the white man, has believed him, and has come to regard himself as ugly, incapable, feminine, in the presence of his white master.*

In "The Primeval Mitosis" Cleaver painstakingly analyzes the relationship between white and black heterosexual men, drawing an analogy to the relationship between mind and body. The mind can be compared to the "Omnipotent Administrator," the white American male, as against the body, or the "Supermasculine Menial," the black American male.

Just as the black homosexual succumbs to the white man's *pretense of virility*, the white man, who is by nature effeminate, is *no less sexually* attracted to the black man's body, according to Cleaver.

Yet, because of the infirmity of his image and being which moves him to worship masculinity and physical prowess, the Omnipotent Administrator cannot help but covertly, and perhaps in an extremely sublimated guise, envy the bodies and strength of the most alienated men beneath him—those furthest from the apex of adminis-

---

* So far as I am aware, this is the first discussion by an American black on the black-white homosexual couple. James Baldwin has described these couples in several of his novels, but he has never attempted to explain the psychological motives that can lead a young black to desire and love a white man.

tration—because the men most alienated from the mind, least diluted by admixture of the Mind, will be perceived as the most masculine manifestations of the Body: the Supermasculine Menials. (This is precisely the root, the fountainhead, of the homosexuality that is perennially associated with the Omnipotent Administrator.)

What such a psychosociological explanation indicates is that sexual relations between a white and black man can exist only on a sadomasochistic level, as Jones and Cleaver hold: the emasculated Black who attempts to achieve virility by identifying with a white man must, by the nature of things, have a love-hate feeling for his master. Like the heterosexual Cleaver, who dedicates a love-hate poem to a white woman, the black homosexual who desires a white man must remember that he is despised by the white race in general, and that he must have his lover. Similarly, the white who loves a black cannot—however liberal he is—forget that his lover has a heritage long degraded and that in loving him, he debases and humiliates himself.

Thus, according to Cleaver, and to Jones, the black homosexual has mistaken appearance for reality; only the white man who dreams of a black knows the source of true virility. Interestingly, a similar view was held by Lawrence, who suggests that Cooper and Melville must have intuited this "fact."

Practice: Interracial Homosexual Relationships in the Work of James Baldwin

James Baldwin, who is a member of two minority groups— black and homosexual—gives the impression in his work of being a man uncomfortable in his black skin, and of trying to convince the reader that everyone can and *should* be bisexual. We have already noted a few of the homosexual elements in Baldwin's work; here, we will analyze the link between his color and his sexual orientation.

LeRoi Jones and Eldridge Cleaver provide a starting point. In his essay "Brief Reflections on Two Hot Shots" (1963) Jones deals rather unkindly with Baldwin and the South African writer Peter Abrahams. Each, he says, is a "Joan of Arc of the cocktail party," and he states, "If Abrahams and Baldwin were turned white, for example, there would be no more noise about them." It seems he believes that Baldwin is homosexual because he wants to be white and has always identified with whites; we have already noted that Jones maintains that all white culture is basically homosexual. Cleaver in *Soul on Ice* is more explicit: "There is in James Baldwin's work the most grueling, agonizing, total hatred of the blacks, particularly of himself, and the most shameful, fanatical, fawning, sycophantic love of whites that one can find in the writings of any black American writer of note in our time."

Commenting on Baldwin's essay on Richard Wright, he states; "Baldwin . . . reveals that he despised—not Richard Wright, but his masculinity. He cannot confront the stud in others—except that he must either submit to it or destroy it. And he was not about to bow to a *black* man." Adding to this literary furor were Black Panther leader Huey Newton's remarks in *Playboy* (May 1973). He reported that when Cleaver met Baldwin, they exchanged a long kiss on the mouth. According to Newton, Cleaver is a repressed homosexual, unsure of his masculinity, projecting his femininity onto another—in this case, Baldwin.

In Baldwin's *Go Tell It on the Mountain,* the homoerotic relationship is between two adolescent blacks, and whites hardly appear. We learn, however, that John Grimes, the hero, is the only member of his family who does not hate whites; in fact he identifies with a white actress and a young white man. His father tells him that "some of them white folks *you* like so much . . . tried to cut your brother's throat."

In *Giovanni's Room* not one black appears. With his protagonist comfortable in his white skin, Baldwin is able to discuss how to be a "normal" homosexual in American society without any violent outcries of revolt, obscenity, or anger. It would appear that where the white homosexual is concerned, every problem is muted, an idle luxury. He sets the story in France, perhaps to abandon, at least temporarily, the role of racial spokesman that America has forced him to assume; very likely it is for the same reasons that he prefers to live in Europe rather than the United States.

In *Another Country* the first homosexual contact between a black and a white man is not sexual but vengeful. Rufus decides not to go to bed with a white man, even though he has paid for his dinner; in effect, he "rolls" him, like the protagonists in Motley and James Jones who roll queers to preserve their virility. We sense that Baldwin is rejoicing in the trick he plays on the white man. Rufus regains a portion of his virility, he wins control, whereas the "virile" white man is made to appear contemptible and scorned, and disappears into the night. However, the emotional relationship between Baldwin and his characters is more complex than this. Since he is a homosexual, the white man also contains something of Baldwin, and the author cannot help feeling some pity for him (i.e., pity for himself, a frustrated homosexual). This is the reason for the tone at the end of the scene: "'You're a good-looking boy,' he said. Rufus moved away. 'So long, mister. Thanks.'"

We can discern Baldwin's duality in all of his black and white relationships. He is a homosexual black locked in a love-hate relationship with a white, wanting to be him. "Homosexual spite" created by envy and frustrated desire is, in Baldwin, an exacerbated condition. His homosexuality seems somehow based on his horror at being black.

The scene in the street leads to a flashback—a device dear to Baldwin—in which we see Rufus with Eric, the southern white man. Here, too, Rufus is having an ambiguous relationship with a homosexual in which friendship, hatred, and some vague sexual attraction are intermingled: "He remembered only that Eric had loved him. He had despised Eric's manhood by treating him as a woman . . . by treating him as nothing more than a hideous sexual deformity. But Leona had not been a deformity. And he had used against her the very epithets he had used against Eric, and in the very same way."

The element of revenge is further brought out by this comparison with Leona, the poor southern white woman whom Rufus sadistically mistreats, reducing her to a despised sex object. For the black, the southern white is the epitome of the white race. If the Southerner is also homosexual, the basically heterosexual black can then doubly despise him. However, since Eric is also Baldwin (as we see in the love scenes with Yves), we later learn, to borrow Cleaver's words, that Rufus has "let a white bisexual homosexual fuck him in his ass." Cleaver seems to be further implying that Rufus's downfall is due to Baldwin's inability to "confront the stud" in the black. Thus, just as Proust—for the same reasons—ended up turning Saint-Loup into a homosexual, Baldwin has a compulsive need to devirilize his studs, to force them to suffer the ultimate outrage. Rufus and Vivaldo both experience this fate. On the other hand, Richard, the novel's heterosexual villain, does not inspire the author's sympathy because he is without the least hint of homosexuality. Thus, Baldwin cannot identify with him.

Vivaldo, the handsome, heterosexual Italian who nevertheless enjoys the "innocent" delights of homosexuality with Eric, admits to him that something might have happened between himself and Rufus. Although sexual relations never actually occurred, the love-hate schema, and the theme of homosexual relations through a female intermediary, are both clear in the following passage, and the flashback it contains: "Somewhere in his heart the black boy hated the white boy because he was white. Somewhere in his heart Vivaldo had feared and hated Rufus because he was black. They had balled chicks together, once or twice, the same chick. . . ." On one occasion, Vivaldo and one of his black friends had displayed themselves to a girl, "but also to each other." Vivaldo is relieved to discover that the black is only slightly larger than he. His fear of black virility—the white man's fear of black sexual "power" that Baldwin, Cleaver, LeRoi Jones, Mailer, and Gore Vidal all mention—is somewhat allayed, but at night he dreams that his black pal is chasing him with a knife, and that he, Vivaldo, must fight back. On both sides, then, the homosexual or homoerotic relationship between white and black is tinged with revenge.

The relationship between Rufus and Eric, which the reader learns about in a flashback, is also colored by the same destructive emotions. Although Rufus is convinced that Eric loved him, we are no longer sure of the *quality* of their love after reading Eric's interior monologue: "But had he ever loved Rufus? Or had it been simply rage and nostalgia and guilt? and shame? Was it the body of Rufus to which he had clung, or the bodies of dark men, seen briefly, somewhere, in a garden or a clearing, long ago, sweat running down their chocolate chests and shoulders. . . . Certainly he had never succeeded in making Rufus believe he loved him. Perhaps Rufus had looked into his eyes and seen those dark men Eric saw, and hated him for it."

We must compare these scenes of homosexual love-hate between a black man and a white with the innocent and pure scenes between Eric and Yves, or Vivaldo and Eric. Here, we find no hatred. When Vivaldo allows Eric to seduce him, out of feelings of friendship, comradeship, the scene is full of ecstatic joy, rediscovered innocence: "Vivaldo seemed to have fallen through a great hole in time, back to his innocence; he felt clean, washed, and empty, waiting to be filled." And if the relationship between Giovanni and David is somewhat tense and may end unhappily, we feel that this is because David represents *Homo americanus*—white, blond, puritanical, stifled by his culture— whereas Giovanni is the incarnation of the virile yet gentle Latin, sensual, warm, the white embodiment of John Grimes. Schöner was also dark, contrasted with the Nordic captain. Vivaldo has this same warmth, the same joy of living. His name is symbolic: this Italo-American is *living*; in other words, according to Baldwin's philosophy, he does not rein in his instincts as do his fellow countrymen.

His next novel, *Tell Me How Long the Train's Been Gone*, does not express hatred, since the homosexual partners are black. Leo and Caleb are brothers who find happiness in mutual masturbation, a situation shared by the love between John and Elisha, or John and David. We come to know Leo in all his psychological complexity because Baldwin has so mingled his own life with that of his character. Interestingly, several of the scenes ring changes on the basic sadomasochistic relationship between white man and black. Most noteworthy is the scene in which Caleb, who has been sentenced to hard labor for robbery, is repelled by the foreman's advances: "Nigger, if my balls was on your chin, where would my prick be?" Caleb becomes wild with rage because the man is white and is taking advantage of his superior position. Here too, racial difference creates tension. The foreman pursues Caleb and tries to molest him, but Caleb

knocks him down with a blow to the head, an act which sends
Caleb to solitary confinement, but because of his racial dignity
he does not give in to the foreman, despite his repeated advance.

In this novel, the only "faggots" are white. In the restaurant
where Leo eventually works are certain special clients: "the brilliant Boston scion who liked to get fucked in the ass and who
threw himself before a subway train. . . . Steve . . . the wayward son of a famous general, and he fell in love with me." The
tones of social revenge in this devirilization of white American
high society are clear. The scene in which Leo, in a movie theater, allows a "blond head" to perform fellatio on him, seems
similarly distorted by spite. Having achieved orgasm, Leo "felt
like murdering the poor white faggot."

Leslie Fiedler, who praises Baldwin, nevertheless regrets that
Another Country is "technically inadequate to its task" and that
Baldwin has waited so long to reveal a "long-kept secret." Indeed, what is so exasperating in Baldwin's description of interracial homosexual relations is his inability to get out of himself and
create coherent, "free" characters. Norman Podhoretz has remarked that Baldwin is inclined to wax sentimental when he
describes racially mixed couples, or male couples, or a homosexual and a woman, "whereas he is visibly skeptical of the validity
of the more standard varieties of sex." And—so it would appear
—for good reason: Baldwin is incapable of identifying with a
white or a black who is *only* heterosexual, or with a homosexual
who is exclusively homosexual, unless he is an adolescent—John
Grimes, for example.

In *Another Country* the characters Eric and Ida both contain
something of Baldwin: one is homosexual (but, of course, virile),
and the other is a *black* woman. Both are sexual partners of
Vivaldo, who is Ida's man but Eric's "woman." Baldwin can thus
possess him twice, but at the price of a certain psychological in-
coherence in the Italian male character, who is purported to be
highly heterosexual despite his continuing desire for Rufus and
his passivity with Eric. Baldwin is uncomfortable unless he casts
himself as a white homosexual loving a white man. It is not
merely by chance that *Another Country* ends on a note of hope
as Eric meets his beloved Yves again.

Thus, Baldwin's novels move between two poles: his settling

of accounts with the white race—since he feels that they are what has forced him to hate himself—and his homosexual love for the white man, with whom he desperately tries to identify. The settlement of accounts is exacerbated by his mission—somewhat grudgingly accepted (cf. *The Fire Next Time*)—as a spokesman for his race. When Leo Proudhammer or Rufus Scott express contempt for poor white faggots, Baldwin is killing two birds with one stone: he is taking his personal revenge, and he is also trying to win the approval of black militants. However, how can he love a heterosexual white man and enjoy his favors under such conditions? The answer is simple: he transforms himself into a black woman (Ida) and becomes the white man's mistress; he then plays upon another facet of his minority status, changes into a "virile" homosexual, and possesses the same white man. He thus has it both ways. What Vivaldo loses in heterosexuality with Eric he makes up for by becoming Ida's lover, with whom he seems determined to have a stable relationship. Vivaldo, the Italo-American, is therefore not Baldwin's virile ideal, but a "substitute ideal." He is American and white, to be sure, but he is also Italian, and this keeps him from being a member of the forces of the hereditary foe. He is a certified heterosexual, but he can—out of friendship for Eric (Baldwin)—cross the line, albeit not permanently. And when he returns to the other, heterosexual, side, he seeks out a black woman, thus a character who has something in common with Baldwin (color and sexuality). All of Baldwin's characters could be analyzed along the same lines.

Tell Me How Long the Train's Been Gone ends at the early stages of a potentially successful love affair between two blacks. One of them, Leo, is a black militant who has earlier been involved with white men, yet comes to find happiness in his own race. The white man seems to have lost his power of attraction for Baldwin, who is perhaps trying to regain credibility with the new generation of young black militants. Have his novels succeeded in curing him of his seeming self-hatred and of his hatred for blacks in general? (His latest novel, *If Beale Street Could Talk*, is a young woman's story of her love affair with a young black militant.)

In the span of the archetype, the black and white couple in

American literature has fallen from the harmonious, silent couple of the frontiersman and the Indian, or the American sailor and the Kanaka, or—according to Fiedler—the slave and his young master in flight from society, to the tortured couples in Baldwin's novels. In the 1960s the American black is no longer the pure, proud warrior of Cooper's novels nor the handsome, virile, *and* androgynous creature described by Dana, Melville, and London. American blacks, descended from slaves kidnapped from Africa, have over the years become incarnations of evil, human animals, devils, in the eyes of the average American. For the fictional American black and white man to love each other is as implausible as *The Tempest* with Caliban and Ferdinand cast as lovers. The twofold obstacle is obvious: a pure young man is given to practice a kind of *homosexual bestiality.*

In addition, Cooper, Melville, Dana, London were all white men, which gave them a certain confidence it would be unreasonable to expect from a ghettoed black American. If Baldwin's interracial novels leave a mixed—and disagreeable—impression, we must seek the reasons for this in his own tortured personality, similar to that of D. H. Lawrence in many ways. The sadomasochism of "The Prussian Officer" expresses the author's inner struggle; it seems that the love-hate between the races in Baldwin's work is also the indication of some inner torment.

In his short story "Desire and the Black Masseur" Tennessee Williams drew the theme of moral and erogenous sadomasochism in black and white relationships to its limits. At the height of pleasure a little white man with the symbolic name of Burns sacrifices his body to a black masseur. The latter "loves" him because he must take revenge on Burns's white body. The expiatory theme, found in all of Williams's plays—as will be discussed—is explicit. Burns experiences orgasm beneath the black's brutal hands, which literally tear him apart. Ejected from the bathhouse, the couple goes on to experience happiness together. The black eventually devours Burns, with the latter's total assent.

Similarly, in *The Confessions of Nat Turner* William Styron describes the abortive relationship between the Reverend Eppes, the white master, and his young slave Nat Turner. Nat has indulged in adolescent homosexuality with another young black, but he rejects the white man, who attempts to sodomize him. Nat thinks that "if [Eppes] had achieved his secondary aim, if I had submitted to his repulsive caresses, he would have gained a toy but lost a slave; it isn't easy to completely dominate someone you have sodomized behind the woodpile, and if I had been the willing receptacle of his desires, it would have been more difficult for him to beat me until my legs seemed to be made of wood."

On the other hand, in *Henderson the Rain King* Saul Bellow does not allow sadomasochism to intrude into the relationship between Henderson and the black King Dahfu: it is a love relationship that is totally harmonious and well balanced. However, Dahfu is not a black American, and the story takes place in Africa.

PART III

Homosexuality and the Theater

Here the frailest leaves of me and yet my strongest lasting,
Here I shade and hide my thoughts, I myself do not expose them,
And yet they expose me more than all my other poems.

Walt Whitman, *Calamus*

Chapter Eight

Tennessee Williams: Theater as Psychotherapy

The childhood and adolescence of Tennessee Williams can be regarded as a classic psychoanalytical homosexual case history. Williams himself has set forth the facts of the "case" in the foreword to his play *Sweet Bird of Youth* and more recently in his *Memoirs*, and his biographers have filled in the details of his introverted childhood. On his father's side his forebears were violent, aggressive people, whereas his mother's family, German Quakers, were "gentle and patrician." His mother's character was "composed and proper to the point of puritanism." From his earliest years, Tom (his original name) had a panic terror of his father which was combined with disgust for his vulgarity. After a bout with diphtheria which left the child partially paralyzed, Mrs. Williams forbade him to play with other children and he grew up "delicate and sissified." In St. Louis, where the family had moved, Tom became the butt of his schoolmates because of his Southern accent and his overrefined manners. Williams recalls that groups of children would follow him home yelling, "Sissy." At home, conditions were little different, since his father made no attempt to hide his contempt for his son, calling him "Miss Nancy." The child responded to this treatment with a violent hatred that recalls the hatred felt by John Grimes for his father in *Go Tell It on the Mountain*. After the birth of a second child, a brother, Tom began to feel that his mother's affection for him had lessened. He took refuge in writing.

At fourteen he won a literary prize offered by *The Smart Set* magazine for an essay on the set subject "Can a Wife Be a Good Sport?" His essay was in the form of a first-person confession. This mental transvestitism is a major key to Williams's art and one of the homosexual artist's principal stratagems for achieving universality. Henry James, D. H. Lawrence, and perhaps even F. Scott Fitzgerald, have had recourse to it.

As soon as he was able, Tom left the family home for New Orleans, where he immersed himself in the underground world of prostitutes, pimps, alcholics, and homosexuals, all the "broken and unloved night creatures who through quirks in fate—or in themselves—were living on the perimeter of life, fraught with desperation and wild despair."

Williams describes himself as a child as a "prim Puritan" in appearance but "a carnal little beast" underneath. Many of the female characters in his plays answer to this description, and underlying the following analysis is our supposition that Williams never treats heterosexuality without embodying himself in the heroine. He is the woman who maintains that a good wife can be a good sport (whether male or female). He is Blanche DuBois as well as Serafina. If he happens to identify with one of his male characters, it is with some victim of American social mores—the young homosexual in *A Streetcar Named Desire* or the passive heroes of *Orpheus Descending* and *Camino Real*.

A Streetcar Named Desire

The homosexual never appears on stage. This is the first thing we note, and it holds true in most of Williams's plays. In *A Streetcar Named Desire* the young homosexual has died before the curtain rises. He committed suicide when his wife, the future nymphomaniac Blanche DuBois, insulted him. Now she carries the burden of his death on her conscience.

Williams introduces the homosexual theme with enormous caution. Blanche's young husband was an adolescent who was different, soft, gentle, but not effeminate. In 1947 novels were depicting homosexual "men," but the theater-going public was not prepared to accept such a character on the stage—or even in the wings. Williams labors to gain the audience's sympathy; the young man is portrayed as a victim, as a person who is sick and seeking treatment: "He came to me for help. I didn't know that," Blanche tells us.

In this play Williams introduces the theme of scandal, of "exposure": "Then I found out. In the worst of all possible ways. By coming suddenly into a room that I thought was empty—which wasn't empty, but had two people in it . . . the boy I had married and an older man who had been his friend for years."

The sparse biographical facts set forth in the preface to *Sweet Bird of Youth* help us to grasp the symbolism of this character. The young, delicate, and poetic boy, "almost too fine to be human!" who is unable to face the harsh realities of life—among them his own psychological problems—is obviously the young poet Tom Williams, attempting to take refuge in his own imagination. The violent, terrifying, and hated father—depth psychology proposes that the ambivalent nature of father hatred is a form of repressed love—who is repulsive but also solid, virile, is obviously Stanley Kowalski, with whom Blanche cannot communicate since, like the homosexual, she is both attracted to and disgusted by this sensual brute.

Blanche, identifying with her dead husband, defends to Stanley the individual's right to live as he pleases, to have inviolable privacy. Her nymphomania recalls the homosexual's obsessive cruising, and her taste for young adolescents is a homosexual taste. She is a female projection of Tennessee Williams, just as her husband is a male projection. One is reminded that Lawrence—who has greatly inspired Williams—"concentrated on the quality of erotic experience as felt particularly by the woman," in critic Signi Falk's words. Baldwin has done much the same. And Charles Jackson, after having written a pair of "homosexual" novels, spoke the part of a nymphomaniac in his next book in order to give free rein to his obsessive fantasies. (On his "sexual clock" in *The Circle of Sex* Gavin Arthur places the loose woman immediately after the insatiable homosexual, whose reincarnation she is.)

The fact that it is easy to categorize Williams's characters in play after play as the aging, frustrated nymphomaniac, the pure *and* oversexed young man, or the handsome brute suggests that all three correspond to aspects of the author's personality, or that they are embodiments of a fantasy. The portrait of the handsome brute was first sketched in *Twenty-Seven Wagons Full of Cotton* in the character of Silva Vicarro, later Silva Vacarro in *Baby Doll*. The character undergoes several metamorphoses in various plays, but he remains basically the handsome and sensual brute, whether as John Buchanan or Stanley Kowalski. All these characters are alike in being the antithesis of Blanche's husband, the delicate and homosexual poet. *They have nothing in common with the author,* but they fascinate both the author and his heroines.

Stanley Kowalski is the Other; he is what Williams is not but would have liked to be. He is the male animal in all his magnificence, "the gaudy seed bearer," to whom one must attach oneself because long ago, in childhood, one was forced to abandon any hope of emulating him, of becoming him. We recall Genet and his neofascist, sadistic, brutal—but attractive—heroes.

Camino Real

The first homosexual to appear on stage in a Tennessee Williams play is the Baron de Charlus. He is one of the characters added to the revised version of *Camino Real*, at a time when the public was finally prepared for a "pervert" on stage—five years after the Kinsey Report and during an avalanche of homosexual novels—and to be separated from him only by footlights. Ironically, though, the playwright is making use of a character who was conceived by another writer forty years earlier and to whom Williams gives a symbolic role: as a decadent, as the habitué of a Dantesque hell of which this play is a modern version. He is a companion in misfortune to the other characters who share similar lurid pasts—Marguerite Gautier or Prudence Duvernoy—against whom Williams sets the ethereal purity of the character of Kilroy. Charlus is thus a disembodied character—a soul in torment surrounded by a halo of unreality and surrealism.

Like Blanche's husband, Charlus is not really *physically* present
on stage because he is part of the literary history of another
country, and because he is in hell.

Charlus, as he was in *Remembrance of Things Past*, is a grotesque. He shares the ridiculous gestures of Proust's character
when cruising Jupien or Morel. Charlus speaks of his masochistic
tastes—which accord with those of Proust's character, and of
Proust himself. "You know the requirements. An iron bed with
no mattress and a considerable length of stout knotted rope. No!
Chains this evening, metal chains. I've been very bad, I have a
lot to atone for. . . ." As was noted in connection with "Desire
and the Black Masseur," Williams links sexuality, and particularly homosexuality, with expiation. Here the playwright employs a theme almost tailored for him by another writer: this is
probably why Williams selected Charlus as his first homosexual
to be offered—briefly—to the public.

The character of Kilroy is a new element in Williams's plays.
Watching him and hearing him speak, we get the impression we
have met him before. First, Kilroy is a typically American young
man, as the author suggests when he describes his body and his
clothing: "He is a young American vagrant, about twenty-seven.
He wears dungarees and a skivvy shirt, the pants faded nearly
white from long wear and much washing, fitting him as closely
as the clothes of sculpture. He has a pair of golden boxing gloves
slung about his neck."

However, the image soon becomes cloudy. The young demigod is a victim who continually complains; boxing has been forbidden him for medical reasons; as for his sexuality, it is all in
the past. This hero is completely devirilized, virtually castrated
—the opposite of Stanley and of Williams's other supervirile heroes. Kilroy becomes like the dramatist himself, like his heroines.
The impression is that Kilroy's former hypersexuality is all talk,
and that his "real true woman, my wife," is no more than an
alibi. The motives put forward to explain his departure are symbolic, to say the least: "My real true woman, my wife, she
would of stuck with me, but it was all spoiled with her being
scared and me, too, that a real kiss would kill me! So one night
while she was sleeping I wrote her goodbye. . . ."

Cat on a Hot Tin Roof

The four overt homosexuals in *Cat on a Hot Tin Roof*, are separated from the spectator. Three of them are dead before the play opens: Big Daddy's former employers, Jack Straw and Peter Ochello, and Skipper, who we are told drunkenly phoned Brick with a confession of his homosexuality before committing suicide. The fourth homosexual is a student to whom Brick makes reference. Though he may not be dead, he never appears on stage.

The portrait of Skipper is sketchy. Maggie reveals that she and Skipper had had sexual relations in order to feel closer to Brick, that Skipper had turned to drink before his death (probably on realizing he was in love with Brick), and that he had enormous difficulty coping with his homosexuality. Just as Blanche Du-Bois's young husband, unable to bear the shock of being discovered a homosexual, committed suicide, Maggie, in a similar scene, is the instrument by which the masks are torn away. The woman kills the homosexual and is sorry ever after.

However, Maggie's character is far different from Blanche's. Despite her nymphomania, Blanche is a frail, refined creature, obsessed with good breeding. Maggie on the other hand is a direct, energetic, almost masculine woman: "Her voice has range and music; sometimes it drops as low as a boy's and you have a sudden image of her playing boy's games as a child." She is the pursuer of Brick, and the audience has the impression that their sex roles are reversed. She mentions that Brick is basically "indifferent" to sex, which paradoxically makes him "wonderful at lovemaking," in the vein of Genet's fantasies of indifferent lovers.

Blanche, obviously, is a thinly disguised projection of the author himself—all sensitivity and unbridled sex—but Maggie appears to be the embodiment of the author's ideal: a woman content with living, at ease in her body, frankly sensual without nymphomania, tolerant and understanding. She is both the ideal American woman, retaining some of the qualities of the Italian

Serafina (*The Rose Tattoo*), and the wife who is also a "good sport." These qualities enable Maggie to understand Greek male friendship—the homosexual dream—and to accuse bitterly repressive society: "It was one of those beautiful, ideal things they tell about in the Greek legends, it wouldn't be anything else, you being you, and that's what made it so sad, that's what made it so awful, because it was love that never could be carried through to anything satisfying or even talked about plainly."

Yet this truth kills Skipper: he commits suicide because society forbids him to acknowledge his true feelings for his friend Brick. In an attempt to force Brick to take hold of himself and return to reality, Big Daddy, Williams's ideal father, tells him: "*You!*—dug the grave of your friend and kicked him in it!—before you'd face truth with him!" Maggie, Big Daddy, and the author all agree. Brick and Skipper's friendship comes to a tragic end because of the world's intolerance.

Brick thus becomes the target of all three characters: his wife, Maggie; his father, Big Daddy; and the ghost of his dead friend, Skipper. These are the three forces that combine to force him to draw the truth—his truth—from the depths of his own heart.

Brick is the virile ideal. Like Cooper's heroes, he is a puritan who is extremely wary of his wife as well as of sex, regarding both with a certain contempt. Brick speaks about virile friendship: "A man has one great good true thing in his life. One great good thing which is true!—I had friendship with Skipper. —You are naming it dirty! . . . Not love with you, Maggie, but friendship with Skipper was the one great true thing, and you are naming it dirty!"

It seems clear that Brick and Skipper never "did" sodomy together; they do not deserve the epithets "sissies," "queers," "dirty old men," "fairies" that Brick shouts to his father. However, we know the extent to which this kind of overreaction is revelatory of an uneasy conscience. As Williams notes, Brick's real problem is that he is a prisoner of conventions and of the *image* of virility American society has imposed upon him. His psychological problems cause him to suffer not at Skipper's death but at Skipper's confession which revealed to him their feelings for each other.

Brick, like so many of Williams's heroes, experiences deep nostalgia for childhood and adolescence, remembered as pure and in-

nocent. In the final analysis, Brick is afraid to enter the adult sexual world. This adult world is symbolized by the family, and
with Skipper dead and Brick's material link with adolescence
thus broken, he refuses to have sexual relations with his wife. To
do so would be to destroy his adolescence.

Brick's homosexuality—whether latent or not—stems from the
ambiguities of his adolescence. Williams thus endows the character with virile purity—a strategy we have seen used by James
Baldwin and Gore Vidal. But his attitude toward Brick is an
ambivalent one: Williams admires his asexual masculinity—
athletic, an excellent lover despite himself; but he condemns
Brick for refusing to search his own heart and for accepting established morality.

Here, as in *A Streetcar Named Desire*, Williams seems to identify principally with the off-stage homosexuals: the student
driven away because of scandal, Skipper through whom the
scandal crept into the Pollitt family, and the former owners of
the plantation. They are American society's true victims who are
given a posthumous absolution by a virile, kind, and loving father
—the unrealizable homosexual fantasy. Most likely Brick is attracted to the tomboy in the sensual, masculine Maggie, which is
the author's way of attempting to seduce Brick, another homosexual fantasy figure. Brick is the embodiment of the sterile,
Anglo-Saxon male character the dramatist is constantly comparing with his sensual, strong, foreign characters—Italians, Poles.
Yet in this play he represents even more: Brick is the symbol of
American hypocrisy that stifles the male personality by refusing
men the right to full expression of their desire to love their
fellows. This is why Brick's character is not completely convincing: he is the focus of his creator's contradictory ideas and emotions; he is Anglo-Saxon sterility and also the American virile
ideal to which Williams has been unable to conform; he is both
adored ("Superior creature!—you godlike being!" Maggie says)
and treated with sympathy for his emotional infirmity. He is the
inaccessible dream and the hated cause of the effeminacy of
"fairies" and "pansies."

He is also the victim of the author's literary form. In his short
stories and poems, Williams writes freely about handsome young
hustlers, Christs of venal love, or about the desperate solitude of

aging homosexuals; however, in a play written for Broadway in 1954, the homosexual had to be kept in the wings and preferably to die before the opening scene. What we do see on stage is a man who "is" and "isn't"—a young athlete too pure to turn to heterosexuality, too virile to tolerate any kind of intimate homosexual relations.

In his preface to this play, Williams admits, "of course it is a pity that so much of all creative work is so closely related to the personality of the one who does it." No one could more openly invite the reader and spectator to regard the characters in his work as projections of their author's demons or fantasies. As he remarks elsewhere, "I guess my work has always been a kind of psychotherapy for me."

Orpheus Descending

Orpheus Descending is set in a small southern town, very like Charity (*The House of Breath*) or Noon City (*Other Voices, Other Rooms*), to which the hero, Val Xavier, comes.

Val is described as "a young man, about thirty, who has a kind of wild beauty about him. . . . He does *not* wear Levi's or a T-shirt, he has on a pair of dark serge pants, glazed from long wear and not excessively tight-fitting. His remarkable garment is a snakeskin jacket, mottled, white, black and grey. He carries a guitar which is covered with inscriptions."

The first portion of the description appears to indicate that Val Xavier is *not* trying to emphasize his sexual attractions. He is no Kilroy but an artist and thus more like Williams than Kilroy was. However, his snakeskin is the outward symbol of his "animalism"; here too, we have the contrast between sensuality and purity.

Williams notes that Val was once a hypersexual, hypervirile man: he had his first heterosexual love affair at fourteen, and since then he has led a dissolute life, without becoming "corrupted" by it. At thirty, however, he has decided he is "through with that route." "Heavy drinking and smoking the weed and shacking with strangers is okay for kids in their twenties." The word "strangers," with its ambiguous neutrality, suggests a sexual indeterminacy, which the author clearly intends. Not only does Val wear a snakeskin—a phallic symbol—but his body too has something animal about it. As he tells Lady, the snakeskin retains his body heat, since his temperature is always two degrees below normal, like a dog's.

His sexual past is somewhat ambiguous—Brick's emotional past was homoerotic without being homosexual—and since *on stage* Brick, Kilroy, and Val do not seem to be particularly enthusiastic about the attractions of heterosexuality, we can reasonably make a connection between them and their author's homosexual fantasies. All three characters are Anglo-Saxon males only in outline, their heterosexual adventures are all in the past. "In the past and off-stage . . ." The formula applies to them as it does to the homosexual characters. Not only that, but the handsome, heterosexual brute is always a foreigner, Polish or Italian —that is, the Other, he who has nothing in common with the author, he who is not the cause of his neurosis, the man with whom he can be a woman—Blanche DuBois, Serafina. In fact, if one of Williams's Anglo-Saxon men is "normal," that is, without sexual problems, he cannot help but be antipathetic because he is the cause of so much suffering. In portraits of Brick, Val, and Kilroy, we find an element of the author's hatred, of revenge, whereas Williams freely sings the praises of Stanley Kowalski or Alvaro Mangiacavallo (*The Rose Tattoo*), who have a healthy and open sex life because they are from different cultures. In such cultures, Williams would not have had the emotional problems that he does.

The female characters, on the other hand, are mostly neurotic, middle-aged nymphomaniacs. Perhaps the homosexual writer is able to describe the anguish of a middle-aged female nymphomaniac more poignantly than others: he need only write about himself, changing the gender of his pronouns. It is not surprising that Williams's "southern gentlewoman," "southern wench," and "desperate hero," to use Signi Falk's terms, are similar in character, or that Mrs. Stone in *The Roman Spring of Mrs. Stone* and the Princess in *Sweet Bird of Youth* are very like aging homosexuals.

In Williams's work we also find that thirst for purity which, in

a heterosexual culture, can be satisfied only by rejecting heterosexuality. (Unless the thirst for purity is a rationalization of
homosexuality.) In any event, we find in Williams what we
might call the Billy Budd complex, which consists in making the
hero a disincarnate creature, in devirilizing him while at the
same time endowing him with enormous strength and undeniable masculine beauty. The hero then becomes the personification
of Innocence, Purity, desexualized Masculinity. Like Billy Budd,
Kilroy and Val have no past. Kilroy does not know where or
when he was born, and Val has never measured his own height
or weighed himself, as he informs Sheriff Talbott. And Talbott
rather reminds us of Claggart in the scene in which he is left
alone with Val after having joined the other small-town men in
beating him up: the stage directions say, "In Talbott's manner: a
curious, half-abashed gentleness, when alone with the boy, as if
he recognized the purity in him and was, truly, for the moment,
ashamed of the sadism implicit in the occurrence."

This stage direction could very well be a description of a scene
in Melville's story, and Val has that strange mixture of virile
beauty and passive innocence that we have discerned in the
younger member of the captain-soldier couple. He too will be
sadistically destroyed. In this case, however, the sadomasochistic
relationship is colored by Williams's social protest. The poet,
Orpheus, is in conflict with the small town, which will pursue
him as the Furies pursued Orestes. We must not forget, as Marcuse has reminded us, that Orpheus is the first homosexual in literature.

Suddenly Last Summer

Like the majority of his homosexual characters, Williams's
Sebastian Venable never appears on stage. And (unlike in other
plays such as A Streetcar Named Desire or Cat on a Hot Tin
Roof) the word "homosexual" is never spoken, nor is "faggot,"
"queer," or "degenerate." This is partly because the characters
who have known Venable have enormous affection for the forty-
year-old poet, who dies in the Enchanted Islands before the play
opens. But it is also due to Williams's fear that even off Broadway

the homosexuality in his play would be badly received: "I was surprised . . . by the acceptance and praise of *Suddenly Last Summer*. When it was done off Broadway, I thought I would be critically tarred and feathered and ridden on a fence rail out of the New York theatre, with no future haven except in translation for theatres abroad." Despite Williams's precautions, critic Richard Hayes reproached him for his "obsessive emphasis on exposure [which] often seems close to a scandalous private fantasy," and Robert Brustein termed the play a "homosexual metaphor."

In fact, the play is structured on the progressive revelation of Sebastian's private life. His reputation is at stake. The mystery surrounding his life is never dispersed. However, from his quasi-incestuous relationship with his mother, his practice of using women (his mother and later Catherine) to attract men, his fear of women, and the lack of precision as to the gender of the young blond persons who surrounded him, we gradually gather that his sensual world was totally masculine. Williams's entire body of work is available to assist in discovering Sebastian's shadowy persona, which owes a great deal to Blanche's husband, to the student driven from the university, and to Skipper. The structure of the play is based on scandal, a common obsession among American homosexuals, and it recalls James Purdy's novel *The Nephew* and all the novels in which the revelation of a character's homosexuality forms the basis for the plot—*A Marriage Below Zero*, *The Lost Weekend*, *The Fall of Valor*, and *Concert Pitch* among others.

The play's two-part structure (the mother's narrative and Catherine's) makes *Suddenly Last Summer* a model of the homosexual scandal and exposure metaphor. The mother's narrative recounts the formation of a future homosexual: an absent father whom the mother loves less than she does her son (whatever she may say) and who is conveniently laid to rest before the action begins; a domineering and faintly incestuous mother, devoted to feminizing and desexualizing her only son, determined to prevent him from growing up. The second narrative, Catherine's, describes the result of such an upbringing: a neurotic and immature adult, fascinated by the morbid and the violent, saddled with an ineradicable guilt complex that he can assuage only through masochistic and fatal ritual sacrifice. By a twisted mysticism the desire for purity is transformed into a fascination with death. The play is replete with allusions to expiation, to redeeming sacrifice, to a cruel God, to cannabalism: such references recall certain of Williams's short stories, "One Arm" or "Desire and the Black Masseur," which also link expiation, masochism, and homosexuality. Maggie Pollitt shows herself to be fully aware of the role death can play in the "preservation" of this "purity," and it is hardly surprising that so many of the overt homosexuals in Williams's plays are dead before the curtain rises: they reveal the author's own guilt complex, his inability to show himself on stage as he truly is.

However, the projection of the author's psychological configuration takes many forms. Note the absent father in *Suddenly Last Summer:* neither George, his cousin, nor Sebastian himself has a father. Both the young men in the play, Dr. Crukowicz and George Holly, are extremely handsome, whereas Catherine is not even described for us. A stage direction, however, suggests that she is less attractive than her brother: George "is typically good-looking, he has the best 'looks' of the family, tall and elegant of figure."

Unlike most of Williams's women, Catherine is apparently young (her age is never mentioned). The fact that she attracts men for Sebastian is largely due, as she herself says, to a lack of timidity rather than to beauty. After all, the elderly Mrs. Venable was also a success in this role. Still, she resembles the nymphomaniacs we have encountered in earlier plays in the way she presses herself against the handsome doctor, crushing her mouth against his: "He tries to disengage himself. She presses her lips to his fiercely, clutching his body against her." Williams seems unable to resist the attraction of the gentle Polish doctor (whereas the young American male is extremely handsome, but antipathetic).

Small Craft Warnings

Small Craft Warnings, written in 1972 (on the basis of a 1971 one-act play entitled *Confessional*),—makes brutally concrete what has hitherto been barely hinted at. Leona, a violent but kind woman, talks about her brother Haley, who is dead before the play begins: he was very delicate and anemic, "too weak to go with a woman," "too beautiful to live." He was an artist, a guitar player. Leona is keeping Bill, Haley's opposite—a hustler, a "nance-slugger," and above all a penis ("Junior"). Violet— which is also Mrs. Venable's first name—is a nymphomaniac with a passion for sailors who spends most of her time "feeling" Bill under the table.

The character of Quentin is the first homosexual to appear in the flesh in a Williams play. He treats the audience to a long, sad monologue on the status of the homosexual in American society. He appears to be a moral masochist who only likes "straight trade"—like Sullivan in *The City and the Pillar*—and who is forced to pay for the favors he receives. He rejects the young and handsome Bobby (T-shirt, bleached-out jeans) because he is too sentimental, too open, not indifferent enough—even though he isn't really "gay." Is Bobby supposed to be the incarnation of the new, sensitive, open, and unprejudiced generation?

Monk, proprietor of the bar in which the drama takes place, speaks of homosexuals disparagingly. In contrast to him, Leona (another version of Maggie Pollitt?) understands Quentin and his kind (asexual rather than effeminate, overrefined but serious; he brings to mind Owen in *Knock on Any Door*). Leona appears to be acting as the author's spokesman, the character who—as in *Camino Real*—is there to describe homosexual bars and the problems homosexuals encounter with the police and the Mafia. The play is almost a documentary, acceptable on the stage after the widespread liberation movements of the 1970s.

Thus, in *Small Craft Warnings* we encounter face to face all of the characters who have populated Tennessee Williams's dramatic work: the pure, delicate (often homosexual or asexual) man; the stud, with his enraptured clientele; nymphomaniac or frustrated women; antipathetic heterosexuals. Williams, who publicly admitted his own homosexuality in 1972,* has indulged himself by playing the role of Quentin, his first homosexual character, on stage.

* See Williams's autobiography, *Memoirs,* published in 1975.

Chapter Nine

William Inge: "Homosexual Spite" in Action

In 1945 William Inge, then a journalist on the St. Louis *Star-Times*, met Tennessee Williams, and the two immediately became friends. While Inge had written very little at the time, his friendship with the author of *The Glass Menagerie* inspired him to turn to the theater. Inge has openly declared his debt to Williams: *The Dark at the Top of the Stairs* is dedicated to him, and his next play, *Natural Affection*, a secondary and conventional character makes a disparaging remark about Williams's *Sweet Bird of Youth*. The similarities in characters and situations in both playwrights' work are obvious: sexual fantasies, frustrated women, the devirilization of studs—"homosexual spite"— homosexual characters studied covertly, etc. However, Inge's plays add to the list of ruses the homosexual dramatist has been forced to employ in depicting his own experience, particularly with regard to "virile friendship," the caustic description of heterosexual relationships, and the portrait of "Mom," the overprotective and castrating woman and mother.

The Stud: His Appearance

The first allusion to the stud, which appears in *Come Back, Little Sheba* (1950), is made by way of his opposite, the middle-aged, worn-out, impotent, and discouraged man who is Lola's husband, Doc: he calls Turk (a name symbolic of the myth of ex-

otic virility) "a big brawny bozo." Even before Turk enters, his
girl friend, the young, pretty Marie, has informed us that he is an
athlete who poses for art students. Turk is a young man with
rough, healthy good looks, undisciplined but not wild, dressed in
the clothes we have already noted on some of Tennessee Williams's heroes: "bleached jeans and T-shirt."

Marie must finish her drawing in Lola's house, where she rents
a room, and Turk undresses in the living room. This is the first of
many stripteases in Inge's plays.

Lola, a frustrated woman, is disturbed by the virility of all
youthful studs—not only Turk but the milkman, who is a kind of
preliminary version of Turk. The milkman is a body-builder,
proud of his newly developed physique, and his brief scene with
Lola gives a foretaste of the scene of Turk's striptease. The milkman has sent his photograph to *Strength and Health*, does forty
pushups before breakfast, and under Lola's fascinated gaze he
"flexes the muscles in his arm and puts Lola's hand on his shoulder." Later, he shows her his picture from the magazine, whose
subscribers are predominantly homosexual.

Hal Carter in *Picnic* (1953) is another version of Turk and the
milkman. He is an "exceedingly handsome youth, dressed in T-
shirt, dungarees and cowboy boots." When he tells his old friend
Alan about his interviews in Hollywood, Hal emphasizes his
body: many pictures were taken of him without his shirt, and he
was told to wear "pants that fit you down here like a glove (Hal
passes his hands over his legs to demonstrate)" (1955 version).
Like Turk, he was a model in college: "They made me pose raw
in front of a whole class" (1955 version). He is also, again like
Turk, an accomplished athlete—a football player, a swimmer, a
parachutist. And while Turk was somewhat undisciplined, but
not wild, Hal has had a much more colorful past, which en-
hances his virility: reform school for having stolen a motorcycle
(sexual symbol), unsavory companions, etc. Thus, Hal is a handsome delinquent whose slightly unsavory past is due to a bad upbringing by an alcoholic father and an unfaithful mother.

To the women who surround them, both Turk and Hal are sex
objects. Mrs. Potts stresses Hal's good looks; the vulgar, frustrated Rosemary pulls up his trousers to see his legs; and Hal
recounts an adventure with a pair of nymphomaniacs who sexu-

ally assaulted him when he was hitchhiking. This last, highly improbable adventure, which Inge deleted from *Summer Brave*, the later version of *Picnic*, reveals the unconscious motives of a homosexual author.* Yet Hal's attractiveness to women is also an outward sign of youth and healthy virility.

And here is the description of the physique and clothing of the hero of *Bus Stop* (1955): "Bo is in his early twenties, is tall and slim and good looking in an outdoors way. Now he is *very unkempt*. He wears *faded jeans that cling to his legs like shedding skin*, his *boots*, worn under his jeans, are scuffed and dusty, and the Stetson on the back of his head is worn and tattered. Over a faded demin shirt, he wears a *shiny horsehide jacket*, and around his neck is tied a bandana" (emphasis added).

Up until the end of Act II, we are led to believe that he too is a lady's man. We know that he has seduced Cherie, that he has spent a night with her, and when she refuses to marry him on the spot, he proudly states, "I got all the wimmin I want. . . . I gotta fight 'em to keep 'em off me." Bo ends up convincing her to marry him, just as the handsome Hal marries the beautiful Madge at the end of *Picnic*.

Rubin, the hero of *The Dark at the Top of the Stairs* (1958), also resembles Hal, Turk, and Bo, and is a contrast to Bruce and Alan (the nice young men in *Come Back, Little Sheba* and *Picnic*), who, although they too are young, are not further described. The playwright is not interested in the physical appearance of these decent young men. They are no more appealing to him than the female characters. Rubin is no longer young: he is married and the father of two teenagers when the play begins; however, he is "quite a good looking man of 36, still robust, dressed in Western clothes."

In his youth, before the advent of the automobile—the play is set in the early twenties—Rubin had been a cowboy like Bo. Now he is reduced to selling saddlery, a job that retains a hint of animal virility (Bo wore horsehide). Like his predecessors, he is a Casanova who cheats on his wife. However, between Rubin and his wife—as between Turk and Marie, Hal and Madge, Bo and Cherie—there exists a powerful physical attraction, one that

---

* These motives would later be illuminated by Gore Vidal in his novel *Myra Breckenridge*.

strongly reminds us of Stella and Stanley in *A Streetcar Named Desire*.

In *Natural Affection* (1963) Bernie is not described physically. He is a city boy, and we are told about his elegant wardrobe: oriental dressing gown, silk tuxedo, Italian shirt, cashmere jacket, gold chain, vicuña shirt. He is the ardent lover of Sue, who describes him to her son as "a fine-feathered rooster" and as a woman chaser, which is also evidenced by his brief "extramarital" fling with Claire, the pretty, flighty, and nymphomaniac neighbor. He is younger than Sue, and she is more or less keeping him, since his salary from his job as a Cadillac salesman is not very large. Bernie has many of the attributes of the gigolo. Claire is attracted to him on an animal level, obviously, and his union with Sue is basically carnal.

The last stud in Inge's gallery is the character Tom in *Where's Daddy?* (1966). His mother-in-law, Mrs. Bigelow, recalls seeing him in television commercials, and that "he's very good looking." Teena, his wife, agrees. His black friend informs us that Tom is a blond, and we hear from Tom himself that his agent considers him to be "the perfect American boy type." He has had "quite a few girls." Thanks to Teena, we know that he is totally heterosexual, i.e., he is good at love-making. When he suddenly begins to wonder whether he might not have homosexual inclinations, his wife "serenely" reassures him. "I've never had reason to think so." Tom, however, is not speaking lightly when he mentions his doubts about himself. In 1966 Inge for the first time mentioned the fateful word "homosexual" when speaking of his stud characters; a careful reading of his plays, beginning with the very first, clearly reveals that the studs have feet of clay: Inge is methodically trying to show us that a virile appearance can conceal a lack of real masculinity.

The Character of the Stud: The Reality

Both Turk and the milkman are only "images," portraits. The milkman symbolically leaves Lola a magazine containing his half-naked picture. He is a masturbatory fantasy—as were Genet's imaginary lovers. Turk is equally symbolic: first and foremost, he is a muscle-bound male model, devoid of any psychological background other than that he is a big, handsome bozo, a good guy, a typically American category. Once she has used him sexually, Marie drops him very quickly to make a good marriage. He too, like the milkman, is no more than a materialized fantasy; he has no real substance. The only difference between the two characters is in the size of their roles: we might say that the milkman is a "sexual image" whereas Turk is a sex *object*.

The character of Hal is more concretely drawn than either Turk or the milkman. However, the character's apparent muscular strength is not accompanied by any exceptional strength of character. On the contrary, he is very unsure of himself: he realizes that he is not overintelligent; he admits that he was able to get into college only on the basis of a football scholarship, that he was not kept on in his fraternity because of his uncouth manners. His delinquent past makes him insecure in the respectable world, and he realizes that women only think of him as a "stud."

The author undermines "apparent virility" just as Genet does—a process Sartre has analyzed, calling it "homosexual spite." The stud whom the homosexual regards with a love-hate emotion is divirilized through various processes which are summed up by Doc, who wants to "fix" Turk, i.e., castrate him. Tennessee Williams uses the same processes, situating the aggressively heterosexual behavior of his handsome American animals in their pasts, but depicting them on the stage as nothing but beautiful bodies whose virility is suspect. A scene in *Picnic* reveals this process: Howard—to amuse himself and to tease Rosemary and the tomboy Millie, who are dancing together—invites Hal to dance. Mincing and gesturing, Hal accepts his invitation. Aside from the fact that a man imitating a woman is always comic, it is interesting to note here that the young, handsome stud is the character who is made to look effeminate.

In the third act of *Bus Stop* it is revealed that Cherie has been Bo's first sexual conquest, even though he is tough and twenty-one years old. Although he has attempted to convince Cherie—and the audience—that he is a real hand with women, as were his predecessors, we later learn through Virgil, his mentor, that Bo has always been "shy as a rabbit." We find this basic fear of women in many of Inge's male characters, a fear that can be evidenced by a lack of sexual relations, or, as in the case of Doc, by putting the woman on a pedestal. In *Bus Stop*, furthermore, the character assigned to Bo is that usually assigned to a woman. He is a virgin and his greatest wish is to marry after his first sexual experience. R. Baird Shuman has commented on this role reversal: "One has the . . . feeling throughout the play that in this satirical presentation of conventional morality in reverse, Bo is pressing, with righteous indignation, towards the shotgun wedding which will make him an honest man."

Two factors contribute to divirilizing the stud in *The Dark at the Top of the Stairs:* the passage of time, and the stud's wife. Rubin loses his job because no one is buying saddlery any more, and he had been forced to sell saddlery because he had to stop being a cowboy. At the age of thirty-six, therefore, despite his physique and his sexual vigor, he is no longer the dashing cowboy who had literally abducted Cora.

The elements that contribute the most to domesticating the male are marriage and women. In *Come Back, Little Sheba* Doc, the married man, was contrasted to Turk, Marie's young lover. Doc was forced to give up his ambitions for a medical career to marry Lola, and after years of marriage, he has been reduced to drinking to forget reality. He has also become impotent. Hal, in *Picnic*, wants to settle down, to marry Madge; and Bo, in *Bus Stop*, attempts to become more civilized by marrying Cherie. What will become of these free-living studs after fifteen years of marriage? Rubin, in an outburst of anger, tells his wife, "I admit in some ways I din wanna marry nobody. Can't ya understand how a man feels, givin' up his freedom?" And *The Dark at the Top of the Stairs* contains another character who symbolizes the plight of the married man: Morris, impotent husband of Cora's vulgar, repressed sister Lottie. He is "a big defeated-looking man of wrecked virility." For the sake of domestic peace, he acquiesces with everything his wife says, thus recalling Doc. However, unlike Lola's husband, Morris does not drink to forget. He takes long, mysterious walks which make him feel depressed. Inge's studs fear turning into a Morris, who acts as an alarm bell, or a scarecrow.

Robert Brustein has noted that Inge's plays frequently end

with a marriage, or in reconciliation between lovers or husband and wife. He sees this as an indication that the dramatist considers marriage the solution to every problem. This is a major misjudgment. Aside from the fact that Broadway audiences like happy endings, Inge's "happy" endings are actually expressions of "homosexual spite." Supreme male emasculation consists in pushing a man into the arms of a praying-mantis female and wife.

Bernie lives with an attractive woman, albeit older than he, and he frankly tells her that he has no intention of marrying her because "I'm not gonna marry a broad who can brag she makes more money'n I do." Other traits add to his devirilization. His attitude to his elegant clothes, about which he talks constantly, is somewhat ambiguous (Sue's clothes are never mentioned). He finds it natural to accept presents from another man, Vince, while his mistress finds this suspicious. He wears perfume, and uses the Cuir de Russie Vince gives him. Our stud, therefore, whose sexual prowess is obvious (with Sue and Claire), is far less virile than one is led to believe. His fastidiousness, his material dependence, his insecurity when deprived of a big car to drive around in, his delicate stomach—all these tend to present an image of him as a man who is *basically* feminine.

The character of Tom recalls studs in earlier plays. He is married, as was Rubin. However, with his wife's grudging agreement, he has decided to get a divorce because they are not yet "mature" enough for the child she is expecting. Although virile in appearance (and in the bedroom), he is basically unsure of himself and prefers to run from responsibility. The child will be turned over to adoptive parents. In addition, his marriage is not good for his acting career, providing him with a conjugal menage instead of masculine freedom. Tom is supposed to represent a young man of the new generation, unable to accept the responsibilities of being an adult. In the end, he returns home. He attempts to adapt to his new role. His outburst against the bonds of marriage and fatherhood is only temporary. Yet Tom is far more interesting in his relationship with Pinky, the middle-aged man, the father substitute, whose character appears in all of Inge's work from *Picnic* on.

The Male Couple: Eros or Agape?

Come Back, Little Sheba describes no friendship between the male characters. Turk is indifferent toward Doc, and Doc loathes him, probably because he is secretly in love with Marie, the pretty boarder, but also because he envies the young man's youth and virility, which are a permanent reproach to his own impotence and domestication. In the latter instance, we may interpret Doc's hatred as an ersatz love, or—at the least—admiration.

We find the same love-hate relations between Hal and Alan in *Picnic*. In college, Hal—the athletic, nonintellectual student—was friends with Alan, the good student, the well-behaved boy. Their friendship is based on mutual admiration. Alan admires his pal's checkered past, his athletic prowess, his female conquests; Hal admires Alan's intelligence and collegiate success. Alan's role vis-à-vis his friend is something like that of an older brother or a father; Hal, although they are the same age, behaves with a certain immaturity. (This relationship between the adult, indulgent "mentor" and the undisciplined youth, an alliance of mind and muscle, of maturity and youth should be noted. It will recur with revelatory regularity throughout Inge's plays.) There is also an element of amorous rivalry between the two that recalls the rivalry between Doc and Turk, and in both cases, it is the wild young man who wins.

In *Picnic*, friendship changes to hatred, a change that is obvious in the comparison of the two scenes of physical contact between Hal and Alan—scenes which also reveal the homoerotic basis of their friendship. In the first, they are reunited after several years. In order for their homoerotic passion not to seem overt, the pretext for their physical contact is an allusion to Hal's "outboard motor": "Hal makes noise of motor starting, Alan jumps up, throws legs around Hal's waist, grabs Hal's nose with one hand, steering him like an outboard motor." Later, when hatred comes to the surface because of their amorous rivalry, physical contact between them takes on the twisted features of sadomasochism. Hal is unwilling to fight with Alan since he is "the only friend I ever had." Alan taunts him until they do finally fight. In their friendship are the ingredients already noted in the various kinds of homoerotic relationships: youth and maturity (mental, in this case), jealousy and rivalry, a desire for physical contact that degenerates into sadomasochistic struggle. On stage, all of this can "get by," especially since there is a heterosexual "happy ending" to help the audience overlook the homosexual theme. However, in his revised version of *Picnic* (Broadway version), *Summer Brave,* Inge allows the love triangle to disintegrate at the end of the play. Madge loses both young men, whose friendship has changed into hatred. Neither the pretty girl nor the young man will end up with the handsome, muscular youth. This should not surprise us, since in the last analysis, neither of them has the author's sympathies.

The most interesting relationship between youth and maturity is found in *Bus Stop,* in which the character of the mature mentor of the handsome young Bo is presented in a highly revealing way. Virgil is virile (tobacco, corpulence, masculine clothing), a poet (he plays the guitar); he acts as both the younger man's father figure and his "adjunct." He is both a wiser version of Bo and at the same time his teacher and admirer. However, the word "adjunct" in the sense of "sidekick," is revealing, since it seems to indicate a kind of symbiotic union between the two men which is emphasized throughout the play. Virgil was once in love, but he has never married, preferring the atmosphere of the bunkhouse where he lives with his pals. He realizes that this is the easy way out, for his heterosexuality is not overly strong, and the homoeroticism of his character is evident. Along with Doc, Alan, Hal, Bo, and a number of Inge's characters, he is timid with "nice women" or with women as a whole. "Yah! Gals can scare a fella," Bo remarks—a leitmotif throughout Inge's work. It seems that Virgil has transferred all his tenderness to Bo. Virgil understands him and gets him out of scrapes (as Alan did for Hal). His tenderness is concealed beneath a rough exterior. However, as a musician, and thus a poet, Virgil is a character who has the playwright's sympathy—as in Tennessee Williams's plays. He might be the author's alter ego—Inge was around forty years of age, like Virgil, when he wrote *Bus Stop.*

In any case, the author's sympathies are such that *the relationship between Bo and Virgil represents the ideal of the mature homosexual.*

In *The Dark at the Top of the Stairs,* there is another form of the homoerotic father-son relationship in the relationship between Sammy and Sonny. Sonny, young and introverted, uncomfortable with friends of his own age, does not like his violent and often-absent father, though he loves his mother a great deal. Treated as a "sissy" by his friends, tied to his mother, indifferent to and even hating his father, Sonny is in a prehomosexual situation (cf. Tennessee Williams, to whom the play is dedicated).

In *Natural Affection* the mysteries of this kind of relationship between an adult and a young man are further revealed. The play is given a homosexual flavor by the introduction of the character of Vince, who is impotent and an alcoholic, as both Bernie and Sue are aware. He is about fifty years old (Inge's age in 1963), and as soon as he hears that Bernie has been in an automobile accident, he arrives with a gift for him. Sue finds it unusual that a man should be so thoughtful of another man. Bernie says, "Vince gives me a present, so he's queer. Is that the way you reason?" Sue's remarks, however, have their effect on Bernie.

In a way, the Vince-Bernie couple is a caricature of the Virgil-Bo relationship. Vince is more overtly homosexual: Bernie—in a friendly way—calls him a "fag," and a "queer." Vince, the older of the two, dreams of giving in to the younger man's attraction, as shown by his falling into Bernie's arms while they are drinking together.

Furthermore, from the beginning of the play, Inge creates a homosexual atmosphere which develops the basic theme by means of allusions that counterpoint the dialogue. In the second scene of Act I, we learn that Sue's son had had difficulties with a homosexual guard at reform school, and that Gil, a young delinquent, has advised him to turn to "wealthy queers" in order to earn some pocket money. In a speech that resembles the words of certain of James Jones's soldiers, or of certain of Willard Motley's characters, Gil says, "Why not? They ain't like Stubby. They treat ya better'n your mother. Give ya all ya want to drink, sometimes take you out to dinner or a show. Then put twenty bucks in your pocket, take-home pay. . . . You're not bein' a queer. You're just doin' it for the money." This chorus, which prefigures certain of the play's major themes, emphasizes the relationship between perverse eros and agape. The "wealthy queers" are, in a way, benefactors, the mentors of young, handsome studs; so Vince showers presents on Bernie, finds a pretext to kiss him, and, since he cannot seduce him himself, gives him his wife.

Pinky is a fiftyish professor, plump, soberly dressed. Since *Where's Daddy?* is a comedy, the character of the mature man must be altered in order to make him a comic figure. However, *this modification for comic effect brings out certain character traits that have always been present in the prototype.* The first scene between Tom and Pinky, his "adopted father," is a further step in the portrayal of physical contact between mentor and handsome youth: Tom throws his arms around Pinky "with boyish affection," and Pinky complains that Tom is always trying "to be seductive" to get his own way.

Pinky recalls his meeting with Tom, who, like Billy Budd, Bo Decker, and many of Tennessee Williams's characters, has no family. However, although Virgil adopted Bo when he was six, Tom is taken on as Pinky's protégé at a much later age, and their meeting is like that of a stud and his client: "When I found you in that disreputable bar—at the age of fifteen—willing to peddle whatever you had that anyone wanted for a warm meal and a place to sleep . . ." (In a later version, this scene is toned down.)

Once he has decided to leave his wife, Tom wants to return to Pinky, to go back to being the little boy he had once been. Pinky refuses, on the basis that the young man must accept his wife and his unborn child, that is, the responsibilities (the burden?) of heterosexuality. The scene between the two is an interesting parody of the separation scene between Bo and Virgil. The female character, Tom's wife, eavesdrops on the scene while busy at the stove, fully aware that she has no part to play in the matter. Tom tells Pinky that he "needs" him. Pinky replies that he is neither his father nor his mother nor his teacher, "or whatever I was in your life." "Suddenly, Tom impulsively grabs Pinky and hugs him. He is close to tears." It is easy to envision Bo appealing to Virgil again after a few years of marriage, and Virgil, like Pinky, refusing to help him. The ambiguity of many of the terms and expressions in this scene indicates the author's thoughts, which are more explicit here than they were eleven years earlier, in *Bus Stop*.

A Prototypical Short Play

Spencer Scranton, the protagonist of *The Boy in the Basement*, is a man of approximately fifty years of age, living with his father and mother in an austere and somber Victorian house. It is both the family's home and place of business, a funeral parlor. Symbolically, Spencer's father is an invalid who sits for days at a time in front of the window; he is little more than a piece of furniture. Mrs. Scranton, his wife, has totally devirilized him and has reduced him to silence. He is a more domesticated Morris. She, on the other hand, is "a very regal-looking woman in her early seventies, still very alert and active." Spencer Scranton too is like Morris, or Doc or Vince, but unlike them, he has never been married.

At the opening of this two-scene play we learn that Spencer has been in some kind of trouble during the past weekend in Pittsburgh, where he makes regular visits. He has had to wake his mother in the middle of the night for her to wire him two hundred dollars immediately. He said he had car trouble.

Spencer's only source of human warmth is his friendship with Joker, a handsome adolescent with the physique of one of Inge's future studs. Joker is a well-adjusted teenager who will never turn homosexual. Girls adore him, he guards his independence, but he plans to get married when he has finished college, which he attends on a football scholarship.

Mrs. Scranton reveals what has happened the past weekend when she returns from her ladies' club meeting, at which, ironically, she has been engaged in upholding the small town's morality. She has learned that the police had raided the Hi Ho Bar, and she quickly comprehends that her son needed the two hundred dollars in order to hush up the scandal. There is no way to deny it, since Spencer has left a book of matches with the bar's name on it lying around.

Here, the theme of discovery, scandal, is used in a highly dramatic way, shedding light on the protagonist's guiding obsession. The domineering mother, who is the cause of her son's problems, is transformed into an accuser, in line with a process familiar to those homosexuals whose mothers one day come to learn the truth. Spencer's mentality sheds light on the psychology of the mama's boys in Inge's plays, all of whom (though they may be married) are embodiments of Spencer, their prototype.

The Boy in the Basement provides a key to and is in effect the nucleus of Inge's work as a whole. His plays written for Broadway are only adulterated and diluted versions of this short play, which has nevertheless been overshadowed by his full-length works. The public for which he wrote forced him to disguise his thoughts and to warp his characters and his themes. Spencer is not only the prototype for Doc, Virgil, Vince, or (from a comic viewpoint) Pinky, but also of all the frustrated female characters, from Lola to Grace (in *Bus Stop*), by way of Mrs. Potts and Rosemary; the male's arrival in the midst of these unsatisfied women recalls the plot of *The House of Bernardo Alba* by the homosexual Spanish poet García Lorca. It is also worthwhile to note that here—as in Tennessee Williams's plays—the women are often older than the young Apollo, and that the "mentors" are middle-aged. Both types are closer to their creator than is the character they idolize, who represents the person the dramatist was unable to be.

In *The Boy in the Basement* the absence of female characters —whether frustrated, fickle, or stupid—and the presence of the "Mother," together illustrate the popular stereotypic schema of the homosexual situation: a totally devirilized father, mentally and physically hen-pecked, a domineering and strong mother, an immature and secretly homosexual son in love with a young, handsome, and heterosexual youth who symbolizes happiness, health, and adjustment. In this sense *The Boy in the Basement* is a literary archetype of the stereotypic homosexual situation. It is the model against which we can compare not only all of Inge's plays, in an attempt to discern their basic formulas, but also Williams's plays, and many American novels with predominantly homosexual themes.

Chapter Ten

Edward Albee: Homosexual Playwright in Spite of Himself

Although now and then a critic makes the suggestion that Williams's and Inge's personal lives may have unduly influenced their philosophies and made their attempts at universalizing their experiences unacceptable, no one has systematically examined their plays for their sexual content. From the very beginning, however, Edward Albee's work has been subjected to relentless psychological analysis. Ironically, of the three dramatists in question, Albee is the one whose work is the least *overtly* sexual: there are few frustrated women; there are no aging young men suffering from Oedipus complexes; yet there are the same magnificent young men who fascinate everyone around them. To discern the psychological basis of these plays, a more subtle analysis must be made of symbols and dramatic situations: this has been done by various well-known critics and novelists, and thanks to their interpretations it is possible to consider Albee in the context of the homosexual American theater.

The Zoo Story

Richard Kostelanetz has written, "At base, Albee describes a failed homosexual pass." He adds that below the surface plot of an apparently harmless meeting which ends tragically, there "runs a homosexual undercurrent." Kostelanetz notes all the homosexual allusions in the speeches of the young semitramp, Jerry, and detects two groups of revealing symbols: animals, and vegetables. Dogs are symbols of masculinity, cats of femininity. According to this symbolism, when Jerry states that he attempted to seduce his landlady's dog, "he symbolically announces his homosexual designs." In addition, an "animal" rejects homosexuality, where a "vegetable" is more yielding. Thus, Jerry makes advances to Peter by tickling him and then pushing him onto a bench, as he says: "You're a vegetable! Go lie down on the ground." The critic translates this as "You're a passive male, so be a female with your back to the ground."

Kostelanetz interprets Jerry's act of despair, impaling himself on a knife he has given Peter, as the final touch in the seduction scene. The knife is held like a phallus, and Jerry "impales himself upon his blade with rhythms suggestive of an orgasm. . . . In his desperate action, Jerry solves his predicament—he finds both the sexual contact to assuage his desire and the death to end it. On one level, then, Albee is writing about the predicament of the lonely homosexual who is never quite sure if the man he tries to pick up is 'gay' and whose possible contacts are limited. On another level, he tells of one man's terrible isolation and his desperate need to break out of his shell."

Michael E. Rutenberg affirms this interpretation of the play, and goes on to emphasize the theme of human loneliness and the impossibility of communication between human beings. He notes that the rooming house in which Jerry lives contains only social outcasts, a Puerto Rican family and a little black queen who spends all his time plucking his eyebrows and going to the bathroom on the landing. Rutenberg analyzes, even more systematically than Kostelanetz, the play's allusions to homosexuality.

Central Park, where the meeting occurs, is a famous twenty-four-hour meeting place for New York homosexuals, and Jerry seems to be well aware of this aspect of the park's amenities. When Peter calls for help, Jerry informs him there are no police in the part of the park where they are: "They're all over on the West side of the park chasing fairies down from trees or out of bushes. That's all they do. That's their function." Rutenberg feels that Jerry is speaking from experience and that he has even been forced to prostitute himself on occasion.

Albee has vehemently denied any homosexual interpretation of his plays, and in particular he has refuted Kostelanetz's analysis. To Michael Rutenberg he stated: "I get rather upset sometimes by all these references to homosexuality in my plays. I'm trying to think if I've ever written about a homosexual at all in any of the plays I've written so far. I don't believe that I have."

Perhaps we should take the author at his word in this statement of intent. Clearly, however, a writer's subconscious frequently plays him false, and furthermore, the homosexual artist —overt or latent—is not free. Generally, writers seek refuge in fiction and try to work out their psychological conflicts by creating characters and situations that will help them objectivize their problems or embody their dreams and fantasies. This is clearly the case in Williams and Inge. In Albee, homosexuality, unconscious or not, also seems to have been forced upon his characters. The author may have been trying to describe an ultimate attempt to communicate, but *he has not been able to help* making so many allusions to homosexuality that even the most innocent spectator is forced to the conclusion that the protagonist is attempting to establish sexual contact with another man.

The sadomasochism inherent in American homosexual literature also sheds light on the play's tragic ending. However, the "message" in *The Zoo Story* is made explicit, perhaps, in the play *Sud,* by Julien Green—who revealed his homosexuality in his autobiography. Green's play, which is set in the South, concerns a young man who allows himself to be killed in a duel with the man he loves; he has instigated the duel himself, and allows himself to be pierced by his friend's sword, since he cannot be pierced by him in any other way. The symbolism is similar to that of *The Zoo Story,* and since Green's play is *overtly* homosexual, it is a model which reveals the pattern, the internal structure, of Albee's play. The American homosexual can cure his neurosis only by death, an extreme solution that illustrates in the strongest possible way the psychological and social distress suffered by a person who refuses to conform to the moral code of a civilization that has made sexual inversion the ultimate taboo.

Who's Afraid of Virginia Woolf?

Both John Rechy and Philip Roth consider *Who's Afraid of Virginia Woolf?* as a play with homosexual overtones. However, Roth has stated that he will not go so far as to say that *Virginia Woolf* is a homosexual play. He has merely suggested that the play seems true only when the characters are considered homosexuals. As men and women, they are not all that interesting. They are, indeed, boring. According to Michael Rutenberg, Ingmar Bergman wanted to produce the play using four men in the principal parts. But Albee insisted to Rutenberg that "homosexuality-hysterical critics . . . seem to find homosexuals under every bed, including their own. . . . No, the play was written about men and women, for men and women."

Although *Who's Afraid of Virginia Woolf?* may not be an overtly homosexual play, it does seem, in the context of Albee's dramatic work, that many passages in it are open to such an interpretation. The remarks about the plays of Williams and Inge, above, can act as points of reference here, and as reminders.

Before analyzing their homosexual content, we must note that between *The Zoo Story* and *Who's Afraid of Virginia Woolf?*, Albee wrote *The Sandbox, The American Dream,* and *The Death of Bessie Smith.* These three plays are also of assistance in confirming the basic homosexuality of Albee's work. In *The Sandbox* the Mommy-Daddy couple are derived from Inge's vision of the heterosexual couple, in *The Dark at the Top of the Stairs* and, above all, the archetypical *Boy in the Basement.* Mommy is the married woman, physically robust, who has totally emasculated Daddy, described as being short and skinny. We encounter the same couple in *The American Dream:* Daddy, a small man who lives in fear of his wife, a mother substitute on whom he has come to depend; Mommy, who dreams of an even more total domination over her husband and who envies Mrs. Barker, who has "an absolutely adorable husband who sits in a wheel chair all the time." We cannot help but be reminded of Mrs. Scranton's husband. Daddy is also impotent, as were Doc and Vince. Mommy informs us that "Daddy doesn't want to sleep with anyone. Daddy's been sick."

In *The American Dream* Mommy and Daddy meticulously proceed to dismember their child, removing in turn his eyes, his nose, cutting off his genitals and his hands. This is a symbolic representation of American parents' emasculations of their sons. Suddenly, the American Dream enters. The physical description of the young man corresponds perfectly to the American virile ideal, as it has been found in so many authors whose works are apparently homosexual. In Albee's plays we meet this blond, muscular beauty in *The Sandbox*, as a well-built youth wearing swimming trunks while exercising on stage—the author calls him "The Angel of Death." The young man in *The American Dream* has a body like one of Inge's studs, or one of Williams's handsome American men. As his grandmother comments, "Yup. Boy, you know what you are, don't you? You're the American dream, that's what you are."

In fact, he is the incarnation of the American *homosexual* dream. However, his body is treated with homosexual spite. We gradually come to learn that he is the twin of the baby that Mommy and Daddy have got rid of, and that he has experienced in his own flesh the tortures inflicted on his brother. He confesses his physical and psychological problems, and he comes to seem the prototype of Inge's studs with feet of clay, of Williams's handsome Americans who are understood to be latently homosexual. Brick Pollitt might be speaking his self-pitying tirade, or Val Xavier, or Kilroy—or Inge's washed-out male characters and studs in the process of being tamed, characters such as Rubin, who is halfway between Turk and Morris or Spencer Scranton. The American mother and American wife is the same character, as Philip Wylie predicted—and as has been amply illustrated in American literature, and especially in the American theater, which, at least until fairly recently, was unable to depict homosexuality openly and was therefore reduced to describing men emasculated by castrating women.

In *The Death of Bessie Smith* the female characters are extremely antipathetic, racist, and narrow-minded: the "First Nurse," who has totally subjugated her father, tries to dominate

an intern, whom she apparently succeeds in getting fired from
the hospital.

The intern is physically like the Angel of Death in *The Sandbox,* and like the eponymous American Dream. He is "a southern
white man, blond, well put-together, with an amiable face;
thirty." Sexually he is a stud, but he is frustrated by the nurse,
who refuses to go any further than "petting." Her function in this
play is to *prevent* the young heterosexual from practicing his heterosexuality, just as Inge and Williams saw to it that the handsome American was prevented from becoming a contented heterosexual.

The author's handsome youths and good-looking blond boys
appear with a monotonous and revealing regularity. Nick, in
Who's Afraid of Virginia Woolf?, is "30 . . . blond, well put-
together, good-looking." He is the twin of the intern in *The
Death of Bessie Smith.* He is also a prototype of the American
dream, a characteristic noticed by George. When science finally
succeeds in creating a man, he says, "everyone . . . will tend to
look like this young man *here.*" He is a virile ideal.

Martha and George recall some of the married couples in
Inge's plays by their habitual bickering and in the basic imbalance of their relationship. Martha, like Mommy or the nurse in
Albee's earlier plays, is a rather awesome character reminiscent
of Mrs. Scranton and Lottie. However, George stands up to her
with more verve than did Daddy, the intern, Morris, or Spencer.
Clearly, however, Martha wears the pants, if only because she is
the daughter of the president of the university at which her husband is merely a professor. She is well aware that in a sense she
is more virile than her husband. When George emits a not very
masculine "Tut, tut, tut," she retorts: "Tut, tut yourself . . . you
old floozie."

Martha has no illusions about the virility of the American stud.
In this regard, she could be speaking for Williams or Inge; she is
almost the alter ego of the playwrights. She confides that making
love with her (with a woman?) requires a great deal of courage
on the part of the man—the American man. "So, *finally* they get
their courage up . . . but that's all, baby! oh my, there is sometimes some very nice potential, but oh my! My, my, my.
(Brightly) But that's how it is in a civilized society."

The dual theme of George and Martha's sterility, on the one hand, and of Nick and Honey's on the other, (an extension of Daddy's impotence) has added fuel to the arguments of those critics who would like to see these four characters as men. The imaginary child that has so misled and irritated these critics, and Honey's nervous pregnancy, would indeed assume a totally different aspect were the four protagonists played by men, two of whom might even be dressed as women. It could then serve as an illustration of the lying—due to early instruction in dissimulation—that is legendary and real with many homosexuals. In addition, many aging homosexuals feel a need to have a child: this is a recurrent theme in Inge's plays. In *Who's Afraid of Virginia Woolf?*, however, the important thing is that the children are imaginary children. Furthermore, Martha, if she is a woman, has all the psychological makeup that is characteristic of the mother of a homosexual. She is both seductive and domineering. George informs his guests that their "son" was made literally sick by his mother's incestuous advances. Martha also shares the aging homosexual's taste for young men: at fifty, she seduces Nick, the American—homosexual—dream.

The play is a lengthy, three-act domestic quarrel; its germ can be found in Albee's earlier work, particularly in *The Death of Bessie Smith*. The critics who regard it as depicting the kind of relationship typical of the homosexual couple have obviously succumbed to a stereotype that has been illustrated in literature by Hemingway in *To Have and Have Not*. Edmund Bergler and Irving Bieber have done much to establish the stereotype of abrasive relationships between homosexuals living together as couples.

In Hemingway's narrative, and in Purdy's *The Nephew*, the argumentative couple consists of a wealthy, middle-aged man and a young man he is keeping. In *Who's Afraid of Virginia Woolf?* Martha is older than George, and it is *thanks to her* that he has kept his job as a history professor at New Carthage College. He would have been fired long ago had he not been the president's son-in-law. The relationship between Honey and Nick, despite appearances, is little different. Although we are not told which of them is younger, we know that he is very handsome, whereas she is described as a small, not very pretty, blonde. Above all, we learn that Nick married her for her money. Here too, in the last analysis, the woman is the real breadwinner. George and Nick are alike in that they share—or shared—a gigolo mentality.

The sterility from which both couples suffer, and which has been variously interpreted as symbolizing the sterility of American life for some—and the stillborn American revolutionary principles for Albee—seems to be the result of "aim-inhibited heterosexuality," a pederastic parody of the Freudian principle of sublimation. All four characters are "unproductive heterosexuals," if not homosexuals, who are sterile by nature. In this sense, they—like some of Williams's and Inge's protagonists—exist at the confluence of their creator's antagonistic psychic tendencies. They are the embodiment of his need to portray men and women in order to reach a broad public and give his message a universal value. At the same time he takes revenge on these characters—and thus on the public—for being forced to disguise his true feelings. In Albee, therefore, virile or unattractive women are actually men in skirts as well as realistic pictures of the mothers of homosexuals, and in addition wicked caricatures of the American woman, while the men are impotent heterosexuals. This explains the violent domestic quarrels, which parody the normal arguments between most couples. The author thus evokes the misunderstanding between parents that, according to psychologists, underlies their child's homosexuality, while at the same time taking revenge on the heterosexual couple by endeavoring to show us that this kind of quarrel is normal.

An even deeper homosexual interpretation of George and Martha's imaginary child is possible. Note that George has accidentally killed both his own parents, and in the third act he "kills" his imaginary son in an automobile accident. Reading this double death in the light of the "Billy Budd complex" as it informs the plays of Williams and Inge, we can hazard that the symbolism of the orphan—or the child of unknown parents—may be deeply rooted in the homosexual psyche. Recall that the homosexual has rejected his father—has refused to identify with him or has been unable to do so—and that wrongly or rightly he believes his father has rejected him. Psychoanalysis has further demonstrated that the Oedipal situation can create patricidal fantasies. In a sense, the homosexual—who has not been successful in resolving the Oedipal conflict—has killed his father and has believed himself killed by his father. *Who's Afraid of Virginia Woolf?* may be the theatrical archetype of this "double murder," which the playwright has taken pains to show us is imaginary, i.e., symbolic. Thus, George represents the homosexual who has killed his parents in order to escape from them; he is also the father who "kills" his homosexual son. The extent to which the character is allegorical is clear. Albee, it might be said, is both George and George's son. As mother and wife, he has created Martha—which ought not be a surprise, for ever since Wylie it has been known that the castrating American woman is "Mom," the domineering wife and mother. Henry James anticipated all of this when he had Morgan die in the presence of both his parents at the very moment in which he was rejecting them, killing them symbolically, in order to go off with Pemberton, who represents Life.

Who's Afraid of Virginia Woolf?, therefore, is a homosexual play from every point of view, in all its situations and in all its symbols. It is a heterosexual play only in outward appearance, since in 1962 it had to reach the mass public, and also because Albee *does not want* to write a homosexual work. However, as is the case with *all* homosexual writers, his obsessions emerge, despite all he can do, to color and to contravene his best intentions.

Tiny Alice

Michael Rutenberg, whose interpretations of Albee's plays attempt to be objective, has remarked that Julian, the protagonist of *Tiny Alice,* is "caught up in the middle of this strange household where Lawyer and Butler call each other 'dearest and darling,' suggesting a homosexual relationship between them. . . . There is another hint of homosexuality as a subsidiary theme in the very first scene of the play. The Lawyer insinuates that the Cardinal is homosexual. I don't believe that homosexuality is a theme inherent in this play, but Albee's slight references do cause critics to write that 'he toys with you, suggesting a homosexual relationship between the lay brother and the Cardinal.' Albee should be more selective, otherwise his audience will pick up a small reference and weave it into a major theme, as did Philip Roth in his very controversial review."

Roth, however, seizing on the homosexual allusions and attempting to connect them to a basic dramatic situation that expresses some psychological disposition of the author's, states, "*Tiny Alice* is a homosexual daydream in which the celibate male is tempted and seduced by the overpowering female, only to be betrayed by the male lover and murdered by the cruel law, or in this instance, cruel lawyer. . . . How long before a play is produced on Broadway in which the homosexual hero is presented as a homosexual, and not disguised as an *angst*-ridden priest, or an angry Negro, or an aging actress; or worst of all Everyman?"

It would be futile to quote all the references in the play which lend themselves to homosexual interpretation—and which therefore tend to corroborate Roth's deductions. However, within the context of American homosexual literature, many of these allusions fall under a more general heading and are thus more interesting. In Albee, we again encounter the influence of D. H. Lawrence on the psychology of American men of letters. Animal symbolism, the eroticism of hands—and especially the thumb—and lips are all found in the conversation between Julian and Miss Alice, indelibly marking the author's work. Julian relates how his young friend and he took two horses and rode for hours, talking together, mutually mesmerizing each other. Upon their return their steeds were in a lather, and they were scolded by one of the stableboys, who had "tufts of coarse black hair on his thumbs." Miss Alice then makes reference to Lawrence's "Love on a Farm," in which is described the sexual attraction of a hand that has the acrid odor of rabbit fur. Julian, "embarrassed," admits, "I suppose . . . yes, I suppose . . . those thumbs were . . . erotic for *me*—at that time, if you think about it; mental sex play. Unconscious."

Julian is a masochist dreaming of martyrdom, of blood and

sacrifice (we are reminded of Sebastian Venable). In this too he is related to the other sadomasochists in American literature. He describes himself with a lucidity that sheds a great deal of light on the psychology of homosexual masochism. To Tiny Alice, the patroness—or patron?—he reveals his adolescent fantasies. When studying Roman history, he imagined himself sometimes as the lion, sometimes as the gladiator, but in each case he was the victim, the sufferer. The gladiator was on top of him and he felt the trident piercing his flesh. Here we note the sexual symbolism of blood. Julian mentions a bloody wound, which is an obvious evocation of the woman's sexual organs, her menstrual blood, as is made clear by the comparison between the martyr and the woman. Equally clearly, the gladiator is the symbol of masculine sexuality—the image of thumbs pressing into the neck —and it is revealing that while in his state of trance, Julian unconsciously mistakes Miss Alice for the gladiator when she wraps her arms around his neck and torso. Thus, we can say that Miss Alice is the sadist and Julian the masochist, which means that Miss Alice is the male and Julian the female element in the couple. In *Tiny Alice* Julian, a man wearing a robe—because he is a brother—a homosexual masochist, is the logical end-product of the devirilization of the American male, which is the basic and sole subject of Williams, Inge, and Albee.

Of course, Albee has rejected Philip Roth's interpretation as having "no validity." In response to Bernard Dukore's article in *Drama Survey*, which noted, "*Tiny Alice* is said to be homosexual slang meaning 'anus,'" Albee retorted, "I don't know where half these people get their arcane information from. It's fascinating information and perhaps I'll be able to use it in a play some day."

A Delicate Balance

Here again, the play contains casual homosexual allusions, and at least one of the characters would appear to be a drag queen. Julia, who was once married to a homosexual (offstage, like Blanche DuBois), mentions "the fags," whom she ranks between gamblers and lechers (three of her husbands). She refers to Teddy, her dead brother, and she believes that had he lived, he would have been like her ex-husband, Charlie. Her father, Tobias, is indignant: "Your brother would not have grown up to be a fag." To which she replies, "Who is to say?" Is Albee trying to tell us that Teddy's parents are the typical parents of a homosexual? Rutenberg believes that Tobias and Agnes are embodiments of the "Mom" and "Pop" who appear in so many of Albee's plays. Tobias recalls the symbolic character of George, who is unable to be husband or father in the true sense of either word. Rutenberg, on the basis of particular passages in the play, explains, "Tobias of his own accord withdrew from the responsibilities of a father and husband, content to let Agnes take his place."

However, although the character of the homosexual husband is carefully kept in the wings, as in Williams's plays, the real "homosexual" in this play is Agnes's sister Claire, whose attitude, appearance, speech, and especially her sense of humor, inescapably evoke the "fag." Claire is Julia's "aunt"—she is called "Auntie Claire"—and she complains that she can't find a man even if she tries. Those she has had have stayed only for brief periods, and "none my own"—the complaint of any aging homosexual. Later, she says that her mother called her "Claire, girl," because she had an uncle who was also named Claire! Her humor is a mixture of spite, contempt, and tag lines from plays, a mixture that is also present in the character of Queenie in John Herbert's *Fortune and Men's Eyes*. This kind of humor conceals a profound despair and permanent frustration.

The Ballad of the Sad Café

"Tell me who you adapt, and I'll tell you who you are." This motto could apply to film-makers and playwrights who adapt someone else's work. No one was surprised when Lucchino Visconti made a film of Thomas Mann's *Death in Venice*, and no one found it strange when Albee adapted for the stage such novels as Carson McCullers's *The Ballad of the Sad Café* and James Purdy's *Malcolm*, and considered adapting *A Separate Peace.*

In bringing *The Ballad of the Sad Café* to the Broadway stage Albee faithfully followed in the novelist's plot and the characters' psychologies. The tomboyish Miss Amelia, the handsome and virile Marvin, and the repugnant little hunchback Cousin Lymon have all retained their original personalities in the transfer from novel to stage. And whether the characters be those of Carson McCullers or of Albee, they are directly linked to the "homosexual situation" as it exists throughout American literature.

McCullers describes Miss Amelia as "a dark, tall woman with bones and muscles like a man. Her hair was cut short and brushed back from the forehead." In both play and novel she wears pants, in the literal and the figurative sense, and her actions and gestures are those of a laborer. Marvin Macy tells her that most of the time he forgets she is a girl. "You so big; you more like a man." She fights with him, after having worked out with a punching bag. Obviously, the character is a caricature of the American woman in general, and of the female character in "homosexual theater" in particular: Miss Amelia unites all the physical and psychological traits that are contrary to the image of the traditionally female attributes of reserve, tenderness, prettiness. (In *Picnic* the tomboy character, Millie Owens, is reading *The Ballad of the Sad Café*.)

Her character is shown in relation to two men: Cousin Lymon and Marvin. It is unclear why she married Marvin, as she has refused to sleep with him since the marriage. The novelist describes him as "the handsomest man in this region—being six feet one inch tall, hard-muscled, and with slow gray eyes and curly hair." The narrator, an addition of Albee's, describes him as "the handsomest man in the region . . . and the wildest." Marvin is astonishingly like one of Inge's studs—a skirt-chaser, over-sexed, a fighter, quick to whip out his razor. However, in order to please Miss Amelia, with whom he is in love, he tries to be tender, to rid himself of his rough manners.

We are made aware of Marvin's sex appeal through the intermediary of Cousin Lymon, the hunchbacked dwarf, a sort of anti-Marvin. In a sense, their relationship is archetypical of the homoerotic relationship between admirer and idol. *It is the basic schema reduced to its extreme concentration.* Lymon is a caricatured, revealing embodiment of Joel, Lymie, Jamie, and all the rest. The frail, un-virile bodies of these young men, all ill-adapted to the role society forces them to play, are transformed into the body of a deformed dwarf, while the bodies of their idols, who are all handsome and well-built, become the body of "the handsomest man in the region." The idol's athletic prowess, his bravado, his contempt for discipline, are transformed into knife fights. We are told that Marvin has cut off his opponent's ear and has done time in prison for it.

All three protagonists are locked in amorous rivalry, and in view of Miss Amelia's masculinity, it can be said that they are, in fact, three men who love each other and who destroy each other, according to the "Andromache principle": thus, Marvin loves Amelia, who loves Lymon, who loves Marvin. This is a typically homosexual love-hate relationship, with sadomasochistic overtones. Amelia is attracted to the hunchback, whom she despises; the hunchback has a crush on Marvin, who insults him from the beginning and treats him roughly; Marvin tries to win Amelia's favors and she openly detests him and has always refused him her bed.

The whole region realizes that a battle will inevitably take place and that this abscess must be lanced, in line with the archetypical captain-soldier schema: "Finally, Miss Amelia has Marvin Macy to the ground, and straddles him, her hands on his throat." Marvin succeeds in overpowering her, thanks to the hunchback, who stifles Miss Amelia. Both men conquer the woman, the caricature of the American Woman, of Mom. The narrator informs us that that evening both men leave town together, after having vandalized Miss Amelia's café.

The Ballad of the Sad Café, written by an American woman and brought to the stage by a "homosexual" playwright, thus represents a basic statement that adds to and clarifies Inge's *The Boy in the Basement* and Williams's *Suddenly Last Summer.* And all of these archetypical plays were offered to the public armed with certain protective devices: in Inge's case, a short,

one-act play; in Albee's case, an adaptation of the work of a female novelist; and in the case of Williams, an offstage homosexual and vague, epicene language.

Malcolm

Albee's second adaptation was based on James Purdy's novel,
a kind of homosexual reverie in which the word "pederast" occurs several times and whose main characters can be divided
into two broad categories between whom young Malcolm fluc-
tuates: on one hand, weak men, and on the other women who
wear the pants. Madame Girard reminds us of Martha, Miss
Alice, and Miss Amelia. Tyrannical and nymphomaniac, she is
surrounded by handsome young men and attracted to Malcolm
because he is good looking; Eloisa, Jerome's wife, runs the house
and says that all the male characters in the book are "fags."

Malcolm is another incarnation of innocence who, symbolically, does not even know what the word "pederast" means. He
confuses its meaning with "astrologer." He is prey to the advances of both male and female characters, and he also suffers
from the "Billy Budd complex," since he has neither father nor
mother. His search for his father forms the framework of the
book. Married at fifteen to the pretty singer Melba, he meets his
father in a men's room in a nightclub, whereupon he embraces
him, only to find himself repulsed by the other man, who calls
the police. "Arrest this pederast," he says to the policeman; "He
attacked me."

This synopsis of Purdy's novel reveals why the playwright was
attracted to it: women who are "Moms" (save for the minor
figure of Melba, who is very much like Inge's Cherie), men with
pederastic tendencies, a Billy Budd figure (Albee is an adopted
child), the quest for a father, etc.

In Albee's adaptation (1966), a character says to Malcolm, "So
. . . you are the boy who is infatuated with his father." A prostitute once married to a nice boy tells of his "shacking up with a
cop picked up one night in a bus depot," for whom he is keeping
house. Malcolm, at certain "parties," has made love in the dark

with people of whose sex he is not too sure, etc. In both Purdy's novel and Albee's play Malcolm reminds us of a girl pursued by men (in this case by Jerome, Eloisa's husband, and by Madame Girard, who has all the earmarks of an aging homosexual male). Malcolm dies of alcoholism and "sexual hyperesthesia" brought about by his activities with Melba.

PART IV

The Circumstances of the Homosexual as Reflected in the Novel and Theater

Are you the new person drawn toward me?
To begin with, take warning, I am surely far different from what
    you suppose;
Do you suppose you will find in me your ideal?
Do you think it so easy to have me become your lover?
Do you think the friendship of me would be unalloy'd satis-
    faction?
Do you think I am trusty and faithful?
Do you see no further than this façade, this smooth and tolerant
    manner of me?
Do you suppose yourself advancing on real ground toward a real
    heroic man?
Have you no thought, O dreamer, that it may be all maya, illu-
    sion?

Walt Whitman, *Calamus*

Chapter Eleven

Small Town and Big City

Behavioral Nonconformity in the Small Town

The American small town is the microscopic slide on which the novelist examines the average American's mental attitudes. In small towns, puritanism, the sense of "what people will say," conformity, all reign supreme. Winesburg, Gopher Prairie, Kings Row, and Peyton Place have much in common: as Sherwood Anderson has written, there are monsters and "grotesques" beneath their unruffled surfaces. Psychoanalysis teaches that these monstrous psychological deformities and frustrations are sexual in origin. Anderson, while apparently not influenced by Freud, came to this realization quite early in the twentieth century.

In all the novels that investigate the hypocritical conformity in small towns, the character of the homosexual holds an important place. In rejecting the only kind of sexual activity condoned, at least until recently, by law and church, the homosexual is also rejecting the *American way of life*. Although in New York, Chicago, or San Francisco the homosexual's life style is more or less ignored, if he succeeds in becoming part of a "secret society" within society as a whole, this is something he cannot do in the restricted society of Winesburg or Gopher Prairie. There, everyone will be curious about his private life, and thus he has three options: he can be open about his tastes and risk being ostracized or even experience physical violence; he can conceal his life and become prey to destructive frustrations; or he can flee to

the big city. In Capote's work, as in William Goyen's, are characters who have chosen the first course and have had either to shut
themselves up at home or take refuge in dream worlds, or—having chosen to become objects of contempt for the town's inhabitants—to face, with foreknowledge and equanimity, the risk of
getting themselves killed.

A sociological study written in 1966, *The Boys of Boise: Furor,
Vice and Folly in an American City,* described the atmosphere of
a small town, Boise, Idaho, which was the site of a homosexual
scandal in 1955. Author John Gerassi meticulously researched
the facts of the affair. The scandal revealed the workings of
a small town, its pettiness, intolerance, and hypocrisy: "I . . . understood, perhaps for the first time, what life in a small town is
really like, and since America is ultimately made up of such
small towns, I understood what America is really like." The scandal uncovered a hitherto unsuspected side of Boise, an isolated
town with mimimal interest in anything outside it. At the time, it
was discovered that several of the town's most important inhabitants, including a banker, had "corrupted" minors. An attempt
was made to use these revelations to depose the mayor and his
reform administration. The town's largest newspapers, among
them *The Statesman,* began campaigns against all the purported
homosexuals in the community and took the position that the
scandal was a conspiracy aimed at destroying the family unit.

The entire town was shaken by a "witch hunt" comparable to
the one Senator McCarthy had engaged in at the national level a
short while before. Just as, in 1950, thousands of people had
called *The Statesman,* the police, and the local FBI unit to
denounce "communists," so in 1955 they called to divulge the
names of homosexuals. The town's bachelors were in a state of
panic. Men no longer dared go out at night without their wives
or their girl friends. All-male poker games were abandoned for
fear of creating suspicion. Mothers were afraid to leave their
sons alone with any man, from mailmen to policemen.

Gerassi's investigation is of assistance in understanding certain
passages in such books as *Winesburg, Ohio, Main Street, Kings
Row,* and *The Nephew.*

Winesburg, Ohio, contains many inhabitants who do not conform, either mentally or physically, to the virile type acceptable

to the small town. In the story entitled "Mother," George, who has a close but silent relationship with his mother, is totally unlike his father, the handsome, virile, ambitious Tom Willard. The father, in turn, considers his son's dreamy temperament as evidence of some illness or effeminacy.

Although the misogynist or feminine characters in *Winesburg, Ohio,* are repressed, hypersensitive creatures, it does not necessarily follow that they are all homosexuals. However, the only feelings of affection they know are those between a son and a father, a man and his friend. In this regard, George Willard— prefiguring Singer in *The Heart Is a Lonely Hunter,* who appears to be basically homosexual—represents a refuge for all these frustrated and unhappy beings. George, who identifies with his mother, appears to be attracted only to other men. Wing Biddelbaum is the prototype of all the other sensitive and "feminine" inhabitants of Winesburg. His affectionate physical contact with his pupils and his taste for daydreaming make him the asocial man par excellence.

In Sinclair Lewis's *Main Street* Raymond Wutherspoon and Erik Valborg typify the relationship between the sexual nonconformist and the small town (in this instance, Gopher Prairie).

In the character of Raymond Wutherspoon, Lewis sets out to describe an effeminate puritan who has stifled his inner sexuality by means of strict self-control. The result is a withering of his personality, narrow-mindedness, unforgivable nastiness. Raymie, "the gentleman hen," in the end becomes a part of Gopher Prairie. Back from the war, somewhat virilized by his decorations, he marries the masculine Vida Sherwin and establishes himself comfortably, sharing the community's views and adopting its attitudes. In fact, he is more Catholic than the Pope. His puritanism, which appears to be a defense mechanism against identification with his mother, is proof of his solidity. He is a good man, a fine American. He stays in Gopher Prairie.

Lewis's attitude toward Erik Valborg is quite different. According to Uncle Whittier, Erik is a "milksop." This remark reminds us of Radcliff, the Noon City truck driver, or of Eddie in *A View from the Bridge:* "Makes me tired to see a young fellow that ought to be in the war, or anyway out in the fields earning his living honest, like I done when I was young, doing woman's work and then come out and dress up like a show-actor! Why, when I was his age—" However, seen through Carol's eyes—herself uprooted and isolated among the narrow-minded and hypocritical farmers—the reader's impression of Erik is quite different; he is like a "visitant from the sun." Carol, who is stifling in the small-town atmosphere, and Erik, who is so handsome and gentle that he seems almost feminine, take refuge in each other. Erik possesses all the attributes Gopher Prairie finds suspect: unvirile elegance, good looks, artistic tastes (he has been an amateur actor), a love for the frivolous.

Despite a partial change in Gopher Prairie's opinion of him, Erik does not stay. He flees to New York, where he becomes an actor. In contrast to Raymond, who represses his femininity, "makes himself virile," and remains in the small town, Erik, all grace and feminine charm, finds his own salvation in flight. The author's evident sympathy for him is a clear indication of which solution he prefers.

Unlike Erik, Jamie, the young, effeminate character in *Kings Row*, does not run away. He remains in Kings Row and conforms to its morality. He resembles Raymond Wutherspoon, who made his adaptation unconsciously. Jamie, however, must consciously stifle his homosexual feelings. He accepts the established, prevailing moral code and does not rebel against it. He believes that others are right and that the homosexual does not have the freedom to live according to his deepest instincts. When he ceases to be an adolescent, Jamie begins to exercise self-control: "There was no longer anyone—anyone with whom he had—nothing of that kind had happened in a long, long time." "No one seemed to sense that Jamie was anything but a shy and reserved young man. . . . A few people called him 'Miss Nancy,' but no one seemed to imply much by the nickname."

Both Erik Valborg and Mark in Blair Niles's *Strange Brother* flee to New York; Spencer Scranton (*The Boy in the Basement*) spends his weekends in Pittsburgh. For generations, young American homosexuals have been taking the same route. And interesting dramatic situations occur when the small town impinges on the new world of the "rebels" who have gone to live in the "other" societies of New York, Chicago, or San Francisco. Two short stories that offer food for such thought are "No Competition" (1947), by Wilson Lehr, and "Fulvous Yellow" (1948), by Stanley Kaufmann.

On a visit to New York, Mary Alice Williams decides to look up Charles Dwyer, a childhood friend who has become an actor. They are both twenty-eight years old. Mary Alice is shy, sensitive, perhaps somewhat narrow-minded—all of which adds to the story's irony. Charles invites her to a party of handsome young men, all well dressed and healthy looking, who pay almost no attention to her at all; she leaves early. The girl from the small town does not understand the truth about Charles's guests. She takes their effeminacy and overrefinement to be New York manners, "theatrical."

The story turns on this ironic description of the gap between the small town Mary Alice represents and the big city in which each group, each community, has its own slang, its own mode of behaving and thinking. Mary Alice is an intruder in New York, just as Erik Valborg was a nonconformist in Gopher Prairie. Both are square pegs in round holes.

A comparison between Jamie's room (*Kings Row*) and the decorated apartment of a New York homosexual is revealing. Jamie, the feminine boy who loves poetry and watching sunsets with young males, has consciously stifled any expression of his own personality. On the contrary, Charles Dwyer, far from Minnesota, can allow himself to throw piles of multicolored pillows on sofas covered in yellow fabric, to cover his walls with photographs of male dancers.

Although Mary Alice does not guess the awful truth, she has but to evoke her home town, and its frame of reference takes over; Charles's friends, placed in the Minnesota context in her mind, remind her of something or someone unpleasant. She thinks of "Mr. Gibson, the instructor in that survey of English history course at college. The one who had been such a great friend of Charles's. She shut out of her mind the evil things people used to say about Mr. Gibson. People she knew just didn't behave like that."

In Stanley Kaufmann's short story "Fulvous Yellow," a color again reveals (as did the lemon-yellow sofa in Charles's apartment) the true nature of the protagonist. This story describes the visit to New York of a middle-aged couple who have come from

Albany to see their son. Ev is working as a designer and living with his boss, Ty, who has just given him the present of a magnificent fulvous yellow scarf.

Again, silk and the color yellow put both the reader and Ev's father on the track. Mr. Sprague does not understand the adjective "fulvous," and it symbolizes for him the gulf between the small town, with its simple and virile tastes, and the big, refined and effeminate city. The adult Ev has not lived up to his father's expectations: "Later, when he undressed for bed, Mr. Sprague took his wallet out of his pocket as was his custom, to put it in a drawer. He remembered a picture of Ev and himself that he carried in his wallet and found it. It had been snapped on an Adirondacks fishing trip. . . . The boy was wearing high top shoes and breeches and a plaid shirt open at the throat. He was grinning and squinting into the sun. In his hands he held the string of bass and pickerel he had caught that day."

At the end of the story, the father's feelings toward homosexuality, symbolized by the fulvous yellow color, are made obvious. In the dining car of the train taking them back to Albany, Mr. Sprague orders pumpkin pie: "He stared at it a minute, then he prodded the viscous, flabby filling with his fork. Then he dropped his fork sharply. His wife looked up anxiously, and after a moment, he spoke. 'Fulvous yellow,' he said."

The reader is made to feel a certain sympathy for Mary Alice, suddenly plunged into a big-city milieu that welcomes her at arm's length. There is a vague sadness in "No Competition," created by the uncomprehension between the two worlds, big city against small town, and the intrusion of the sophisticated, homosexual world into the world of a middle-class, small-town girl. The contemptuous, ironic behavior of the homosexual actors is unpleasant, snobbish. This disagreeable impression is accentuated in Kaufmann's story; his tale of the loss of a son is narrated with an ironic discretion that heightens the father's poignant sorrow. In this sense, "Fulvous Yellow" is the antithesis—and much more realistic it is!—of "Pages from Cold Point," the short story in which Paul Bowles described the incestuous relations between a father and son.

In his novel *The Nephew* (1960), James Purdy satirically (but with humor and without viciousness) describes Rainbow Center, a small town in the Midwest. There are two inhabitants of Rainbow Center who live on the fringe of society: Vernon Miller and Willard Baker. The two men's difference is clearly indicated by their distinctive clothing. (Gopher Prairie was uncomfortable with Erik's silk shirts.) Even today, overelegant dress is suspect in the American small town: "Nobody else in Rainbow Center had ever dressed this expensively among the men or even, perhaps, among the women."

A man in Rainbow Center either is one of the boys, or he is not. Professor Mannheim, whose reputation in the town is certainly not of the best, since he has had adulterous adventures with some of his students, has been the recipient of Cliff's confidences. Cliff is the nephew of Alma and Boyd (conformist small-town types), and has been reported missing in Korea. With Vernon Miller, Mannheim appears to be the inhabitant of Rainbow Center who knew Cliff best, but he does not talk about him with anyone, not even his wife, who is the first person to pronounce the fateful word: "Everybody in town knows that Willard Baker and Vernon Miller are homosexuals," Rosa says, thinking that her statement can explain everything. "And I imagine Cliff must have known it too."

Cliff and Vernon, the two young men, are reincarnations of all the Adolf Myerses, Erik Valborgs, Jamie Wakefields, etc.; they are militant rebels to a degree, and in *The Nephew*—as in all the other novels—*rebellion is linked to homoeroticism*. Vernon and Cliff were close; they each represented a refuge for the other. *The homosexual and the pure young man are alike*, if only in their shared hatred for the American small town, and in their basic innocence. The two stood alone in the world against Established Order, against puritan morality, destructive prejudice. Their friendship (which was love on Vernon's part) grew on poisoned ground, the poisoned ground of Rainbow Center. However, far from running away, Vernon ends by conforming to the American small-town virile ideal and gets married. Cliff is reported missing in Korea. His flight is ironic on two counts: when he leaves Rainbow Center, it is to join the army and then disappear in the war.

Politician and Big City

The average homosexual either flees from the small town or conforms to its way of life, whatever the cost. In the American small town, no one can be anonymous, everyone lives in a glass house, and the homosexual lives in perpetual fear of being found out, of creating scandal. In literature that deals with the small town, scandalous discovery is an ideal dramatic ploy: the purulent abscess that finally bursts functions like the catastrophe in Greek drama. The entire novel is built around this deflagration. In a small town, the dressmaker, schoolteacher, music teacher are synonymous with vice and threaten the foundations of society. In the hurly-burly of New York, Chicago, or San Francisco, the average homosexual suddenly loses his explosive, destructive force. The bomb is defused. An anonymous member of a secret society within society as a whole, he can live his life without much danger of being "discovered" if he is careful not to behave immodestly—in parks and public places—that is, not to flaunt his peculiarity in the face of the heterosexual world. Although in most of the states, the law can still ferret him out in the depths of his secret society or in the intimacy of his bedroom, the cases in which the law interferes with someone who is not flouting *public* modesty are rare.

The most public figure in a big city is the politician. For him there is no question of belonging to a secret society: as with the average small-town American, the private life of a political figure is everybody's business. Responsible as he is for the proper running of the country, and therefore of its morals, the politician cannot both represent the people and its culture—that is, its prejudices—and be a rebel, a person who, in Marcuse's phrase, symbolizes the "Great Refusal." In Western society—and particularly in American society—politics and homosexuality are antinomical. When they coincide, they must by their very nature destroy each other. The politician, should he be a homosexual, must conceal his tendencies, like the small-town inhabitant, or risk destroying his career and himself at any moment. In a sense, for the politician the entire country is a small town. His enemies and his rivals will search out his private habits to use them against him if at all possible. In *The Hero in America* Dixon Wecter recalls that "Martin Van Buren failed of his reelection in 1840 after the public had grown tired of his lace-tipped cravats and morocco shoes, and a ribald whig politician had exposed his use of a lotion called 'Essence of Victoria.'" "Effeminacy is fatal," Wecter concludes. Peter Fisher has noted that despite the courage shown by the few declared homosexuals who stand for election, the "widespread intolerance toward homosexuality in politics can be traced in part to the role of the politician. Politicians are expected to be male. Our educational system presents politics as a predominantly male occupation." Even the professions from which most of the nation's politicians are drawn in Fisher's text are predominantly male: "law, the military, industrial management, and in rural areas, farming."

One allusion to the link between politics and homosexuality dates from 1932. In *Studs Lonigan*, Studs, the young Irishman who is desperately trying to embody the American virile ideal, tells about the feelings of the "silent majority" in this regard. He says that "Wilson's gonna get skunked" because he is a "morphodite . . . like fat Leon."

In *It Can't Happen Here* (1935) Sinclair Lewis described fascist homosexual police whose fear of scandal persists, even though the example set for them is the overtly homosexual president. The public, however, would not condone their president's denial of the very bases of the culture he is supposed to symbolize—thus the police arrest homosexuals for offenses against public morals. And when the people learn that their president has "favorites," they are shocked. An all-powerful Secretary of State commits murder to stop gossip. Lewis appears to believe that even in a fascist America controlled by homosexual tyrants, the fear of scandal, of "being found out," will be ineradicable and that even despots will suffer from it.

Democratic America is the context for James Barr's play *Game of Fools* (1955). Barr, an avowed defender of homosexuality, depicts how a candidate for a small-town mayorality tries to destroy his opponent by proving that the latter's son is homosexual. He succeeds. Denunciation and the political use of scandal are not themes restricted to fiction. In *The Boys of Boise* John Gerassi writes, "Some thought that they could use the scandal to rock City Hall, which was then in the hands of a fairly decent, reformist administration, the winner of nonpartisan election." In 1950 Senator Joseph McCarthy tried to destroy the Truman administration by attacking the State Department, and later all government agencies: approximately ninety homosexuals—"sexual perverts," as the senator called them—were fired without appeal. (Gore Vidal brought political homosexual scandal to the stage in his play *The Best Man*.)

In *Advise and Consent* (1959) Allen Drury gives an outstanding description of the crisis produced by homosexual scandal in politics. To make his story more dramatic and the catastrophe more spectacular, Drury has made his hero, Brigham Anderson, an embodiment of all the "American" virtues: he is the American virile ideal, *handsome, athletic, masculine; he represents an American state; he has a wife and children*. The American dream unfolds in this character's past history and his physical description. He is an intellectually precocious adolescent and becomes the captain of his football team. In the war, stationed in Honolulu, he yields to the bliss of a homosexual relationship in an attempt to come to terms with himself. After the war he marries a girl who is *shy and unattractive* whom he attempts to make happy even though he is not in love with her. Like any good American he is athletic, mentally mature, a former soldier, a husband, and a father. He forces himself to repress his tendencies, and when his inner "peace" is disturbed by his memories of the past, he ruthlessly thrusts them aside and devotes himself to his home and his career.

His career as a United States senator is as public as any career can be. When a rival senator manages to find his friend from Honolulu, now in need of money, and obtains a full and signed confession from him, the scandal explodes: the ensuing events culminate in Brig's suicide.

Although the novel (638 close-packed pages) is principally a fond satire of the American Senate and a denunciation of the actions of the President's investigative commissions, it should be noted that the author has made Brig's story the central theme of the book, showing that *the homosexual is the system's favorite victim.* This young, basically homosexual, American god, successful in the most prominent and symbolic career open to *Homo americanus*, is paradoxically in conflict with the Supreme Court, the symbol of law. Since he is too much a part of American culture to flout it, Brig thinks himself unfit to live because he is a homosexual. His political career was doomed from the beginning to the fate of Icarus because of his real and deepest emotional tendencies. The author has endowed him with all the ideal qualities of the American hero in order to make his fall from his place in the sun all the more spectacular, and also to emphasize the extent to which American society, symbolized by its political and judicial mores, can be cruel and unjust.

Chapter Twelve

Three Categories of Homosexuals

The Queen (and His Stud)

To the majority of people, the term "homosexual" evokes the stereotype of the effeminate youth with dyed hair, a swish walk, female gestures, and a high-pitched voice. This is the extreme stereotype of "men who are fleeing from manhood," as D. W. Cory and J. P. LeRoy, authors of *The Homosexual and His Society*, have described it. We will refer to such men as "queens," for unlike other terms—"fairy" or "pansy" for example—it is not really pejorative. A kind of amused tenderness tempers the word "queen," for this epithet is associated with witty, arrogant remarks, and the burlesque movements of a male body attempting to imitate a woman. The queen is an amusing character, and although he can also be a character living in despair, the queen most often manages to mask his despair with apparent gaiety.

The queen must be carefully distinguished from another stereotype: the effeminate man attempting to remain within the heterosexual sphere but betrayed by his appearance, his gestures, his overintent stare. Leon in *Studs Lonigan*, Campion and Dumphry in *Tender Is the Night*, the cook in Hemingway's "The Light of the World," all the many characters who are treated with contempt by heterosexual heroes, are not queens. Although some of the characters in the works in which they appear insult them and call them "fairies," "pansies," and "fags," they do not use the gentler name of "queen." (In his story "The Mother of a

Queen" Hemingway does give this term a clearly pejorative sense; however, in 1938 a title with a less ambiguous word would have been impossible.)

The queen is the most dangerous of creatures. He is always on the verge of threatening a man's virility. This is not solely because the queen represents a man's antithesis, the extreme evil to be avoided at all costs (American education as a whole being devoted to making boys different from girls), but because the queen is so nearly a woman that even a hidebound heterosexual may make a mistake. There is nothing like the humiliation of discovering one has been attracted to a "male." When Studs Lonigan encounters three effeminate men who are too well dressed to be "real men," he is momentarily tempted to make a pass, out of curiosity. However, he is quickly overcome with disgust and changes his mind. Studs could never have been tempted by Fat Leon. In 1931 Blair Niles created Nelly, the drag queen, whom she described with a certain sympathy. The author of *Strange Brother* also described a drag ball in Harlem. Dos Passos gives a brief glimpse of a queen in the character of "Gloria Swanson," the black prostitute who appears to receive Dick Savage's favors, and in his "girl friend," Florence. The author of *The Big Money* treats the scene humorously, and Gloria Swanson (like Tony the Cuban) remains in the reader's memory as an amusing, albeit sketchy and only partially realized, character.

In H. C. McIntosh's novel *This Finer Shadow* (1940) a detailed description of the queen's world is given for the first time. McIntosh describes a drag ball to which all the characters in the novel come dressed as women, their names suddenly feminized. During the evening these homosexuals reveal their true characters: gestures turn effeminate, voices rise a tone, conversation is like that at an afternoon tea. This scene is preceded by a description of the lengthy preparations, the choosing of dresses, the careful makeup at their dressing tables, etc.

To the theater, John Herbert and Mart Crowley have introduced Queenie and Emory, who embody all the characteristics of the queen.

This type of homosexual, the extreme stereotype, according to Cory and LeRoy, is as much despised by "normal" homosexuals as he is by heterosexuals. They reproach the queen for being neither man nor woman, and for giving a bad name to the community as a whole. In *The Boys in the Band* the host, Michael, continually insults Emory. One of the queen's distinctive characteristics is that one never knows whether to speak of him in the masculine or the feminine, he or she. Genet has warned, "I will speak to you about Divine, mixing masculine and feminine as my mood dictates." (In French, of course, the problem is intensified.) The first lines of Hubert Selby's story "The Queen Is Dead" in *Last Exit to Brooklyn* are: "Georgette was a hip queer. She (he) didn't try to disguise or conceal it with marriage and mans talk."

The queen's gestures imitate those of a woman and, frequently, caricature them. Cory and LeRoy, who have nothing but contempt for the type, mention limp wrists, swaying hips, and the mincing walk of those who are as unable to resemble men successfully as to pass themselves off as women. Those who do succeed in this are rare. According to the narrator of *The City of Night*, "Of all the queens I will meet in L.A., Trudi has most accurately been able to duplicate the female stance so that, unlike most other queens, she has not become the mere parody of a woman."

Not just anyone can become a "girl-queen," to use Genet's phrase. Clothes do not make the queen. A special psychological makeup is required. The queen in flight from virility, constantly attempting to identify himself with a woman, is attempting to repress all of his male qualities. In *Last Exit to Brooklyn* the characters Georgette, Alberta, and Regina are exclusively interested in studs, in tough guys, in delinquents who will eventually get married but who live with queens *without losing any of their own virility*. Georgette is in love with Vinnie, who is a hood, and he experiences all the sufferings of any pure young girl in love with a handsome and indifferent man.

The queen's despair—the despair of Georgette (and Genet's Divine)—may arise from the feeling of having been deceived or abandoned. However, this type of suffering is common to all mortals, men or women. In the case of queens, however, despair is usually due more to the profound and inescapable feeling of being a hybrid, of no longer belonging to either sex. The despair created by this split in personality is concealed beneath a veneer of superficial gaiety which is most clearly expressed by the queen's "humor." Listening to the conversation of the guests in *This Finer Shadow*, of the characters in "The Queen Is Dead," of Queenie or Emory, of Roy in *Something You Do in the Dark*, or of Genet's girl-queens, one is struck by the brilliance of the repartee, the telling remarks, the witty phrases—and also by the nastiness employed to destroy a rival and to humiliate him by constant allusions to his lack of grace, his age, or his vulgarity. In Farrell two queens abuse each other like fishwives before deciding to join forces to seduce Studs—and in *Fortune and Men's Eyes* Queenie never misses an opportunity to taunt Mona, the weaker character.

The language of queens is not a slang. Of course, queens employ words and phrases far different from the language of Shakespeare or Racine, but it is the intonation, the tone, the syntax of their language, more than the vocabulary *per se*, that distinguishes their language from the language of the studs. Harry, Malfie, and Vinnie, all of whom are studs, do not talk like Lee, Camille, or Georgette. To convince himself of his femininity, the queen refers to himself in the feminine. Georgette gets even with her brother Arthur by calling him a "fairy."

Queens hold more or less honest jobs of all types in order to live. They are prostitutes, they work part-time in bars; some are women's hairdressers or hospital orderlies. According to Cory and LeRoy, "Most of these would-be females come from the lower socioeconomic brackets: they seek only to live in the most carefree manner for the remainder of their lives." The queens in *City of Night* and *Last Exit to Brooklyn* "cruise" the sidewalks of all the large cities. Their studs spend their time at the movies. As long as they are young and attractive, the girl-queens can be kept by the rare studs who are not kept by them as their pimps.

In "Strike" (*Last Exit to Brooklyn*) Alberta and Regina are kept by Harry Black. Harry meets Regina at a drag dance. They enter into a sort of liaison. He often invites Regina to his home, and takes him out as a man does a woman. Harry is content because Regina is "a little different than the others." The real difference between Regina and other queens soon becomes apparent to Harry, to his sorrow. *Regina has so completely iden-*

tified with the American woman that she also adopted all her defects. Between Regina and Mary, his wife, there is no difference at all. Both are members of the Cinderella category established by Philip Wylie. For such assimilated American women, the man is Prince Charming; he will change their life, he will give them a luxurious house, a convertible. Cinderella's dream has been Americanized: the castle is a house in the suburbs, the coach is a Mustang with glittering chrome.

Regina remains with Harry so long as he freely spends money out of union funds—so long as he gives her shirts or some bauble or other, chauffeurs her around in cabs, and takes her to dinner in restaurants. When the strike ends and the money supply dries up—Harry can no longer draw from the union's petty cash—Regina drops him without a hint of scruple for another "trick." Harry's dream of a woman who is not a "ballbreaker" evaporates into thin air. The queen is not the fabulous creature dreamed of by Melville, with all the qualities of a man and with a woman's beauty. *Billy Budd is the dream: Regina is the reality.* Harry's normality, his appearance, his average-American mind are what make Regina a perfect example of the American "ideal" of femininity. Regina, more than the attractive Trudi, is the character who succeeds in becoming more than a mere caricature of a woman.

The Average Homosexual

Cory and LeRoy describe men who can be classed as "normally masculine homosexuals," but who from time to time evidence "a slight mannerism here and there . . . as a sort of password." The majority of homosexuals probably fall into this category. They are men who wear masks during the day, whose private lives begin after working hours. They are part of the "scene" to varying degrees. Many of the characters in American novels and plays are of this type, among them some of the protagonists of Vidal and Baldwin, some of the characters sketched in Hemingway's novels and in Inge's plays, etc. The prototype of this category is probably the professor who is the protagonist of

Christopher Isherwood's *A Single Man.* The same sort of character appears also in Isherwood's *The World in the Evening,* as a doctor who, with his boy friend, leads a typically middle-class American life in a small town that accepts them because they are not blatant. In these characters, the average homosexual is as far removed from the queen as from the rough trade or the hustler, whose psychology will be dealt with later.

Here we are not dealing with the psychological problems that emerge out of the inner conflicts of the homosexual who is unable to come to terms with himself, as described in such characters as John Grandin or Don (both protagonists in Charles Jackson's novels), or with sadistic captains, with soldiers rejecting homoerotic liaisons, or with latent or repressed homosexuals, such as Raymond Wutherspoon.

The Etiology of Homosexuality

THE MOTHER-SON RELATIONSHIP

Several critics have noted the passionate attachment between Melville's *Pierre* and his mother, Mrs. Glendinning. The psychiatrist H. A. Murray speaks of the "enduring mother fixation" that explains the "repressed homosexual component" of Pierre's personality, throwing light on his "flight from marriage, his preference for almost sexless women," and his seeking refuge with his cousin Glen Stanley, his boyhood idol. In Waldo Frank's *The Dark Mother,* Tom Rennard and David Markand, whose relationship is homoerotic, are caught in the toils of an Oedipus—or rather, Jocasta—complex. Elliott Paul, the author of *Concert Pitch,* has described the incestuous feelings of the latent homosexual Robert Maura for his mother. Jamie, the "sissy" in *Kings Row,* chafes at his mother's cloying affection. The mother of Steve La Cava, the young homosexual lieutenant in Loren Wahl's *The Invisible Glass,* wants him to look on every girl as the Virgin Mary, obviously in order to protect him from all women. The narrator of *The City of Night* speaks of his mother's "ferocious love" from which he has had to escape in order to discover his own identity. In *This Day's Death,* another of Rechy's novels, the mother, Mrs. Girard, is an incarnation of the possessive, castrating mother we have met in *Suddenly Last Summer*, *The Boy in the Basement*, *The American Dream*, and *Game of Fools*. Michael, the host in *The Boys in the Band*, complains of his mother's stifling love which has, according to him, made him a homosexual.

In all these works, the authors appear to be indicating that a principal cause of homosexuality is an overly close relationship between a son and a possessive, domineering mother.

A few authors, however, do trace the homosexual character's sexual orientation to hostile or indifferent mothers. James describes Mrs. Moreen ("The Pupil") as being a mother whose demonstrations of affection for her son conceal actual hostility. Jim, the protagonist of *The City and the Pillar*, feels that his mother no longer loves him as she once did. In *The Season of Comfort* the mother is openly hostile to her son. In *Another Country* Baldwin describes the mother of Yves, the young Frenchman, as devoid of maternal instincts. In the theater, the only mother of a homosexual who openly rejects her son is Queenie's mother (*Fortune and Men's Eyes*), who abandoned him as a child.

All of these authors, homosexual or heterosexual, have more or less deliberately adopted the tenets of psychoanalysis, and regard the mother as one of the principal causes of their characters' homosexuality. It should be noted that it was not until long after the popularization of psychoanalysis in America that the first "psychological case histories" were sketched out in American literature.

THE FATHER-SON RELATIONSHIP

In *Pierre*, *The Turn of the Screw*, and *Other Voices, Other Rooms* the father is absent. In *Reflections in a Golden Eye* the captain is an orphan. The father of Morgan ("The Pupil") prefers his elder son and is often away from home. He also appears to be incapable of providing for his family, and his wife is the head of the family. In the theater, fathers rarely figure in the work of the homosexual Tennessee Williams and William Inge. In Edward Albee's plays the father has often been devirilized by a castrating wife.

James Baldwin, in *Go Tell It on the Mountain*, has probably best described the adolescent son's combined hatred and fear of the father who forces him to withdraw into himself and reject identification with the father, thereby imperilling his sexual identity. Jim Willard, the teenager in *The City and the Pillar*, feels a strong hatred for his father. Similarly, as a young man General Cummings in *The Naked and the Dead* was terrified of his father, whom he hated. In his novel *Something You Do in the Dark* Daniel Curzon describes a violent scene between a father and his homosexual son. The father, a laborer in a Detroit suburb and thus a real American "he-man," discovers his son with a lover he has picked up and brought home, under his own roof. After this poignant scene, which is related calmly and without melodramatics, the father throws his son out.

Often fathers are described not as overtly indifferent or hostile but merely as lukewarm in their relationships with their sons. David's father (*Giovanni's Room*) is unable to offer his son a role model because he is an alcoholic, irresponsible and incapable. David says, "He thought we were alike. I did not want to think so." Similarly, Lymie, the "sissy" in *The Folded Leaf*, is unable to identify with his father, who is a fickle old skirt-chaser.

On the other hand, we have the incestuous father of "Pages from Cold Point," the narrator's father in *City of Night* who intimately fondles his son, and Dennis Vaccaro in James Kirkwood's *Good Times/Bad Times* (1968), who is initiated into homosexuality by his father.

SIBLING RELATIONSHIPS

Although Jim (*The City and the Pillar*) dislikes his brother, and although Georgette, the queen in *Last Exit to Brooklyn*, hates his brother Arthur (and the feeling is mutual), the protagonists in James Baldwin's and Charles Jackson's novels love their brothers. Leo Proudhammer (*Tell Me How Long the Train's Been Gone*) experiences his first taste of erotic pleasure with Caleb, his brother, and Don (*The Lost Weekend*) appears to feel an incestuous attachment to his brother. In *A Meeting by the River*, a novel by Christopher Isherwood, Olivier has experienced incestuous desire for his (bisexual) brother Patrick.

THE PREHOMOSEXUAL CHILD

Irving Bieber has described the child in a prehomosexual situation (the "sissy"). More than half the homosexuals he analyzed had evidenced such behavior during childhood and adolescence: "He is reluctant to participate in boyhood activities thought to be potentially physically injurious—usually grossly overestimated. His peer group responds with humiliating name calling and often with physical attack which timidity tends to invite among children." Merle Miller and Tennessee Williams both experienced such problems. In *The Invisible Glass* Steve La Cava prefers playing with girls, because the boys make fun of him. In *Something You Do in the Dark* the following dialogue occurs between a father and his homosexual son: " 'You were always sort of afraid to fight when you was a little boy.' 'I'm sorry. I guess I was a disappointment to you in most ways.' 'You'd never fight 'em back; they'd chase you right up here on the front porch, and you wouldn't fight 'em back.' " Mention also might be made here of the name-calling to which Tom, in *Tea and Sympathy*, is subjected by his schoolmates; Sonny, the child in Inge's *The Dark at the Top of the Stairs* is chased by children who taunt him with his girlish tastes.

However, the effeminate boy is not the only prototype for the future homosexual man. Jamie, Lymie, Joel, John Grimes, the young General Cummings, Steve La Cava, and so on can be contrasted with the many young men who avoid girls but who are nonetheless at ease with their peers: some of the adolescent characters in Baldwin and Vidal are meant to destroy the "sissy" stereotype. Jim Willard is an athlete, as are his counterparts in *A Thirsty Evil* and *The Season of Comfort*. Baldwin's Leo Proudhammer has an almost normal childhood.

INITIATION

Initiation—the first homosexual experience—plays an important part in many novels and plays. Such is the case with the protagonist of *Kings Row*, and Vidal and Baldwin describe sexual exploration between adolescents.

Initiation by an older man occurs in *Other Voices, Other*

Rooms and *The House of Breath;* symbolically, it represents the moment of the younger character's entry into the homosexual world. In predominantly heterosexual literature the figure of the potential adult seducer recurs with revealing frequency: Farrell's Pole and Leon, Hemingway's cook, Piot in Elliott Paul's *Concert Pitch,* the man in the bar in Merle Miller's *That Winter.* The two protagonists in John Updike's novels *Rabbit, Run* and *The Centaur* are both wary of older men. Harry, who has himself aroused the suspicions of the young basketball players, wonders for a moment whether his former coach, Tothero, is trying to seduce him. Peter, the teenager in *The Centaur,* expresses the fears shared by most adolescents who are still uncertain as to their sexual identity: "I felt, as long as my love of girls remained unconsummated, open on that side—a three-walled room any burglar could enter."

Social Adaptation

Psychologically, the average homosexual exists on the outskirts of society. His social life overlaps only partially. Yet he must fulfill his needs. In *The Turn of the Screw* the "homosexual" is a servant, which is proper and fitting. Hemingway's cook in "The Light of the World" may also be classified as a servant. More often, however, at least in literature—whether it be heterosexual or homosexual—the homosexual character is an artist: Leon Piot (*Concert Pitch*), Winston Hawes (*Serenade*), Leon (*Studs Lonigan*) are all musicians; Jim's lover Ronald Shaw (*The City and the Pillar*) is a Hollywood actor. In Baldwin's novels, Leo Proudhammer and Eric are both actors. Erik Valborg, the effeminate young man in *Main Street,* becomes an actor, and Mailer makes Teddy Pope a film star. There are countless examples. Some professions have always been more tolerant toward sexual deviation (unless, as Freud appears to indicate, homosexuality and the artistic temperament are closely related—but that is a question outside the scope of this study). Suffice it to say that the homosexual, whether a music teacher, actor, decorator, or model, is not for that reason, properly speaking, a stereotype. Indeed, it is true that such professions attract young people who feel uncomfortable in the aggressively heterosexual business world. Speaking of American customs in the nineteenth century, Henry Steele Commager, in *The American Mind,* emphasized that "women . . . largely dictated the standards of literature and art and clothed culture so ostentatiously in feminine garb that the term itself came to have connotations of effeminacy." In *The Popular Book* James D. Hart states, "Men were busy with money-making, politics, and all the other so-called practical affairs of the day; women took over the arts, social deportment, and domestic standards."

In literature, teaching is often categorized as being a "homosexual profession." In the chapter "Teacher and Pupil" we dealt with several teachers with homoerotic tendencies. However, a distinction must be drawn between professors of the humanities and professors of the sciences. Louis Terman and C. Cox Miles have placed engineers in the dyed-in-the-wool heterosexual category as he-men, and physics or mathematics professors are their first cousins (cf. *Sex and Personality*). Hank (*The Boys in the Band*) is a math teacher and looks so virile that Alan (the outsider) refuses to believe he is a homosexual! Henry Fuller, John Rechy, Gore Vidal, and Robert Anderson (*Tea and Sympathy*) have all created homosexual professors without laying any particular stress on the teacher-pupil relationship, but at the same time they hint that even among these "solid citizens" there are a few followers of Uranus.

Jim Girard, the protagonist of *This Day's Death,* is studying to be a lawyer; Charles Kennedy (*The World in the Evening*) is a doctor; in *This Day's Death* and in *Something You Do in the Dark* Rechy and Curzon both seem to be hinting that the policeman who arrests Jim (or Cole) is a repressed homosexual (Cole is arrested in a men's room). And then there is the large cast of sailors, soldiers, and officers that appears throughout American literature. A roll-call of these military men would be far too lengthy; it reveals the attempt of homosexual authors to virilize their protagonists, to break away from the stereotype and to reestablish warrior homosexuality on the Greek model. James Jones, Allen Drury, John Horne Burns, etc., have shown that in the army and aboard ship the antihomosexual prejudices of American males are somewhat relaxed. Furthermore, the public is more willing to accept this kind of "forced" homosexuality.

Whatever the homosexual's profession, he must at all costs avoid coming into conflict with society. He has somehow to manage *to give the impression that he is socially well-adjusted*. Not until *Advise and Consent* (1959) do we find Senator Anderson's heterosexual friends supporting him in his struggle before the investigating committee.

Many homosexual spokesmen have denounced society's hostility toward those who do not adopt its sexual standards. Evidences of this hostility are to be found in many novels and plays. In *From Here to Eternity* the Army undertakes a sweeping investigation; in *Advise and Consent* an American Senator is accused; in *It Can't Happen Here* homosexual dictators live in fear of public opinion. Cory, Vidal, and Goodman have constantly denounced the harmful and cruel prejudices with regard to sexuality prevalent in America. They have looked for support to Freud ("Letter to an American Mother"), Kinsey, Ellis, and others. However, the American sexual establishment has been slow to change its mind: Nelly's legal problems (*Strange Brother*) and those of Jim Girard (*This Day's Death*) and Cole (*Something You Do in the Dark*), as well as the troubles experienced by the boys in *Game of Fools* (James Barr) or Mona (*Fortune and Men's Eyes*) continue to occur.

Sexual Adaptation

In light of such hostility on the part of society—and obviously for a variety of complex reasons as well—it is natural that some homosexuals do attempt to conform to their country's sexual morality—without great success. Raymond Wutherspoon, virilized by his stint in the army, marries late (and he marries an authoritarian, masculine woman); Captain Penderton marries the seductive Leonora, whom he abandons; Don, hero of *The Lost Weekend*, is unable to face heterosexual contact without the support of alcohol; Professor John Grandin (*The Fall of Valor*) neglects his conjugal responsibilities; David, Giovanni's lover, forces himself to have sex with women out of a panic fear of some homosexual hell; Hank, the virile homosexual in *The Boys in the Band*, is getting a divorce; and Cole (*Something You Do in the Dark*) tries to "change" by having an affair with

Angie, a girl, to whom he cries out "Save me, Angie!" Most of the
officers who are obsessed by the animal grace of the soldiers
under their command attempt to get rid of their guilt feelings
by paying an occasional tribute to heterosexuality. All of these
protagonists play hide-and-seek with their deeper instincts, and
they find in the heterosexual relationship an alibi with which,
they think, to ease their conscience.

Another mental ploy consists in interposing a woman between
oneself and another male: Cliff Hauman and his friend in *The
Fall of Valor*, Vivaldo and his black friend in *Another Country*,
Roger and Gib in Robert Phelps's *Heroes and Orators*, etc. From
the point of view of novelistic technique, the presence of a
woman—wife or mistress—lends more depth to the psychological drama. In *Serenade, The Fall of Valor, A Long Day's
Dying, Giovanni's Room, Advise and Consent*, etc., the woman is
society's representative: her reaction mirrors that of the small
town which drives out Adolf Myers ("Hands") and it is all the
more vivid and striking in that wife and mistress, without knowing it, have had intimate contact with the enemy. John Grandin's
wife, Brigham Anderson's wife, and Giovanni's mistress show little tenderness to their unfaithful spouses.

There are few tolerant women in American literature of the
homosexual. Apart from Alma in *The Nephew*, there is the tolerance expressed by Maggie (*Cat on a Hot Tin Roof*) and Blanche
(*A Streetcar Named Desire*). Christopher Isherwood, in *The
World in the Evening* (1954), created two tolerant women: the
wife of the bisexual narrator, who forgives her husband his homosexual infidelity with the young and handsome Michael, and
the narrator's aunt, who—although she is a respected citizen of a
small town—ends up understanding the feelings between
Charles Kennedy and his friend, Bob Wood. Angie tries to help
her friend Cole in *Something You Do in the Dark*.

The homosexual in American literature rarely finds a permanent partner. Idyllic liaisons that appear stable are often brought
to a sudden end by the death of one of the partners. In *Quatrefoil* the commander dies just as he is beginning a promising
relationship.

Even when describing more or less permanent unions, authors
often stress their negative aspects. In *To Have and Have Not*

Hemingway eavesdrops on the bitter arguments between Wallace Johnston and Henry Carpenter, which prefigure the disputes between Willard and Vernon in *The Nephew*. The liaison between Dr. Charles Kennedy and his boy friend Bob in *The World in the Evening* is not without its problems and difficulties of all kinds. Jim cannot remain long with the actor Ronald Shaw, because he is not seeking a "father" but rather a "brother"—whom he will never find. George's relationship in *A Single Man* was apparently cloudless, but it is being remembered for us after the death of his lover, and we never see them together. The love affair between Eric and Yves in *Another Country* is fragile from the very beginning because of the couple's basic nature: despite the novel's optimistic ending (Yves's arrival in the United States), the reader realizes that their real cohabitation is just beginning—the French episodes occurred in a vacation atmosphere. And cohabitation by David and Giovanni is obviously impossible. In *The Boys in the Band*, Hank and Larry manage to stay together only at the cost of many concessions. Daniel Curzon makes it clear that Cole's liaison with his boy friend does not outlast Cole's term in prison.

No character in *The City and the Pillar* dares enter into a permanent relationship. Jim leaves Ronald Shaw to continue searching for Bob, or for some successor to his "dream-lover." He soon admits to Paul Sullivan that he is spending his nights in bars, where he picks up five or six partners a week, "and none of it means anything, but afterwards I feel so peaceful and clean . . . you know what I mean." Paul Sullivan, an intellectual, has long ago given up all hope of finding an ideal lover—that is, a "normal" homosexual—and relies on one-night stands with men he meets in bars.

Burns, Rechy, Vidal, Wahl, Curzon, and all the other authors who describe the hidden society of the homosexual use bars as one of the basic institutions of this underground world. Burns, Motley, Baldwin—and earlier, Fitzgerald—describe the atmosphere of these hangouts, which consists of superficial gaiety masking an underlying frustration, anxiety, and despair. In the theater Williams in *Camino Real* and Crowley in *The Boys in the Band* make reference to the lack of human warmth.

Apart from bars, the preferred meeting places are parks, public lavatories, YMCA showers, steam baths, and certain streets or squares in the large cities. John Rechy, all of whose novels are in part documentary and often reminiscent of homosexual guidebooks, describes all these locales. In Mart Crowley's play, Hank meets his first sexual partner in the public lavatory at Grand Central Station; this is the same location where the German student is discovered in Saul Bellow's *Herzog*. Daniel Curzon gives descriptions of a park, a bar, and in particular a Detroit bathhouse.

In *Numbers* Rechy was the first to examine the psychological state of the cruising homosexual seeking a partner for a brief adventure, or for a night; the hero, Johnny Rio, back in Los Angeles after a visit to his family in Laredo—where he had remained chaste—revisits all the cruising locales, in particular Griffith Park, where innumerable young men, on foot or in cars, wander about in search of sexual contact.

By making his hero an Adonis, Rechy attempts to show that whatever his outward appearance, the homosexual is basically a person who is unsure of himself, a person constantly in search of acceptance. He continually relives the initial crisis, the trauma of parental rejection—as James so well understood in "The Pupil." The homosexual, the "cruiser," is an eternal Morgan in search of his Pemberton. The monotony of Rechy's novel, which might be considered a technical defect, marvelously evokes the obsessive nature, the emptiness, of such contacts, and the cruiser's monomania. For the cruiser, cruising is not only a favorite pastime but a vital activity. He has the impression that he does not exist unless he can attract a partner: "The first one today! Johnny thinks. I'm alive!" And this thought makes us aware that the search for a partner is an act of *survival*, and that nothing can appease it, neither finding an ideal lover, who is quickly cut down to human dimensions, nor the feeling of satiety that many sexual conquests can provide: "One rejection—real or imaginary—can slaughter Johnny Rio, even among one hundred successes." While cruising in a park, Cole, the hero of *Something You Do in the Dark*, "felt his body aroused again. Alive! He was thoroughly alive, a delectable, welling joy. How could anyone not understand? Yet perhaps they did understand—that was why Keel and the other policemen went beating through the blackened parks with their chains, flaying the exposed flesh, to subdue, to chastise, to destroy!"

Not all homosexuals are seeking the same erotic experience. *City of Night* is enlightening on this subject. The novel contains a gallery of different types. We encounter many "solid citizens" whose sexual pleasures are similar only insofar as their partner must be a man. The novel offers many glimpses into the sexual habits of the disciples of Socrates. Yet compared to pornographic works on this subject, which however make no claim to be literature, the novel is fairly mild. Only William Burroughs has surpassed Rechy in the description of violent and exotic lovemaking.

Three Characteristics of the Average Homosexual: The Sense of Loneliness, the Fear of Aging, and the Fear of Scandal

The first time the boy Nick sees Owen in Willard Motley's *Knock on Any Door*, he appraises him as "the unhappy man." In Owen the author portrays a melancholy, lonely man who sees Nick as both son and lover, but above all as someone to cherish and to love. Gore Vidal, describing the character of the intellectual Paul Sullivan, whose defense mechanism makes it impossible for him to express his real feelings, makes the connection between the loneliness of this type of homosexual and the "psychic masochism" Bergler describes; he describes the pleasure Sullivan experiences at being tortured by his loneliness.

George, in *A Single Man*, is a lonely creature—as the title indicates—who is prey to morbid, somber thoughts. He feels his solitude more acutely because he is no longer young. Yet Bob, who is a young, virile, and proud homosexual in *The World in the Evening*, ex-sailor, fighter, militant homosexual, also suffers from this loneliness.

Human loneliness is the underlying theme that gives unity to the picaresque *City of Night*, a feeling that is if anything more pronounced among the hustlers, the queens, and their scores. At the outset of his journey into the lower depths of the New York homosexual world, the narrator senses the force that impels the clients in certain movie houses to engage in sordid sex acts: it is the need for human contact, however degrading. In the johns, he sees "body fusing with mouth hurriedly, momentarily stifling that sense of crushing aloneness that the world manifests each desperate moment of the day—and which only the liberation of Orgasm seemed then to be able to vanquish, if only momentarily."

The sordid world around Pershing Square, Times Square, in the bars, is the real world of "Lonely-Outcast America," a world in which superficial gaiety, the provocative posing of the queens, and the tough stance of the hustlers are all in reality forms of concealment of a frustrated need for love, of an immense despair. The narrator himself, who acts tough and pretends to be a hustler with his "scores" or with his friends, admits to two companions in New Orleans—where the carnival season creates a temporary freedom—"No, I'm not the way I pretended to be for you—and for others. Like you, like everyone else, I'm scared, cold, cold, terrified."

Time is the homosexual's Enemy Number One. Encounters are possible only between desirable young men, and the aging man must gradually—like Divine, still longing for the "pleasures of bed and hallway"—begin to pay his "lovers." In his short stories Tennessee Williams evokes the isolation felt by the homosexual who is beginning to lose his looks: the queen in "Two on a Party" is far more aware of the passage of time than his middle-aged friend, Cora, with whom he cruises sailors. In "Hard Candy" an old man haunts the balcony of a sordid movie theater, picking up boys to whom he offers candy—until the day one of these handsome youths murders him. In this story Williams beautifully expresses the sorrow of the homosexual old man, who has neither a family nor a home where he can live in peace, surrounded with affection. The same movie theater is described in "The Mysteries of the Joy Rio," where one of the frequenters is Pablo, middle-aged, once handsome in the days when he was the lover of Kroger, a watchmaker whose business he has taken over. Now, his good looks gone, Pablo tries to people his solitude by means of sexual contacts in this flea-pit. Isherwood's professor also goes through the "crisis of aging" (Evelyn Hooker) alone, after Jim's death. He replaces anonymous adventures such as those of the old men at the Joy Rio with his students, attempting to form intimate relationships with them in order to drink at the spring of their youth, like the professor in Frederick Buechner's *A Long Day's Dying*.

John Rechy, himself obsessed with the idea of growing old, constantly alludes to the loss of youth and beauty. All of his protagonists share the same anxiety over the passage of time that slowly kills. Skipper, an ex-hustler, always carries photographs taken in his youth and passes them around. The narrator considers "the end of youth . . . a kind of death. You die slowly by the process of gnawing discovery. You die too in the gigantic awareness that the miraculous passport given to the young can be ripped away savagely by the enemy Time." Michael, the host in *The Boys in the Band,* is obsessed by the idea of growing bald and remarks that when it comes to age, queens are worse than women: life is over at thirty. In *Suddenly Last Summer* Mrs. Venable says that her son, Sebastian, had resisted the ravages of time out of stubbornness; and Chance Wayne, who is a gigolo employed by women, shares his creator's obsessions and speaks of time as Enemy Number One.

Cruising is the means by which the homosexual is reassured concerning his sex-appeal. Unfortunately, in the United States sexual solicitation is illegal. Thus, the homosexual's psychology is characteristically guilt-ridden. Scandal and exposure lie in wait for the cruising homosexual around the corner of a bathhouse hallway, at the bend of a path in a park. Bob, the literary prototype of the militant homosexual, informs the narrator that he is a "professional criminal"; and in *A Single Man* Christopher Isherwood says that "like everyone with an acute criminal complex, George is hyperconscious of all bylaws, city ordinances, rules and petty regulations. Think of how many Public Enemies have been caught just because they neglected to pay a parking ticket! Never once has he seen his passport stamped at a frontier, his driver's license accepted by a post-office clerk as evidence of identity, without whispering gleefully to himself, *Idiots*—fooled *them again!*"

The Hustler

The hustler sells himself to men. In the United States he usually dresses as "rough trade." He often wears cowboy clothes, as in *The Boys in the Band*. James Leo Herlihy has coined the phrase "midnight cowboys." Mart Crowley makes us realize that William Inge's young heroes were patterned on these handsome delinquents haunting Times Square and Sixth Avenue. Rechy, in *City of Night*, describes the hustler's pose as follows: ". . . the stance, the jive-talk—a mixture of jazz, joint, junk sounds. The almost disdainful, disinterested, but at the same time, inviting look; the casual way of dress." Melville's impressed sailors adopted exactly the same stance before the officer choosing them (cf. *Redburn*).

The first hustler glimpsed in the course of this study was Nick in *Knock on Any Door*. His characteristic trait is narcissism. He spends hours before his mirror, admiring his virile good looks, which he uses to "play the phoneys." He is fifteen and very successful. The money he earns is spent on girls. In spite of his scruples and the shame which sometimes overcomes him, he persists —for money. However, the author suggests that it is his unhappy childhood and his thirst for love and virile friendship—satisfied both with the heterosexual Grant and the homosexual Owen— joined to his narcissism and his inability to love his wife (whom he unconsciously pushes to suicide), that impel him, thus revealing strong homosexual tendencies which Nick denies with the hustler's habitual excuse: "I do it for money." (One of Inge's minor characters, Gil—among others—uses the same alibi.)

Jones's soldiers, like Nick, "chase the queers" for the sake of the money, for a drink, for an invitation into a comfortable home. Jones reveals that some of them enjoy it, despite their vehement denials. Even the aggressively heterosexual Prewitt ends up showing a high degree of tolerance, and we suspect that the military police investigation comes at an opportune time for putting an end to his new activities.

Tennessee Williams has also examined the psychology of the

hustler. He has noted the narcissism of young men who require the homage (financial or otherwise) of another man. (For Sartre, the desire to please is an indication of a prepederastic state.) Women do not have social and economic importance enough to provide the social recognition they are searching for. In "One Arm" Oliver, a handsome hustler, now in prison, receives many letters from his former clients. Like Nick, and in the same circumstances, he lovingly explores his own body: "Autoerotic sensations began to flower in him. . . . Lying nude on the cot . . . his one large hand made joyless love to his body, exploring all of those erogenous zones that the fingers of others, hundreds of strangers' fingers, had clasped with a hunger that now was beginning to be understandable to him." Like Nick's, this beautiful body will burn in the electric chair. The hustler will perish for his sins—perish, not wither. Nick wanted to "live fast, die young and have a good-looking corpse."

Rechy dazzles us with a whole series of young, handsome males, indifferent and virile, who—like Genet's Mignon—"turn tricks for cash." Pete, Skipper, Chuck, names hard and tough as a sock in the jaw, sell their bodies for a fistful of dollars. Although they go to bed with men, it is *only* because they want to live well, and male clients are easier to come by than female, as Herlihy's midnight cowboy quickly discovers. (Paolo, Mrs. Stone's gigolo in her Roman Spring, goes from men to women.) Although they sleep with queens for pleasure, their virility remains intact, since queens are not really men. Similarly, in Selby's book, Harry, Vinnie, and Malfie do not feel that their masculinity has been diminished just because they make love to Georgette, Ginger, Lee, Alberta, or Regina. In Rechy's world, hustlers sometimes set up housekeeping with queens, but they earn their living from "average homosexuals," from "johns."

In both Rechy's books and those of his predecessors, the hustler's psychology is based on his refusal to be ranked as a homosexual. In *City of Night* the narrator attempts—fairly unsuccessfully—to have relations with Barbara, and he refuses to kiss his partners, or to "reciprocate." As soon as he begins to feel some attachment for another man, he runs away. The motive force in all of Rechy's novels has remained the same: John (*City of Night*), Johnny Rio (*Numbers*), or Jim (*This Day's Death*) all have the hustler mentality. They attempt to prove that they are looking for men solely for money, or to assure themselves that their charms still operate. The stories end when the masks are removed and the protagonists finally admit that they prefer men.

Chapter Thirteen

Between the American Woman and
the American Virile Ideal

Prior to the appearance of such militant feminists as Betty
Friedan, Diana Trilling, and Kate Millett, to name only the better
known, the loudest voices raised against the traditional role of
women were those of misogynist men. In *A Generation of Vipers*
(1942) Philip Wylie violently attacked the role of "Mom" as the
symbol of American matriarchal society. Wylie's thesis was a familiar one: the American woman devirilizes; she is an octopus
strangling her child and preventing him from developing mentally, morally, or sexually. According to Wylie, this explains why
the American man never becomes an adult. When he marries, it
is because he sees his wife as a mother-substitute—as has been illustrated by the playwrights Tennessee Williams, William Inge,
and Edward Albee.

Margaret Mead, in *Male and Female*, developed this thesis;
she enlarged it to include the role played by the "big sister" in
the American family, a figure representing "law and order" as
does the mother. Fiedler made the same assertions in *Love and
Death in the American Novel*. He situates the role of the American woman within the Judeo-Christian tradition, in which
woman is the Canaanites' idol, the Whore of Babylon—or Eve,
the reason for man's fall. Fiedler quotes Geoffrey Gorer, whose
conclusions are in line with those reached by Wylie or Mead:
"modesty, politeness, neatness, cleanliness—come to be regarded
as concessions to feminine demands, and . . . as such they are

sloughed off—with relief but not without guilt—whenever a suitable occasion presents itself . . . the stag poker game, the fishing trip, the convention."

All of these American authors reach the conclusion that the American male associates all the moral fetters by which he is bound with women, and he seeks refuge in the virile world of the fishing trip, which becomes the symbol of virile friendship in a place removed from the devirilizing American woman. According to Freud and his followers, this desire for exclusively male company is a form of homoeroticism, of sublimated homosexuality. On the other hand, the boy who allows himself to be dominated by a woman, whether mother or sister, risks identifying with her and becoming an overt invert. The extent to which the American woman represents an omnipotent peril is obvious: between overt homosexuality and homoeroticism there is merely the difference in the form taken by the defense mechanisms that are set up by the ego of the American male, crushed beneath "Mom's" weight.

The tendency to combine femininity with restricted freedom has been attacked by feminists; Betty Friedan is one example: in *The Feminine Mystique* she set out to denounce male chauvinism and to restore the image of the American woman. Her book was the starting gun in the feminist movement, which some men have also joined. Kate Millett in *Sexual Politics*, a book which quickly became a best-seller, treated all these themes and singled out the homoeroticism of male groupings that are the outgrowth of the male's basic misogyny in whatever society he lives.

Following their analyses, all of these authors, on the one hand, deduce that American culture is a misogynist culture, restricting the woman either to the role of asexual mother or prostitute, and that the American man therefore experiences great difficulty in considering the woman as an equal partner with whom he can share life's joys and sorrows; and, on the other hand, they stress the problems present-day American males face when they attempt to fill the preordained role of the virile, strong, courageous, dominant head of the household. This role is a restrictive one, and many American men, like Rabbit, prefer to "give up," either by seeking refuge in the homosexual world—in a world of male substitutes—or by grabbing at any opportunity to leave their homes. Even in James Fenimore Cooper's day, his male heroes were extremely reluctant to marry.

The expression "the American virile ideal" has been used frequently. This ideal haunts the imagination of the homosexual, because it forms the basis for his renunciation of virility. Joel (*Other Voices, Other Rooms*) is fully aware that "his danger had already been," that is, the die had already been cast. The American Dream sooner or later makes his appearance in all works by homosexual authors, to a greater or lesser extent. In Albee and Inge, he is present to a high degree: Inge represents the Dream in the character of Bo (*Bus Stop*) or Hal (*Picnic*). Albee borrows him from Carson McCullers and turns the character into a prototype in *The Ballad of the Sad Café*. Some authors attempt to domesticate the American Dream, *and thereby devirilize it*. This is the case with Charles Jackson in *The Fall of Valor*, in which Cliff Hauman is shown to have some inner flaw, as does Brig Anderson (*Advise and Consent*) or the American Dream himself in Albee's play of the same name.

The American virile ideal is the ideal of a country that was once a land of pioneers. Its indispensable characteristics are youth, strength, "Caucasian" beauty, purity, a thirst for unlimited freedom, and physical and moral courage. These we recognize as the characteristics of Cooper's heroes. Long before Leslie Fiedler, D. H. Lawrence noted these ideal characteristics in Deerslayer and in many other Cooper heroes. Natty Bumppo, the Deerslayer, is a prototype that recurs throughout virile American literature. He is the quintessence of the pioneer, that is, of the American virile ideal. The American will be considered masculine insofar as he resembles this strong and courageous being who is in harmony with untamed nature, who is unfettered in every way, free of all ties.

A survey of novels with pioneer heroes makes it very clear that Deerslayer, chaste as he may have been, was nonetheless the father of a host of offspring! The novels written after the disappearance of the frontier—1890—teem with handsome men, blond and blue-eyed, dark with green or steel-gray eyes, all devoted to total freedom, all contemptuous of the civilization symbolized by the East, the small town, and woman. And although the American male could no longer realize this ideal in any concrete way—by setting off on adventures in which he might prove his virility—he could still dream of it.

In novels written after the disappearance of the frontier that reflect nostalgia for an ideal forever lost, women are of little importance. The female is either an Indian with whom the hero takes some furtive pleasure, or whom—if he lives with her—he reduces to the status of slave or mistress, or she is a temptress of whom he must beware if his ideal freedom, his virility, is to be protected.

The ideal man must be a "man's man," a man who is at ease among other men who admire him, who are his friends. In Cooper's novels and those of his successors, friendship plays a major role. Lawrence remarked of Cooper that the one love of Natty Bumppo's life is his love for Chingachgook: a love that is silent, deep, abstract, tacit, but that nevertheless amounts to an actual embrace.

It is obvious that the lack of sexuality, of overt heterosexuality, in the novels preceding the First World War is the result of the American puritanism Waldo Frank denounced in *Our America*. As the evolution in morals began to permit greater freedom of expression, the "pioneer novel" began to put an increasing emphasis on sexuality. The new hero abandoned himself to sensual pleasure much more freely than his forerunners, but the woman still represented a constant threat.

The typically American pioneer hero was one who knew neither fear nor weakness and who was totally at ease in a male world. However, he proved his heterosexuality with Indian women or with "loose women." Today, the young American still must conform to this ideal. From childhood on, he must participate in team sports, be completely comfortable with his peers, and inspire their admiration—their envy. We recall Phineas and Spud, the young heroes of John Knowles and William Maxwell. The conquest of the West is replaced by the conquest of the athletic trophy; the struggle against the Indians becomes the bodily contact of football or boxing. And although he has to surround himself with men and allow women only a peripheral importance, the young American must go out with girls, according to the "dating" code. In his life, the Indian maidens of pioneer days are replaced by young American girls. Marriage is both an end and a beginning. It is the end of carefree and virile youth and the beginning of an inevitable but formidable bourgeois domestication. Rabbit illustrates this dilemma for us; Leslie Fiedler has linked it with the Rip Van Winkle myth.

The young American boy must not derive pleasure from female company. If he does, he is a "sissy." The quiet, introverted boy, the "good boy," is a suspicious figure in American life, since the pioneer ideal is based on a love of freedom that approaches anarchy. Leslie Fiedler has written, "The Good Bad Boy is, of course, America's vision of itself, crude and unruly in his beginnings, but endowed by his creator with an instinctive sense of what is right. Sexually as pure as any milky maiden, he is a roughneck all the same, at once potent and submissive, made to be reformed by the right woman." The sensitive, well-dressed, polite boy who is fond of reading is by definitive anti-American. Even in Harlem in the 1950s, "real boys" distrust the good, intelligent, dreamy John Grimes. There are many other examples, from Farrell's young Irishmen to the playmates of the young Tom Williams.

Homosexual authors dream of the virile ideal of the "Good Bad Boy." Since they have become homosexuals because of their failure to achieve this ideal, they depict it in their work with obsessive regularity. However, they also deform it. This they do in two ways: by accentuating its libertarian anarchy, on the one hand, and by twisting its chastity into homosexuality or impotence. At its extreme, *the homoerotic delinquent boy becomes the caricature of the American virile ideal*. The most extreme example is the handsome and delinquent Marvin Macy (*Ballad of the Sad Café*), who is admired, loved, adulated, by cousin Lymon, the deformed homosexual. Hal (*Picnic*) and Nick, Willard Motley's young hero, also embody this ideal. The hustler, the character who must fend for himself, who lives outside the law and struggles along in the jungle of cities, is the final embodiment of the pioneer, the lone man against the elements, against adversity. Thus it should not be surprising that the hustler dresses like a cowboy, wears worn clothing, and adopts the attitude of a diamond in the rough. Inge's plays are full of first cousins of Marvin Macy.

In the works of homosexual writers, the "American Dream's" abstinence entails—to borrow from Albee—a constant threat of becoming homosexual. Seizing on the lack of aggressive heterosexuality in Natty Bumppo and his kind, the homosexual American novelist or dramatist has transformed it into a rejection of the female, into latent or overt homosexuality. There are countless examples of such handsome, virile, American males, all blond, well-built, athletic, occasional heterosexuals but fundamentally homoerotic, who still retain traces of the original model. At random, there are Cliff Hauman (*The Fall of Valor*), Brig Anderson (*Advise and Consent*), Brick (*Cat on a Hot Tin Roof*), and, perhaps less obviously, some of Inge's heroes: Hal, Bo, and above all Tom (*Where's Daddy?*).

The American virile ideal, as seen through the eyes of a homosexual writer, is a handsome delinquent whose past is full of adventure but who is now found to have become amenable, who appears to be ready to enter into a relationship with some friend or mentor. Hal finds his Alan (*Picnic*), as Nick finds his Owen (*Knock on Any Door*) and Marvin Macy finds Cousin Lymon. This is a masochistic ideal, although the sadist has to make some adjustments in order for a relationship to exist. Yet the ideal retains the aura of a free-living outlaw—the one that Cousin Lymon, for example, finds so ravishing. Stanley Kowalski, the Polish-American, appears to represent Williams's sensual virile ideal, whereas Val Xavier, Kilroy, and Brick Pollitt are his desexualized virile ideal, obviously more like the ideal Anglo-Saxon pioneer. Nick (*Who's Afraid of Virginia Woolf?*), the Intern (*The Death of Bessie Smith*), the American Dream (*The American Dream*) all have the health, strength, and Anglo-Saxon handsomeness of the pioneer, but their chastity has been bastardized to emasculation. Woman has performed her castrating task to the very limit.

Thus, what Williams's plays so magnificently illustrate can be better understood in light of the American virile ideal. The American male must strike a balance between the homoeroticism of all-male groups (athletics, the business world—the modern version of the frontier), which must never be mentioned, the heterosexuality of a Don Juan with a list of conquests, yet not be made effeminate by women, and also "operable" heterosexuality within the controls of marriage. He has to repulse every threat to his freedom—synonymous with virility—since the pioneer must remain free to combat nature and the Indians; and yet he must be tamed, must set up a household, must take an active part in twentieth-century society, in which it is no longer necessary to clear land but rather to build. This apparent dilemma is worked out in the following way: youth is devoted to team sports and to various experiences with girls; it is a condensed version of the youth of American civilization itself. Once tribute has been paid to the country's ideal, maturity is devoted to building a family and a career. The first phase represents the dream; the second is the reality.

The boy who cannot achieve the first phase will dream of it all his life. However, since he will be neurotic, he will spoil the dream as he looks back on it through the complex network of his psychological problems. He will be a moral masochist, like Genet, who will make sadism and the sadist his god. This sadist, however, will be domesticated, tamed—a sadist with homosexual tendencies in order that he can represent some hope of contact. Whence the two-fold perversion, at first glance contradictory, of the American virile ideal as described by Motley, Jackson, Inge, Williams, and others. The hero is "tough," a fighter, a delinquent; but at the same time there is something questionable about his abstinence: he seems to be making a virtue out of a necessity.

Proust understood the homosexual's dilemma completely. Although he was writing about the European homosexual, his words apply equally as well—perhaps better—to the American homosexual, who is more strongly influenced by the pioneer ideal than his European counterpart, whose uncivilized past is lost in the mists of antiquity. Of Charlus, Proust wrote, "He belonged to that race of beings, less paradoxical than they appear, whose ideal is manly simply because their temperament is feminine." And later, he described "lovers from whom is always precluded the possibility of that love the hope of which gives them the strength to endure so many risks and so much loneliness, since they fall in love with precisely that type of man who

has nothing feminine about him, who is not an invert and conse-
quently cannot love them in return."

The task of the homosexual novelist or dramatist consists in
bringing his hero to the limit at which, while remaining a real
man—and even a hypervirile man—he can embody the hope of
which Proust is speaking.

PART V

Latent Homosexuality:
Short of and Beyond
True Heterosexuality

Fast-anchor'd eternal O love! O woman I love!
O bride! O wife! more resistless than I can tell, the
 thoughts of you!
Then separate, as disembodied or another born,
Ethereal, the last athletic reality, my consolation,
I ascend, I float in the regions of your love, O man,
O sharer of my roving life.

       Walt Whitman, *Calamus*

Many psychologists, psychiatrists, and psychoanalysts have attempted to define "latent homosexuality." The term was first employed by Freud, and adopted by his disciples and the public at large. A latent homosexual is a man *who is unaware* of his homoerotic desires but whose mental and emotional attitude reveals his basic nature to be homosexual, despite the ruses he employs to conceal it from himself. All "heterosexuals" who "interpose" a woman between themselves and another man, in whatever manner, in order to attain the other male with impunity, are latent homosexuals.

Bill, the "he-man" teacher in *Tea and Sympathy*, can be taken as the prototype of the latent homosexual, the man who is so strongly attracted (albeit unconsciously) to the pit of inversion that he adopts a violently homoerotophobic attitude, to such a degree that he *caricatures* the virile ideal to which he is aspiring in his gestures and his speech. Bill is obviously more "homosexual" than the adolescent Tom. Like all the "nance-sluggers" of whom Philip Wylie speaks, and of whom we have already noted many examples, Bill is able to maintain his precarious heterosexuality only by denigrating the effeminate, the sub-males, the faggots, the grimacing travesties of his deepest self, his ego.

However, Tom is also a type of latent homosexual: gentle, feminine, attracted to an older woman who is a substitute for the mother he has lost, the boy falls short of true heterosexuality, just as Bill, in his attempts to appear masculine, goes beyond it.

Bergler has noted that the Caspar Milquetoast type is more like the "he-man" than he appears: the difference lies in the intensity and the direction of his defensive reaction against homosexuality. The he-man "protests too much," whereas Milquetoast, identifying with his mother, but not consciously homosexual, adopts a passive, masochistic attitude to cajole his father, whom he both hates and loves. Bloom (*From Here to Eternity*)—who finally commits suicide—represents the hypervirile latent homosexual who cannot face the revelation of his own personality. He is like the characters described by Charles Jackson in *The Fall of Valor*, or Tennessee Williams in *Cat on a Hot Tin Roof*. Sinclair Lewis, on the other hand—he himself was a "sissy" as a child, but did not become an overt homosexual—appears to link the femininity of two of his characters, Erik Valborg and Raymond Wutherspoon, to their latent homosexuality.

There are, therefore, *two types of latent homosexuality* which exist on the borderline of overt homosexuality: one falls short of true heterosexual masculinity, and the other goes beyond it, beyond the understated, well-balanced virility that we see in Tennessee Williams's foreign heroes and in Big Daddy, his dream father. Real masculinity is neither brutal nor passive: it is able to coexist with the kind of tolerance Big Daddy manifests, a tolerance that differentiates him from his "he-man" son, who is a quintessential nance-slugger.

Chapter Fourteen

Henry James: The Feminine Masochist Syndrome

Spiritual Transvestism

The inspired intuition of the prehomosexual situation in Henry James's "The Pupil" is no coincidence, nor is it the result of outside observation. James lived this situation himself, anticipating the same experiences lived fifty years later by such a total invert as Tennessee Williams. It may seem presumptuous or sacrilegious to draw a parallel between the authors of *The Turn of the Screw* and *Cat on a Hot Tin Roof*, yet the two writers are alike in more than one regard: as children, they were both "sissies," both sought refuge in literature, both feared women, both are fundamentally androgynous, both give evidence of "spiritual transvestism," and both are obsessed by a particular unattainable virile ideal. In the case of Williams, the neurosis that grew out of his familial situation led to an overt homosexuality which he frenetically practiced in the underworld societies of the large American cities, whereas it would appear that James "came out" at a fairly late date: the time in which he lived, his education, and his temperament all seem to have kept his instincts reined in, to have kept his homophilia within the confines of homoeroticism, of either latent or voluntarily repressed homosexuality.

The Childhood of a "Sissy"

James's father, although an active man with a robust constitution, was an "anti-Calvinist philosopher" who appeared to his son to be a weaker and more passive character than the boy's mother, who took care of her husband with the same maternal solicitude—disguising the desire to manage everything her own way—with which she surrounded her children. Mary James dominated the entire household: a temperamental and authoritarian woman, she was the real head of the family, and everyone —including her husband—obeyed her.

In addition, the James children—and especially Henry and William (whose emotional equilibrium was to be precarious throughout his life)—resented the incongruities in their father's personality. To them, his "profession" was the symbol of his nonconformity to the American virile ideal. In *Notes of a Son and Brother*, Henry James wrote:

> I remember well how when we were all young together we had, *under pressure of the American ideal* in that matter, then so rigid, felt it tasteless and even humiliating that the head of our little family was *not* in business, and that even among our relatives on each side we couldn't so much as name proudly anyone who was. [Emphasis added.]

No "virile" ideal with which to identify; a domineering and suffocating mother and a weak father indulgent toward his children: this imbalance alone would be enough to explain the atrophy of masculine feelings from which Henry James appears to have suffered all his life. However, his situation was further complicated by his inferiority complex with regard to his older brother William, whom he had unsuccessfully tried to equal in the art of drawing. Leon Edel has carefully traced the history of this complex, which contributed to making James both passive and feminine and from which he was never able to free himself, even after he had gained fame in the field of literature.

As a child, James was the prototypical "sissy." While William played with "real" boys, Henry stayed at home with his sister Alice. In *A Small Boy and Others* he admits, "It wasn't that I mightn't have been drawn to the boys in question, but that I simply wasn't qualified. All boys, I rather found, were difficult to play with." These words might well have been spoken by the young John Grimes (*Go Tell It on the Mountain*), who watched his half-brother playing with "real boys" in Harlem, while he stayed at home among his books and his daydreams, looking out the window. Steele Mackaye, a famous actor of the time, recalled that boys had called James a "sissy" (reported by Edel).

The Civil War made his inferiority complex and feelings of inadequacy even more firmly seated: whereas the two younger brothers enlisted, the older boys went off to Harvard. In *Notes of a Son and Brother*, James speaks of a wound that made him unfit to bear arms. His choice of words and the circumstances lead us to believe there had been some kind of emasculation, but Leon Edel gives credible evidence that the wound was in fact no more than a back injury, from which, for that matter, James was to suffer throughout his life. James's biographer believes that he was attempting to excuse his "cowardice" by inventing a wound that clearly made him unfit for military service, but it seems that the actual fact—pain in the lumbar region—should have been enough to convince the reader. Cannot this *obvious desire to pass for a eunuch* be read as an attempt to make excuses for James's attitude toward women and his lifelong bachelorhood by a completely involuntary physical accident, one that occurred when he was engaged in the brave act—the virile act—of helping to extinguish a fire? Is this not a means of forestalling an accusation of homosexuality? In fact, when James came to write his memoirs, England had been shocked by the Oscar Wilde trial, and James had already assiduously pursued a great many handsome young men.

A Woman's Man

James's attitude toward women stems from his relationship with his mother and his identification with his sister. Dominated by Mary James, rejected by William, unable to identify with either father or brother, James stayed at home with Alice. In his novels, the mothers are either terrifying and domineering or passive and withdrawn. Edel says that "both types mirror the two aspects of Mary James." We recall Morgan's mother, whose maternal love conceals indifference and latent hostility toward her son. In "The Author of *Beltraffio*" Mrs. Ambient "loves" her son so much that she allows him to die rather than live to read the books of the husband she loathes. In *The Ambassadors* Mrs. Newsome is a domineering and strict mother; Mrs. De Grey, in "De Grey: A Romance," on the other hand, is all affectionate (perhaps incestuous) tenderness, as is Mrs. Acton in *The Europeans.*

Edel notes that James's relationships with his mother and his sister created in him a "fear of women and worship of women." Both were placed on a pedestal in order better to be kept at a distance. James's affection for Minny Temple reveals Platonic veneration more than anything else, and despite the pain it caused him, her death in 1870 brought him a "concealed emotional relief." Once dead, Minny could be adored without any danger. She could also serve as an alibi—like the invented devirilizing wound. In "Longstaff's Marriage" Diana Belfield dies shortly after her marriage with the handsome Reginald Longstaff. Her friend Agatha tells the young man that Diana died to free him. Likewise, in "Maude Evelyn" Marmaduke, rejected by Lavinia, falls in love with a dead girl. He "marries" her. Like Longstaff, he pays a symbolic tribute to heterosexuality.

Henry James spent a great deal of time with women, but it was always as a solicitous, somewhat distant, friend. According to Edel, all the women with whom he associated were domineering and often cruel. Mr. Nadal, undersecretary of the American Legation in London, revealed his understanding of James's attitude toward women when he noted in his *Journal* that James "seemed to look at women rather as women looked at them. Women look at women as persons; men look at them as women. The quality of sex in women, which is their first and chief attraction to most men, was not their chief attraction to James" (quoted by Edel). And Régis Michaud believed that James, had he been a woman, would have made an excellent "chaperone" (quoted by Oscar Cargill in *The Novels of Henry James*).

Handsome Young Men

Perhaps James was what Jean-Paul Sartre has called a "homosexual vestal." However, it seems obvious that he was "taken" with many young men, particularly toward the end of his life.

Gus Barker, whom he saw posing in the nude one day in the studio of William Hunt, appears to have been the prototype of all handsome young men, completely virile and at ease in the world. In *Notes of a Son and Brother* James recounts the scene and the trauma it produced:

> . . . the beautiful young manly form of our cousin Gus Barker . . . perched on a pedestal and divested of every garment. . . . This was my first personal vision of the "life," on a pedestal and in a pose, that had half gleamed and half gloomed through the chiaroscuro of our old friend Haydon; and I well recall the crash, at the sight, of all my inward emulation—so forced was I to recognize on the spot that I might niggle for months over plaster casts and not come within miles of any such point of attack. The bravery of my brother's own [drawings] in especial dazzled me out of every presumption; since nothing less than that meant drawing (they were not using colour) and since our genial kinsman's perfect gymnastic figure meant living, truth, I should certainly best testify to the whole mystery by pocketing my pencil.

Gus later died in the Civil War, and James carefully preserved the drawing William had made of him. The young and virile beauty that he saw was doubly inaccessible to the adolescent James: it was on a pedestal, and it could not be rendered tangibly with pencil and paper. *The renunciation of drawing is a renunciation of virility* brought about by the belief that he is incapable of emulating either Gus or William. Gus's death obviously finalized Henry's realization that he would never be a man, in the American meaning of the word.

Just as they haunted his novels, handsome young men also made their appearances throughout Henry James's life. Wolcott Balestier and Jonathan Sturges prefigure the young, handsome sculptor Hendrik Andersen, whose friendship appears to have been an emotional turning point in the Master's life: Andersen "was strong and handsome and full of energy," Edel informs us. At first glance, James was struck by his physique. Although they spent only three days together at James's house at Rye, the Master lived on the memory of those idyllic days for a long time afterward. Hendrik, who was a mediocre sculptor but an avid social climber, went back to New York leaving an observer with the impression that his attentions to his new friend had been largely determined by self-interest. James, however, began to write him letters that vibrate with actual, physical love, letters in which one senses his sorrow at Andersen's absence. The two were to meet again a dozen or so times, at Lamb House, in New York, and in Rome. James's passionate letters to Hendrik employ a vocabulary unique in his correspondence. One example will suffice: in 1902, after the death of the sculptor's brother, James wrote, "I wish I could go to Rome and put my hands on you (oh, how lovingly I should lay them!) but that, alas, is odiously impossible. . . . I am in town for a few weeks but I return to Rye April 1st, and sooner or later to have you there and do for you, to put my arms round you and *make* you lean on me as on a brother and a lover!" The correspondence continued in this vein until 1913, when the letters begin to take on a disillusioned and melancholy tone when James came to realize that he had no hope of seeing Hendrik again.

Henry James's attitude toward overt homosexuality is an ambiguous one. Although his novels and short stories are highly homoerotic, full of passionate admiration for certain handsome Anglo-Saxon males, it seems evident that his *public* attitude with regard to professed homosexuality was fairly distant. The Oscar Wilde affair simultaneously fascinated and repelled him. When Edmund Gosse showed James the book *A Problem of Modern Ethics* by the militant homosexual J. A. Symonds, James thanked Gosse for having shown him "those marvelous outpourings." However, he refused to write an appreciation of Symonds after the latter's death because of the latter's "strangely morbid and hysterical" side: to do so, James said, would be "a Problem—a problem beyond me."

Dr. Collins, whom James consulted in 1911, stated that the writer had "a large dose of femininity in his character." Dr. Collins might well have given the same diagnosis with regard to many of James's protagonists: it would have applied to the "light man," the androgynous creature who acts as an adopted mother-

father to the two children, who has once been involved with the
father of one child and the mother of the other—or to Roger
Lawrence, whose timidity is almost pathological, and who is so
strongly contrasted to the handsome ruffian Herbert Lawrence.
Above all, it could have been applied to Lewis Lambert Strether,
who, according to Leslie Fiedler, is "the most maidenly of all
James's men." A study of the protagonist of *The Ambassadors*
and his relationships with women, on the one hand, and with the
novel's young hero, on the other, gives a better understanding of
James's position in the "masculine-feminine continuum."

Strether—the Homosexual Search for Virility

Lambert Strether is a widower. He had married young, but
both his wife and son are dead. In short, he is a bachelor who
has paid his tribute to heterosexuality with no more difficulty
than did Marmaduke or Longstaff. In the town of Woollett, he
frequents the home of Mrs. Newsome, a widow and the mother
of two grown children. She is, first and foremost, a *mother*. The
friendship between Strether and Mrs. Newsome is not intimate:
"There had been no little confronted dinner, no pink lights, no
whiff of vague sweetness, as a preliminary." Later on, he senses
that Sarah Pocock, the daughter, considers him incapable of discovering the woman who is preventing Chad Newsome, the
brother, from leaving Paris: "Hadn't she, at the best, but a scant
faith in his ability to find women? It wasn't even as if he had
found her mother—so much more, to her discrimination, had her
mother performed the finding."

The Ambassador to Paris is entrusted with the mission of
bringing Chad back to Woollett, and of discovering the reason
for his prolonged stay in Europe. The Newsome family believes
that the only reason possible is a woman. Chad is twenty-eight
years of age; it appears that in the United States he was a lively,
superficial young man, and a fairly ordinary one. He is another
of the handsome youths who haunt James's work, young men
such as Clifford and Felix in *The Europeans*, or De Grey, in the
story of the same name—to cite but a few out of many examples.

Chad does not make his appearance until near the end of the

first quarter of the novel. His entrance is meticulously arranged, as is that of Saint-Loup in Proust's novel. At the theater, Strether wonders whether Chad will resemble one of the actors. We are next introduced to his friend, Little Bilham, whom Strether mistakes for Chad, a Chad totally transformed by his stay in Europe, when Strether arrives at Chad's house on the Boulevard Malesherbes. On the balcony above, he sees a young man. The older man—he is over fifty—is placed in the position of an admirer raising his eyes to the creature he admires. The two men's respective positions remind us of the positions of Gus Barker and the young Henry James in Hunt's studio. Gus symbolized unattainable life, virility, beauty, and *joie de vivre* for the adolescent, prehomosexual James. An analysis of this scene in *The Ambassadors* shows us that Strether, suddenly become an admirer of youth, desires to attain his idol, who is set almost beyond his grasp but who is *suddenly seen as being accessible* because he has become Europeanized and thus is closer to him than the youthful Chad could have been in Woollett. Little Bilham—youthful, well-meaning, and civilized—attests to the fact that Chad has improved and that he will probably have drawn closer to the passive, calm, wise man with the guarded manner who is his mother's friend.

In this scene, Strether's feelings are given symbolic, "material" form by two settings: the Parisian apartment of Miss Gostrey, his friend and "sister" ("They might have been brother and sister"), his alter ego who is perhaps a mother figure, and by the hotel where he is staying with his old friend, the solid but slightly boring American Waymarsh. Miss Gostrey's apartment is pleasant and in good taste; it is the apartment of a person no longer young, with whom Strether finds it pleasant to have cultural and intellectual conversations but who is unable to keep him in Paris at the end of novel—no more than can Grace, the owner of the diner in which the characters in Inge's *Bus Stop* are forced to spend the night, keep Virgil with her after Bo's departure. The other dwelling in which Strether can seek refuge is a dull, cold hotel room, filled with the presence of Waymarsh, who has left his wife whom he married at thirty.

Strether, therefore, is at a crossroads: on the one hand, there is affection for a woman who has not yet made her appearance and friendship for a man of his own age who no longer entertains him, and, on the other hand, there is his desire to penetrate to the intimacy of a young man, either Little Bilham or Chad, a desire born of "friendship at first sight," and based solely on admiration for the physical appearance of this young man set up on high, a symbol of happy youth, now suddenly seen to be accessible. Strether enters the house.

Chad's sudden appearance in the box at the theater where Strether and Miss Gostrey are seated is a theatrical effect: "The fact was that his perception of the young man's identity—so absolutely checked for a minute—had been quite one of the sensations that count in a life." Chad is elegant, at ease, youthfully virile; he possesses the art of living that Strether lacks. As for Strether, he sees Chad in the same way the masochistic, passive, and homosexual Proust saw Saint-Loup.

In Europe Chad has become the embodiment of adult virility. He has broken all his ties with his past adolescence, spent under his mother's devirilizing influence. James seems to be indicating this when he notes that Chad's face has completely lost all resemblance to his mother's. Chad's alteration is primarily physical, and secondarily only moral: "Chad was brown and thick and strong, and, of old, Chad had been rough." However, he is now "smooth" as the "taste of a sauce or . . . the rub of a hand." And he has grown more handsome: his eye is brighter, his complexion clearer, his white even teeth are more brilliant, his voice is more melodious and his smile more full of joy. "The phenomenon—Strether kept eyeing it as a phenomenon, an eminent case—was marked enough to be touched by the finger. He finally put his hand across the table and laid it on Chad's arm."

For the passive, timid Strether—an unconvinced heterosexual—Chad represents the epitome of the virile male who is liked by women and who loves them in return. Most of all, Strether is struck by Chad's "massive young manhood," his "pagan"—we might almost say "animal"—side, a quality that has proved attractive to so many homosexual novelists and playwrights. Strether, who would appear to be a moral masochist, is well aware that there is something "abnormal," "perverted," "beyond access," about his idol, all of which corresponds to a masochist fantasy: a touch of "latent" "pagan" sadism. In short, the rela-

tionship between Marvin Macy and Cousin Lymon is a carica-
ture of the relationship between Chad Newsome and Strether.
"Pagan—yes, that was, wasn't it? what Chad *would* logically be.
It was what he must be. It was what he was," Strether muses.

It is equally likely—according to Leon Edel, that Hendrik Andersen made James suddenly understand that life was to be lived
actively, not merely through the intermediary of art; so too
Strether's meeting with Little Bilham and Chad, the "young
Pagan," makes him understand that his life has hitherto been the
life of a living corpse. He gives Little Bilham the famous advice
to experience life to its full. "Live all you can; it's a mistake not
to. It doesn't so much matter what you do in particular, so long
as you have your life."

This scene takes place in the garden of the sculptor Gloriani,
who represents success in the spheres of art, society, and European aristocracy. Strether admires him, as he admires the duchess toward whom the sculptor advances and shares with him his
liveliness of spirit, his "latent insolence." "There was something
in the great world covertly tigerish, which came to him, across
the lawn, in the charming air, as a waft from the jungle. Yet it
made him admire most of the two, made him envy, the glossy
male tiger, magnificently marked." Strether says to Little Bilham,
"I know . . . whom *I* would enjoy being like!" And Little Bilham
asks, "Gloriani?" Strether, however, hesitates, since:

> He had just made out . . . something and somebody
> else: another impression had been superimposed. A
> young girl in a white dress and softly plumed white hat
> had suddenly come into view, and what was next clear
> was that her course was toward them. What was clearer
> still was that the handsome young man at her side was
> Chad Newsome, and what was clearest of all was that
> she was therefore Mlle de Vionnet, that she was unmis-
> takeably pretty—bright, gentle, shy, happy, wonder-
> ful. . . . What was clearest of all indeed was something
> much more than this, something at the single stroke of
> which—and wasn't it simply juxtaposition?—all vague-
> ness vanished. It was the click of a spring—he saw the
> truth. He had by this time met Chad's look; there was

more of it in that; and the truth, accordingly, as far as Bilham's inquiry was concerned, had thrust in the answer. "Oh, Chad!"—it was that rare youth he should have enjoyed being "like."

Thus Strether's hesitation. Which does he want to be like, Gloriani or Chad? He chooses insouciant, unproductive youth rather than the great and middle-aged artist. If we read the text carefully, however, there is justification for believing his hesitation to be even greater than it appears on the surface. Two sentences stand out: "Yet it made him admire most of the two, made him envy, the glossy male tiger," and, "He had just made out . . . something and somebody else . . . a young girl. . . ." He hesitates because of the sight of the girl, and only afterward at the sight of the handsome young man at her side. Strether's mind appears to waver, and the juxtaposition of images provides him with his answer. He would have liked to resemble the duchess (the epitome of the aristocratic European women of high society whom James assiduously frequented, as Proust the Duchesse de Guermantes), or Gloriani, a famous artist, an admired creator (a Master), or the pretty girl who is admired by young men (James's spiritual transvestism), or even Chad, the essence of happy virility, the American virile ideal (Gus Barker) made somehow accessible by his Europeanization, which is symbolized by a sprinkling of gray in his hair. (James also used the word "truth" to describe Gus.) Leon Edel refers to James's overwhelming desire to be a real boy, like Miles, which was thwarted by the feminine passivity his family situation had given him. The scene at Gloriani's appears to be the novelistic embodiment of what Edel has revealed concerning James's ambivalent temperament.

For that matter, Miss Gostrey tells Strether that he is more indebted to women than is any other man of her acquaintance, and he himself is fully aware that he belongs to a feminine world. When Mrs. Pocock arrives in Paris with her husband, Jim, and her sister-in-law, Strether suddenly realizes that "the society, over there, of which Sarah and Mamie—and, in a more eminent way, Mrs. Newsome herself—were specimens, was essentially a society of women, and that poor Jim wasn't in it. He himself, Lambert Strether, *was,* as yet, in some degree—which was an odd situation for a man."

It is not surprising, therefore, that Strether, far from urging Chad to return to the United States in accordance with the mission with which he has been charged by Mrs. Newsome, urges him to stay in Paris. He himself ardently wishes to remain in this city where, in company with Chad and his friends, he has been awakened to life. He explains to Miss Gostrey that Chad's case interests him, that he doesn't want to "give him up." In fact, Strether wants to stay in Paris in Chad's company because, since he cannot become him—no more than the professor could become a student in *A Long Day's Dying* or than Gene could take Phineas's place in *A Separate Peace*—he must attempt to enter into intimate contact with his idol. This is the deeper significance of the scene in which Strether visits Chad, finds him out, and remains alone in the apartment on the Boulevard Malesherbes, standing "a long time on the balcony." He "hung over it as he had seen Little Bilham hang the day of his first approach." Strether realizes he has come to the apartment to discover the freedom that may help him recapture his own youth, the youth he had not known how to enjoy.

On the same evening, alone with Chad in the apartment, Strether remarks that Chad's superiority is due to his sense of life: "He surrendered himself, accordingly, to so approved a gift —It was in truth essentially by bringing his personal life to a function all subsidiary to the young man's own that he held together. And the great point above all, the sign of how completely Chad possessed the knowledge in question, was that one thus became, not only with a proper cheerfulness, but with a wild native impulse, the feeder of his stream."

On this evening, then, Strether understands that he must submit to Chad, that he ought to submit, to surrender. Having been unable to resemble Chad, to become him, he can keep him only by becoming one of his "feeders." *Strether is the forerunner of all the homosexual characters, latent or overt, passive and masochistic, who seek a virile man to whom they must submit since they cannot become him.*

When Strether comes to understand that Chad's relationship with Mme de Vionnet is not "virtuous," when he understands that Chad and the mother of the pretty girl he met at Gloriani's are lovers, his reaction turns to jealousy. He is glad that he has not been forced by circumstances to give them "his blessing." He fully realizes that his lucid and objective alter ego, Miss Gostrey, will ask him, "What on earth—that's what I want to know now—had you then supposed?" Finally, he recognizes "that he had really been trying, all along, to suppose nothing. Verily, verily, his labor had been lost." Later, attempting not to feel bitter, "he wishes to do everything because he was lucid and quiet," and, hoping to see Chad one last time before leaving for America, Strether repeats to himself, "You've been chucked, old boy." However, "It would have sickened him to feel vindictive."

After a final interview with Chad, who has been in London and is thus perhaps already losing interest in Mme de Vionnet, Strether leaves for Woollett and its society of women, of which, we know, he is an integral part. He thereby abandons his alter ego, his soul-sister or blood-brother, Miss Gostrey. He also realizes that he has lost Mrs. Newsome. His European experience has obviously enriched him, but he has also come to realize that he has discovered life too late. *The virile ideal will remain fixed on its pedestal.* It seemed momentarily attainable because, transported to Europe, the ideal had become somehow tamed, civilized. However, Chad escapes Strether, as Hendrik Andersen escaped Henry James. Strether remains passive and feminine, unable to win Mrs. Newsome by accomplishing the mission that was set to test his virility.

Leon Edel links the publication of *The Ambassadors* very precisely with James's meeting with Hendrik Andersen. He also believes that there is a great resemblance between Little Bilham and Jonathan Sturges on the one hand, and between Waymarsh and William James on the other. Maria Gostrey and Marie Vionnet are maternal images (Mrs. James's first name was Mary), and Edel finds it significant that the novel contains no actual father.

For the present purpose, *The Ambassadors* is above all an allegory of James's emotional life. Mrs. Newsome represents the dominance of the mother, as Edel has suggested, and Waymarsh that of the brother from whom James had to free himself by entering Chad's apartment, by becoming a real man. Chad symbolizes the essence of virility that James had attempted to attain in all the young men with whom he had close friendships. Chad does not allow women to interfere with him; he dominates them or he uses them. Meeting Chad, Strether, the introverted, passive, feminine man, understands that he has not known how to live, that he has repressed his emotional and sensual life for too long, and that he could have come closer to the virile ideal. Now, however, it is too late to recapture time lost. Unable to become Chad, to conform to the American virile ideal he had renounced upon seeing the youthful Gus Barker posing on a pedestal—and William's portrait of the scene—James may yet enter into a symbiotic union with him, become one of his "feeders." However, Chad rejects Strether, despite his kindness and his solicitude. As an incarnate homosexual fantasy, Chad must *by his very nature* reject the feminine and passive adorer *because* he is a virile man —i.e., *a man who prefers women.* So long as his heterosexuality was thought to be "virtuous," unrealized, as in some of Tennessee Williams's heroes, Chad could embody a ray of hope, could be thought of as accessible. Strether feels younger; Chad has something adult about him and still represents a "young Pagan," the antithesis of the "Good Boy" of the Judeo-Christian tradition. To keep such a man, however, Strether would have had to have been a girl—Jeanne de Vionnet, or the girl Chad may have gone to London to see. It is possible—probable—that Chad has had his fill of thirty-eight-year-old Mme de Vionnet, the mother who has polished, formed, and tamed him. And Strether feels that he, too, has had a hand in this transformation, just as the mentors in Inge's plays form their roughneck protégés. Although Strether has been so entranced by the young man that he endows him with qualities that neither Mrs. Pocock nor Miss Gostrey (Strether's lucid alter ego) can see, once he has been rejected he sees Chad in a new light. Perhaps Mme de Vionnet was right after all in her fear she would lose Chad: "She had but made Chad what he was—so why could she think she had made him infinite? She had made him better, she had made him best, she had made him anything one would; but it came to our friend with supreme queerness that he was none the less only Chad."

Which recalls Sartre, commenting on Genet: "One of the dominant features of the homosexual is . . . his wanting to dupe himself and to take revenge for being a dupe by sudden recurrences of cynicism."

Chapter Fifteen

Francis Scott Fitzgerald: Self-virilization and Its Failure

The "Sissy" and His Hero

Biographers of the author of the Basil stories agree that the young F. Scott Fitzgerald was a "sissy." Mizener relates that as an adolescent at Newman Academy, Fitzgerald was so pretty that he won a "quick reputation as a sissy." Henry Dan Piper mentions the hats, coats, and warm clothes which Mrs. Fitzgerald, a typical "overprotective" mother, piled on him, and quotes one of his friends as remarking that when he was eleven or twelve years old, "Scott was handsome but we thought him a sissy." Fitzgerald was not a member of the "gang." At seventeen, according to Mizener, Fitzgerald was short, "slight and slope-shouldered in build, almost girlishly handsome, with yellow hair and long-lashed green eyes." During his childhood and adolescence, Fitzgerald's condition was typical of the prehomosexual: a domineering, commanding, and possessive mother, a passive and indulgent father. He had difficulty being accepted by his friends. In 1933 Fitzgerald wrote John O'Hara that in his youth he had suffered from an inferiority complex.

All of his biographers have hinted at Fitzgerald's femininity. The famous Triangle Club anecdote is symbolic. Fitzgerald had had to relinquish his feminine role in the annual performance by the Princeton club, and he donned his costume and attended a dance at the University of Minnesota with his old friend Gus Shurmeier. Mizener describes Fitzgerald's behavior at the dance as follows: "He spent the evening casually asking for cigarettes in the middle of the dance floor and absent-mindedly drawing a small vanity case from the top of a blue stocking. This practical joke made all the papers, but it was an inadequate substitute for the flower he had looked forward to as 'the Most Beautiful "Show Girl" in the Triangle Club.' " Andrew Turnbull called Fitzgerald a "woman's man." He mentions his weak character, his liking for psychological analysis and nuances, his feminine intuition (which recalls D. H. Lawrence, who also had a "feminine strain" he was able to employ in his art).

When Hemingway met Fitzgerald, the latter was, symbolically, in the company of a Princeton athlete. Turnbull regarded him as a "chronic hero-worshipper," and Mizener gives a list of his "heroes," from Sam White to Buzz Law and Hobey Baker, football champions whose figures haunt his novels and short stories. In his adolescence, Fitzgerald discovered that if one could not be the "hero," then one must hymn his exploits in order to attract him, to make contact with him. Having played poorly during a football game, "he tried to atone for this humiliation by writing . . . a thirty-six-line poem in praise of football." The poem was printed in the school newspaper.

However, Fitzgerald's attempt at self-virilization was not doomed to total failure. At Newman Academy he ended up playing left halfback, and was successful enough to win a highly prized trophy. Once he had gained the respect and esteem of his friends, he overcame his reputation as a sissy, and girls began to take an interest in him, and he in them. It seems clear nonetheless that Fitzgerald never effected a natural and definitive introjection of the virile image: throughout his life, he continued to search for heroes with whom he might identify, and his virility was always precarious if this support failed him. In *The Crack-Up*, he wrote, "When I like men I want to be like them—I want to lose the outer qualities that give me my individuality and be like them. I don't want the man; I want to absorb into myself all the qualities that make him attractive and leave him out." This is a perfect definition of that adolescent identification which seems so suspect in an adult man; it attests to the failure of introjection, which is the basic cause of overt or latent homosexuality.

Margaret Mead has written of these "rabbity men" who homoerotically attach themselves to lions because of American society's failure to instill in them the notion that a tender, graceful and sensitive man—like Fitzgerald—can yet claim to be a real man. Mizener, Turnbull, Piper, and Carlos Baker—among others—have all described the close friendship between Fitzgerald, temperamental, charming, imaginative, and Ernest Hemingway, solid, a fighter, a "he-man." In A *Moveable Feast* Hemingway describes Fitzgerald as a disturbingly and teasingly handsome young man, and the description of their trip together to Lyons to pick up Scott's car is a masterpiece of humor, in which can be glimpsed all too clearly Scott's femininity as he plays with Hemingway the role he had formerly played with his devoted friend Gus Shurmeier. Fitzgerald is capricious; he insists that Hemingway make all the decisions, that he care for him and coddle him, etc. As Carlos Baker clearly shows us in his biography, Hemingway came to represent for Fitzgerald the male to be imitated, and also the male upon whom he could lean, as a woman leans on a man.

Hemingway is something like Spud and Fitzgerald something like Lymie (*The Folded Leaf*), and the intimacy between them has a strong flavor of repressed homosexuality: Fitzgerald's mouth "worried" Hemingway because it might have been the mouth of a girl, and an episode in their friendship related in A *Moveable Feast* is revealing in its candor: Zelda, who was jealous of her husband's work—according to Hemingway—told Scott that he would never succeed in satisfying a woman. Fitzgerald asked Hemingway to examine him. Hemingway reassured him: he was "perfectly fine." This scene occurs in the men's room of a Parisian café. Is this desire of Fitzgerald's to exhibit himself to Hemingway—rather than consulting a doctor, as he says—not a clear indication of homosexuality? Or perhaps even an unconscious desire to make Hemingway tell him that he is *not* made to love women. "It is not," Hemingway writes, "basically a question of the size in repose. . . . It is the size that it becomes. It is also a question of angle." The next step would have been a comparison of their individual erections. Perhaps this is what Fitzgerald was unconsciously hoping for!

The Compromise

Fitzgerald's choice to attend Princeton is also highly revealing of his psychology. Firmly convinced that Harvard students were "sissies," which he was attempting not to be, Fitzgerald also decided against Yale because he imagined that students there were "brawny and brutal and powerful." He enrolled at Princeton because he considered Princeton students to be "slender and keen and romantic."

From childhood on, Fitzgerald stood at the junction of three roads: the road toward which everything about him seemed to point, the road of the prehomosexual "sissy"; the road of his heroes, the handsome, indifferent, virile—brutal—athletes; and, finally, the road he eventually took, a kind of compromise between the ideal and the real, the road symbolized by Princeton, the Alma Mater of slender, keen, romantic students—that is, of very few Americans in the America of the early twentieth century.

Basil Duke is attracted to the girls who are most popular with popular boys, and we note that Hubert fascinates him more than does Imogene. Although Fitzgerald was attracted to girls from adolescence on, it was never a direct attraction. *The woman is always a means, an intermediary who enables him to attain another goal.* It might be said that Fitzgerald was saved from the pitfall of homosexuality by his eternal desire to be accepted by his friends, and by his social ambitions. In order to make himself liked by his friends, an adolescent boy has to exert a more or less successful effort to engage in virile sports, or to praise such endeavors. *However, the red badge of virility can be truly won only through the conquest of a female.* As an adolescent, Fitzgerald dated many girls. He is supposed to have been in love with Marie Hersey, but it is revealing that he adds that Marie "is the most popular with T. Ames, L. Porterfield, B. Griggs, C. Read, R. Warner, etc. and I am crazy about her." In his student days he fell in love with Ginevra King. Ginevra was one of the four most beautiful debutantes in Chicago, and Turnbull flatly states that "with Ginevra, part of the attraction had been the society she came from." Her social position gave her an appeal that fascinated the son of lower-middle-class parents who had decided to gain admission to American high society at any cost.

Zelda obviously represented Fitzgerald's ideal. The daughter of an excellent southern family, she allied youthful female beauty with the masculinity of a tomboy. Both Turnbull and Nancy Milford have described her boyish appeal, her unfeminine tastes, her androgynous beauty. In addition, she and Scott were enough alike to be twins, which was not displeasing to her narcissistic suitor.

Fitzgerald's attitude toward sexuality—heterosexuality—is symptomatic: Turnbull explains that the young Fitzgerald was inhibited by a kind of "shy fastidiousness" and, "as he later described it, despair more than lust now drove him into a woman's arms." He was disgusted by Frank Harris's pornographic "memoirs," and he told a woman friend: "It's disgusting. It's the kind of filth your sex is often subjected to, the kind of lavatory conversations men indulge in. It bores me—you don't know how disgusting men can be!" Fitzgerald was something of a woman's activist, and one suspects he preserved his heterosexuality by means of the unconscious strategy Havelock Ellis called "eonism." The anecdote of transvestitism at Princeton would indicate this. Ellis held that eonism is always linked with homosexuality, but that the subject "identifies himself . . . not merely in dress, but in general tastes, in ways of acting, and in emotional disposition," with the opposite sex. Even after marriage, the eonist seldom has a "vigorous sexual temperament." Should he enjoy wearing female clothing, he does so with "complete success," and "with a minute and almost instinctive adoption of feminine ways, which, [he feels], come to [him] naturally." The eonist's intelligence is usually higher than average, and he "may attain distinction as [an] author or otherwise."

This description of the eonist's psychology seems strikingly applicable to Fitzgerald. Fiedler has put implicit emphasis on it, remarking that "Fitzgerald has come to seem more and more poignantly by the girl we left behind." He makes much of the fact that in a sketch for *Tender Is the Night,* "Rosemary was indeed a boy, who was to kill his mother according to the original plot." He adds that Fitzgerald, "like one of his own epicene coquettes . . . postured and flirted with all comers."

Fitzgerald's work is full of hints of his basic femininity; throughout his life he played the dual and exhausting game of identifying with he-men on the one hand, and with a woman on the other, so as to be able to make love to her. It is as though, adolescent identification having failed, the subject still refuses to eroticize his passionate admiration for his idol and must as a result, and at whatever cost, eroticize his feelings for women. It might even be suggested that Fitzgerald, an effeminate, prehomosexual child who out of social ambition desired to conform to the American virile ideal, narcissistically loved women and thereby kept up appearances—a schema that is not heterosexual, but sapphic. From this point of view, his work cannot help but be reminiscent of some of Henry James's novels and short stories.

Autobiographical Works

At the beginning of *This Side of Paradise*, Amory Blaine is in a typical prehomosexual situation, able to identify only with his mother: "Amory Blaine inherited from his mother every trait, except the stray inexpressible few, that made him worth while. His father, an ineffectual, inarticulate man with a taste for Byron . . ." Amory's apparent masculinity results from a deliberate effort on his part: he imagines himself making excuses: "My *dear* Mrs. St. Claire, I'm *frightfully* sorry to be late, but my maid"—he paused here and realized he would be quoting—'but my uncle and I had to see a fella.'" Like the young Fitzgerald, Amory is a narcissistic flirt. He thinks he is "exceedingly handsome."

From this first novel, the various features of the "hero" are clearly discernible. First, there is Dick Humbird, whose physique is fascinating: he is slim, well-built, dark; he is charming and has a sense of honor; he is not overly intelligent. Later on, Amory comes to admire Burne Holiday, who attracts him mainly because of his intelligence, whereas hitherto he has been held in thrall by his heroes' "immediate magnetism." For Amory, the body has a disproportionate importance: blonds are a privileged class, regular features an indication of undeniable superiority. Whitman, Tolstoy, Carpenter, are "ugly looking," as though they have come out of an "old men's home."

Amory's attitude to sexuality sets the pattern for all of Fitzgerald's later protagonists and reflects the author's: sexuality stops at the face. Maxwell Geismar has noted that the libido of the characters in Fitzgerald's novels is "centered around their lips." Amory is disgusted by Myra's first kiss, recalling the reactions of some of Sherwood Anderson's misfits. Although later he becomes a real lady's man, this is not so much because he is attracted to women but rather because he is determined to assert himself, to be a real man, like his heroes. He decides to seduce Isabelle, but he is aware that he has no feelings for her at all; yet, her coldness angers him: "If he didn't kiss her, it would worry him. . . . It would interfere vaguely with his idea of himself as a conqueror."

The novel's androgynous tone is intensified by the presence of the character of Monsignor Darcy, a character based on Monsignor Fay, Fitzgerald's own mentor. Obviously asexual—an androgynous bachelor—Darcy is depicted as a mixture of the Shakespeare of the Sonnets and Oscar Wilde. Evoking the "paternal instinct" dormant in every man, Darcy says he wishes Amory were his son, and writes a very ambiguous sonnet to him. A psychoanalyst would obviously regard Darcy as both father and mother substitute, a kind of androgynous compromise to which the young Amory becomes attracted because he feels no irresistible attraction for women and yet cannot or will not eroticize the adoration he feels for his heroes. Darcy, desexualized despite his charm by his age, his intellect, and his status as a man of the cloth, become the young man's spiritual father "at first sight." Darcy is the forerunner of Pinky, Tom's mentor in Inge's *Where's Daddy?;* he also reminds us of Henry James.

The protagonist of *The Beautiful and the Damned,* Anthony Patch, is at sixteen a far cry from the American virile ideal. He has all the characteristics of the sissy, "an inarticulate boy, *thoroughly un-American,* and politely bewildered by his contemporaries." His personality resembles that of two of James Baldwin's characters, the young Eric in *Another Country,* and the young black, John Grimes. Like Eric, he likes to dress up in luxurious fabrics, in satins and brocades, and parade before the mirror; like John Grimes, he looks out of the window and dreamily listens to the sound of children playing, "realizing dimly this clamour, breathless and immediate, in which it seemed he was never to have a part." Anthony becomes an actor in the Hasty Pudding Club, the Harvard student theater group, in which female roles are taken by men. Although his good looks are not "Aryan," he is charming and "he was yet, here and there, considered handsome." Overly thin despite his broad shoulders, he has a sharp nose and his mouth droops when he is unhappy; however, his blue eyes are full of charm. He is "passive" by temperament, although he does not realize he is "merely the sensitive plate on which the photograph was made."

Anthony's love for Gloria is passive: "Some Gargantuan photographer had focussed the camera on Gloria and *snap!*—the poor plate could but develop." Yet Gloria is far from being the ultimate in femininity. To a non-Aryan like Anthony, she is like a Nordic Ganymede. Maxwell Geismar has noted—anticipating Leslie Fiedler—the inversion of sexual roles in Fitzgerald's work: "Fitzgerald's mythological reference is apt: and clinging to this shining, hard, dominant Ganymede . . . Anthony Patch himself takes on the role of the volatile, uneasy, and even perhaps betrayed, un-Nordic woman."

Gloria is a tomboy: this is dictated both by the period in which the story occurs and by the novelist's personal tastes. Her hair is bobbed long before this became fashionable; she is sadistic and cruel; she awakens in Anthony a latent masochism which he resists. Between them there is a sadomasochistic struggle faintly reminiscent of the struggle between captain and soldier: "Instead of seizing the girl and holding her by sheer strength until she became passive to his desire, instead of beating down her will by the force of his own, he had walked, defeated and powerless, from her door."

Just as we have noted the mixture of feminine passivity and masculine aggressiveness in both partners of the sadomasochistic couple, so in Anthony and Gloria we note an androgyny emphasized by the characters themselves. Gloria says they are "twins," and later she declares that she has a "man's mind," to which Anthony replies, "You've got a mind like mine. Not strongly gendered either way." (Nancy Milford reports that Fitzgerald had told Dr. Rennie that Zelda looked on him "as a woman" and that "all our lives, since the days of our engagement, we have spent hunting for some man Zelda considers strong enough to lean upon.") Such youthful narcissism, reminiscent of the narcissism of Amory, or of Fitzgerald himself, such a desire to find one's own double, is obviously the result of the author's inability to objectivize his sexuality.

Gloria is nothing but a compromise between Amory's deep, secret, and unconscious desires and his determination to adapt to the standards of American society. Like Amory and like his creator, Anthony owes his salvation to his social ambitions and to his need to be accepted by the rich and the "beautiful." All these characters are helped to convert to heterosexuality by the androgynous nature of the Aryan women they want to possess in order to attract the attention of other men. This holds true for Amory, and it is the case with Anthony. Before the "Nordic Ganymede" Gloria, "the doors of the Ritz would revolve, the crowd would divide, fifty masculine eyes would start, stare, as she gave back forgotten dreams to the husbands of many obese and comic women." It would be difficult to choose a passage that better sums up Anthony's psychology—and the author's: masculine eyes dazzled by the beauty of a girl-ephebe walking out of the most elegant—and expensive—hotel in New York. And the men thus seduced will dream of being young and androgynous beings.

Many critics have noted the passivity, cowardice, and immaturity of the narrator of *The Great Gatsby*. A. Le Vot states that "Nick is always in an inferior position," that he is "over shadowed by Tom's magnificence," and "admiring" before Gatsby's. A retarded, "immature" adolescent who is unable to play a virile role, Nick tries to find stability and inner balance by the familiar masochistic process of identification and symbiotic union with a seemingly stronger, more virile, man than himself—Tom Buchanan or Jay Gatsby.

In a letter, Fitzgerald's editor Max Perkins regretted that Gatsby was not better described: "Gatsby is somewhat vague. The reader's eyes can never quite focus on him, his outlines are dim. . . . couldn't *he* be physically described as distinctly as the others, and couldn't you add one or two characteristics?" In his reply to Perkins, Fitzgerald made two points: "*I myself didn't know what Gatsby looked like or was engaged in* and you felt it. . . . My first instinct after your letter was to let him go and have Tom Buchanan dominate the book (I suppose he's the best character I've ever done . . .) but Gatsby sticks in my heart."

The fabulously wealthy Gatsby is a young man who is vigorous, virile, self-assured, elegant, and also unpolished in appearance. In a flashback, we are told the story of his youth as a tramp, "a salmon-fisher," " a clam-digger," living by his wits. He is a very virile and untamed young man, whose "brown, hardening body" is comfortable in the wild. He is also a lady's man, but he despises his overeasy conquests. We see how closely Gatsby is related to the typical he-men described by London, Hemingway, and Mailer: courage, strength, virile beauty, an eventful past, indifference to other people, a frantic narcissist—all of these are the usual characteristics of the portrait of the hero admired by a passive and feminine man, in this case Nick Carraway. In addition, Fitzgerald's hero is charming, as evidenced by his smile, replete with happiness and confidence: "He had probably discovered that people liked him when he smiled."

At over thirty years of age, Gatsby possesses both the qualities of the Fitzgerald hero: virile, self-confident beauty, and social position. Yet he has the smile and the charm that belong not only to the idols but also to the men who adore them—Amory, Anthony, and Fitzgerald himself. The character is a narcissistic projection of his creator, an "ideal self" much closer to the author's ego than is the hero he sought in the Princeton or Yale football players. Gatsby also shares with Fitzgerald his rapid rise in society and his desire to dazzle and conquer women with his wealth. It has been said that the story of Gatsby and Daisy is the fictionalized version of the story of Fitzgerald and Ginevra King.

Tom and Gatsby are joined through a woman, Daisy, whom they both love and who loves both of them. However, they are also linked by the hate-love feelings of Nick Carraway. *They embody two very similar facets of the same hero.* This is the basic reason why one of them—Tom—is very painstakingly drawn, while Gatsby is merely a sketch. In other words, had Gatsby too been minutely described, he would have been too much like

Tom's twin, and the characters in the novel would have seemed less individualized. In this respect, it is interesting to note that Daisy goes from one to the other without any difficulty, like Alcmene going from Amphitryon to Jupiter, who has assumed her husband's features to seduce her. If Fitzgerald doubled his hero —unconsciously—it was obviously to emphasize in each character one of the two qualities that so fascinated him in men: Tom is a concentration of virile, rough beauty (merely suggested in Gatsby), while Gatsby symbolizes fabulous wealth that has been quickly acquired (Tom is also extremely wealthy).

Tom Buchanan is the all-American man, like the athletes Fitzgerald adored. At Yale, Tom was one of best football players. His first appearance in the novel is symbolic: "He had changed since his New Haven years. Now he was a sturdy straw-haired man of thirty with a rather hard mouth and a supercilious manner. Two shining arrogant eyes had established dominance over his face and gave him the appearance of always leaning aggressively forward. Not even the effeminate swank of his riding clothes could hide the enormous power of that body—he seemed to fill those glistening boots until he strained the top lacing, and you would see a great pack of muscle shifting when his shoulder moved under his thin coat. It was a body capable of enormous leverage—a cruel body."

Tom's body, his posture and his clothing all combine to make him a character of almost superhuman strength, touching on cruelty and sadism, and the narrator adopts in his regard the masochistic attitude of an inferior flattered to be admitted into a superior's condescending presence. Furthermore, Tom's actions toward Nick are revealing: he sometimes put his hand on Nick's shoulder in a friendly way, but more often the gesture reveals his desire to dominate the other: "Wedging his tense arm imperatively under mine, Tom Buchanan compelled me from the room as though he were moving a checker to another square." Or: "He jumped to his feet and, taking hold of my elbow, literally forced me from the car." Or again: "With his authoritative arms breaking the way, we pushed through the still gathering crowd." Whenever he mentions Tom, the narrator cannot avoid evoking his strength and muscles with a monotony approaching obsession: "Tom flung open the door, blocked out its space for a moment with his thick body, and hurried into the room." His arms are "powerful," his fingers "thick," his enormous muscles play beneath his jacket, his "bulkiness" is "wholesome," his walk is "aggressive." The picture of the he-man—not unlike the studs in Inge's plays—is completed by racism, which he shares with London's heroes, and with London himself.

Nick both admires and hates the novel's two "heroes," Tom and Gatsby, and he has a platonic affair with Jordan, a small-breasted woman with "erect carriage," which she accentuates "by throwing her body backward at the shoulders like a young cadet." She is athletic, a champion golfer, uncomfortable in her feminine clothes; she is like Zelda. The flirtation ends as quickly as it begins, and it seems fairly obvious that Nick is not truly attracted to Jordan but that she is present in the novel for the form, as a counterweight to Nick's dual hero worship for the reader—and perhaps for the author himself. There is also something weak, diluted, and disincarnate about Gatsby's love for Daisy. The only time their relations are touched with any sensuality is—revealingly—when they are "reflected" by other men: "It excited him, too, that many men had already loved Daisy—it increased her value in his eyes. He felt their presence all about the house, pervading the air with shades and echoes of still vibrant emotions." (An anecdote reported by Turnbull gives a good illustration of the female element in Fitzgerald's sensual universe: at a party "he had overheard an ex-Princeton athlete propose to the debutante of the year, and he was so intoxicated that he 'was all for becoming engaged to almost anyone immediately.'" The important thing is to do as the hero, the champion athlete, does.)

Tender Is the Night contains the same virile hierarchy noted in the earlier novels, here further developed and more completely worked out. The following gradation is established: overt homosexuals, effeminate men, and "heroes." Mention has already been made of those on the lowest rung on the ladder, Campion, Dumphry, and Francisco. More interesting here is the resemblance between Nick and Dick, on the one hand, and Tom Barban and Tom Buchanan, on the other; the resemblance is emphasized by the similarity of names. Noteworthy too is the fact that the effeminate man is split into McKisco and Dick: Fitzgerald maneuvers between these two poles, the former a weak, cowardly creature who thinks himself a failure, the latter a weak man who *almost* raises himself to the "hero" level through his willpower and charm. Basil, Amory, and Anthony all belong in the second category, and the husband of Tom Buchanan's mistress, a minor character, is separated from the homosexuals Campion and Dumphry by only a very thin line. Francisco, however, is almost on a level with Dick.

Dick owes some of his traits to the character Francis Malarky, who was supposed to be the novel's protagonist. Francis (a name with a feminine sound) was saddled with a possessive, "close-binding" mother, so stifling that he has to kill her at the end of the novel in order to free himself. Francis, with his "conventional beauty," also had all the candor and temperament of Fitzgerald's other young males. Expelled from West Point for a breach of discipline, rejected in Hollywood, where he had worked as a film editor, Francis was forced to leave the United States to avoid jail. His boyhood can easily be imagined, caught between a criminal, imprisoned father and a vulgar and domineering mother. Although one cannot go so far as to regard such crimes as sexual infractions, in a novel which is a panorama of sexual perversions of all kinds it is not out of place to suggest such a possibility, particularly since the character of Francis is transformed into Rosemary and also provides materials for certain facets of Dick Diver, while—as Michel Fabre notes—"the ardent Brugerol gives way to Tommy Costello, a mutation towards the male Barban" in the later versions of the novel.

Dick's character is feminized at the outset. While still barely acquainted with him, Nicole writes to him: "Moreover, you seem quieter than the others, all soft like a big cat. . . . Are you a sissy?" On the beach, Dick appears in "trousers of transparent black lace. Close inspection revealed that actually they were lined with flesh-colored cloth." Mrs. McKisco contemptuously remarks, "Well, if that isn't a pansy's trick!" He then quickly turns to Dumphry and Campion and adds, "Oh, I beg your pardon." The remark links Dick with the homosexuals Dumphry and Campion.

When the novel begins, Dick is a young, married man. He is Rosemary's virile ideal; she is subject to his *virile charm*. Although his voice is melodious and persuasive, the girl senses the "layer of hardness in him, of self-control and of self-discipline." On the deepest level, however, like all of Fitzgerald's fictional alter egos, Dick is weak, passive, and unable to control his own destiny. The symbol of Dick's passivity and emasculation is the money he accepts from Nicole's sister, Baby Warren, to set up his psychiatric clinic. This makes him feel he has "been swallowed up like a gigolo," and the novel is the chronicle of his disintegration, culminating in his ultimate destruction. Fitzgerald describes his protagonist as a young man of athletic appearance, intelligent, cultivated, with "all the talents, including especially great personal charm." He is "a superman in possibilities," but he "lacks that tensile strength—none of the ruggedness of Brancusi, Leger, Picasso." In describing his hero's appearance, Fitzgerald drew on Gerald Murphy, Ernest Hemingway, other men he admired—and himself. "He looks, though, like me," he said (quoted by Matthew T. Bruccoli).

So Dick, too, is a projection of Fitzgerald himself, with additional characteristics borrowed from his real-life heroes; however, he retains the passivity, weakness, and charm of the original model. Michel Fabre has noted that Dick is a "bitter and lucid" spectator, so "vulnerable that he is subject to many temptations and harbors in himself all the corruption he discerns in others; sick, a seducer, gradually losing his virility, violent, alcoholic, a failed writer, he is even accused of homosexuality and incest." The fluid nature of his personality recalls the sexual imprecision to be found in Amory or Nick. In all these things, Dick is a contrast to Tom Barban, the "hero" of the novel.

Barban is a perfected version of all of Fitzgerald's earlier heroes. He is the handsome football player, muscular and aggressive, and indifferent to his admirer's homage. He is the watered-down American cousin of the desirable brutes who populate Jean Genet's world. "Effeminate" writers with masochistic tendencies are first obsessed by their hero's physique. Barban—his symbolic name prefiguring the barbarian Croft—is an anti-Dick Diver (civilized man), just as he is an anti-McKisco, the failed, cowardly writer, and an anti-homosexual (Dumphry, Campion, Francisco). He has none of the passivity that is characteristic of Dick, nor does he have the soft body that seems to be the hallmark of Fitzgerald's homosexual characters. At first glance, he appears to be "conventionally handsome—but there was a faint disgust always in his face which marred the full fierce lustre of his brown eyes." He is "less civilized" than the other men with whom Rosemary is acquainted, a mercenary who is always willing to sell his services to fight in a war, "any war." Barban has "worn the uniforms of eight countries." At the outset, he reveals, "My business is to kill people." Both Dick and the author believe that Tom Barban "was a ruler, Tommy was a hero." Dick sees him in a Munich cafe, "laughing his martial laugh. . . . As a rule, he drank little; courage was his game and his companions were always a little afraid of him."

As soon as Dick—who in the beginning is almost on Barban's level of virility—sinks on the scale, Nicole turns to Tom Barban. Like Desdemona, she is attracted by this man who reminds us of the barbarian Othello seducing the naïve Venetian girl: "His handsome face was so dark as to have lost the pleasantness of deep tan, without attaining the blue beauty of negroes—it was just worn leather. The foreignness of his depigmentation by unknown suns, his nourishment by strange soils, his tongue awkward with the curl of many dialects, his reactions attuned to odd alarms—these things fascinated and rested Nicole." Later, Barban brags of having "brutalized many men into shape," and with his scars and arching eyebrows, he is described as a "fighting Puck, an earnest Satan."

Gatsby and Buchanan both love the same woman, who loves each of them in turn. Similarly, Dick and Barban both love Nicole, who "rests" from one of them with the other. Fitzgerald at one time considered allowing Tom Buchanan to dominate *The Great Gatsby* to Gatsby's detriment; in *Tender Is the Night,* Dick deteriorates and falls apart, while Tom Barban becomes increasingly strong and virile. This happens because all of an author's projections—whether they are realistic or utopian—are firmly linked to the personality of their creator or, rather, to his personalities. When Dick abandons virility and becomes an alcoholic, Tom takes over more and more of the hero's characteristics and wins Nicole's love; when Tom Buchanan succeeds in winning back his wife by an act of will, Gatsby's personality withers, disintegrates, and dies.

The most solid of the connections that link the protagonists is the female. Nick Carraway, the narrator of *The Great Gatsby*, shared such feelings with regard to his two heroes: he resembled Daisy. Similarly, Dick is so close to Nicole that at the beginning of their love affair they each sign the letters they exchange with the same fanciful name, "Dicole." The play on names reveals the interpenetration of their personalities: Dick-Nick-Nicole, are the three faces of the author who chose as his own wife the Montgomery, Alabama, tomboy who so much resembled him. Since Francis Melarky turned into Rosemary and Dick, since Rosemary loves Dick, who is himself so close to Nicole that they become one person; and since Nicole loves both Dick and Barban, both of whom are projections to the author, may one not wonder whether, by making Nicole yield to Tom Barban, Fitzgerald was not pursuing to its logical conclusion the love-admiration felt by Basil for Hubert Blair, or his own feelings toward Hemingway, by way of Nick's feelings toward Tom Buchanan? Schematically, here is the basis on which we can posit a deeper friendship between Basil Duke and his heroes than might appear at first glance:

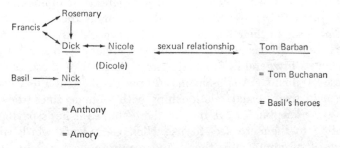

The pivotal point of this schema, its keystone, is Nicole, or "Dicole." She has sexual relations with Tom Barban, the ultimate version of Basil's indifferent and athletic "heroes," and she is also linked with Dick (Dicole). Since Dick himself is the combination of Francis and Rosemary, he thereby becomes feminine, and certain aspects of his temperament recall the passive and masochistic Nick Carraway. Basil, like Dick, is the alter ego of the young Fitzgerald. Thus, through the intermediary of the fictional, masculine-feminine character "Dicole," Basil has sexual

relations with Tom Barban, the "hero." And just as the women of
Basil, Anthony, Gatsby—and Fitzgerald—gained in charm and
sexual attraction because they were desired by other men, so
Nicole is an innocent intermediary between Dick and Barban,
between Fitzgerald and his "hero"; however, here the relationship goes much further, and the subterfuges of the unconscious threaten to be laid bare,

The fighter, warrior homoeroticism tacitly present in Barban's
character is revealed by a brief anecdote that has apparently
been overlooked by Fitzgerald's critics. A young Englishman of
the kind who "were always jumping around cornices and bal-
conies, as if they thought they were in the rigging of a ship," tells
of a boxing match with his best friend "in which they loved and
bruised each other for an hour." Dick laughs at him. "'If you
don't understand, I can't explain it to you,' said the young
Englishman coldly."

Only a Barban, a D. H. Lawrence, a Jack London, a real he-
man, would understand the young Englishman. Dick is no more
part of the homoerotic warrior race than was Fitzgerald himself.
His feminine passivity employs other means to achieve its ends.
Although *apparently* heterosexual, Fitzgerald's feminine-masoch-
istic protagonists love women only insofar as the women bring
them closer to their heroes, and it is no accident that, as Maxwell Geismar has noted, heterosexual relations occur only at
lip level. Fitzgerald's "realistic projections"—like those of Tennessee Williams's Anglo-Saxons—do not display any great enthusiasm in their sexual relationships with women, since they are
too busy keeping an eye on the "hero" to see if he is paying attention to them, to see—to use Nick Carraway's words about
Tom—if he appreciates them, and wants to be loved by them.
Having forgone his "superman" fate and wanting "above all to
be brave and kind," Dick "had wanted, even more than that, to
be loved." We may be sure that in his subconscious it was not by
either Nicole or Rosemary.

Chapter Sixteen

The Feminine-Masochist Temperament in Certain Jewish Characters

Weak Jew and Muscular Gentile: Sexual Attraction

In Bruce Jay Friedman's *A Mother's Kisses* Joseph's mother is the typical Bieber "domineering" and "seductive" mother. Although not a newcomer to American literature, her portrait was finally painted realistically in 1964: she is depicted as sensual, possessive, and vulgar. Such novels as Friedman's—or Philip Roth's *Portnoy's Complaint*—have firmly established this type of woman as the typical Jewish American mother. From Philip Wylie we know that such "Moms" are precisely the type of woman who engenders sexual inversion in her son, particularly if the father is practically nonexistent, as is the case with Joseph's father. Joseph is not only passive and timid; he feels a *truly sexual attraction* for the strong, muscular male body, a virility symbol that both attracts and repels him. He is most forcibly struck by the strong, brutal male's strong, muscular legs, members which psychoanalysis tells us are phallic substitutes.

In *A Mother's Kisses* and *Stern* (1962) muscular legs are a symbol of erotic virility. The director of the summer camp where Joseph is employed is a man with "great bulging thighs," but his voice is so weak that Joseph has the impression that "so much power had been poured into his legs there was none left for his voice." When Salamandro emerges from the shower in his robe and sits down, "crossing his great bearlike legs," Joseph finds them "beefily seductive." He cannot resist "looking inside them, checking for nudity, hoping there was no way for anyone ever to know his thoughts. He prayed that years later he might not admit in a drunken slip that he had found a camp director's legs sexy." He also notices the legs of his colleague, Dick Kensie, an ex-GI: they are "hairy, chipper, combat toughened legs."

Stern, the adult version of the adolescent invert, feels the same attraction for the muscular, vigorous legs of the men who impress him, of the fireman who comes to sell him tickets to a dance. The man he fears and whom he thinks is persecuting him appears to be a muscular Gentile whose powerful muscles ripple beneath the light fabric of his T-shirt.

Friedman, in an interview with Pierre Dommergues (cf. *Les U.S.A. à la Recherche de leur Identité*), admitted his hero's "passivity" and "femininity." He linked both these characteristics with the Jewish condition, noting that his man both frightens and attracts him; we can see here the ambiguous feelings the homosexual experiences toward the male figure, the image of the feared and desired father. (With his boss, who is a father image, Stern is ill at ease and timid.) Stern also "fears" and "hopes" that his wife will be attacked by the man, with whom he will then have a sexual relationship *through* a woman, in line with a schema that has occurred in several American novels, a schema which psychoanalysis has fully investigated. However, Stern, whose masochistic makeup is emphasized by the author, is not consciously homoerotic; he has nothing but contempt for the homosexuals he encounters. Joseph's and Stern's passivity and femininity, according to a psychiatrist Friedman quotes, are inherent in the Jewish faith; masochism, a feminine temperament, and latent homosexuality can all be found in the protagonists of at least one other Jewish novelist, Saul Bellow.

Bellow analyzed the homoerotic relationship between the masochistic Jew and the sadistic Gentile in 1947 in his novel entitled *The Victim*, which describes the relationship between Asa Leventhal, a Jew, and Kirby Allbee, a Gentile. The latter accuses the Jew of having cost him his job as a newspaperman (which is partly true). He tracks him down, subjugates him, and ends up moving in with him while the "victim's" wife is, symbolically, out of town on vacation.

The narrative is like the chronicle of a paranoid obsession. Leventhal—like Stern—feels real terror in the presence of his tormentor. Although his own conscience is clear, he is unable to resist the Gentile. He agrees to take him in and lends him money up until the final crisis: one day he gets hold of himself and, awakening from his masochistic torpor, throws Allbee out. Leslie Fiedler has indicated the homoerotic element in Asa and Allbee's relationship. Noting that Bellow's true universe is "a world of men in boarding houses, men whose wives are ill, or have left them, or have gone off on vacation," he continues, "But in no book does the involvement of mates quivering between poles of attraction and repulsion take on a more crucial importance than it has in *The Victim.*" Asa Leventhal discovers his enemy-lover in his own bed—not with his wife, but with a common prostitute. The bond between the men is not the ambivalent link between a deceived husband and his wife's lover, but the link that exists between Jew and Gentile. Fiedler goes on to mention the "terrible physical intimacy" whose nausea Bellow describes so thoroughly.

Such a description of the Jewish-Gentile couple tends to confirm the notion of the basic sadomasochism of American homosexuality: captain and soldier, black and white, older boy and younger boy—all the men who love each other and destroy each other in a civilization that frustrates their most pressing instincts and turns love into hatred when it is thwarted by the conscience, by the superego. Freud described the relationship between paranoia and homosexuality: Asa is a paranoid whose obsessional neurosis is rooted in his minority status (like Stern), and Bellow is to be congratulated for having, in 1947, noted the attraction and repulsion the slave and master, minority member and WASP, feel for each other. The novel is replete with this emotional ambivalence on the part of both victim and tormentor. It ends in an orgiastic scene, the familiar scene of struggle that solved the complex relationship between enemy-lovers in "The Prussian Officer," in William Styron's *Set This House on Fire* (1960), or in *Of Time and the River.* Fiedler comments, "It is the consummation: an orgasm of violence, entailing a separation."

The Quest for a Father

The structure of the novel *Seize the Day* (1956) is also based on male relationships. Tom Wilhelm, the protagonist, is a retarded adolescent over forty years old who is unable to assume the role expected of a man in American society. He is likable and kind; we sense he is seeking a father figure. Like Stern, Joseph, and Asa Leventhal, he suffers from an ineradicable inferiority complex and is a failure in everything he undertakes. He loves and fears both his own father and Dr. Adler, who refuses to continue helping him. Tom then seeks a father substitute in Tamkin, a megalomaniac, a liar, a swindler, and a poet. Our concern is with his relationship to these two "fathers." Wilhelm's mistress, Olive, is no more than a dim figure, and his wife is present only as a voice on the telephone.

Halfway into the novel, the theme of overt homosexuality is introduced indirectly, *negatively*. However, it makes a revealing counterpoint to the protagonists' homoerotic relationship. The father, aware of Tom's immaturity, appears to accept the fact of his son's possible homosexuality: asking him if he has been fired because of a woman, he receives a negative answer. He continues, "Maybe it was a man, then." Shocked and angered, Tom protests.

Toward Tamkin, Tom Wilhelm has the attitude of a younger boy to his "hero," an attitude that combines masochistic passivity and the desire to be dominated by a person regarded as being more adult, more experienced, than oneself. He is happy that the "doctor" "cared about him," and he wants "kindness, mercy." When he perceives that Tamkin has tricked him, he thinks, I was the man beneath; Tamkin was on my back, and I thought I was on his. He made me carry him." In "Caliban on Prospero: A Psychoanalytic Study of the Novel *Seize the Day*, by Saul Bellow," Daniel Weiss makes much of the "back" image, which recurs several times in the book, and he links it to the theme of submerged, repressed homosexuality.

Herzog, Prototype of the Masochistic Minority, the Latent Homosexual

In *Herzog* (1964) all of Bellow's favorite themes are developed. It is the novel in which the relationship between masochism and the Jewish temperament is most clear and meaningful. The psychology of the character Herzog, a minority member, can be summed up as follows: inferiority complex and guilt complex, coupled with the masochistic desire to be accepted by the community.

Herzog attributes the impression some Jews have of being unfit for American reality, composed as it is of aggressiveness, violence, and ostentatious virility, to the education the Jewish immigrants provided for their children. Young Jews were "brought up on moral principles as Victorian ladies were on pianoforte and needlepoint." This inferiority complex and feeling of guilt has already been noted in many homosexual characters, notably in the protagonist of Isherwood's *A Single Man*.

A minority member's desire to achieve integration into the hostile society in which he is forced to live is described in several ways. Herzog is a college professor and has enough money to enable him to live the American dream. As a second-generation immigrant, he is caught between his unassimilated parents, who are poor inhabitants of the slums in which the new arrivals settled and the completely integrated Jews Herzog calls "Reality Professors"—Shura, Himmelstein, Shapiro, Madeleine, etc.—all of whom have become real Americans with hardly a trace of minority mentality. Herzog's children will be third-generation immigrants, hence ordinary Americans.

The desire to gain admittance to a milieu superior to one's own always includes a certain amount of moral masochism. The Uncle Tom—the black, Jew, or homosexual who is trying to "pass"—will do anything to please, will risk rejection at every turn, will attempt to achieve intimacy with those who despise him. Herzog feels the same love-hate toward the "Reality Professors" that we find in the homosexual vis-à-vis the virile, heterosexual male. Herzog attends the questioning of a young black and two homosexuals in court, and he attempts to dissociate himself from such "victims," and to ingratiate himself with the representatives of the law. His difficulty in achieving this reveals his minority complex: he thinks of his elegance, of his apparent self-possession, his charm, and he tells himself that a man like himself "is immune to lower forms of suffering and punishment." When he gets up to leave, however, he turns pale, his pulse races, and he has the impression that the judge is expecting him to salute him; he escapes.

Can sexuality counteract such a neurosis? In *Herzog* sexuality runs the gamut of human possibilities in this regard.

Descriptions of the human body occupy an important place in the book. Herzog contemplates his own body on several occasions. He admires his strength and vigor, while sadly noting the first indications of age: he is losing his hair, putting on weight. He has an almost feminine coquetry. He enjoys dressing well, wearing bright colors, looking at himself in mirrors.

Althought the female body is also described in detail (particularly the bodies of Ramona and Madeleine), it is more interesting to note the extent to which Herzog is fascinated by the male body, and particularly the body of his wife's lover, Gersbach, which has an aura of both brutality and tenderness. Gersbach's thick, red hair and his wooden leg make him strangely attractive to Herzog, who notices his "deep," "hot" eyes, "full of life," his "long, dark" eyelashes, full of vitality, his "bearishly thick" hair, his self-assurance, his narcissism: "He knew he was a terribly handsome man. He expected women—all women—to be mad about him. And many were, weren't they? Including the second Mrs. Herzog." Herzog is overwhelmed by Gersbach's sensuality, just as Leventhal was by Allbee's. The sexual aura rises from male bodies and forces itself on the senses of other men: "His face was all heaviness, sexual meat. Looking down his open shirt front, Herzog saw the hair-covered heavy soft flesh of Gersbach's breast. His chin was thick, and like a stone axe, a brutal weapon. And then there were his sentimental eyes, the thick crest of hair, and that hearty voice with its peculiar fraudulence and grossness."

Herzog is also a lady's man. He has been married twice, he has two mistresses, and he never misses the opportunity to make another conquest. However, his tastes are special: he is attracted to authoritarian, cruel, sadistic women. In Grand Central Station he sees a woman with "bitch eyes" which express "a sort of female arrogance which had an immediate sexual power over him." In Turkey he is attracted by the "trousered, mannish Turkish women," and he recalls the prostitutes in Hamburg who wore "black lace underthings . . . German military boots, and rapped at you with riding crops on the windowpanes." Madeleine, his wife, the woman he still loves and who has most influence over him, is the epitome of the type of femininity to which Herzog is attracted. She "swings her weight like a male." She is the "arch-bitch" in a riding habit in a picture of her taken at twelve years of age. The choice of words used to describe this photograph evokes sadism: Madeleine looks as though she were "craving for revenge," she is wearing boots and appears to have "the power to hurt." This aura of cruelty is what has attracted Herzog: "There was a flavor of subjugation in his love for Madeleine." In a letter to Shapiro, Herzog describes himself as "your friend Herzog writhing under his sharp elegant heel," for Madeleine is "stronger than Wellington" and wants to "kick his brains out with a murderous bitch foot." Cutting hair before the mirror, she looks like she is "discharging a gun," and when applying lipstick in a restuarant, she peers into the blade of a knife.

Herzog will be cured (temporarily) of his neurosis by his mistress, Ramona. Although he actually feels castrated by virile and aggressive women—who are the ones to whom he is attracted sexually—and although he is totally uninterested in feminine, conventional, passive women (such as his first wife, Daisy), he believes that in Ramona he has found the right mixture of strong character and femininity: "She entered a room provocatively, swaggering slightly, one hand touching her thigh, as though she carried a knife in her garter belt." Ramona can be dominant and remain feminine, she can shift from independence to sensuality. The colorless Hoberly, whom she sadistically rejects, is also subject to her charms.

Herzog is a paranoid who fears and desires sexual aggression.

The paranoia that infects his relationship with Gersbach (as was the case with Leventhal and Allbee) is clearly sexual: writing to Gersbach about Madeleine, he says, "Enjoy her—rejoice in her. You will not reach me through her, however. I know you sought me in her flesh. But I am no longer there." Phoebe, Gersbach's wife, tells him that her husband "fell for" him, and that he "adored" him.

Herzog identifies with the victims of the law he sees in court (particularly with the young prostitute Aleck-Alice, the symbol of a corrupt society) because in his childhood he had had a traumatic experience that has led to his panic fear of possible sexual aggression. As a child, he was attacked by a man dressed in a military cape who practically raped him. J. J. Clayton, who regards this scene as one of the principal keys to the character's passive, feminine, homoerotic character, writes that Herzog wants his father to use him so that he may escape castration: "This scene is crucial in the development of Herzog's guilt: his sense of sex as filthy and of himself as a whore."

Moise Herzog's childhood was spent within a family that was happy, despite its poverty. The child found love and comfort within the family between a tender, loving mother and a father who was full of human warmth and goodness but completely ineffectual. Many symbols, particularly those of the house and the pistol, demonstrate that Herzog has not successfully resolved his Oedipus complex: he is always trying to introject the image of his father and to escape from the toils of the Oedipal situation. Obviously, this is the familiar family situation which engenders homosexuality. An episode employing the odor of fish reveals the importance of the Oedipus complex in the protagonist's emotional development. Passing a fish store, Herzog notices the fish piled up and the lobsters pressed against the window. Leaving the elevator, which gives directly onto the sidewalk, he "received the raised pattern of the steel through his thin soles; like Braille. But he did not interpret a message." The author continues: "The fish were arrested, lifelike, in the white, frothing ground ice. The street was overcast, warm and gray, intimate, unclean, flavored by the polluted river, the sexually stirring brackish tidal odor." Madeleine, who asks him in a "peremptory" tone why he is lagging behind, receives the reply: "Well, my mother came from the Baltic provinces. She loved fish."

The metaphors speak for themselves; the message the character has been unable to decipher (the steel message that links the Oedipus complex and masochism) is brought out by the author: Herzog's sexuality is arrested at the Oedipal stage, which explains his passivity with men (the father) and his sexual problems with women, whom he prefers hard, mannish. *His masochism is a redhibition of passive homosexuality.* It is therefore not surprising that his attitude toward sexuality is unhealthy. When he mentions it, he blushes and feels oppressed and ill at ease. The irony in his speech is clearly a defense mechanism: he makes fun of Ramona's sensuality and of physical love, which seems to him "comical," "absurd," "the very essence of slavery." His guilt complex, created by an unresolved Oedipus complex and a traumatic experience (traumatic because it has touched such a vital nerve), makes him find all sexuality repugnant. The fish are "brackish," the street "unclean," the river "polluted"—but the odor is "sexually stirring." The prostitute Aleck-Alice says that his clients like him better when he is dirty; the prostitute Herzog meets at the police station is probably successful because of her "dirty ways."

Thus we have all of Stern's psychological problems, with the difference that in *Herzog* the "Reality Professors," the well-integrated, virilely aggressive males, are Jews and not Gentiles. However, they are Jews with all the characteristics of Anglo-Saxon Protestants, and they are all devoted to the American dream. Shura, his brother, Sandor Himmelstein, his wife's lawyer, Aunt Zipporah, et al., have all adopted the philosophy of the taxi driver who is ready to "bust the sonofabitch on the head" with his jack if he touches his cab. Herzog, in spite of his respectable profession, his intelligence, and his many heterosexual experiences, will always be a child with homoerotic tendencies. There is little difference between Bellow's character and William Maxwell's Lymie. Herzog can no more bridge the gap that separates him from the hockey players (an eminently virile sport, like boxing or football), than Lymie can *become* Spud, his handsome, athletic, well-adjusted hero. Passive, masochistic, erratic, maladjusted to American reality, Herzog will never be one of these vigorous and healthy young men, "swift, padded, yellow, black, red, rushing, slashing, whirling over the ice."

It is only fitting that the subject of masochistic passivity has been taken up by some Jewish novelists: from the beginning of history, the Jew has been the prototype of the passive victim of Judeo-Christian society, a victim who—according to such authors as Irving Howe or Theodore Reik—actually needs his tormentor. The "Jewish novel" made its appearance in American literature in the 1930s after Dreiser, who paved the way for second-generation American novelists. The Jews then began to speak up, as Leslie Fiedler has noted in his retracing of the history of the Jewish novel.

The Jewish protagonists of Daniel Fuchs, Nathanael West, and Philip Roth are all victims, antiheroes. The Jew came into his own in American literature after World War II, and Jewish writers began to play a predominant role. Jews became critics, dramatists, and novelists—Philip Rahv, Arthur Miller, Leon Uris, Irwin Shaw, Herman Wouk, Saul Bellow, Philip Roth, Bruce Jay Friedman, and others. However, the protagonists of Shaw, Uris, or Wouk bear no resemblance to the protagonists of Miller, Friedman, or Roth. Just as Gore Vidal destroyed the stereotype of the passive, effeminate, timid homosexual, Irwin Shaw made Noah Ackerman into an antischlemiel. He is brave, violent, and a fighter. Greenwald, in *The Caine Mutiny*, is more Anglo-Saxon than the Anglo-Saxons. One must thus avoid overgeneralization when placing certain Jewish novelists in the feminine-masochist continuum. Although it is obvious that Joseph, Stern, Leventhal, or Herzog are of the feminine-masochist type, it is equally obvious that other Jewish protagonists have been depicted as being just as brutal, aggressive, and pugnacious as the Gentile males that fascinate, appall, and attract the Sterns and Josephs. Bellow has depicted both types of Jew, for that matter: in Herzog, we have the Jewish "Reality Professors," who are on a par with Allbee, the tormentor in *The Victim*—or with Fitzgerald's handsome brutes. Stern, Joseph, Leventhal, or Herzog, however, are moral or erogenous masochists, with obvious homosexual traits. Friedman and Bellow both connect this feminine passivity to the Jewish religion and Jewish upbringing; it is not surprising that the descendants of persecuted forebears should adopt a masochistic attitude toward their tormentors. And just as certain American homosexuals, having gained awareness after Vidal, have forced themselves into an aggressive stance, just as masochism can at any moment turn into its opposite, sadism—as psychologists since Krafft-Ebing have been well aware—so the Jew contains both tendencies, one of which will take precedence according to the socioeconomic status of the country in which he lives. (Cf. Leslie Fiedler, "Saul Bellow," in *The Prairie Schooner*, Summer 1957.)

Chapter Seventeen

Jack London: The Hypervirile Syndrome

The Work

The Hero's Body

Jack London's hero is an *incarnate* hero: he forces himself upon weak, civilized, readers by the muscular weight of his virile presence. Meeting him is a chastening experience, for he makes us discover all of our own shameful, submasculine softness. Every inch of this athlete is explored: our eyes travel over the features of his face, our fingers test the weight of his shoulders, the curve of his thigh, the hardness of his calves. The actions of this demigod mean less than the way he moves, his raised arm with its bulging biceps, his inflated chest, the tension in his legs. Wolf Larsen, Joe, and Pat Glendon all have, as Maxwell Geismar has noted, "the same kind of body essentially which you find glorified by popular 'health cults.'"

Wolf Larsen's body fascinates the narrator of *The Sea-Wolf*. We are constantly being told that he is "beautiful in the masculine sense." The epithets employed to describe him are "savage" and "terrible." When the narrator sees him naked for the first time, he gasps: before him stands a superman, a "god." The narrator is an expert in masculine anatomy! Picked up after a shipwreck by a vessel under Wolf Larsen's command, the narrator is ordered to sleep on the forecastle with the other sailors, and he observes their bodies with lively interest. He notes that no matter how muscular they are, they all have defects: "an insufficient development here, an undue development there, a twist or crook that destroyed symmetry, legs too short or too long, or too much sinew and bone exposed, or too little." Wolf Larsen, on the other hand, is perfection incarnate, and when he raises his arm, his muscles play beneath his skin. Firmly ensconced on the deck of his ship, he grips the surface with his toes, bringing into relief all the muscles in his legs. He orders Humphrey to feel them: "They were as hard as iron," sighs the conquered narrator.

The eponymous Martin Eden is perhaps less superhuman in appearance, but he has little to envy Wolf when it comes to muscles and virility. With his muscular bull's neck, his health and strength, he feels his biceps with his hand while standing in front of his mirror, and when he raises his arm in front of Ruth—always the same gesture—the muscle swells up and becomes "heavy and hard." Brissenden, the skinny intellectual who plays vis-à-vis Martin the same role Humphrey plays vis-à-vis Wolf Larsen, cries out in admiration, "Ah, you young Greek! . . . I wonder if you take just pride in that body of yours? You are devilish strong. You are a young panther, a lion-cub."

London scarcely bothers to vary his descriptive vocabulary or tone. Burning Daylight, in the novel of the same name, is also "eminently handsome, magnificently strong, almost bursting with a splendid virility." And the father of Pat Glendon, the young boxer in *The Abysmal Brute*, invites Stubener to admire his son's body: "'Tis the true stuff. Look at the slope of the shoulders, an' the lungs of him. . . . you're looking at a man . . . the like of which was never seen before. Not a muscle of him bound." There are many other examples in any one of London's works. Joe, Hans Welson, and all the rest strike us first by their athletic builds, like those of Greek gods, as beautiful animals the author describes for us in minute detail (cf. *The Game*, and "The Unexpected").

Yet London's hero must not be merely strong and robust; his body must also be graceful. Ponta and Powers are only heavy, brutish animals, and London compares them unfavorably to the masculinity of their adversaries, Joe and Pat. The hero in *The Game* is described by animal metaphors—he is a lion-cub, a tiger, and a wolf—yet he also has traits that soften and *feminize* him. His enormous muscles are covered with the softest skin imaginable. Wolf Larsen's skin is like satin, and "his body, thanks to his Scandinavian stock, was fair as the fairest woman's." Joe's cheek is "soft and smooth as a girl's," and Genevieve thinks him "pretty" when she sees him for the first time. (She quickly retracts this, however, when she becomes fully aware of his undeniable masculinity: "He must be handsome, then," she says to herself.) Later we are given a more precise description, and we see the ambiguous face of a cherub on the body of a boxer: "girl-cheeked, blue-eyes, curly-headed," the skin of his body "fair as a woman's, far more satiny." Martin Eden can also pride himself on the fact that there are "few pale spirits of women who could boast fairer or smoother skins than he"; his mouth "might have been a cherub's mouth." The severity of the hero's face is almost always softened by a "curl" at the corner of his lips: Burning Daylight, Dick Forrest, Pat Glendon, Joe, and others all have this firm yet tender mouth, "the lips of a fighter and of a lover."

Thus, with an interesting regularity, Jack London introduces some feminine feature here and there in his hypervirile hero. The androgynous creature with muscles of steel beneath a woman's skin, his lips either "full and sensual" or "stern and harsh, even ascetic," seems to be created from a familiar dream, doubtless the same dream that impelled Melville to create the character of Billy Budd, the beautiful, androgynous sailor, and to cherish the memory of Jack Chase.

In *The Game* Joe is described through Genevieve's eyes as she watches him half-naked in the ring. Without quite realizing why, she is moved, and she hardly dares look at him because she feels it is "sinful." When she finally summons her courage, she contemplates a beautiful demigod. Ruth also feels strong attraction intermingled with guilt when she looks at Martin Eden's sensual body. Maud Sangster, the heroine of *The Abysmal Brute,* becomes a woman at the touch of Pat's hands. Pat, whom his father describes from a "technical" point of view, is revealed sensually through the girl's eyes: "She studied his fine countenance, the eyes clear blue and wide apart, the well-modelled, almost aquiline, nose, the firm, chaste lips that were sweet in a masculine way in their curl at the corners."

The Embrace

When London wants two men to embrace, he makes them fight, or, in a world without women, dance together. Most often, the heroes are intertwined in a struggle, in hand-to-hand combat. In the ring, Joe and his adversary fight before Genevieve—who has slipped into the arena disguised as a boy. The referee has difficulty keeping the boxers apart: "It took all his strength to split those clinging bodies, and no sooner had he split them than Joe fell unharmed into another embrace and the work had to be done all over again. In vain when freed, did Ponta try to avoid the clutching arms and twining body. . . . each time Joe . . . caught him in his arms" We are not quite as disconcerted as the innocent Genevieve, who wonders what pleasure her boy friend can possibly find in this "brutal" struggle, in these "fierce clutches," in such "terrible hurts." For her part, she offers "rest," "content," "sweet, calm joy," and yet, when Joe holds her in his arms, he turns his head to "listen to that other and siren call she would not understand." This is a very Laurentian dilemma, reminding us of Rupert's vacillations between his love for Ursula and the homoerotic attraction he feels for Gerald. The wrestling scene in *Women in Love,* obviously homosexual, sheds light on the scene in *The Game.* The "other call" Joe hears announces the attraction of masculine love that Rupert Birkin will also experience. The same situation is also described in a letter from London to his future wife, Charmian:

> I have held a woman in my arms who loved me and whom I loved, and in that love-moment have told her, as one will tell a dead dream, of this great thing I had looked for, looked for vainly, and the quest of which I had at last abandoned. And the woman grew passionately angry, and I should have wondered had I not known how pale and weak it made all of her that she could ever give me.
>
> For I had dreamed of the great Man Comrade . . .
> [Quoted by Charmian London, *The Book of Jack London,* Vol. II, p. 81.]

For Jack London, dancing is the same as struggle. Although Burning Daylight avoids dances where women are present, he likes dancing with a man—"upon whose arm was tied a handkerchief to conventionalize him into a woman"—until his partner falls from exhaustion. In the frontier world, where there were few women, dancing was always "a test of endurance for one man to whirl another down." Burning Daylight, with revealing haste, without even catching his breath, "still reeling and staggering and clutching at the air with his hands . . . caught the nearest girl and started in on a waltz." Although he is careful to choose a male partner who will be worthy of him, he catches "the nearest girl." She restores the character's virility, imperiled by a homoerotic embrace; the author uses her to mitigate the ambiguity of the embrace and to make it acceptable to the reader, and perhaps to himself as well.

The Woman's Role

The typical London hero is a man without women. As a youth, he is frightened of sexuality, of heterosexuality. For Joe, in *The Game*, "woman had no part in his cosmos. His imagination was . . . untouched by woman." When Joe sees Genevieve for the first time (he is twenty years old), London uses the following words to describe his hero's amazement: "He had never dreamed a girl could be so beautiful."

Burning Daylight is not a lady's man either, although all women are attracted by his virile beauty. He is, first and foremost, a "man's man," at home in the saloon or among the prospectors, and—like Martin Eden—he regards women as "toys," as "playthings, part of the relaxation from the bigger game of life." Although he will dance with either men or women, he prefers the company of men, since he is wary of love: "But comradeship with men was different from love with women. There was no servitude in comradeship . . . comradeship was different. There was no slavery about it." There is some justification for stating that Burning Daylight places love for women and male comradeship on the same level, as though it were merely a question of coolly choosing between these two types of human relations.

Burning Daylight's treatment of women as sex objects indicates his basic fear of women. The author gives the primal reason behind his panic: at sixteen, "Queen Anne," a girl of easy virtue (obviously modeled on "Queen Mamie," London's first conquest), seduced him, and he found their love-making grotesque. Furthermore, he was born in a gold prospectors' camp, and his mother died when he was a baby. Thus he goes out with girls only out of "masculine pride," in order to act like a real man: "No lamb had ever walked with a wolf in greater fear and trembling than had he walked with them."

Pat Glendon is an earlier version of Carson McCullers' soldier and of Bo Decker, the hero of *Bus Stop*. His father explains to Stubener that "he's woman-shy—they'll not bother him for years. He can't bring himself to understand the creatures, and damn few of them has he seen at that." When a schoolmistress makes advances to him, Pat runs away into the woods, where he hides all night, and he begs his father to burn the letters she has written to him.

Before their Encounter with Woman, London's heroes are pure to the point of asexuality, and they take their pleasure (offstage, as it were) merely to be like other men—but without evincing any enthusiasm whatsoever—or merely to satisfy their sexual needs; they do not form attachments with females. All the heroes would appear to follow the advice Pat's father gives him (advice repeated by the father of the soldier Williams), according to which women are "death an' damnation." Pat's father adds, "But when you do find the one, the only one, hang onto her." The one woman will be Maud Sangster for Pat, Ruth Morse for Martin, Dede Mason for Burning Daylight, Genevieve for Joe, Maud Brewster for Humphrey.

The typical London heroine is either an ethereal young girl, a princess in a tower, or a tomboy. We need not point out at this stage that these are hardly unfamiliar types in American literature. (Maxwell Geismar, among others, has done this for us. Genevieve experiences carnal desire upon seeing Joe's half-naked body *while she is dressed as a boy*. Dede, with whom Burning Daylight finally comes to experience conjugal bliss, is his "comrade and playfellow and joyfellow," and has "a boyish way of throwing her head back" when she laughs. His declaration of love is ambiguous: he tells her he is looking for "a real friend, man or woman, the kind you chum with, you know, that you're glad to be with and sorry to be away from." Maud Sangster is also a tomboy: she is a journalist, an athlete, a tennis player, and plays polo on a male team. She has had little interest in men before succumbing to Pat's charms. Yet she is also "daintily feminine." In other words, she is androgynous, as are so many of London's heroines, in particular Frona Welse (*A Daughter of the Snows*), Edith Nelson ("The Unexpected"), or Joan Lackland (*Adventure*).

The Sea-Wolf

Humphrey is picked out of the sea by a captain who is hypervirile to the point of sadistic brutality. The narrator describes himself in images that lend him a feminine aspect. He is violently attracted to the body of his host-tormentor, and once subjugated, in thrall to his masculine beauty, he abandons himself to adoration of his hero. The narrator knows or senses that this dazzling virility is of a kind to "fascinate and dominate women till they surrender in a gladness of joy and relief and sacrifice." However, the reader knows that Humphrey has never been sensually interested in women and that in his emotional life he has been "a monkish fellow." And he is inordinately interested in the male body: under an aesthetic pretext he compares the sailors' bodies with the eye of a connoisseur. When he sees Wolf Larsen's naked body, he gasps: he drops the roll of bandage he is holding to bind the captain's wounds, "unwinding and spilling" it on the floor. Gradually, through contact with Captain Larsen and his rough crew, he himself becomes more virile, though he regresses many times. When he falls exhausted while participating in maneuvers, he says, "I gave up like a woman."

The child learns to assume responsibility and his masculine role through the psychological process of introjection and identification. Humphrey, in order to become worthy of his father, of Wolf Larsen, imitates him and takes inspiration from his strength and his courage, while at the same time he hates and fears him. Humphrey wants to kill Wolf to free the "family," and the struggle which they engage in over Maud (who is later compared to a mother) reflects the love-rivalry between father and son in the Oedipal conflict. By becoming an adult, the child becomes virile and able to objectivize his sexuality. The narcissistic projection that impels Humphrey to homoerotic admiration for the physical beauty of Wolf and the crew—and to find himself, by comparison, unworthy and effeminate—is metamorphosed into heterosexuality. Soon, he can admire women *sexually*, whereas before he had "failed . . . in grasping much of the physical characteristics of love."

At the beginning of their relationship, he regards Maud as "a creature goddesslike and unapproachable." He finally attains sexual (heterosexual) maturity when, having escaped from Wolf and arrived on the island, he kills the seals in order to make a shelter with their skins. This last, virilely aggressive act finally makes him completely masculine. Henceforth he will protect his companion and allay her fears: "I shall never forget, in that moment, how instantly conscious I became of my manhood. . . . I felt myself masculine, the protector of the weak, the fighting male." Humphrey becomes a true adult, and he is freed, to all intents and purposes, from his complexes when he ties Wolf up and Wolf dies.

The novel is almost a *Bildungsroman,* a chronicle of sexual maturation. Humphrey emerges from the ambiguities of adolescence by following the route from narcissism to sexual objectivization. The symbolic events along this route are easily discernible: he is *reborn* when he is rescued and enters a new world of primitive brutality. His attraction to Maud's grace and tenderness is natural, since she represents the world in which he was raised. They become civilized accomplices seeking escape from the primitive world. In the meantime, however, Humphrey becomes masculinized, *animalized,* and he henceforth feels able to fulfill his true role as a man, as a male, as the protector of his companion. In other words, he overcomes his inferiority complex, which is the frequent cause of thwarted emotional development, and frees himself from fear of the father, which has prevented his emotional and sexual development. However, since his maturation occurs well after adolescence (he is thirty-five), we can read *The Sea-Wolf* as a description of the passage from homoeroticism to heterosexuality.

Adventure

The central figure in all London's novels is always the same: it is Woman. We have already noted that this woman is often masculine and of an independent nature. In *Adventure* she is so much the tomboy, and the author dwells so insistently on her masculine characteristics, that her characterization as "transvestite"—hinted at by the author himself—is irresistible.

On her arrival in the Solomon Islands, Joan Lackland is wearing a Stetson cowboy hat and sporting a Colt 38 on her hip. London quickly adds that she, too—despite her masculine disguise—is "deliciously feminine." Before long, Sheldon—the protagonist—begins to feel that she is "not a woman at all," and to regard their relationship as so pure that "he might have been her brother, or she his brother." Entranced by her androgyny, he considers her "the most masculine and at the same time the most feminine woman he had ever met." Yet he continues to emphasize her masculinity. He notices her "boy's eyes," her fingers "brown with tan . . . exceedingly boyish" that "delighted in doing what boys' fingers did." Mentally and physically she enjoys "swimming and violent endeavor of all sorts." Although she is daring, she "dared no farther than boys' adventures," and she delights in "a sexless *camaraderie* with men." Joan's sexual neutrality reminds him of that of a choirboy. He wonders whether he can awaken the sensual feelings of such a creature, with her (masculine) woman's body and her boyish soul and mind, a girl who dives as well as a man, who is so beautiful and yet not "really a woman."

In fact, he realizes he loves her when he begins to love her masculine attributes, her Stetson, her cartridge belt, her long-barreled gun, and he is then irritated that he has fallen in love with a woman who walks roughshod over conventions and who is so far from his feminine ideal (which is not described). The girl he first loves for her clothing "wasn't really a woman. She was a masquerader. Under all her seeming of a woman, she was a boy, playing a boy's pranks, diving for fish among sharks, sporting a revolver, longing for adventure." He suddenly wonders if he would have loved her in the same way had she been truly feminine, with nothing boyish about her: "Then it rushed in upon his consciousness that he really loved her for what she was, for all the boy in her and all the rest in her."

Sheldon has had little experience of women. In fact, this is only his second experience with love, and on the first occasion "he had been more wooed than wooing; and the affair had profited him little." We are reminded of Pat and Humphrey. Like the latter, Sheldon is isolated among "savages," and therefore the girl must play the role of sexual catalyst. She is more than a sexual companion; she is the representative of a more advanced civilization, of Civilization itself. Even after he discovers he loves her, virile images continue to crowd into his mind: "He nearly told her that she was a most adorable boy. But he checked all such wayward fancies." Sheldon is aware of the suspicious ambiguity of his feelings, for he states, "and such is the perverseness of human nature—I am frank you see—I love you for that, too." In response to her expression of disgust, he goes on: "You have no right to recoil from the mention of my love for you. Remember, this is man-talk. From the point of view of the talk, you are a man. The woman in you is only incidental, accidental, and irrelevant. You've got to listen to the bald statement of fact, strange though it is, that I love you."

He then asks her to marry him, and, to seal the bargain, he offers her his hand "as between men."

Aside from being merely an exotic adventure story, the novel can be summed up as follows: a man living alone among savages, who has little interest in women, falls in love with a tomboy. He is well aware that she is more boy than woman, but after some initial hesitation, after a more or less conscious attempt to repress his love for this "transvestite," this virile—but not overly heterosexual—male admits he loves her for her sexual ambiguity itself. The obsessive repetition of the word "boy" cannot be due entirely to the clumsiness of a thirty-four-year-old, experienced novelist, but would appear to indicate the author's more or less conscious desire to transmit some deeper message.

Although in 1910 the tomboy character was far from a novelty in American fiction, it nevertheless has additional interest in conjunction with London's male characters, with their athletic bodies beneath their feminine flesh, their Greek-god faces that are at once masculine and feminine, their fear of women and quest for purity. It would appear that—like Melville—London dreamed of an androgynous race in a world in which one could be attracted to maleness and still remain a paragon of aggressive virility. (London wrote to Anna Strunsky that male and female were both descended from some androgynous being.)

In both *The Sea-Wolf* and *Adventure*, which share the same confessional atmosphere, the plot is based on a single theme: the ending of sexual deviation or of arrested emotional development. Humphrey escapes from his ambiguous, retarded adolescence by ridding himself of his Oedipus complex—although Maud is in fact only a mother substitute (she is compared to the Earth that replenished Antaeus' strength). Sheldon awakens to heterosexual love through Joan Lackland, an ephebus. In both instances, the transformation occurs under favorable circumstances, since in a world of brutes or savages, the man will sorely feel the lack of civilization and turn to the woman for it. What Humphrey and Sheldon find is more than just a woman; she is a soul-sister, a beloved brother, a brother-spirit. The change is effected by subterfuge: Maud is a companion, and also a mother; Joan is a wife, but also a companion.

The Man

The Author's Body

In looking at photographs of the young Jack London, it is easy to recognize in him the faces of his many similar heroes. The photographs show a blond young man with light eyes, a well-defined mouth drawn back at the corners, a strong chin. In a letter written to Cloudesley Johns dated February 22, 1899, London paints a self-portrait of himself as blond, tan, with gray eyes. Modestly—or with an eye to his masculinity—London does not mention his "beauty," but he tacitly stresses the hallmarks of virility: he tends to gain weight when he lives an outdoor life, and his face is tan "through many long-continued liaisons with the sun." Although he is a bit short, it is because "sailor life shortened me." His face is scarred, and he is missing his front teeth, both defects suggesting he has been in many fights. (In fact, London lost his teeth because of scurvy.) Later, when he had put on weight—like an aging Burning Daylight—and lost his "lean runner's stomach," London fondly remembered his body as a young man's and continued to project into his novels the vigorous and supple figure that had formed the basis for his narcissism. Charmian London, his second wife, quotes a letter an admirer wrote about Jack's body, and his biographer, Richard O'Connor, recalls the words of James Hopper, a student at the University of California, Berkeley, who thought London resembled a "cross between a seagoing Swede on the beach and a Greek god."

Self-virilization

At the age of six, Jack London learned he was a bastard. The fact that he made this discovery through the children of the neighborhood made it all the more traumatic. Richard O'Connor depicts him at ten years of age as a "silent, ingrowing, shy and hesitant" child, with something "tremulous, almost haunted, about his features." London himself, in *John Barleycorn*, tells how ardently he wished to become a man among men; to attain his goal, he frequented with the sailors around the port in Oakland, California, took up sailing as a teenager, and drank in the company of "real men." "As a youth, by way of the saloon I had escaped from the narrowness of woman's influence into the wide free world of men." One perceives his fierce desire to conquer his inferiority complex, created by the circumstances of his birth and by the emotional imbalance in his home life, which was dominated by a harsh, violent, and insensitive mother, a spiritualist adept; his step-father was soft, passive, weak, and incapable. At fifteen London had become a "man among men," a beer-drinker, a daring fighter. He became an "oyster pirate" and bought the *Razzle Dazzle*, a boat which was sold with Queen Mamie, the sixteen-year-old tomboy who introduced him to sex. She is probably the model for Queen Anne, who initiates and *traumatizes* Burning Daylight.

It was during this period that London first became interested in girls. However, his comments and the details he later gave about the awakening of his heterosexual instincts are extremely revealing. He made friends, with a boy of his own age who was an inveterate girl-chaser: "I didn't know anything about girls. I had been too busy being a man. This was an entirely new phase of existence which had escaped me. And when I saw Louis say good-bye to me, raise his hat to a girl of his acquaintance, and walk on with her side by side down the sidewalk, I was made excited and envious. I, too, wanted to play this game." Thus, *the woman is of secondary importance* in this deliberate process of virilization, *but she is a necessary part of it.* Speaking with Joseph Noel about homosexuality, London said—despite his desire to appear tolerant—"A man should love women, and plenty of them."

Several aspects of London's ideas concerning relations with the opposite sex are brought out in *The Kempton-Wace Letters.* He states that although marriage is "the whole life of the woman," for the man it is only an "episode," "a mere side to his many-sided life." He denounces love as "pre-nuptial madness," on which no permanent union should be based. "Conjugal friendship" should be a mixture of "affection" and "comradeship," as lucid and rational as the love between two brothers. London, an only son, obviously somewhat idealized this kind of love.

There are unflattering references to women throughout London's work. In *John Barleycorn* he writes of their "silly superficial chatterings," stating that they are "as primitive, direct, and deadly in their pursuit of biological destiny as the monkeys women were before they shed their furry coats and replaced them with the fur of other animals." In *Mammonart* Upton Sinclair reveals that London had hoped to write another book called *Jane Barleycorn* (to be signed with the pseudonym Jack Liverpool), in which he was planning to denounce female treachery, a poison as noxious as alcohol. He would express his "tragic disillusionment and his contempt for woman as a parasite, a creature of vanity and self-indulgence." Other witnesses have stressed Jack London's contempt for "Jane Barleycorn." Adela St. Johns, in *Final Verdict* (1963), speaking of her visits to London's home, Glen Allen, states that "He never saw women as people. Women weren't really important to him, nor was sex. I never saw Jack particularly attentive to or engrossed by a woman. He was more interested in the men in any gathering."

Above all, London regarded women as tools for procreation. All his life he wanted a son, and he was violently disappointed at the birth of each of his daughters. He drowned his disappointment in alcohol. In August 1904 he wrote to Blanche Partington that he liked women because he had to reproduce. His sexual desire for women was linked to the desire *to reproduce himself*, in the narcissistic sense of the term. As Montherlant has noted (cf. *Les Jeunes Filles*), this is a homosexual desire.

After courting Mabel Applegarth in his youth, London married twice, first Bess Maddern then Charmian Kittredge. His three official relationships with women can be summarized as follows: Mabel was a princess-in-a-tower type, from a more exalted social sphere than his own, and he described her in the character of Ruth in his novel *Martin Eden*. Richard O'Connor speculates that, because of his class complex and his avid desire to improve himself socially, London may have been more in love with Mabel's social position than with Mabel herself. (We are reminded of Fitzgerald.) Bess was chosen for her broad hips: she might have been the mother of "seven sturdy saxon sons and seven beautiful daughters." Charmian was the ideal, androgynous creature that haunted his novels long before London met her in the flesh. Charmian was not pretty; she was a tomboy, and she boxed and fenced like a real man; she was also five years older than London. Indeed, of the three, she best represents the realization of London's twofold dream: an ideal comrade and ideal woman. In this he anticipated D. H. Lawrence.

The Ideal Comrade

It is obvious from London's letters that his search for the ideal comrade was a real emotional need, a need that may in part explain his socialist tendencies. In 1899, at the age of twenty-three, he spoke of his quest to Cloudesley Johns—whom he had not yet met, but whose letters had led him to hope that he might be a possible incarnation of his Ideal. "All my life I had sought an ideal chum—such things as ideals are never obtainable, anyway. I never found the man in whom the elements were so mixed that he could satisfy, or come anywhere near satisfying my ideal. A brilliant brain—good; and then the same united with physical cowardice—nil. And vice versa. So it goes and has gone."

He never achieved this hoped-for intimacy with Cloudesley Johns, but he came close to realizing it with the poet George Sterling, whose handsome Greek profile was widely admired. Joan London, Jack's daughter, describes the evolution and the tone of their friendship in interesting terms. She describes George as "tall, slender and graceful." His profile was so perfect that London nicknamed him "Greek." She admits—not without some difficulty—the evident homoerotic aspect of their mutual attraction. "It seems probable that the emotional interplay which continued between them for a number of years revealed this latent homosexuality of which neither was aware." She adds that both men "naively declared their love for each other." London's letters to Sterling, although terse, confirm their readiness to state their affection for each other. In June 1903 London tells him he is sorry not to know him better; they have never "touched the intimately personal note." He attempts to understand Sterling and "to lay hands on the inner side" of his friend. During the voyage of the Snark, he ends a letter thus: "Charmian sends loads of love. I send you all mine." What, we wonder, was left for Charmian, the ideal wife?

In an earlier letter London was even more explicit: he wrote to Charmian, his future wife, that he had always dreamed of a friend who would have been "one with me." And he continues:

> As I say, I abandoned the dream of the great Man-Comrade who was to live youth with me, perpetual Youth with me, down to the grave. And then You came . . . into my life. It was not long before I began to find in you the something all-around that I had failed to find in any man; began to grow aware of that kinship that was comradeship, and to wish you were a man. . . .
>
> And then, by the time I was convinced of the possibility of a great comradeship between us, and of the futility of attempting to realize it, something else began to creep in—the woman in you twining around my heart.

It was inevitable. But the wonder of it is that in a
woman I should find, not only the comradeship and
kinship I had sought in men alone, but the great
woman-love as well; and this woman is You, You!

This letter clearly reveals London's narcissism, his desire to
love someone like himself—which Adela St. Johns mentions—
and which is the reason for the sameness of the bodies and characters of his heroes and heroines. The desire to melt into another
man, the desire to "be one" with him—we are irresistibly
reminded of Erich Fromm's symbiotic union, a union that *would
not be* sadomasochistic, that would not be based on the masculine-feminine heterosexual schema. London, the hypervirile intellectual, would be united with another hypervirile intellectual.
Arthur Calder-Marshall, however, has lucidly remarked that "the
sort of Man-Comradeship of which Jack London had dreamed
would certainly be impossible outside the bonds of homosexual
marriage, and most improbably within them." Jack London's letter to Charmian is of course a love letter, but it is obvious that
*the woman is regarded as an androgynous substitute for the
ideal male friend.*
    In the light of his letters to Anna Strunsky, Cloudesley Johns,
George Sterling, and Charmian Kittredge we can better understand the meaning implicit in London's "androgynous novels,"
particularly *The Sea-Wolf*, which was written at the time of his
meeting with Charmian, and *Adventure*, written ten years later.
The portraits of both Maud and Joan are based on Charmian,
the woman who reconciled—temporarily—Jack London to
Woman. In *The Sea-Wolf*, the ideal androgynous being's feminine side is emphasized, whereas in *Adventure*, it is her tomboy
side. Humphrey is unable to achieve virility unless the woman is
extremely passive; a tomboy could have played merely the same
devirilizing role Idabel plays vis-à-vis Joel in *Other Voices, Other
Rooms*. The gentle Maud allows him—at little cost!—to be the
active partner. However, the virile but chaste Sheldon finds in
Joan Lackland all the delights of male love, Greek-style, that
"anti-feminine ideal of complete manliness" mentioned by Henri
I. Marrou, an ideal that fascism attempted to hold up for the
modern world.

Racism, Fascism, and Homosexuality

Jack London's racist notions are well known; they may have originated in the warnings his mother, Flora, gave him with regard to "brunette races" who will "stab you in the back" if you allow them to. They may have been given substance by his avid reading of Kipling and by the virulent antioriental feeling prevalent in California during his youth, when the phrase "Yellow Peril" was spoken with terror. The authors who had the greatest influence on London's philosophy of life were Darwin, Spencer, Nietzsche, and Marx. Spencer's theory of "natural selection" attracted this young man, entranced as he was with strength, vigor, and virility; Marx's economic theories suited the son of poor parents who was forced to work from the age of eleven; and Nietzsche's Superman became an Ideal for which to strive. As a correspondent during the Russo-Japanese War, London allowed his antioriental feelings full play, going so far as to state before the Oakland chapter of the Socialist Party, of which he was a member: "What the devil! I am first of all a white man and only then a Socialist." During his marriage to Bess Maddern, London hoped—against all genetic logic—that he would be the father of "seven sturdy saxon sons," and his first heroine, Frona Welse, firmly believes in the supremacy of the descendants of the Viking race.

It is hardly surprising, therefore, that in book after book London emphasizes the whiteness of his heroes' skin. Although a tanned face is the symbol of an outdoor life, of virility, the hero's body is whiter than a woman's: London tells us that Wolf Larsen's "bronze ended with his face. His body, thanks to his Scandinavian stock, was fair as the fairest woman's." When Martin Eden looks at himself in the mirror, he is surprised by "the brown sunburn of his face. . . . He had not dreamed he was so black, he rolled up his shirt-sleeve and compared the white underside of the arm with his face. Yes he was a white man after all."

London's work always contains a contrast between the dark and graceless Latin and the light-eyed blond (who may be suntanned): Joe fights an opponent "lacking in intelligence and spirit," "swarthy to blackness, and his body . . . covered with a hairy growth that matted like a dog's on his chest and shoulders." Pat Glendon fights Powers in front of Maud, who compares "the thoroughbred" Pat with Powers, the brunet, the "abysmal brute," his body covered with thick brown hair.

A few colored men find favor with London, but they always have flaws. Oofty-Oofty, the Kanaka in *The Sea-Wolf*—a character straight out of Melville, who was one of London's favorite authors—is extremely handsome, almost as perfect as Wolf Larsen, but whose features, "in so far as [they] pleased, that far had they been what I would call feminine." Burning Daylight's Indian companion, Kama, is virile, strong, and brave, but "he knew the other was the better man, and thus, at the start, he was himself foredoomed to defeat. . . . His attitude toward Daylight was worshipful. . . . No wonder the race of white men conquered, was his thought, when it bred men like this man."

Two other half-breed characters reveal both London's contempt for the nonwhite and his admiration for male physical beauty, *no matter how tanned the skin*. Here is Christian Young, a minor character in *Adventure*: "The blended Tahitian and English blood showed in his soft eyes and tawny skin, but the English hardness was there, and it was what enabled him to run his ketch single-handed and to wring a livelihood out of the fighting Solomons." In *The Road*, we have a handsome, twenty-year-old mulatto who is beaten by the prison warders for trying to defend his human dignity. In real life, Jack and Charmian London gave a home to Nakata, a thirteen-year-old Japanese boy who acted as a substitute son. When he left his masters in 1915 to become a dentist, London felt he had lost a true son: Richard O'Connor writes, "The gap he would leave in Jack's life specially would never be closed."

Although both London's work and his public statements reveal an obvious racism, and although much has been written about his contempt for Orientals and the colored races, he could still make exceptions when physical beauty appeared in a nonwhite.

According to Richard O'Connor, Nazism was "The monstrous but logical culmination of [London's] ideas about Nordic superiority." In *The Psychology of Fascism* Peter Nathan has described the fascist mentality and has shown the extent to which the Nazi ideal is, in fact, a homosexual ideal. (This has also been shown in *The City and the Pillar* and *City of Night*.) Among certain German intellectuals, Nazism was considered a movement that was a direct outgrowth of Spartan civilization, and Jean Genet was fascinated by Hitler's young soldiers. Lawrence, too, flirted with fascism. Nathan's essay seems to be so applicable to London's ideas and his work that it could serve as a conclusion to the analysis of the homosexual component in London's works, especially with regard to their overemphasis on virility, on the woman's role, on the *Führer* mystique, on the sadomasochism of male relationships, their emphasis on chastity, etc.

London was fascinated—as was D. H. Lawrence—by the primitive, animal element in man's nature. In his stories of wolves and dogs he dons an animal's skin. He lauds the brutality of primitive man and violent sexuality, both of which he regarded as the natural expressions of noncivilized man or woman. The male in an English slum is right to beat his wife—it is a natural act. The less civilized the male, the closer he is to the beast. However, as an artist London was unable to indulge himself completely in his yearning for unalloyed brutality; thus the compromise of his burly and tender heroes, who are at once violent and robust and have a feminine sensitivity in their eyes. Joe's gesture of abandoning himself in his opponent's arms in the ring, in the arms of the primitive brute, is a symbolic one. He is Jack London himself, homoerotically seduced by the sirens of complete, primitive, animalistic virility, and performing before the woman he loves, the gentle, pure Genevieve, dressed as a boy. Psychological conflict like this—which prefigures the conflict of Birkin and of Lawrence himself—is allowed no outlet by Western civilization.

Alcohol

The insoluble dilemma of the latent homosexual in Judeo-Christian civilization leads to a neurosis that some men attempt to drown in alcohol. Marie Bonaparte, in a painstaking examination of the homosexual component in Edgar Allan Poe's work, has written, "Poe . . . used to drink, as is generally the case, because of a latent homosexuality. He never drank alone, but always with boon companions." Making a clear distinction between overt homosexuality and Poe's latent homosexuality the Freudian analyst adds: "As is the general rule with all hard drinkers, the homosexuality he gratified with boon companions was latent but deep-rooted."

London's case is similar. In his introduction to London's antialcoholic tract, *John Barleycorn,* Arthur Calder-Marshall connects London's dipsomania to a neurosis caused by his traumatic discovery of his illegitimacy and by his unstable home life. Richard O'Connor remarks that London—although his stated aim was to fight alcoholism—described with a certain nostalgia "the warm comradeship engendered by drinking, of the exhilarating atmosphere of the saloon." Since its publication, *John Barleycorn* has been made the subject of psychoanalytical comment, and the conclusions reached anticipate those of Marie Bonaparte with regard to Poe. In an article entitled "John Barleycorn Under Psychoanalysis" Wilfrid Lay finds in the tract, and in London's work as a whole, "traits of Sadism-Masochism, homosexuality and extraversion to a high degree."

This confirms the general impression derived from London's works and his life. Although London probably never had homosexual relations, since that would have destroyed his ideal of virility, he spent his life searching for a way out of this impasse: how can a man realize his basic, homoerotic desires in a civilization in which, *according to a cultural postulate,* the homosexual is a subhuman effeminate? Jack London's search for a comrade, for a "double" (which Marie Bonaparte links to homosexuality), his two marriages illustrative of his attitude toward women, his promiscuity, his fierce determination to be "a man among men," his narcissistic, racist, protofascist adulation of a Superman with a woman's skin, his alcoholism, his desire to "reproduce himself in a son, his fondness for primitive and brutal animalism (cf. the actual "bodily" relationship between Buck and his master in *The Call of the Wild,* which the conscience accepts more readily than if the relationship were between two men), his socialist ideas—everything about London can be explained by his latent and persistent homosexuality.

Joan London maintains that London was unconscious of it. This is entirely possible, if we recall that Freud's work did not begin to appear in translation in the United States until 1910, and that London read Freud and Jung around 1915. Charmian London nevertheless believes that her husband began to write dog stories in 1915 partly because "they took his mind off people, whose murkily sex-motivated depths he had so recently come to suspect." Thanks to Joseph Noel, however, we now know that London was familiar with homosexuality as early as his first sea voyage at seventeen. Michael Monahan, we are told, expressed the opinion that all homosexuals ought to be hanged, but London replied, "Sailors are that way too. Prisoners in cells are also that way. Wherever you herd men together and deny them women their latent sex perversions come to the surface. It's a perfectly natural result of a natural cause." And he went on to describe the "fo'castle lovers," as he called them.

So London was aware of what homosexuality was all about; like Melville, he had seen sailors practice it. It is also likely that his stay in the Niagara Falls jail had opened his eyes, as he seems to suggest in *The Road*. Both experiences appear to have led him to associate homosexuality with brutality and violence. As a civilized man and as a writer, he had to dissociate himself from such "unprintable" and "unthinkable" horrors (*The Road*). At the same time, he dreamed of a virile, intimate, ardent, total, *but pure* love with an alter ego who would be both virile and tender. His desire to be a "real man," to reproduce himself, *forced* him to heterosexuality, although his basic sexual instinct was probably homosexual.

Jack London is one of the most striking examples of a psychological conflict between the homosexual instinct, fostered by childhood emotional insecurity, and the fervent desire to be a man among men in a society that relegates the homosexual to the status of an effeminate submale, a woman. Although London attempted to sublimate his homosexuality by dissociating it from effeminacy on the one hand, and from the "fo'castle lovers"—primitive and brutal—on the other, his attitude toward women and his narcissistic adoration of the male's white and muscular body, along with his search for masculine love, clearly show that he failed in his task—not of virilization, for he was virile, but of objectivizing his sexuality. His subterfuges are many and varied, but in the end they merely shed an even brighter light on the insolubility of his problem. Charmain London was perhaps correct when she linked his discovery of Freud and psychoanalysis to the psychological depression that was undoubtedly one of the reasons for his suicide.

Freud's *Three Essays on the Theory of Sexuality,* which appeared in translation in 1910, explains the human "perverseness" —sexual ambiguity—of which London wrote in *Adventure.* Recalling that it was at this same period that London was planning to write a ferocious denunciation of women, we wonder whether London did not later realize—at forty—that all his life he had been playing games with the truth, the truth about himself.

Chapter Eighteen

Ernest Hemingway: The (Almost) Total Sublimation of the Homosexual Instinct

In Part I, I mentioned the typical homosexual figure in Ernest Hemingway's work: the author of "The Mother of a Queen" was not overfond of the effeminate man, and in his eyes every homosexual was effeminate and vice versa. Carlos Baker, one of his biographers, confirms this impression, and relates several anecdotes in which Hemingway is shown to have been a pre-eminent "nance-slugger." Tennessee Williams was also aware of this reputation, but nevertheless he showed up for a meeting with Hemingway that had been organized by Kenneth Tynan, even though he demurred that Hemingway "usually kicks people like me in the crotch."

As fate would have it, however, Hemingway was obliged throughout his life to combat the rumor that underneath his hypervirile exterior he was a follower of Socrates. Zelda Fitzgerald so accused him to her husband, and Fitzgerald passed on to him some remarks made by Robert MacAlmon; at one time a homosexual posing as Hemingway gave lectures coast to coast, and spent several weeks at the Explorer's Club in New York lunching with various young men. (Hemingway believed that this deception was the cause of his doubtful reputation.) Virginia Woolf, in her essay *Men Without Women*, found something unnatural about Hemingway's virility, and Max Eastman, writing in *The New Republic*, stated that the author of *Death in the Afternoon* was posing as a virile male because he was not really a "full-sized man." One critic described Hemingway's style as like "false hair on the chest." Hemingway had constantly to defend himself against such accusations, often going so far as to beat up his detractors.

The Hero

Philip Young has pointed to the mixture of passivity and tenderness in the adolescent Nick Adams, the Hemingway hero par excellence. Nick is both "tough" and "wounded." William Bysshe Stein has noted that the Freudian list of phallic, symbolic wounds in Hemingway's work is interminable. "Nick is injured in the leg and Robert Jordan in the thigh. Harry in 'The Snows of Kilimanjaro' dies of a gangrened limb; Colonel Cantwell wears a scar on his knee; Harry Morgan in *To Have and Have Not* loses an arm; Lieutenant Henry in *A Farewell to Arms* and Jake Barnes in *The Sun Also Rises* are comparably afflicted." Georges-Albert Astre has linked this fictional wound to the wound Hemingway himself received in the First World War and to his resultant castration anxiety, as well as to a horror of sex, and its corollary, a desire for purity that cannot be realized as long as man desires women. A short story entitled "God Rest You Merry, Gentlemen," supports this interpretation, depicting the torture of an adolescent who demands to be castrated to put an end to his impure thoughts.

Hemingway's male protagonists are rarely described physically. Though we know Nick Adams is an adolescent, healthy in mind and body, we are not told how he looks. The description of Pedro Romero (*The Sun Also Rises*), the bullfighter who symbolizes strength, courage, and virility, is meager compared to the precision with which a Jack London hero is described. All we are told is that "his black hair shone under the electric light," and that he is "the best-looking boy" the narrator has ever seen. Everyone, from Montaya to the narrator, including the heroine, Lady Brett, is enthralled by his virile beauty. The narrator, Jake Barnes, on several occasions stresses the fact that Romero is the most handsome boy he knows. Hemingway's descriptions of his heroes' physiques are singularly terse and ridden with cliches. In *A Farewell to Arms* Frederick Henry's Italian friend is introduced lying on his bed in the room they share: ". . . with his eyes closed. . . . He was good-looking, was my age, and he came from Amalfi." Robert Jordan, the protagonist of *For Whom the Bell Tolls,* has a disincarnate, lean body. At forty, he is "tall and thin, with sun-streaked fair hair, and a wind-and-sun-burned face."

Philip Young has drawn a careful distinction between the two types of Hemingway heroes: the "code-hero" and the "Hemingway hero." The former is the embodiment of the virile ideal that has inspired the latter, who is the author's alter ego. Thus, Pedro Romero and Santiago (*The Old Man and the Sea*) are code-heroes, whereas Jake, Frederick, and Robert Jordan suffer from the doubt, fear, and anxiety of their wounds. A third category of male characters, submen, womanly men, contains the homosexuals, the effeminate men, and the cowards. The categories are not rigid, however, as is shown by the vivid metamorphosis of Francis Macomber, or by the rapid breakdown of Pablo in *For Whom the Bell Tolls.*

"Heterosexualization"

Francis Macomber, the eponymous protagonist of "The Short Happy Life . . ." is thirty-five years old, as was Humphrey in *The Sea-Wolf.* He undergoes the same process of belated virilization. Physically he is a fine figure of a man, a sportsman, an accomplished big-game hunter, the perfect 1930s American—up to and including his crew-cut hair. His deeper nature, however, suddenly comes to the fore during a lion hunt: he shows himself, "very publicly, to be a coward." In the past, this aspect has been hidden behind the face of a retarded adolescent with regular features and "fine eyes, only faintly shifty." Like the Prussian officer, his eyes indicate the inner flaw beneath the rigid carapace.

In this story, the virile ideal is personified by Wilson, the guide, with his exemplary courage and his healthy sexuality. The gun symbolism makes this clear—it is both an emblem of courage and an emblem of virility: "Robert Wilson came up then carrying his short, ugly, shockingly big-bored 505 Gibbs and grinning." The ugliness and shocking size of the gun says a lot about the author's ambivalent sexual feelings: a mixture of admiration and of fear. Macomber, who has just publicly demonstrated his cowardice by fleeing from a lion, is obviously impotent, in line with the Hemingway principle that equates courage with sexual power. In Wilson's eyes, cowardice immediately evokes homosexuality: Francis Macomber seems to be a "poor beggar," a "poor sod," a "fag." However—and the point is revealing—Wilson is so firmly established in his impregnable virile fortress that, far from making fun of Francis, he is able to pity him and retain his affection, while, although he uses Margot Macomber, Francis's wife, sexually, he despises her as a bitch who in his eyes, embodies all the bad qualities of the American woman.

Wilson is something like Wolf Larsen insofar as he embodies the father model with whom one must identify. His weapon, so cruel in appearance, gives him a sadistic appeal; Francis (whose name, as Robert W. Lewis reminds us, is almost feminine) is similar to Humphrey Van Weyden, who acquired virility through contact with the virile ideal. Although Humphrey clearly appeared to be a latent homosexual, this is not so obvious in Francis's case; the important thing, however, is that in the father's eyes—in Wilson's eyes—the son's weakness is naturally linked to adolescent sexual ambiguity, or to the impotence of the latent homosexual. "Look at the beggar now, Wilson thought. It's that some of them stay little boys so long, Wilson thought. Sometimes all their lives. Their figures stay boyish when they're fifty. The great American boy-men." When Macomber earns virility by killing a lion, thereby becoming an adult and thus "heterosexual," Wilson deduces that this "probably meant the end of cuckoldry too." In Hemingway, as in London, retarded virilization is linked to the passage from latent homosexuality to active heterosexuality. In Hemingway, cowardice is always the symptom of a latent homosexuality, as in *For Whom the Bell Tolls*.

The Loss of Heterosexuality

At the beginning of the Spanish Civil War, Pablo, Pilar's husband, was one of the chiefs of the Republican resistance; he was virile, cruel, and feared. As the novel opens, he is shown in a different light: he has acquired some horses by stealing them from the fascists, and now would prefer to leave the guerrillas and live as a solid private citizen. Just as Francis Macomber, prior to his virilization, was the opposite of Wilson, in this novel Pablo is the contrast to Robert Jordan, the courageous and heterosexual hero (he is the only male character in the novel to have sexual relations). Pablo is described by two characteristics: he is *flojo* (flaccid), and he loves horses. His wife, Pilar, who has assumed all the virile qualities as her husband has abandoned them, is now the hard, "active" element of the two (as was Margot Macomber). The first character in the novel to employ a sexual image to describe Pablo's cowardice is Old Anselmo: "'But since a long time he is *muy flojo*,' Anselmo said. 'He is very flaccid. He is very much afraid to die.'" To be afraid to die is to be unvirile and not an active heterosexual. Later, Anselmo speaks of Pablo's glorious past deeds and thinks, "And now he is as finished and as ended as a boar that has been altered." Robert Jordan makes reference to Pilar's husband's "lost eggs." Pilar is even more precise and openly talks about his devirilization, his cowardice, and homosexuality. "Take your bad milk out of here, you horse exhausted *maricon*." (*Maricon*=faggot.)

Obviously, Pablo has become disinterested in his wife as he has lost his courage (i.e., his virility), and has turned his love toward his horses. The first image of him is revealing: he is looking tenderly at the horses. Later, he speaks to one of his stallions, calling him his "lovely white-faced big beauty. . . . Thou art no woman or a fool." Agustín calls Pablo a "horse lover" and accuses him of "befouling" his steeds. When Pablo captures the horse of a dead fascist, he rubs his leg affectionately against the beast's flank. Thus, Pablo's is an overt homosexuality transferred from man to horse, to the stallion, in accord with his loss of courage and its Hemingway corollary, loss of sexual virility. While Francis Macomber, according to Wilson, becomes "heterosexual" through an act of courage, Pablo becomes "homosexual" because of his growing cowardice. Pilar, a true "code-hero," is always giving certificates of heterosexuality and rescinding them at the least sign of weakness. She is the one who calls Pablo a *maricon*, and who treats Fernando like an "old maid" because he speaks "primly." When Pablo and Jordan are reconciled and converse amicably together before dynamiting the bridge, Pilar asks, "What are you two doing? Becoming *maricones*?"

The Heroine

The Androgyne

Pilar is far more virile than she is feminine. Robert W. Lewis has noted that her love for Maria is ambiguous, to say the least. Pilar seems perfectly aware of it, for that matter, and although she tells the girl, who has reminded her that there is "nothing like that" between them, that she is not a *tortillera* she adds, "There is always something like that. . . . There is always something like something that there should not be." Lewis would appear to be correct in his statement: "She caresses Maria, and her feeling for her is sexual, though in her own mind she denies it." Pilar's androgyny is obvious in her speech and her actions, in her role as chief of the guerrilla band, and her courage, "code"-inspired as it is, is only the extreme manifestation of an androgyny that has been present in all of Hemingway's previous novels.

The mannish Lady Brett uses a man's vocabulary ("Hello, you chaps," "Hello, gents," "I say, give a chap a brandy and soda"), and her hair is "brushed back like a boy's." This is the sexual independence of the 1920s "flapper." She is naturally at ease in a world of men (Jack, Bill, Robert, and Mike), all of whom accept her as a member of the group, one of the boys in the band.

Despite her extreme femininity, Catherine Barkley (*A Farewell to Arms*) talks about cutting her hair and suggests to her lover, Frederick, that he allow his to grow longer: "We'd be just alike only one of us blonde and one of us dark. . . ." She desires to be her lover. Maria, whose love affair is typically short and happy, has her hair cut short all over her head and dresses like her lover in a khaki shirt. She has very small breasts and her body is thin. Jordan repeats Catherine Barkley's suggestion:

> "But in Madrid I thought we could go together to the coiffeur's and they would cut it neatly on the sides and in the back as they cut mine and that way it would look better in the town while it is growing out."
>
> "I would look like thee," she said and held him close to her. "And then I never would want to change it."

One of Robert Jordan's sexual fantasies is Greta Garbo, whom Susan Sontag has called a "camp" figure and whose beauty is androgynous. Brett, Catharine, and particularly Maria are all fairly asexual young women who, with their air of Greek ephebuses, remind us of Joan Lackland, London's heroine. In Hemingway's novel *The Old Man and the Sea* the woman is painlessly metamorphosed into a boy who is the companion of the old fisherman Santiago. When virility no longer has to be a synonym for active heterosexuality, the conscious mind no longer has to have recourse to the tomboy with her firm body, small breasts, and short hair. Eros turns to agape: active heterosexuality melts into sublimated homosexuality (Robert W. Lewis has examined the development of this process).

Philip, the hero of *The Fifth Column*, manages to combine eros and agape by rejecting the American woman in favor of Anita, a Spanish semiprostitute, and his pal Max, whom he loves like a brother and whom he also respects, whereas Dorothy is only "a commodity you shouldn't pay too high a price for." Maria, the total androgyne in *For Whom the Bell Tolls*, is loved only during the space of a brief encounter preceding death, and Jordan frankly tells her that his feeling for her is more fraternal than sexual: "I love thee as I love all that we have fought for. I love thee as I love liberty and dignity . . . and I love all my comrades that have died. . . . But I love thee as I love what I love most in the world and I love thee more." In *The Old Man and the Sea* the author often writes that the boy "loves" the old man, and that the latter "loves" the boy. Here, of course, there is no question of sexual love but merely of deep affection, of totally sublimated sexuality in an atmosphere of complete purity, adrift on the androgynous sea. Philip Young writes of this metamorphosis of the heroine into an ephebus: "In a way we have known the boy before, for in providing that sentimental adulation which is his need for love and pity the other hero once required, Manolin has taken over some of the functions hitherto performed by the heroine." Manolin feeds Santiago and offers him a completely disinterested love. And it is of course no accident that in *Across the River and Into the Trees* Colonel Cantwell calls Renata "Rimbaud," to which she replies, "You'd make an awfully funny Verlaine." This exchange merely maintains the basic imprecision of sexual categories in Hemingway's work.

Hemingway was married four times: Hadley, Pauline, Martha, and Mary. His first two wives, whom he married when he was aged twenty-two and twenty-eight, respectively, were eight and four years older than he. Agnes, his first love, was eight years older. Martha and Mary, who were thirty-seven and forty years old when he met them, were both younger than he at marriage. It is as though Hemingway had first sought a maternal figure and later, when he had become "Papa" Hemingway, had rid himself of his Oedipus complex. Pauline's hair was short like a boy's, and Martha was an active and independent journalist—like Maud in London's *The Abysmal Brute*—who was assigned to the front during the war, and who was a real virile rival to her husband, as Carlos Baker's description of her reveals.

In Hemingway's work, the female character plays various roles, all very like those played by females in London's novels. The woman is a "trap," a sex object or—if she is enough of a tomboy—a companion.

The Trap

The female trap is present throughout *In Our Time*. Bill, Nick Adams's friend, sums up the philosophy all Hemingway's heroes share when he says to his friend, "Once a man's married he's absolutely bitched. . . . He hasn't got anything more. Nothing. Not a damn thing. He's done for." This is also the philosophy of the entourage of Pedro Romero, the bullfighter who cannot marry because he must remain pure to personify the virile ideal. When his mistress becomes pregnant, Frederick Henry feels "trapped," and she frankly admits she wants to "ruin" him. Philip, the hero of *The Fifth Column*, quickly drops Dorothy, who is trying—like any good Anglo-Saxon woman—to fill the primary place in his life, because he must devote himself to the Cause and to his comrades. Similarly, Robert Jordan, at forty, is unmarried and makes several frank statements about women in general, and against his mother, in particular. Quoting at random: "I have no time for any woman." "I like them very much, but I have not given them much importance." And so on. One might also mention Helen, in "Cross-Country Snow," who symbolizes America and the responsibilities of parenthood, and Margot Macomber, who murders her husband when she sees he has become a real man. Margot is the "bitch" prototype, the "female trap" who would rather kill her man than no longer be able to "ruin" him, which is something Catherine Barkley also wants. Hemingway's female trap varies from the gentle Catherine, whose fantasies include the destruction of the male, to Margot Macomber, who carries her fantasies to their logical conclusion. Brett or Maria, the tomboys, are not true traps, since neither is a complete woman; both make a timely exit from the hero's life. Harry in *To Have and Have Not*, the male character in "Hills Like White Elephants," and the protagonist of "The Snows of Kilimanjaro" are all aware that they are being destroyed by a woman (and by money).

The Sex Object

Many of Hemingway's male protagonists—Krebs, Robert Jordan, Philip, etc.,—share Martin Eden's or Burning Daylight's attitude toward women. In "Soldier's Home" Krebs's thoughts recall London's confidences in *John Barleycorn*. Krebs "would have liked to have a girl but he did not want to have to spend a long time getting her. He did not want any consequences. . . . Besides, he did not really need a girl. The army had taught him that. It was all right to pose as though you had to have a girl. Nearly everybody did that. But it was not true. You did not need a girl."

Philip avoids Dorothy and the responsibilities that a liaison with a "nice girl" entail to take carnal and uncomplicated pleasure with the brunet Anita. Leslie Fielder has commented on this aspect of sexuality in Hemingway's work: "The seed-extractors are Indians or Latins, black-eyed and dusky in hue, while the castrators are at least Anglo-Saxon, if not symbolically blond."

Before encountering Woman, Robert Jordan treated women as sex objects, and seemed not to feel much need for active heterosexuality. His partners have all been prostitutes. To Pilar he makes the following London-like confession: "But I have not

found one that moved me as they say they should move you."
This holds true until he meets Maria, the Woman, the same
woman Pat Glendon's father promises his son—and they each
look like a boy endowed with enormous feminine tenderness.

In Hemingway's work, however, eternally happy heterosexual
love is almost completely absent. Catharine Barkley dies in
childbirth; Brett is in love with a bullfighter who must flee the
trap she personifies; Maria *has* to give up her lover, who *must*
die; etc. The heterosexual idyll is short and dull, as in *The Fifth
Column*, or short and passionate, as in *A Farewell to Arms* or
For Whom the Bell Tolls. Eternal love, love that is not destroyed
by events, is reserved for friends, for comrades: this is why neither Santiago (the hero as an old man) nor Manolin (the
ephebus without his female disguise) die at the end of *The Old
Man and the Sea*.

Comrades

In Hemingway's work, the woman is always the "wet blanket,"
the spoiler. In "The End of Something," Nick, the adolescent, no
longer loves Marjorie because he no longer has "fun" with her.
Having sketched for him a frightening picture of conjugal life,
his pal Bill tells him, in "The Three-Day Blow," that had Nick
not got rid of his girl, they wouldn't be together, drinking whis-
key and planning their fishing trip for the next day. With satis-
faction, Bill concludes, "So long as it's over that's all that mat-
ters," adding, "I tell you, Wemedge, I was worried while it was
going on." In "Cross-Country Snow" Nick is with another comrade, George; they enjoy skiing in Europe together because "they
were fond of each other." George, however, must return to the
States to continue his studies. They imagine a wonderful life in
which both would be far from college and wives. (Nick is married, his wife expecting a child.) Their ideal life would be a life
of sports in the company of other men. "Don't you wish we could
just bum together? Take our skis and go on the train to where
there was good running and then go on and put up at pubs and
go right across the Oberland and up the Valais and all through
the Engadine and just take repair kit and extra sweaters and

pyjamas in our rucksacks and not give a damn about school or anything."

"Anything" is Helen, the unborn child, American society . . . who knows what else? George, like Bill, represents the siren call of perpetual comradeship, and Nick answers "No," despite his lack of enthusiasm about returning to the States: "No. Not exactly." But he is unable to explain why it is not really hell for him to have to go back to his wife and expected child. When George asks him to "promise" they will ski together again some day, Nick remarks bitterly that "there isn't any good in promising." They put on their skis once more and pull on their mittens: "Now they would have the run home together."

Sport is again the "link" that unites—*in purity*—the male characters in *The Sun Also Rises* (1926). Like skiing, the fishing trip brings men together and momentarily cuts them off from destructive women. Bill is able to confess his love to Jack without its seeming suspect. For that matter, he says, "Listen. You're a hell of a good guy, and I'm fonder of you than anybody on earth. I couldn't tell you that in New York. It'd mean I was a faggot." In "The Death of Love in *The Sun Also Rises*," Mark Spilka has noted the religious flavor of this male comradeship: "A few days later, when they visit the old monastery at Roncevalles, this combination of fishing, drinking, and male camaraderie is given an edge over religion itself."

The friendship between Henry and Rinaldi (*A Farewell to Arms*) is more emotional because Rinaldi is an Italian. As long as there is a difference in nationality, male contact can go as far as kissing. Rinaldi, in fact, kisses the hero on many occasions, but we note that *the latter never returns his kisses*. On the one occasion the Latin asks Henry to kiss him, the Anglo-Saxon hero replies, "I never kiss you. You're an ape."

The tone of the conversations between these two men who share the same room would be impossible were they both Americans. Rinaldi, a lady's man, appears to lack all the puritan rigidity Bill Gorton referred to. During the war, in Italy, the Anglo-Saxon protagonist allows his Italian comrade to kiss him, to embrace him, to call him "baby," and to tell him he loves him. And it is no accident that Frederick speaks of his friend's beauty as he lies on his bed, while Frederick is washing himself, naked to the waist: "I took off my tunic and shirt and washed in the cold water in the basin. While I rubbed myself with a towel I looked around the room and out the window and at Rinaldi lying with his eyes closed on the bed. He was good-looking, was my age . . ." This is clearly sexual sublimation, which is made even clearer during the scene in which Frederick has come back from the hospital after a knee operation:

> "Well, baby," he said. I sat up on the bed. He came over, sat down and put his arm around me. "Good old baby." He whacked me on the back and I held both his arms. "Old baby," he said. "Let me see your knee."
> "I'll have to take off my pants."
> "Take off your pants, baby. We're all friends here."

Professionally—Rinaldi is a doctor—he probes his friend's knee, while Frederick notes his "fine surgeon's hands," his hair shiny and parted smoothly." Rinaldi later calls Frederick a puritan and reproaches him for being unable to reconcile his sexual needs and his moral sensibilities. Each time Frederick returns from the brothel, he brushes his teeth, "trying to brush away the Villa Rossa from your teeth in the morning. . . . Every time I see that glass I think of you trying to clean your conscience with a toothbrush." He came over to the bed. 'Kiss me once and tell me you're not serious.'"

Rinaldi represents the affectionate Italian without complexes and without sexual problems. He prefigures Giovanni, who reproaches the American David for his Anglo-Saxon rigidity and his ineradicable guilt complex.

When the scene shifts from Italy to Spain, *machismo* regains its prime status. Robert Jordan, caught up in the Spanish Civil War and entrusted with a dangerous mission, has no time either for women or for affectionate masculine friendships. There is nothing of the affectionate and sentimental Italian doctor in Old Anselmo or young Agustín, his Spanish comrades, and Pilar would probably have treated Rinaldi and Henry as *maricones*. Male friendship is evidenced in *For Whom the Bell Tolls* in a more purified, "virile" way. It is interesting that Pablo's homosexuality has been diverted away from men and toward horses, whose flanks he can caress, whose beauty he can brag about, just as the Prussian officer turned from his hated mistresses to long rides on horseback.

Affection among men can only be manifested by gestures. Robert Jordan expresses his affection by putting his hand on the gypsy's shoulder, or by giving Old Anselmo a friendly slap on the back. When Jordan and Agustín spy a group of enemy cavalry, "Robert Jordan noticed he was sweating. He reached over and put his hand on his shoulder. His hand was still there as they saw the four horsemen ride out of the timber and he felt the muscles of Agustín's back twitch under his hand." He also puts his hand on Primitivo's shoulder in order to help him face the fact that it is impossible to save El Sordo's band, which has come under fascist attack. And although he kisses Maria, he puts his hand on Pilar's shoulder, demonstrating that he thinks of her as an equal, as a real guerrilla. If the male character is very young, the entire arm goes around his shoulders. Likewise, when Anselmo, who is old, has stayed at his post in the cold after his relief has failed to turn up, never dreaming of shirking his duty, Jordan indulges in the book's most affectionate gesture of all: "He put his arm around Anselmo's shoulder and held him tight as they walked and shook him."

The supreme mark of affection between these modern versions of Achilles and Patroclus is not the killing of the comrade's murderer but killing the comrade himself if he is so badly wounded that he cannot recover or escape. In the same breath, Robert Jordan sincerely says that he "cared very much" for the Russian Kashklin, and that he killed him. The gypsy recalls that he too had promised the Russian demolitions expert to perform this most exalted rite. In the same manner, after Jordan has been wounded and the fascists are attacking, Agustín, who is Jordan's "disciple," asks him, "'Do you want me to shoot thee, Ingles?' . . . leaning down close. 'Quieres? It is nothing.'" The words are vibrant with affection and tenderness.

When speaking of the fascists, Jordan usually adopts the neutral tones of a technician with a difficult mission, his words are dispassionate; however, his tone becomes emotional when he tells—with discretion—of a friendship between two of Franco's young soldiers. Paco Berrendo has lost Julian, his best friend, who has been killed by El Sordo's men. The author, in brief touches, allows us to glimpse the young man's emotion. Paco is shown as intelligent and a sensitive young officer, able to control his immense grief.

In *The Old Man and the Sea*, friendship is more affectionate; Santiago readily muses that he "loves" the young Manolin with a love that resembles that of master for disciple. "The old man had taught the boy to fish and the boy loved him." Their love is expressed by timid bodily contact. Manolin wakes Santiago by placing his hand on the old man's knee, and Santiago wakes Manolin by taking the boy's foot between his hands and holding it until the child opens his eyes. When the youngster is awake, Santiago makes the same affectionate gesture as Jordan with Agustín, placing his arm around the boy's shoulders. He realizes that Manolin keeps him alive by bringing him food, and by offering him affection in his solitude.

Pablo related his homosexual desires for his horses, which are prime sex symbols: in Hemingway's work, lions, bulls, and fish are also symbols of virility. Robert W. Lewis makes much of the lion and bull in "The Short Happy Life of Francis Macomber," and of the bulls in *The Sun Also Rises*, which are compared to the "steers" who are asexual as old maids. In *The Old Man and the Sea* Santiago's mental linkage between the lion, sexuality, and the boy is clear. The old man "only dreamed of places now and of the lions on the beach. They played like young cats in the dusk and he loved them as he loved the boy. He never dreamed about the boy. He simply woke, looked out the open door at the moon and unrolled his trousers and put them on. He urinated outside the shack and then went up the road to wake the boy."

Sublimation is at work not only with the lions, but also with fish. In *The Sun Also Rises* the fishing party was a symbol of a rich love between comrades, in contrast to the deleterious and impure life of the city; in *The Old Man and the Sea* the battle between Santiago and the fish reminds us of the loving struggle in which love and hate intermingle: "'Fish,' he said, 'I love you and respect you very much. But I will kill you dead before the day ends.'" Carlos Baker quotes a comment made by Janet Flanner which aptly sums up one of the aspects of this love between comrades in Hemingway's work. Speaking of the death struggle between Santiago and the fish, she wrote, "It was the extremest virile sentimentality both in emotion and in writing style that I ever saw. Only hardy Ernest could have two males fighting to the death and loving each other because that's what they are doing."

Throughout Hemingway's work, male comradeship thrives on love and death. Jake Barnes is wounded in the war and able to love both Brett and Bill *purely,* because his sex has become sterile. Rinaldi and Frederick embrace in the atmosphere of the Front, the hospital, and Max and Philip live in the shadow of guns and the torture chamber; Robert Jordan and his guerrillas are aware that death hovers above their cave. Danger, combat, and death are powerful sublimating agents. There is no ambiguous tenderness—which can lead to decadence and make even the strongest man a prey to his senses, to his id. In close contact with danger and death men's bodies become hard, their desires are purified, affection becomes entirely spiritualized. For this reason, Pablo, who dreams of peace, "fouls" his horses and becomes a *maricon.* Against this "perverted" attitude is placed the ideal of virile friendship, symbolized by the act of the warrior who fires a bullet into his wounded friend's head, or by Paco Berrendo, who *does not touch* his friend, who says a prayer for him.

Although London's latent homosexuality is abundantly evident, there is no reason to believe that the accusations of Zelda Fitzgerald—and others—have any basis in fact. On the contrary, Hemingway is the most striking example we have in American letters of the (almost) *perfect sublimation of the homosexual instinct.* We can discern the three facets of latent homosexuality in his work: the cult of pure male friendship, the contempt for women (the counterpart to blatant promiscuity), the constant, conscious effort to be a man among men. However, in Hemingway, all of this appears to be effortless. By comparing the androgynous Maria with Joan (*Adventure*), we can gauge the distance that separates the author whose conscious mind must resort to tricks, and the resolutely heterosexual man who at the same time loves somewhat boyish women. A similar comparison between Humphrey's "heterosexualization" and Francis Macomber's, which are allegories of the passage from latent or overt homosexuality to heterosexuality, reveals the basic difference between homosexual masochism, which derives pleasure from brutality, and the mere anxiety of a man who fears being unworthy of the "code-hero," of the virile ideal he has set for himself.

London and Hemingway represent *two stages of sublimation achieved within American civilization.* London is the repressed homosexual whose conscious mind must find countless excuses—including racism, protofascism, androgyny—to relieve the ego of its guilt complex; Hemingway is the all-American boy who is at ease with his comrades, a big-game hunter, an experienced fisherman, avid for dangerous adventures far from the company of women, narcissistically attracted to strength and masculinity, who only notices a man's beauty if the man has something tender and feminine about him, as in the case of Rinaldi. In Hemingway there is no masochistic admiration for a man such as Wolf Larsen, since Hemingway is perfectly at ease with his own virility, which he carries—like Baldwin's sailor—as naturally as his skin. However—and here is the irreducible paradox of Greco-American virility—the "antifeminine ideal of complete virility" is impossible without a certain contempt for everything that is uniquely feminine. Thus Hemingway's taste for women who are tomboys to some extent, his cult for male sports, his desire to reduce heterosexuality to a brief adventure with no aftereffects. The chronicle of the tender love between an old man and an ephebus ends not in death but in a dream populated by the lions he loves as much as he loves the young fisherman seated beside him.

I am tempted to wonder whether Hemingway might have been the Ideal Comrade for whom Jack London longed. They had the same taste for adventure on sea and on land, the same talents of sailor and war correspondent, the same attitude toward danger, the same love of boxing and other virile sports. Both men, separated by a twenty-three-year gap in age—and who never met, London dying when Hemingway was an adolescent—nourished the same feelings toward women and assigned them identical roles: wife, mother, sex object. Both feared the female's destructive power. One could go on listing points of comparison between these "hypervirile" men, drawing parallels between their sexual bragging, their contempt for "inferior" races, their desperate desire to be a "man's man," which can be summed up in three words: sport, alcohol, and women. Indeed, upon reflection, Melville (whom London greatly admired) might also have been London's ideal comrade. Melville, too, sought throughout his life an ideal comrade, an ideal he thought at one point to have found in Hawthorne. (In this regard, the reader is referred to the excellent spiritual biography of Melville by Edwin Haviland Miller.)

However, although London searched for years for a comrade with whom to share his life, and although he did have such a love-friendship with George Sterling, the same was not true for Hemingway, who was never intimately linked with any man and who inevitably quarreled with his friends. Only toward the end of his life did he form attachments with various young men—Aaron Hotchner or the bullfighter Ordonez—precisely at the time he was engaged in writing *The Old Man and the Sea;* it was as though he were attempting to recapture his youth through a third party, or as though the fact of having become "Papa" Hemingway, of being the father of three grown sons, had in some way liberated his feelings for his comrades.

Chapter Nineteen

Norman Mailer: The Overt Latent Homosexual

Norman Mailer is the descendant of Jack London and Ernest Hemingway. The latter is his hero, the man to whom he most often refers, whom he has consciously imitated—as an individual more than as a writer, since Mailer, having learned at the feet of Dos Passos and Farrell, quickly found his own, personal style, one more reminiscent of Henry Miller or D. H. Lawrence. Mailer began writing during the Second World War, and participated in the "sexual revolution" under Wilhelm Reich's banner. His hypervirility is manifested not only by his resolute desire to be a "man's man," a reporter dealing with public life (like London and Hemingway), but also by expressions of hypersexuality which his predecessors, owing to the times in which they wrote, were forced to edit from the printed page. London, however, did complain bitterly about the prudish literary morality of his own era, and he bragged excessively about his own sexual exploits. And Hemingway's first short story, "Up in Michigan," which had trouble getting past his publisher's censorship, is clear indication that at any other period he would have gratified his readers with many explicit erotic scenes.

Mailer's work has kept up with the liberalization in American sexual mores: it has become increasingly explicit, and the obscenities suggested or bowdlerized in *The Naked and the Dead* (like those of Hemingway) are vigorously detailed in the pages of *Why Are We in Viet-Nam?* In the early novels, the erotic scenes are rare and expurgated, but such scenes increase in number over the years, reaching full force in "The Time of Her Time," and make up the key moments in *An American Dream* and *Why Are We in Viet-Nam?*

The special theme of homosexuality appeared sporadically in the earlier novels, where it was concentrated in certain characters to whom it added somber dimension. As Mailer managed to free himself of his fear of homosexuality, as he carefully analyzed himself and came to realize that there is a homosexual component in all men, the theme was enlarged with each successive work—novels, essays, narratives—and has now assumed quite considerable proportions. It is more interesting, therefore, to analyze his last story, *Why Are We in Viet-Nam?*, in order to examine, as in a magnifying mirror, what was nascent in the earlier novels. For in this novel, Mailer—hyperlucid as ever when it comes to other people and also to himself—has given us a magnificent key for deciphering not only his own obsessions but also those of his masters, Hemingway and London.

Why They Were in Vietnam

The adolescent D.J. and Tex are introduced to the reader as typical American boys: they are middle-class and live in Texas, the American state par excellence. They are both handsome, athletic, and virile. Their portrait must have been inspired by those of Nick Adams, Bill, or George, Hemingway's pure and solid adolescents. Mailer, however, dares to plumb their unconscious minds.

As the novel opens, D.J., who is the narrator, is eighteen years old, and is imagining his mother on a visit to her Jewish analyst. The latter tells Mrs. Alice Hallie Jee Jethroe that her son is "a latent homosexual highly overheterosexual with onanistic narcissistic and sodomistic overtones." (A perfect description of Mailer's heroes, by the way, from Croft to D.J., by way of Rojack and Sergius O'Shaugnessy!) The mother—the narrator is still imagining the scene for the reader—describes the friendship of her son and his pal Tex in the following manner: "But they're stuck to each other like ranch dogs in a fuck. Hunting together, playing

football together on the very same team, riding motorcycles together, holding hands while they ride, studying karate together,
I bet they can't even get their rocks off unless they're put-putting
in the same vaginal slime." This comment has the merit of
frankness, and it masterfully sums up the homosexuality through
the intermediary of a woman who has been mentioned repeat-
edly through this study; it also introduces the theme of the
homoeroticism of hunters, motorcyclists, and wrestlers.

D.J., like all of Mailer's male characters, is a mother's boy, retaining traces of femininity in his features and in his psychological makeup. He is the feminine element in the D.J.–Tex couple: "D.J., as you may have divined, is a manly clean-featured
version in formal features of his mother." D.J. and Tex complement each other perfectly, and reproduce the father-mother pair:
"Tex is a looker, like D.J. He's tall, got a whippy old body, 6–1,
168 pound, all whip leather. . . . He and D.J. are lookalikes, except for expression, cause D.J. is full of mother-love . . . whereas
Tex is full of ape shit daddy-love."

There is a reason for this: Tex's father, Gottfried Hyde, is a
real, virile, oversexed Texas male; that is, he "fucks" anything
that moves, man, woman, child, "any old hole." It is not surprising, therefore, that his offspring's language is crude: Tex
threatens D.J. that he will "suck your cock and bite it off." However, despite their pederastic talk, our teenagers are real little he-
men: "And all that pederastic palaver? Hell, yes. They is crazy
about each other. They even prong each other's girls when they
can, but fear not, gentle auditor, they is men, real Texas men,
they don't ding ding ring a ling on no queer street with each
other, shit, no, they just talk to each other that way to express
Texas tenderness."

On a hunting trip to Alaska, away from the adults, they go
into the underbrush and there, in the wilds of nature, they get a
hint that God is a ferocious animal. Freed from the taboos of
city, family, and the anthropomorphic Christian God, the young
Texans' primitive instincts emerge with unwonted violence. They
want to unite with this animalistic God. That night, D.J. realizes
that if Tex has never tried to "prong" him, it is because if he
were to do so, "D.J. once become a bitch would kill him and
D.J. . . . knew he could make a try to prong Tex tonight, there

was a chance to get it in and steal the iron from Texas' ass and
put it in his own and he was hard as a hammer at the thought
. . . and Tex was ready to fight him to the death, yeah, now it
was there, murder between them under all friendship, for God
was a beast, not a man, and God said 'Go out and kill—fulfill my
will, go and kill,' . . . and they were twins, never to be near as
lovers again, but killer brothers."

This scene is highly important to an understanding of Mailer,
on the one hand, and of all homosexually inspired American literature, on the other. It is a description of the "sublimation" of
homosexuality into violence. D.J. and Tex love and desire each
other, but they both fear that the fulfillment of such desire will
transform them into "softies," into subhumans, non-Americans.
Although they believe—as do Genet's studs—that "fucking" a
man makes one doubly a man, and incorporates one's partner's
virility into oneself, there is always the risk that the partner will
suddenly turn on you. So the desire to possess another male
changes into hatred and violence. The repression of homosexual
desire finds its outlet in murderous combat, according to the captain-soldier schema. Thus a pact is sealed: one's hatred and murderous fury are turned against the enemy, against the Nazi, the
Japanese, the Cong. The hunters will satisfy their homosexual
desires by hunting together, by killing both beasts and men, together. This explains the combination of eros and thanatos in
Hemingway and D. H. Lawrence. The "heterosexualization" of
D.J. and Tex explains the sublimated homosexuality of the guerrilla comrades in For Whom the Bell Tolls, of London's boxers in
their hand-to-hand combat. All will seal their pact in blood, as
did Gerald Crich and Rupert Birkin in Women in Love.

Narcissism and Homosexuality

The desire to be a real man entails an attempt to conform to
an "ideal self" and hence to be preoccupied with "self." All
hypervirile males, from London to Mailer, are fanatical
narcissists, occupied with proving their masculinity both mentally and physically. Hemingway boxed, skied, courted danger

and even death. He despaired when his baldness became irremediable, and he committed suicide when his wasted body no longer corresponded to his image of a real man. London ended his life in part for the same reasons.

Narcissism takes a similar form in Norman Mailer: he is an athlete, a boxing enthusiast, a pilot, proud of his physical prowess; he detests pacifism and nonviolence, since nonviolence is not virile. What is more interesting: although half Jewish, he imagines himself in Aryan bodies, in Croft and Rojack.

Croft is the earliest of Mailer's characters to exhibit overt narcissism. He is a violent, misogynist barbarian who lives the "antifeminine ideal of complete virility" to the full. *"I hate everything which is not myself."* Sergius O'Shaugnessy, the protagonist of *The Deer Park,* describes himself as follows: "I had my blond hair and blue eyes and I was six feet one. I was good-looking and I knew it. I had studied the mirror long enough." Here is the hero of "The Time of Her Time": "I had my good looks, my blond hair, my height, build." In this short story, the hero's narcissism is laid bare, as are the thoughts of every hypervirile male:

> That was the kick I could find, that a year from now, five years from now, down all the seasons to the hours of her old age, I would be the one she would be forced to remember, and it would nourish me a little over the years, thinking of that grudged souvenir that would not die in her, my blond hair, my blue eyes, my small broken nose, my clear mouth and chin, my height, my boxer's body, my parts—yes, I was getting excited at the naked image of me in the young-old mind of that sour sexed-up dynamo.

Woman is only a pretext: Sergius, the fake Irishman, *in fact makes love to himself*—which is the very definition of narcissism and of homosexuality. His partner is in no way deceived; she calls him a "phallic narcissist." In *An American Dream* Rojack looks at himself in a mirror after he has killed his wife, and he discovers his beauty, his blond hair, his blue eyes, which remind him of the beauty of one of the German soldiers he has killed.

Woman

Mailer is fully conscious of his own misogyny. In an interview reprinted in *The Presidential Papers*, he says that he imagines "most men who understand women at all feel hostility towards them. At their worst, women are low sloppy beasts."

All of Mailer's male protagonists are misogynists. Croft, whose wife cheats on him, is an unsurpassed lover (as are all of Mailer's heroes), and he thinks of all women as "fugging whores." Brown, another character in *The Naked and the Dead*, maintains, "There ain't a woman you can trust." Sergius would rather his partner would just disappear after a night of sex and that he could "start the new day by lowering her in a basket . . . six floors down to the garbage pile . . . wave my hand at her safe landing and get in again myself to the blessed isolations of a man alone." Rojack is afraid to admit to Cherry, his girl friend, that he is afraid of women and that when he is in bed with a woman he has the impression that he is a "pirate sharpening up a raid on life." After he has killed his wife, he tells himself that he has not been so happy since he was twelve years old.

However, Mailer's hero—like the heroes of London and Hemingway—badly needs a woman. His choice is revealing, and not surprising in light of the choices previously made by the heroes of *Adventure* or *For Whom the Bell Tolls*. Sergius O'Shaugnessy's partner has "a long thin nose, dark eyes, and a kind of lean force, her arms and square shoulders had shown the flat thin muscles of a wiry boy." Ruta, the German, is primarily seen as a female Nazi in the narrator's eyes, or rather, to a soldier who has himself killed four Germans, she is a *male* Nazi: Rojack, who regards murder as a sexual act and the sexual act as a fight to the death, exclaims, "There was a high private pleasure in plugging a Nazi." Deborah, his wife, is no weakling either: "She was a handsome woman, Deborah, she was big. With high heels she stood at least an inch over me." Rojack compares her to a bull, which is—for Mailer as for Hemingway—the ultimate virile symbol: "She was up like a bull and like a bull she charged. Her head struck me in the stomach . . . and then she drove one powerful knee at my groin (she fought like a prep-school bully) and missing that, she reached with both hands, tried to find my root and mangle me."

The description of Cherry, the girl he really loves, is even more interesting. Where as Deborah and Ruta give him neither comfort nor solace, Cherry symbolizes femininity and the prospect of a happy love affair. Her voice is "warm, strong, confident, almost masculine," and when Rojack hears her singing in the nightclub where she is appearing, "she looked at different instants like a dozen lovely blondes, and now again a little like the little boy next door. A clean tough decent little American boy in her look. . . ." Later, he is again struck by her "delicate boy-girl face." Getting rid of her former black lover, the singer Shago Martin, she speaks "with a strong male voice, some small-town Southern mill boss or politician—her brother, I realized then." (The brother in question is a sheriff.)

So the typical heroine in Mailer's novels tends to resemble the tomboys that populate the novels of London, Hemingway, and Scott Fitzgerald.

For Mailer (as for London), the woman is first and foremost an instrument of procreation. In *The Presidential Papers* Mailer states: "The prime responsibility of a woman probably is to be on earth long enough to find the best mate possible for herself, and conceive children who will improve the species."

Yet this is not the role Mailer's heroines play in fact. In his stories, women are mainly sexual tools, as they are in all of Hemingway's work, and in certain of London's narratives. The woman, preferably androgynous, is principally *an intermediary between the hero and all the men she has known previously*. In line with a previously noted schema, which is given its clearest expression in Mailer's work, the woman is merely a catalyst between one male and other males—at the furthest limit, *between the protagonist and himself*.

Mailer's work abounds with examples of homosexuality through the intermediary of a woman. In the story "The Time of Her Time," Sergius's Jewish girl friend comes to see him a second time having cut her hair and wearing jeans, and still carrying with her the odor of her lover Arthur. Although Sergius tries to convince himself that he is excited by the feminine side of Denise's lover, the reader is forced to admire his ingenuity and lucidity in discerning the imprecision of sexual boundaries.

Later, in *An American Dream*, Rojack, the Harvard football star, admits one of his reasons for marrying Deborah: she has had a horde of admirers: "politicians of the first rank, racing drivers, tycoons, and her fair share of the more certified playboys of the Western world, she had been my entry to the big league." Kissing Cherry for the first time, he thinks, "It was not the nicest kiss I ever had, but it was certainly the most powerful, there was something in it of the iron motor in the hearts of a good many men she must have kissed."

There is also a hint of homosexuality in his interview with Kelly, Deborah's father, with whom she has had an incestuous relationship. Kelly has also been the lover of Cherry and Ruta. There are three women between Kelly and Rojack—thus the very strong sexual attraction they feel for each other. Kelly and Rojack are tempted to make love through the intermediary of the dead Deborah, the absent Cherry (who is dying), and the German Ruta, who is in the next room and can thus act as a concrete go-between for carnal contact between the two men.

Struggle and Sexuality

Mailer's heroes are attracted as much to persons of the same sex as to those of the opposite sex because for them sexuality is a synonym for virile struggle, for combat to the death. The more ferocious the partner, the more "masculine," the more the hero's equal, the more interesting the combat will be and the more triumphant the final victory. In *Why Are We in Viet-Nam?* the reader witnesses the metamorphosis of sexuality—of homosexuality—into the killer instinct; it is in *An American Dream*, however, that Rojack utters the key sentence: "Besides, murder offers the promise of vast relief. It is never unsexual."

In *An American Dream*, there are many examples of sexual struggle and warrior sexuality. The tone is set at the outset: Rojack's first murder changes his life:

The grenades went off somewhere five or ten yards over
each machine gun, *blast, blast,* like a boxer's tattoo,
one-two, and I was exploded in the butt from a piece of
my own shrapnel, whacked with a delicious pain clean
as a mistress' sharp teeth going "yummy" in your rump
and then the barrel of my carbine swung around like a
long fine antenna and pointed itself at the machine-gun
hole on my right where a great bloody sweet German
face, a healthy overspoiled young beauty of a face,
mother-love all over its making, possessor of that over-
curved mouth which only great fat sweet young faggots
can have when their rectum is tuned and entertained
from adolescence on, came crying, sliding, smiling up
over the edge of the hole, "Hello death!" blood and
mud like the herald of sodomy upon his chest, and I
pulled the trigger as if I were squeezing the softest
breast of the softest pigeon which ever flew, still a
woman's breast takes me now and then to the pigeon on
that trigger.

Following this episode, which reveals Rojack's attitude, toward murder, combat, and death on the one hand, and their connection with sexuality—homosexuality—on the other, all the
other scenes of love-making in the book will evoke sodomy and
mortal combat, every scene of struggle will recall a sexual embrace. The fight between Shago, Cherry's black ex-lover, and
Rojack is like a sublimated sodomy based on the many scenes of
struggle mentioned earlier—in "The Prussian Officer," between
adolescent boys, the fight between Starwick and Eugene Gant,
etc.

In Rojack's long interview with his father-in-law, Kelly, sexuality is again combined with the notion of death, murder, and suicide. Rojack thinks of throwing himself off Kelly's terrace to put
an end to his unhappy life, and this temptation leads him to recall the mixture of fear and excitement an adolescent boy feels
when he is about to have his first sexual experience. Kelly's tacit
invitation to share Ruta leads to a walk along the parapet of the
skyscraper's terrace. A brush with death can replace homosexual

contact, as does bear-hunting or Cong-hunting in *Why Are We in Viet-Nam?*

Mailer, who is prolix and ready with explications with regard both to his work and to his own personality, and who sees the world around him with a fair degree of clarity, was one of the first writers to note the relationship between contact sports— American football or boxing—and homosexuality. Kate Millett writes, "In an essay on football, Mailer explains that it is the suppressed sexuality in the players' habitual gesture of bottom slapping (which he traces ingeniously to its origin in homosexual flirtations), plus the act of centering the ball 'in the classic pose of sodomy,' which 'liberates testosterone' and enables the player, by the 'prongsmanship and buggery at the seat' of his 'root' to carry on and hit hard in the 'happy broil.'" There is a similar linkage between combat and homosexuality in Mailer's description of the Griffith-Paret match. There had been gossip that Griffith was "gay," and on the morning of the match Paret insulted him, "touching him on the buttocks, while making a few more remarks about his manhood." In the ring, Griffith violently attacked Paret, who died shortly afterward.

Sodomization

In prison—as in the army or on shipboard there are no women and—the male's androgynous nature rises to the surface. In *The Prisoner of Sex* Mailer states, "One's ass is one's honor in prison. Men commit murder to defend that ass or revenge it if it has been raped. One's ass becomes one's woman, one's honor is that she is virginal."

Sodomization plays a major role in the sex lives of Mailer's characters. A boyish partner, an attempt to unite with a woman's previous lovers through her, the temptation an "All-American" boy feels to fuck another adolescent or to be fucked by him, the basic misogyny of the male characters, their contempt for women —all these elements combine to make Mailer's male characters men who *choose* not to submit to their deeper instincts in order to preserve their masculine identity in a society that equates virility with heterosexuality. Were they born in prison, in a place removed from society, these males would be no more troubled by Bloom's complex (*From Here to Eternity*) than are Melville's Kanakas or Polynesians.

Sodomizing a woman thus becomes an additional ruse by which homosexual pleasure can be experienced outside homosexuality, a means of covertly attaining the Greek ideal of total virility unrealizable in Judeo-Christian civilization. Writing of things that Melville, London, or Hemingway would never have dreamed of putting on paper, Mailer describes several scenes of sodomy by which the hero acquires a kind of accrued virile strength. In "The Time of Her Time," published in 1959, Sergius sodomizes the Jewess with the boy's body, whom he nicknames "Commissar." The German Ruta in *An American Dream* reminds Rojack of the Nazi with the handsome fuckee's face; this is clearly why he digs for gold in her "ass," with the same purpose as he has drawn steel from Cherry's masculine kisses. D.J. dreams of getting all the Texas "iron" from Tex's ass to put in his own. D.J. wants both to be sodomized and to sodomize. Sergius sodomizes Denise after she has sodomized him with her finger. His first reaction is one of fury; however, because the sex act is really a boxing match, a corrida, his rage is erotic: "Well, she had been right, that finger tipped the balance. . . . I worked on her like a beaver for forty-odd minutes or more, slapping my tail to build her nest."

Sodomization restores vigor—this is the meaning of the mineral metaphors in *Why Are We in Viet-Nam?* and *An American Dream*—because it allows us to escape from the castrating trap set by the female sex. Again, we have the old dream of a virility that can be achieved without female intervention—a dream that our society makes impossible. (Jake in *The Sun Also Rises* embodies this dream because of his wound, which enables him to be chaste without being unvirile; London's heroes live this fantasy up until the day they encounter a tomboy.)

In this regard, the figurative sodomization of Shago is highly significant because it marks a determinant stage in Rojack's psychological development. He is seeking in the black man's ass neither pirate gold nor Texas iron, but the virile and sexual strength of the black race as a whole. Cherry has told him that "Shago's a *stud,* Mr. Rojack," and Mailer elsewhere has spoken at length about the hypersexuality of blacks and the white jealousy that has been aroused because of it (cf. "The White Negro"). Shago's umbrella, which Rojack discovers after he has thrown Cherry's former lover out, becomes a phallic symbol that enables him to face Deborah's father, to stand up to him—and to regain the ground after having walked the parapet of the Waldorf Towers. Barry H. Leeds has noted that Stephen Rojack has acquired stored-up virile strength from his symbolic sodomization of Shago Martin, in line with a principle that underlies all of Mailer's work. As the hypervirile adolescent Tex, a liberated spokesman for his predecessors brutally expresses it, the "asshole," because it is "harder to enter than cunt," is "reserved for the special tool." Unfortunately, in American culture, this statement is one that the virile hero can put into practice only if his partner is a (masculine) woman.

Gaining Virility

"All men are homosexual but for their choice not to be." This statement by Mailer also applies to London and Hemingway: *virility must be gained, and it is acquired by heterosexual means.* In *John Barleycorn* London described his frantic efforts to become a man, and how his virilization was rewarded with heterosexuality.

Carlos Baker—among others—has explained that Hemingway's hypervirility, his fondness for danger and violent sports, were based on his fear of not being as virile as he would have liked. Mailer, who has made a searching analysis of D. H. Lawrence's complex personality, uses similar words to diagnose that of his hero, Hemingway. In *Cannibals and Christians* he recounts an anecdote told by Morley Callaghan in his book *That Summer in Paris,* according to which Hemingway was almost beaten in a boxing match by a smaller opponent because Fitzgerald, who was acting as timekeeper, had allowed the round to run overtime. Mailer explains Hemingway's fury with Fitzgerald: "What is more likely the truth of his long odyssey is that

he struggled with his cowardice . . . all of his life. . . . There
are two kinds of brave men: those who are brave by the grace of
nature, and those who are brave by an act of will. It is the merit
of Callaghan's long anecdote that the second condition is suggested to be Hemingway's own."

Hemingway's work plainly reveals that he considered cowardice to be a symptom of latent homosexuality, and it is possible
that he regarded any sign of weakness on his own part as a start
down the long and fatal road to sexual inversion. Mailer has constantly evoked the heroic figure of the author of "The Short
Happy Life of Francis Macomber," and has deliberately followed in his footsteps. In *The Presidential Papers* he sets Hemingway in the pantheon of American heroes, between Jack London and Joe Louis, and in *Advertisements for Myself* he reveals
his desire to imitate Hemingway in his conclusion that "it was
more important to be a man than a very good writer." Being a
man is being able to "keep my nerve."

Everything in Mailer is explicit. His statements and his novels
clarify the work of his predecessors in American letters, as do the
novels of Carson McCullers and James Purdy that take up the
theme of captain and soldier and decode *Billy Budd*. London
describes boxers fighting and embracing; Hemingway and his
fish struggle with each other and love each other; in *Tender Is the
Night* the young Englishmen's love for each other increases as
they fight; Mailer compares Sergius and his mistress to a pair of
boxers. Hemingway sought increased virility in contact with
bulls and bullfighters, Mailer makes Sergius a teacher of *in camera* bullfighting who sees the sex act as a corrida in which he is
alternately bullfighter and bull. He also recommends the Mexican practice of eating the bull's testicles as a means of gaining
virility. Even a feminine man can gain virility by swallowing this
"delicacy"; unless of course he is afraid of becoming too virile
(again there is the double equation: courage=heterosexuality,
cowardice=nonvirility=homosexuality): "What freezes the homosexual in his homosexuality is not fear of women so much as
the fear of the masculine world with which he must war if he
wishes to keep the woman."

In Mailer, therefore, there is the conviction that virility is
gained, earned, that is is derived from a *conscious* repression of

cowardice, of the femininity *natural* to all men, and of his homosexuality, which is an integral part of the adolescent personality
he must sublimate—as do D.J. and Tex—in violence. The residue
that remains after this quasichemical transformation will be male
friendship, sealed in the blood of comrades-in-arms, of brothers
who are, at one moment, nearly lovers. From this it is easy to see
how, in the imagination of Jack London, Wolf Larsen and his sadomasochistic crew were born, and why Hemingway's imagination created comrades to fish, hunt, and fight together. The value
of Mailer's stories and statements is that, having profited from the
liberalization of American morals and from the consequences of
the "sexual revolution" on both the personal and the literary
level, they show us in slow-motion the mechanism of the sublimation of natural homosexuality in violence. Thus we can arrive
at the equation that tacitly underlies the life and works of these
three hypervirile writers: *virility=violence=outrageous heterosexuality*. Underlying this equation, however, is an infrastructure
that is concealed with considerable cleverness: *hypervirility=
forced repression of homosexuality*. As Mailer writes in *Cannibals and Christians*, "Masculinity is not something given to you,
something you're born with, but something you gain."

CONCLUSION

Another Country

American society, according to Wainwright Churchill and George Weinberg, is characterized by its homoerotophobia. Although homosexuality has never been advocated in Europe, Europe has always seemed more tolerant to Americans, less aggressively virile. Henry James, William Styron, and Hemingway have all indicated this in various works. American laws have made this panic fear of inversion, of "crimes against nature," official, whereas France, since the beginning of the nineteenth century, has dropped any mention of this offense from its Napoleonic Code. In England, on the other hand, this example was not followed until the second half of this century.

The affectionate Rinaldi (*A Farewell to Arms*) is the forerunner of all the homoerotic or homosexual Italians that appear in the works of J. H. Burns and James Baldwin. A virile American like Hemingway seemed to think that in Italy his alter ego, Frederick Henry, could allow himself to be kissed by a young and handsome Italian with impunity; Captain Joe and Orlando, the handsome Florentine, appear to be inseparable; David falls passionately in love with Giovanni. These homosexual tendencies are given play in foreign countries, in another country, thereby attesting to the suppression or repression American civilization exerts on man's instincts. To free oneself of that repression, it is not enough to "project" homoerotic desires onto some contemptible man who has renounced virility, onto an effeminate male, a broken creature, an outcast and a derelict, or to link perverse temptation with something evil. Such feelings will still live in every American male, in every male, and in particular in two kinds of apparently heterosexual males—the feminine-masochist man (James, Fitzgerald, etc.) and the hyper-virile man (London, Hemingway, Mailer).

Until the 1940s, the portrait that American writers drew of the overt homosexual was primarily negative: no matter what distancing methods were used—consciously or unconsciously—whether he was a major or a minor character, the homosexual was the antithesis of Good, i.e., of the American virile ideal. Charles Jackson, to make his "latent" homosexual palatable, had to portray the overt homosexual as an effeminate stereotype, the underside of the American dream, a nightmare to terrify his protagonist. In almost all the novels written before World War II, the invert served to enhance the hero's good looks, his purity, and above all, his masculinity. This is the role he plays in the works of Farrell, Dos Passos, Fitzgerald, and London.

Sexual inversion made its appearance in the American novel by way of adolescent sexual ambiguity, a condition recognized by American psychologists and psychoanalysts since the beginning of the century, and by way of the self-hating latent homosexual, as in the novels of Bellaman and Jackson. Even after the decisive turning point in 1948, Vidal and Baldwin depict the invincible self-hatred from which the American homosexual must suffer. Jim (*The City and the Pillar*), David (*Giovanni's Room*), and Eric (*Another Country*) all have enormous difficulty in fully accepting themselves: all three are tortured creatures, like Michael, their theatrical counterpart in *The Boys in the Band*.

The inner conflict in which the American homosexual's ego is engaged, the antagonism between his deepest instincts—released in infancy through the imbalance of his familial situation—and the sexual ideal of his society, have been masterfully described by D. H. Lawrence, who obsesses American homosexual writers. It is no coincidence that the archetypical captain and soldier—higher centers (hierarchical superior) against lower (hierarchical inferior)—have been described not only by Melville and Purdy, but also by Hemingway, McCullers, and Mailer. Allegorically, the Prussian officer is the extreme limit of the Nordic virile ideal of warlike brutality, hard-heartedness, self-control, while

the soldier—dark, "Mediterranean," the reincarnation of
Cooper's Indians (about which Lawrence had such penetrating
things to say)—symbolizes animal sensuality, joy of living, the
Freudian id, the polymorphous-perverse that the intellect must
succeed in stifling. The dilemma of the Prussian officer, the antagonism between id and superego, is the key to the human condition of the Western homosexual, and especially the American
homosexual. The thirst for normality characteristic of all homosexual novels—in particular those of Baldwin and Vidal—is the
thirst to conform to the American virile ideal. Homosexuality,
however, is the most categorical rejection of that virile ideal,
which must of necessity be gained heterosexually. To be homosexual is to be relegated to nonconformity, to be cast among the
subhuman, the pariahs, the girlish, whose adolescent prototypes
are such characters as Jamie, Lymie, Joel, John Grimes, and of
whom Dumphry, Campion, and Fat Leon are the finished prod-
uct.

Men who have, willingly or unwillingly to varying degrees,
abandoned the quest for virility find themselves attracted to men
who are overwhelmingly forceful, indifferent, or sadistically
aggressive, men whom they simultaneously desire and hate, since
they love them only because they are unable to be them. The
conflict that destroys the Prussian officer is waged within *all* homosexuals in American literature: in Claggart and Captain Vere,
in Penderton and General Cummings, and in the blatantly
effeminate men who search for men *who do not resemble them,*
an incontestable proof of their need to rid themselves of themselves. The difference between the captain and Lymie, between
Bill (*Tea and Sympathy*) and Regina or Alberta (*Last Exit to
Brooklyn*) is only apparent: the former are trying to convince
themselves and their society that they have not renounced virility (American style), and the latter have chosen to abandon
artifice and to accept their true sexual identity.

The postwar novel that best illustrates this thesis is a best-
seller that will not, one supposes, be regarded as a literary masterpiece—John Knowles' *A Separate Peace*. Gene, the narrator,
accomplishes a deed that is hinted at in the novels of London,
Hemingway, and Mailer: the mutilation of the American virile
ideal, its reduction to human dimensions. Gene has no choice: ei-

ther he falls into the pit from which all overt homosexuals are leering up at him, or he belittles the American virile ideal. His cruelty and his killer instincts arise from his refusal to eroticize his admiration for Phineas's beauty, his strength, his contented animal nature, his refusal to follow the road to damnation taken by John Grimes (Baldwin) and Lymie (Maxwell), who are erotically attracted to Elisha (or David) and to Spud. It is a defense mechanism of the same type as London's promiscuity: although an adolescent need not prove his heterosexuality, the adult London must resist the appeal of masculine beauty by forcing himself to make love to many women, rather than loving woman: quantity conceals the lack of quality.

Judeo-Christian society is misogynistic: woman is always an inferior, contemptible, devirilizing creature. Mailer sees this clearly: in the end, the ideal sexual partner, the preferred companion, will be a man. Yet sexual relations with a man are devirilizing! Thus, the only acceptable compromise is to pay lip service to heterosexuality to rid oneself of guilt, in order that one can then be free to indulge in erotic male company with impunity. Cooper and London both sensed this, if they did not consciously understand it. The dream of an ideal comrade—an ideal that is, as London states, unattainable—is clearly expressed in his letters to Cloudesley John and George Sterling. The letters are the clearest expression of London's desire for a symbiotic union, a union that is homosexual but not homogenital! When reality intervenes, however, the dream falls to pieces.

In fact, symbiotic union is an unconsummated homosexual marriage. The American dream is, in the end, of men living for each other, through each other, *within each other*, without any sexual intervention. Vere, Claggart, and Billy Budd are joined in death: Claggart is killed by Billy, who is condemned to death by Vere, who dies murmuring the name of the Beautiful Sailor. Ishmael regrets that his body and the bodies of the other sailors cannot melt together. Eugene Gant considers Starwick an integral part not only of his life but of his very body. Gene dons Phineas's pink shirt in order to *become* his friend-enemy, and Phineas thinks of Gene as a extension of himself. John wants to "usurp" Elisha's body.

In an aggressively heterosexual culture, the only type of symbiotic union that can—perforce—*seem* viable is the union of a feminine male, a female replacement, and a real man. Lymie and Spud, John and Elisha (or David) *temporarily* reproduce the schema of a heterosexual couple. Once adolescence is over, however, society accepts the real men and abandons the effeminate to their unhappy, outcast lot. Sissies do not become virile, they grow old. "Divine had not become virile; she had aged," Genet writes in *Notre-Dame des Fleurs*. The apparent masculinity of the homosexual professor or officer is only a façade. American—Western—reality established such categories at an early stage. But the flaw persists beneath the veneer of masculinity in Isherwood's professors, or in Buechner's, and in the officers of Melville, Mailer, or McCullers. In their students and their troops such men seek the assurance, strength, and basic masculinity they lack: the Spartan, pedagogic, or warrior homosexual ideal is not viable in American reality. The homosexual captain and professor are seeking a father because the boy becomes homosexual because of his failure to interiorize the father image, the virile model.

Men who refuse to renounce virility will seek refuge from inversion in sadism; according to Krafft-Ebing and Freud, sadism is hypertrophied masculinity. To brutalize a man physically is to have bodily contact with him while seeming to be more virile than other men. Struggle, man-to-man combat, occurs in all homoerotic American novels: it has a clearly sexual tone in Wolfe, Styron, Baldwin, and Vidal, but once again it is Lawrence who, in "The Prussian Officer" and in *Women in Love*, best described its basic schema and its psychological motivation. London too delighted in describing the boxing matches between Joe and his opponent: their embrace is at once tender and brutal. These embraces, these "clinches," are the expression of a desire for symbiotic union with another supermale, a union that can be *corporal without being genital*, one that subsumes all the mythology of fighter and warrior. The brutal embrace reflects both the desire for bodily symbiotic union and the refusal to make such a union into an erotic one. The fighters appear to be saying, "Hate is the opposite of love." "If I fight with him, if I strike him, how can I be accused of loving him?" However, John actually fights Elisha (as Lymie does Spud) before being "con-

verted," through religion, to homosexuality. The orgasm of
hatred that shakes Eugene as he brutalizes Starwick, or of Cass
when he murders Mason (in Styron's *Set This House on Fire*), is
an orgasm of disguised love.

The American male cannot love his counterpart, his brother.
The difference between them, which is inherent in the heterosexual couple, must be established in some other guise, no matter
what that may be. All the homoerotic couples in American
literature exhibit this difference, inspired by the heterosexual
couple. Even James Barr and Loren Wahl, both of whom attempt
to depict two soldiers or sailors who love each other *tenderly*,
describe in the first instance an older man and a younger man,
and in the second, a black and a white man, a lieutenant and a
soldier.

Even with this difference, however, there is no guarantee that
the couple will be a viable one. Male couples are threatened by
time (in Baldwin, for example) or by death (particularly in
Wahl and Barr). In play after play, William Inge depicted male
couples according to the schema older-younger, mentor-disciple,
but always broke up such liaisons at play's end. Hatred, which is
society's envoy within the unnatural union, is always in the background ready to replace love, and the homoerotic embrace always seems to be on the point of changing into mortal combat.
The union between two men cannot occur under the aegis of
tender love. There can be no relief other than in the paroxysm of
hatred.

Thus, from work to work, American novelists and dramatists
who have dealt with the theme of male homosexuality have illustrated the basic conflict between society's sexual morality and
man's unsuppressed instincts. A whole gamut of stratagems has
been employed to appease the conscience. The superego of the
white adult male reader has been flattered by using distancing:
dehumanizing, depersonalizing, and "abstracting" the homosexual character, who is turned into a foreigner, a Negro, an adolescent, a creature more woman than man whom we must pity,
hate, or make fun of. Even when the difference seems closest to
that of heterosexuality—as in the novels of Selby, in which "real
men" live with creatures so feminine they might easily be
mistaken for women—the liaison is not happy.

"Disimbrication" of American reality can also take the form of the Billy Budd myth: a creature is created without any links with reality, born of unknown parents, endowed with all the characteristics of virility yet pure and innocent so that his asexuality is palatable, a creature both angel and beast, superman and pretty girl. All these characteristics are to be found in certain of Williams's male characters (Brick, Kilroy, Val, Xavier, etc.), and in London's novels. In the latter, the male's androgyny is reflected by the woman's: each seems to be taking a step toward the other to meet in midstream in a dream world, far from civilization (an island, a ship), where American reality cannot reach them. The same androgyny is to be found in Fitzgerald, whose protagonists (like their creator) see the masculine woman as the means by which they can, indirectly, abandon themselves to homosexuality with impunity. The interposed woman also allows the male to be attained without any trauma of conscience. In Fitzgerald, however, the protagonist's feminine masochism will reveal his homosexual tendencies: although he loves Gloria, Daisy, or Nicole, he is in fact aiming at Tom Buchanan and Tom Barban.

The American homosexual is caught between two types of homosexuality: that symbolized by D. H. Lawrence, entailing total acceptance of the Prussian virile ideal, which is the extreme version of the Western virile ideal (brutality, sadism, rejection of all effeminate tenderness), the versions adopted by the American pioneer in his struggle against a hostile environment; or that symbolized by Jean Genet, the pure and simple acceptance of the femininity that exists in every man. Genet is the essentially feminine and masochistic man who dreams of union with his opposite, the fascist brute. Unable to be a "man among men," a "Man's man," he becomes one of the passive lovers and will be a "man for men." Like Cousin Lymon, he has perverted the Western virile ideal into that of a gangster, a delinquent, a sadistic fascist, into one who must be desired and submitted to if one cannot become him. In Genet's view, any trace of sympathy or tenderness from the handsome tough would cast him into the abyss too, and he would become another Anacleto, Cousin Lymon, Strether, etc. The handsome and sadistic tough is to be found in the work of James, Fitzgerald, Bellow—and in London, as Wolf Larsen. The author of *The Sea-Wolf* split himself in two: having successfully avoided becoming the latent, feminine-masochist homosexual nascent in Humphrey Van Weyden, he took as his ideal the Nietzschean Superman he did not quite manage to become.

Lawrence shows clearly that the sadistic captain is basically only a weak woman, and that from his mother, the Polish countess, he has inherited more than mere aristocratic refinement. He would like to be "penetrated" by the handsome Schöner, just as Lieutenant Seblon dreams of abandoning himself in the strong arms of the handsome sailor Querelle. The American homosexual is continually caught between the captain and Divine, between Seblon and Alberta, between Lawrence and Genet, according to whether he attempts to conform, at whatever cost, to the American—Western—virile ideal, or whether he rejects it and dresses in frills and laces.

Edward Albee—among others—also demonstrates this antagonism between ego and superego. His shocked and vehement denials—which remind us of Whitman's denials of J. A. Symonds's accusations—resemble those of Brick Pollitt, whom Maggie and Big Daddy attempt to corner. They also resemble Gene's refusal to eroticize his feelings for Phineas. From *The Zoo Story* to *Tiny Alice*, Albee has written his "internal narrative." The American dream is always a handsome young blond male, mutilated and devirilized by the dramatist out of revenge, a revenge that is the sign of the author's inner conflict. The loving-hate for this ideal, which will cause suffering to anyone who cannot attain it, is easy to detect in Inge, in Williams, or in the queens who refer to their friends in the feminine. Despite the apparent rejection of virility by such characters as Divine, Alberta, Ginger, or Trudi, any queen who manages to retain a few ounces of masculinity (as Genet remarks with regard to Divine) will envy the stud he cannot be.

Williams's work reflects this love-hatred for the American virile ideal. The dramatist mutilates or symbolically castrates his handsome Anglo-Saxon protagonist by placing his sexuality in the past, offstage, but he has an enormous erotic admiration for the foreigner, the character who is not like him: the Italian and the Pole both represent *truly* heterosexual masculinity. James,

who was so uncomfortable in the United States, also European-
izes Chad, the "perverse pagan," long before Strether thinks of
becoming intimate with him. Baldwin makes David a sterile
creature and exalts the sensual, living beauty of Giovanni; Richard, the American heterosexual in *Another Country*, is antipathetic, but the author extolls the liberated vitality of Vivaldo, the
homoerotic Italian-American "warrior." Driven by love and
hatred, homosexual writers will always be prey to a frustration
seeking to vent itself in revenge. The settling of accounts with
society occurs in all homosexual novelists and dramatists: Albee,
Inge, Williams—and also James and Fitzgerald—all describe the
heterosexual couple (whose unloved rejects they are) with the
same ill-will that Hemingway brings to his descriptions of the
homosexual couple. Baldwin takes revenge against his white
Anglo-Saxon characters because he is short, ugly, and black:
David, some minor characters in *Tell Me How Long the Train's
Been Gone*, and Richard (*Another Country*), are all the fruits of
the author's self-hatred. Daniel Curzon, in the excellent novel
Something You Do in the Dark, also uses this "homosexual
spite." The scenes between Bud, the handsome, "normal" boy
who is healthy in mind and body, and Cole, the militant homosexual who has been skinned alive, recall the relationship between Alan and Michael in *The Boys in the Band* and that of
Brick and Skipper (*Cat on a Hot Tin Roof*). Bud, who is clearly
homoerotic, is engaged to Cathy-Lynn, who reminds us of one of
Tennessee Williams's shrews. Bud, handsome, kind, affectionate,
and tolerant (a homosexual fantasy), will have an unhappy married life. Like some of Inge's studs, he will be *punished by marriage* for having refused to indulge his homoeroticism (in spite
of a brief experience at college).

The best illustration of an author's getting even with society—
and with the American virile ideal—is Gore Vidal's novel *Myra
Breckinridge*, which deals with the desire to lose oneself, to be
the other, to usurp the other's body. Unable to appease his thirst
for virility by "possessing" many men because these men, by giving in to him, even for money, accept devirilization only to survive, Myron becomes a woman through a sex-change operation.
This is an extreme example of the mental transvestism to be
found in many homoerotic novelists, from Henry James to James

Baldwin, including Lawrence and London. Vidal has worked his fantasies out to the end, and has probed deeply into himself. The dream lover represented by Bob (*The City and the Pillar*) cannot, the author knows, be found in American reality. Jim takes revenge for his failure by raping Bob, and Myron—having become Myra—rapes Rusty, the embodiment of the handsome American stud, a first cousin to William Inge's studs. Myron finds inner peace by becoming a woman and by raping—with a dildo—the American virile ideal, who, traumatized by the experience, becomes a homosexual. (In Baldwin and in Proust all the virile men end up by becoming homosexuals. The supreme revenge of an all-powerful creator.)

Vidal's novel is a confession; it is the confession of failure. "Normal" homosexuality cannot exist in American reality, despite all the examples one can cite, despite all the defenses of the bisexuality "natural" to all human beings that fill the works of the author of *The Season of Comfort*. Having settled his accounts with the American virile ideal he had—until *Myra Breckinridge*—hoped to attain, having "freed" himself by Rusty's rape—as did Jim by savagely possessing Bob—he still cannot live happily and at peace with himself in American civilization. Dreams and fantasies are not enough: one must leave America, that mixture of Gopher Prairie, Rainbow Center, and Marshall Town (where Merle Miller grew up). And flight into dreams or into another country is an admission of failure and defeat. The virile, normal homosexuals of "The Zenner Trophy" are viable— and the point bears stressing—only for the span of a brief short story.

The present generation, however, is bringing everything into question once again. In 1972, George Weinberg wrote *Society and the Healthy Homosexual*, in which he convincingly demonstrated that normal homosexuality can be viable in American society if homosexuals can cease to consider themselves as either sick or as outcasts. Liberation movements have again attacked the American virile ideal and have made a breach in the American, Prussian, notion of masculinity. It is quite possible that coming generations, gradually freed from entrenched American reality, will be able to transform the America of tomorrow into that other country dreamed of by the hero of Waldo Frank's parable

The Dark Mother, a parable that also illustrates Melville's and Baldwin's dream. Although mired in American reality and subject to the spectators' superegos, Mart Crowley was still able to attack the Broadway public in 1968. His action had national dimensions, although the apparent winner in the play is the "heterosexual" Alan, who represents the American spectator on stage.

Today, however, no harmony can exist between the homosexual dream (Billy Budd, Spud, Bob, the students of Buechner and Isherwood), and American reality, still imprisoned in its myths and its taboos—and this despite the liberation movements. The homosexual fantasy has not yet been made flesh, it is not yet based in reality. The inability to create viable couple archetypes is the most tangible proof of this failure: as soon as homosexual writers try to deal realistically with such couples, their homoerotic warrior turns into an effeminate masochist, and Erastes, far from educating or guiding Eromenos, attempts to extract his elixir of virility, seeing him as an "invulnerable" creature who wears his virility as naturally as he does his skin and as an image of the father they never succeeded in interiorizing, long ago and far away, when everything was still possible. The homosexual Proust was wrong: lost time cannot be recaptured. Although far from America the relationship of Pemberton and Morgan could be both pure and emotional and the master could protect, guide, and educate his pupil, George, Isherwood's professor living in California in 1965, still dreams of Kenny as Lymie dreamed of Spud. It is revealing that *A Single Man* ends with masturbation. The American homosexual, like Genet, can do no more than "evoke" his ideal lover.

Even today, the Western homosexual novel is replete with self-deception, with "wishful thinking" that must, sooner or later, face reality. The handsome, young, misogynistic and homosexual Michael, who is the *narrator's* lover in *A World in the Evening,* is the most visible incarnation of such wishful thinking. Isherwood's narrators are always loved by such typically American, chosen creatures; we meet them in *A Meeting by the River, Down There on a Visit,* and the "Berlin Stories." Charles Jackson tacitly implied that Cliff Hauman really loved John Grandin, and Captain Vere, Melville's alter ego, the symbol of his deepest ego, is blessed by Billy Budd, the Handsome Sailor. Melville, Isherwood, Baldwin, Jackson, and others take pleasure in the love that Billy Budd, Michael, Vivaldo, and Hauman, the Marine, *really* feel for them. Yet such love is doomed from the beginning, since American society, sooner or later, will act to separate two men who love each other. Homosexual authors, perpetual "orators," masochistic worshipers of the American virile ideal, can only rebel against their society in dreams, outside of reality, on board ship, on far-off islands, in the wild away from cities, in Europe—or at least such was the case until very recently.

And is the European homosexual so different from his American counterpart? In a comparison of the personality of Oscar Wilde with Verlaine, an overt homosexual, and Baudelaire, a "latent" homosexual, Robert Merle came to the same conclusions: "We find the same oscillation," he writes, "between the pleasure of inflicting pain and the pleasure of suffering," and his remarks on Wilde's "European" sadomasochism could also apply to the torments of all the Prussian officer's American offspring: "For though he has the courage to attack, he does not have the courage to counterattack. Although he is aggressive, he is not combative: he passively abandons himself to the repression he has himself brought about. Not that he lacks courage. Yet his sadism is joined with a profound masochism, central and incurable. Wilde is not, primarily, a tormentor in search of a victim. He temporarily assumes the role of tormentor only to become, finally, the victim of the person he has provoked."

The difference between the European homosexual and the American homosexual is not a question of nature. What varies is the intensity of the repression of femininity. The European virile ideal is less extreme than the American: it can tolerate refinement, elegance, tenderness, as Margaret Mead has noted, and as James illustrates in *The Ambassadors*. The homosexual in Europe is less ashamed of being "crazy about fabrics," as was Erik Valborg. Latent European homosexuals Lucien de Rubempré or Des Esseintes, the protagonist of *A Rebours*, are not subject to overwhelming self-hatred, since they apparently are able to see themselves as not that much different from Frédéric Moreau or Fabrice Del Dongo. (And one must take into account the differences between the various countries of Europe: the

German and Anglo-Saxon virile ideal is much more exalted than the French or the Mediterranean.)

Although self-hatred seems less virulent in the European homosexual, it exists nonetheless. Proust has masterfully observed the lot of men like Charlus, who love only supermales, sadistic brutes, dangerous thugs. Montherlant, who frequented bullfights and fought bulls in his pursuit of the Spartan virile ideal, is like the Prussian officer or like the sadistic captain in Purdy's novel. Gide castigated European inversion and dreamed of virile homosexuality, antique style. A character in a novel by Michèle Perrein (*Le Petit Jules*) explains, as did Proust, that the Western homosexual is continually forced to indulge in self-delusion. Lorca, the Spanish homosexual writer, spoke of "the evening dew that seems to fall for the dead and for lovers gone astray, which is the same thing!" and in his ode to Walt Whitman, whom he seems to have taken for a virile homosexual, Lorca attacks the "queens of all the world's cities" who give boys "drops of filthy death with a bitter poison," concluding with an evocation of "handsome Walt Whitman," asleep by the Hudson. A fair return: the American homosexual believes he will find inner peace in Europe, and the European homosexual believes that the Homosexual Grail is to be found in America, in a union of virility and sexual inversion. Despite a deep questioning of traditional values, both American and European, the "other country" that we glimpse in the "beat" and "hip" movements and in the new militancy of racial or sexual minorities as yet exists only in artificial Edens, or in more or less voluntary self-delusion. "And besides, the wench is *not* dead."

As this book was being readied for its French edition, an ex-Marine saved the life of President Ford by diverting a gun that was aimed at the President. The prime representative of American culture thus owed his life to a representative of American virility. However, the ex-Marine is a militant homosexual.

I. BIBLIOGRAPHIES

Young, Ian. *The Male Homosexual in Literature: A Bibliography* (Metuchen, N.J.: The Scarecrow Press, 1975).

Weinberg, Martin S., and Bell, Alan. *Homosexuality: An Annotated Bibliography* (New York: Harper & Row, 1972).

II. FICTION

Anderson, Sherwood. *Winesburg, Ohio: A Group of Tales of Ohio Small-Town Life,* 1919 (New York: The Modern Library, 1947).

Baldwin, James. *Go Tell It on the Mountain,* 1953 (New York: The Dial Press, 1963).

———. "The Outing," 1953, *Going to Meet the Man* (New York: The Dial Press, 1965), pp. 29–57.

———. *Giovanni's Room* (New York: The Dial Press, 1956).

———. *Another Country* (New York: The Dial Press, 1962).

———. *Tell Me How Long the Train's Been Gone* (New York: The Dial Press, 1968).

———. *If Beale Street Could Talk* (New York: The Dial Press, 1974).

Barr, James. *Quatrefoil: A Modern Novel* (New York: Greenberg, 1950).

Bellaman, Henry. *Kings Row* (New York: Simon & Schuster, 1940).

Bellow, Saul. *The Victim* (New York: The Vanguard Press, 1947).

———. *Seize the Day,* 1956 (New York: The Viking Press, 1961).

———. *Henderson the Rain King* (New York: The Viking Press, 1959).

———. *Herzog* (New York: The Viking Press, 1964).

———. *Mr. Sammler's Planet* (New York: The Viking Press, 1969).

Bourjaily, Vance. *The End of My Life* (New York: The Dial Press, 1947).

Bowles, Paul. "Pages from Cold Point," *Pages from Cold Point,* 1949 (London: Peter Owen, 1968), pp. 7–35.

Bromfield, Louis. *Mr. Smith* (New York: Harper & Brothers, 1951).

Buechner, Frederick. *A Long Day's Dying,* 1949 (London: Chatto & Windus, 1951).

Burns, John Horne. *The Gallery* (New York: Harper & Brothers, 1946).

———. *Lucifer with a Book* (London: Secker & Warburg, 1949).

Burroughs, William S. *Naked Lunch*, 1959 (London: John Calder, 1964).

———. *Nova Express* (New York: Grove Press, 1964).

———. *The Soft Machine* (New York: Grove Press, 1966)

———. *The Ticket That Exploded* (New York: Grove Press, 1967).

———. *The Wild Boys: A Book of the Dead* (New York: Grove Press, 1971).

Cain, James. *Serenade* (New York: Alfred A. Knopf, 1937).

Capote, Truman. *Other Voices, Other Rooms* (New York: Random House, 1948).

Cocteau, Jean. *The Grand Ecart*, 1923 (tr. L. Galantière, New York: Howard Fertig Inc., 1925).

———. *The Holy Terrors*, 1929 (tr. R. Lehmann, New York: New Directions, 1957).

Cory, Donald Webster, ed. *21 Variations on a Theme* (New York: Greenberg, 1953).

Curzon, Daniel. *Something You Do in the Dark* (New York: G. P. Putnam's Sons, 1971).

———. *The Misadventures of Tim McPick* (Los Angeles: John Parke Custis Press, 1975).

Dale, Alan [pseud. of A. J. Cohen]. *A Marriage Below Zero* (New York: G. W. Dillingham, 1889).

Dana, Richard Henry, Jr. *Two Years Before the Mast*, 1840 (New York: The Modern Library, 1945).

Donleavy, James Patrick. *The Ginger Man*, 1958 (New York: Delacorte Press, 1965).

Dos Passos, John. *The Big Money*, 1936, *U.S.A.* (New York: The Modern Library, 1937).

Drury, Allen. *Advise and Consent*, 1959 (London: Collins, 1960).

Farrell, James T. "A Casual Incident," *Calico Shoes and Other Stories* (New York: The Vanguard Press, 1934), pp. 140–47.

———. *Studs Lonigan: A Trilogy* (New York: The Modern Library, 1938) [*Young Lonigan*, 1932; *The Young Manhood of Studs Lonigan*, 1934; *Judgment Day*, 1935].

Faulkner, William. *Absalom, Absalom!* (New York: Random House, 1936).

Fitzgerald, Francis Scott. *This Side of Paradise*, 1920, *The Bodley Head Scott Fitzgerald* (London: The Bodley Head, 1960), vol. III, pp. 9–270.

———. *The Beautiful and the Damned*, 1922, *ibid.*, vol. IV, 1961, pp. 7–393.

———. *The Great Gatsby*, 1925, *ibid.*, vol. I, 1958, pp. 162–163.

——. "Basil: The Scandal Detectives," 1928, *ibid.*, vol. VI, 1963, pp. 13–35.

——. "Basil: The Freshest Boy," pp. 55–80.

——. "Basil: The Captured Shadow," pp. 105–127.

——. *Tender Is the Night,* 1934, *ibid.*, vol. II, 1959.

——. *The Crack Up, with Other Uncollected Pieces, Notebooks and Unpublished Letters,* ed. E. Wilson (New York: New Directions, 1945).

Frank, Waldo. *The Dark Mother* (New York: Boni & Liveright, 1920).

——. *The Death and Birth of David Markand: an American Story* (New York: Scribner's Sons, 1934).

Friedman, Bruce Jay. *Stern* (New York: Simon & Schuster, 1962).

——. *A Mother's Kisses* (New York: Simon & Schuster, 1964).

Fuller, Henry Blake. *Bertram Cope's Year* (Chicago: Ralph Fletcher Seymour, the Alderbunk Press, 1919).

Genet, Jean. *Our Lady of the Flowers,* 1943, 1951 (tr. B. Frechtman, London: Panther Books, 1966).

——. *Funeral Rites,* 1953 (tr. B. Frechtman, New York: Grove Press, 1969).

——. *The Thief's Journal,* 1948 (tr. B. Frechtman, New York: Grove Press, 1973).

——. *Querelle,* 1953 (tr. Anselm Hollo, New York: Grove Press, 1974).

Goodman, Paul. *Parents' Day* (Saugatuch: The 5×8 Press, 1951).

Goyen, William. *The House of Breath* (New York: Random House, 1950).

Hemingway, Ernest. "The End of Something," *In Our Time,* 1925 (New York: Charles Scribner's Sons, 1930), pp. 35–41.

——. "The Three-Day Blow," *ibid.*, pp. 45–61.

——. "Soldier's Home," *ibid.*, pp. 89–101.

——. "Cross-Country Snow," *ibid.*, pp. 139–47.

——. *The Sun Also Rises,* 1926 (New York: The Modern Library, 1930).

——. "A Simple Enquiry," *Men Without Women* (New York: Charles Scribner's Sons, 1927) pp. 162–67; *The Short Stories of Ernest Hemingway* (New York: Charles Scribner's Sons, 1938), pp. 327–30.

——. *A Farewell to Arms,* 1929 (New York: Charles Scribner's Sons, 1957).

——. *To Have and Have Not* (New York: Charles Scribner's Sons, 1937).

———. "The Short Happy Life of Francis Macomber," "*The Fifth Column*" *and the First Forty-Nine Stories* (New York: Charles Scribner's Sons, 1938), pp. 108–36.

———. "The Battler," *The Short Stories of Ernest Hemingway*, pp. 127–38.

———. "The Light of the World," *ibid.*, pp. 385–91.

———. "The Mother of a Queen," *ibid.*, pp. 415–19.

———. *For Whom the Bell Tolls* (New York: Charles Scribner's Sons, 1940).

———. *Across the River and Into the Trees* (New York: Charles Scribner's Sons, 1950).

———. *The Old Man and the Sea* (New York: Charles Scribner's Sons, 1952).

Herlihy, James Leo. *Midnight Cowboy* (New York: Simon & Schuster, 1965).

Holmes, Oliver Wendell. *The Psychiatric Novels of Oliver Wendell Holmes*, abridgment, introduction and psychiatric annotations by Clarence P. Oberndorf, M.D., 1943 (New York: Columbia Univ. Press, 1946) [*A Mortal Antipathy*, pp. 200–64].

Isherwood, Christopher. *Mr. Norris Changes Trains*, 1935 (London: Hogarth Press, 1956).

———. *Goodbye to Berlin* (New York: Random House, 1939).

———. *Down There on a Visit* (New York: Simon and Schuster, 1961).

———. *A Single Man* (New York: Simon and Schuster, 1964).

———. *A Meeting by the River* (London: Methuen & Co., 1967).

Jackson, Charles. *The Lost Weekend* (New York: Farrar & Rinehart, 1944).

———. *The Fall of Valor* (New York: Rinehart & Co., 1946).

———. "Palm Sunday," *The Sunnier Side: Twelve Arcadian Tales* (New York: Farrar, Strauss & Co., 1950), pp. 85–106.

———. "By the Sea," *ibid.*, pp. 201–17.

———. *A Second-Hand Life* (New York: Macmillan, 1967).

James, Henry. "De Grey: a Romance," 1868, *The Complete Tales of Henry James*, ed. Leon Edel (New York: J. B. Lippincott, 1962), vol. I, pp. 387–428.

———. "A Light Man," 1869, *ibid.*, vol. II, 1962, pp. 61–96.

———. "Longstaff's Marriage," 1878, *ibid.*, vol. IV, 1962, pp. 209–42.

———. *The Europeans: A Sketch* (Boston: Houghton, Osgood, 1879).

———. "The Author of 'Beltraffio,'" 1884, *The Complete Tales . . .* , vol. V, 1963, pp. 303–55.

———. "The Pupil," 1890, *ibid.*, vol. VIII, 1963, pp. 409–60.

———. "Collaboration," 1892, *ibid.*, vol. VIII, 1963, pp. 407–32.

———. *The Turn of the Screw*, 1898, *ibid.*, vol. X, 1964, pp. 15–138.

———. "Maud Evelyn," 1900, *ibid.*, vol. XI, 1964, pp. 43–75.

———. "The Great Good Place," 1900, *ibid.*, pp. 13–42.

———. *The Ambassadors*, 1903 (New York, Harper & Brothers, 1948).

Jones, James, *From Here to Eternity* (New York: Charles Scribner's Sons, 1951).

Kaufmann, Stanley. "Fulvous Yellow," *21 Variations on a Theme* (New York: Greenberg, 1953), pp. 186–96.

Knowles, John. *A Separate Peace* (New York: Macmillan, 1960).

———. *Phineas: Six Stories* (New York: Random House, 1968).

Lawrence, David Herbert. "The Prussian Officer," 1914, *The Prussian Officer and Other Stories* (London: Martin Secker, 1929), pp. 1–33.

———. *Women in Love*, 1920 (New York: The Modern Library, 1950).

———. *Aaron's Rod* (London: Martin Secker, 1922).

Lehr, Wilson. "No Competition," 1947, *21 Variations on a Theme* (New York: Greenberg, 1953), pp. 227–36.

Lewis, Sinclair. *Main Street*, 1920 (New York: Harcourt, Brace & World, 1948).

———. *Babbitt* (New York: Harcourt, Brace, 1922).

———. *It Can't Happen Here* (New York: The Sun Dial Press, 1935).

London, Jack. *The Sea-Wolf* (New York: Macmillan, 1904).

———. *The Game*, 1905, *The Fitzroy Edition of the Works of Jack London* (London: Arco Publications, 1967), pp. 13–64.

———. *The Road*, 1907, *The Bodley Head Jack London*, vol. II, 1964, pp. 319–454.

———. "The Unexpected," 1907, *ibid.*, vol. IV, 1966, pp. 314–36.

———. *Martin Eden*, 1909, *ibid.*, vol. III, 1965.

———. *Burning Daylight* (New York: Macmillan, 1910).

———. *Adventure* (New York: Macmillan, 1911).

———. *The Abysmal Brute*, 1913, *The Fitzroy Edition of the Works of Jack London* [with *The Game*] pp. 67–142.

McCullers, Carson. *The Heart Is a Lonely Hunter* (Boston: Houghton Mifflin, 1940).

———. *Reflections in a Golden Eye* (Boston: Houghton Mifflin, 1941).

———. *The Ballad of the Sad Café*, 1951, *Collected Short Stories and the Novel The Ballad of the Sad Café* (Boston: Houghton Mifflin, 1955), pp. 1–54.

———. *Clock Without Hands* (Boston: Houghton Mifflin, 1961).

McIntosh, Harley Cozad. *This Finer Shadow* (New York: The Dial Press, 1941).

Mailer, Norman. *The Naked and the Dead* (New York: Rinehart, 1948).

――――. *Barbary Shore* (New York: Rinehart, 1951).

――――. *The Deer Park* (New York: G. P. Putnam's Sons, 1955).

――――. "The Time of Her Time," *Advertisements for Myself* (New York: Rinehart, 1959), pp. 478–503.

――――. *An American Dream* (New York: The Dial Press, 1965).

――――. *Why Are We in Vietnam?* (New York: G. P. Putnam's Sons, 1967).

Mann, Thomas. *Death in Venice,* 1924 (tr. K. Burke, New York: Knopf, 1965).

Maxwell, William. *The Folded Leaf* (New York: Harper and Brothers, 1945).

Mayne, Xavier [pseud. of E. I. Prime-Stevenson]. *Imre: a Memorandum,* 1906 (New York: Arno Press, 1975).

Melville, Herman. *Typee,* 1846 (Boston: L. C. Page, 1950).

――――. *Redburn: His First Voyage,* 1847 (Boston: L. C. Page, 1924).

――――. *Omoo,* 1847 (Boston: L. C. Page, 1951).

――――. *White-Jacket, or The World in a Man-of-War,* 1850 (Boston: L. C. Page & Co., 1950); New York: Grove Press, 1956.

――――. *Pierre; or, The Ambiguities,* 1852, ed. by H. A. Murray (New York: Hendricks House, 1949).

――――. *Billy Budd, Sailor (An Inside Narrative),* 1891, ed. H. Hayford & M. Sealts, Jr. (Chicago: University of Chicago Press, 1961).

Miller, Merle. *That Winter* (New York: William Sloane, 1947).

Montherlant, Henry de. *The Girls: A Tetralogy of Novels,* 1936–39 (tr. T. Kilmartin, New York: Harper & Row, 1968).

――――. *Les Olympiques,* 1924 (Paris: N. R. F. Gallimard, 1954).

――――. *Les Garçons* (Paris: N. R. F. Gallimard, 1969).

Motley, Willard. *Knock on Any Door* (New York: D. Appleton-Century, 1947).

Murphy, Dennis. *The Sergeant* (New York: The Viking Press, 1958).

Niles, Blair. *Strange Brother* (New York: Liveright, Inc., 1931).

Paul, Elliot. *Concert Pitch* (New York: Random House, 1938).

Perrein, Michèle. *Le Petit Jules* (Paris: Julliard, 1965).

Phelps, Robert. *Heroes and Orators* (New York: McDowell, Obolensky, 1958).

Pine, Hester. *Beer for the Kitten* (New York: Farrar & Rinehart Inc., 1939).

Proust, Marcel. *Remembrance of Things Past* (tr. Scott Moncrieff, New York: Random House, 1934).

Purdy, James. *Malcolm,* 1959 (London: Martin Secker, 1930).

——. *The Nephew* (New York: Farrar, Strauss, Cudahy, 1960).

——. *Eustace Chisholm and the Works* (New York: Farrar, Strauss & Giroux, 1967).

Rechy, John. *City of Night* (New York: Grove Press, 1963).

——. *Numbers* (New York: Grove Press, 1968).

——. *This Day's Death* (New York: Grove Press, 1969).

Salinger, Jerome David. *The Catcher in the Rye* (Boston: Little, Brown, 1951).

Schorer, Mark. "Long in Populous City Pent," 1937, *21 Variations on a Theme* (New York: Greenberg, 1953), pp. 290–95.

Selby, Hubert. *Last Exit to Brooklyn* (New York: Grove Press, 1964).

Steinbeck, John. *Of Mice and Men* (New York: Covici Friede, 1937).

Styron, William. *Set This House on Fire* (New York: Random House, 1960).

——. *The Confessions of Nat Turner* (New York: Random House, 1967).

Sutherland, A., and Anderson, P., eds. *Eros: an Anthology of Friendship* (London: Anthony Blond, 1961).

Trocchi, Alexander. *Cain's Book* (New York: Grove Press, 1960).

Updike, John. *Rabbit, Run* (New York: Alfred A. Knopf, 1960).

——. *The Centaur* (New York: Alfred A. Knopf, 1963).

Vidal, Gore. *In a Yellow Wood* (New York: Dutton, 1947).

——. *The City and the Pillar* (New York: Dutton, 1948).

——. *The Season of Comfort* (New York: Dutton, 1949).

——. *The Judgment of Paris* (New York: Dutton, 1952) [revised edition: Boston: Little, Brown, 1965].

——. "The Zenner Trophy," *A Thirsty Evil* (New York: The Zero Press, 1956), pp. 68–80.

——. "Pages from an Abandoned Journal," *ibid.*, pp. 130–31.

——. *The City and the Pillar Revised* (Boston: Little, Brown, 1965).

——. *Myra Breckinridge* (Boston: Little, Brown, 1968).

——. *Two Sisters, a memoir in the form of a novel* (Boston: Little, Brown, 1970).

Wahl, Loren [Lawrence Madalena]. *The Invisible Glass* (New York: Greenberg, 1950).

Williams, Tennessee. *The Roman Spring of Mrs. Stone* (New York: New Directions, 1950).

——. *One Arm and Other Stories*, 1950 (New York: New Directions, 1954).

——. *Hard Candy*, 1954 (New York: New Directions, 1959).

Wolfe, Thomas. *Of Time and the River: A Legend of Man's Hunger in His Youth* (New York: Charles Scribner's Sons, 1935).

Wylie, Philip. *Opus 21: Descriptive Music for the Lower Kinsey Epoch of the Atomic Age, a Concerto for a One Man Band, Six Arias for Soap Operas, Fugues, Anthems and Barrel House* (New York: Rinehart, 1949).

——. *The Disappearance* (New York: Rinehart, 1951).

III. DRAMA

Albee, Edward. *The Zoo Story*, 1959 (New York: Coward-McCann, 1960) [with *The Death of Bessie Smith, The Sandbox*].

——. *The American Dream* (New York: Coward-McCann, 1961).

——. *Who's Afraid of Virginia Woolf?* (New York: Atheneum, 1962).

——. *The Ballad of the Sad Café* (New York: Atheneum, 1963).

——. *Tiny Alice* (New York: Atheneum, 1965).

——. *A Delicate Balance* (New York: Atheneum, 1966).

——. *Malcolm* (New York: Atheneum, 1966).

——. *Everything in the Garden* (New York: Atheneum, 1968).

Anderson, Robert. *Tea and Sympathy* (New York: Random House, 1953).

Barr, James. *Game of Fools* (Los Angeles: One, Inc., 1955).

Crowley, Mart. *The Boys in the Band* (New York: Farrar, Strauss & Giroux, 1968).

Herbert, John. *Fortune and Men's Eyes* (New York: Grove Press, 1967).

Inge, William. *Come Back, Little Sheba*, 1950, *4 Plays by William Inge* (New York: Random House, 1958).

——. *Picnic*, 1953, *ibid.*, Dramatists Play Service, 1950.

——. *Bus Stop*, 1955, *ibid.*

——. *The Dark at the Top of the Stairs* (New York: Random House, 1958).

——. *A Loss of Roses* (New York: Random House, 1960).

——. *Splendor in the Grass* [Scenario] (New York: Bantam Books, 1961).

——. *The Boy in the Basement, Summer Brave and Eleven Short Plays* (New York: Random House, 1962).

——. *The Tiny Closet; A Murder; A Call, ibid.*

——. *Natural Affection* (New York: Random House, 1963).

——. *Where's Daddy?* (New York: Random House, 1964); Dramatists Play Service, 1966.

Jones, LeRoi. *The Baptism and The Toilet*, 1964 (New York: Grove Press, 1966).

Miller, Arthur. *A View from the Bridge* [with *A Memory of Two Mondays*] (New York: The Viking Press, 1955).

Vidal, Gore. *The Best Man* (New York: Little, Brown, 1960).

Williams, Tennessee. *The Glass Menagerie* (New York: Random House, 1945).

——. *A Streetcar Named Desire* (New York: New Directions, 1947).

——. [with David Windham]. *You Touched Me!* (New York: Samuel French, 1947).

——. *Summer and Smoke* (New York: New Directions, 1948).

——. *The Rose Tattoo* (New York: New Directions, 1950).

——. *I Rise in Flame, Cried the Phoenix* (New York: New Directions, 1951).

——. *Camino Real* (New York: New Directions, 1953).

——. *Cat on a Hot Tin Roof* (New York: New Directions, 1954).

——. *Orpheus Descending* [with *Battle of Angels*] (New York: New Directions, 1958).

——. *Suddenly Last Summer* (New York: New Directions, 1958).

——. *Sweet Bird of Youth* (New York: New Directions, 1959).

——. *Period of Adjustment: High Point Over a Cavern, A Serious Comedy* (New York: New Directions, 1960).

——. *Small Craft Warnings* (New York: New Directions, 1972).

IV. GENERAL LITERARY CRITICISM*

Aldridge, J. W. *After the Lost Generation: A Critical Study of the Writers of the Two Wars* (New York: McGraw-Hill, 1951).

Arnavon, C. *Histoire Littéraire des Etats-Unis* (Paris: Hachette, 1953).

Auden, W. H. *The Enchafèd Flood or the Romantic Iconography of the Sea* (London: Faber and Faber, 1951).

Chase, R. *The American Novel and Its Tradition* (New York: Doubleday, 1957).

College English

De Mott, B. "But He's a Homosexual . . . ," *Supergrow: Essays and Reports on Imagination in America* (New York: New American Library, 1967), pp. 17–34.

Dommergues, P. *Les Ecrivains Américains d'Aujourd'hui* (Paris: P.U.F., 1965).

——. *Les U.S.A. à la Recherche de leur Identité: rencontres avec 40 écrivains américains* (Paris: Grasset, 1967).

*Fiedler, L. *Love and Death in the American Novel* (New York: Criterion Books, 1960).

——. *Waiting for the End* (New York: Stein & Day, 1964).

* Works indicated by asterisks have been especially helpful in the preparation of this book.

*Geismar, M. *Writers in Crisis: the American Novel, 1925–1940* (Boston: Houghton Mifflin, 1942).

*——. *The Last of the Provincials: the American Novel, 1915–1925* Boston: Houghton Mifflin, 1949).

*——. *Rebels and Ancestors: the American Novel, 1890–1915,* 1953 (London: W. H. Allen, 1954).

Hoffman, F. J. *Freudianism and the Literary Mind* (Baton Rouge: Louisiana State University, 1945).

——. *The Art of Southern Fiction: A Study of Some Modern Novelists* (Carbondale and Edwardsville: Southern Illinois University Press, 1967).

Karolides, N. J. *The Pioneer in the American Novel: 1900–1950* (Norman: University of Oklahoma Press, 1965).

Kempf, R. *Sur le Corps Romanesque* (Paris: Seuil, 1968), 189 p.

*Lawrence, D. H. *Studies in Classic American Literature,* 1923 (New York: The Viking Press, 1964).

*——. *The Symbolic Meaning: The Uncollected Versions of Studies in Classic American Literature,* ed. Armin Arnold (Fontwell, Arundel: Centaur Press, 1962).

Lewisohn, L. *Expression in America* (New York: Harper & Brothers, 1932).

Mathiessen, F. O. *The American Renaissance: Art and Expression in the Age of Emerson and Whitman* (London, Toronto, New York: Oxford University Press, 1941).

Mauron, Ch. *Des Metaphores obsedantes au Mythe Personnel, introduction a la psychocritique* (Paris: Jose Corti, 1962).

*Millett, K. *Sexual Politics* (New York: Doubleday, 1971).

Moore, H. T., ed. *Contemporary American Novelists* (Carbondale: Southern Illinois University Press, 1964).

Ruitenbeek, H. M. *Homosexuality and Creative Genius* (New York: Obolensky, Astor-Honor, 1967).

Waldmeir, J. J., ed. *Recent American Fiction, some critical views* (Boston: Houghton Mifflin, 1963).

V. BOOKS AND ARTICLES ON NOVELISTS: BIOGRAPHIES, MEMOIRS, LETTERS

Aldridge, J. W. "A Boy and His Mom," *Saturday Review of Literature,* XXXII (Jan. 15, 1949), pp. 19–20 [on Vidal].

——. "America's Young Novelists: Uneasy Inheritors of a Revolution," *Saturday Review of Literature,* XXXII (Feb. 12, 1949), pp. 6–8, 36–37, 42 [on Vidal].

Arvin, N. *Herman Melville* (William Sloane Associates, 1950).

Asselineau, R. *Ernest Hemingway* (Paris: Seghers, 1972).

Astre, G. A. *Hemingway par lui-même* (Paris: Seuil, 1959).

Baker, C. *Ernest Hemingway, a life story* (New York: Charles Scribner's Sons, 1969).

Baldwin, J. *No Name in the Street* (New York: The Dial Press, 1972).

Beaver, H. "Introduction," *Billy Budd, Sailor* (London: Penguin Books, 1970), pp. 9–50.

Bittner, W. *The Novels of Waldo Frank* (Philadelphia: University of Pennsylvania Press, 1958).

Bonaparte, M. *The Life and Works of Edgar Allan Poe: A Psychoanalytic Interpretation* (London: Imago Publishing Co., 1949).

Bowen, M. *The Long Encounter: Self and Experience in the Writings of Herman Melville* (Chicago: University of Chicago Press, 1960).

Branch, E. M. *James T. Farrell* (Minneapolis: University of Minnesota Press, 1963).

Brandy, L., ed. *Norman Mailer: A Collection of Critical Essays* (Englewood Cliffs, N. J.: Prentice-Hall, 1972).

Breit, H. "James Baldwin and Two Footnotes," *The Creative Present: Notes on Contemporary Fiction*, ed. by Nona Balakian & Charles Simmons (New York: Doubleday, 1963), pp. 16–17.

Bruccoli, M. *The Composition of "Tender Is the Night"* (University of Pittsburgh Press, 1963).

Calder-Marshall, "Introduction," *Martin Eden, The Bodley Head Jack London*, pp. 5–18.

Cargill, O. *The Novels of Henry James* (New York: Macmillan, 1961).

Chase, R., ed. *Melville: A Collection of Critical Essays* (Englewood Cliffs, N. J.: Prentice-Hall, 1962).

Clayton, J. J. *Saul Bellow: In Defense of Man* (Bloomington: Indiana University Press, 1968).

Cleaver, E. "Notes on a Native Son," *Soul on Ice* (New York: McGraw-Hill, 1968), pp. 97–111 [on Baldwin].

Dommergues, P. *Saul Bellow* (Paris: Grasset, 1969).

Dupee, F. W. *Henry James: His Life and Writings* (New York: Doubleday, 1956).

Eckman, F. M. *The Furious Passage of James Baldwin* (New York: Evans, 1966).

*Edel, L. *Henry James* (Philadelphia: Lippincott); vol. I: *The Untried Years, 1843–1870* (1953), vol. II: *The Conquest of London, 1870–1881* (1962), vol. III: *The Middle Years, 1882–1895*

(1962), vol. IV: *The Treacherous Years, 1895–1901* (1969), vol. V: *The Master, 1904–1916* (1972).

Evans, O. *Carson McCullers: Her Life and Work* (London: Peter Owen, 1965).

Fabre, M. *"Tender Is the Night," Francis Scott Fitzgerald* (Paris: Armand Collin, U/U2, 1969) pp. 214–357.

Fiedler, L. "Some Notes on F. Scott Fitzgerald," 1955, *F. Scott Fitzgerald: A Collection of Critical Essays,* ed. Arthur Mizener (Englewood Cliffs, N. J.: Prentice-Hall, 1963) pp. 70–76.

Ford, G. H. *Double Measure: A Study of the Novels and Stories of D. H. Lawrence* (New York: Norton, 1965).

Geismar, M. *Henry James and the Jacobites* (Boston: Houghton Mifflin, 1963).

Harper, H. M., Jr. *Desperate Faith: A Study of Bellow, Salinger, Mailer, Baldwin, and Updike* (Chapel Hill: the University of North Carolina Press, 1967).

Hemingway, E. *A Moveable Feast* (New York: Charles Scribner's Sons, 1964).

Hendricks, K., and Shepherd, I. *Letters from Jack London* (New York: The Odyssey Press, 1965).

Hotcher, A. E. *Papa Hemingway: A Personal Memoir* (New York: Random House, 1966).

Howe, I. "Black Boys and Native Sons," *A World More Attractive: A View of Modern Literature and Politics* (New York: Horizon Press, 1963), pp. 98–122 [on Baldwin].

Hyman, S. E. "Blacks, Whites and Grays," *Standards: A Chronicle of Books for Our Time* (New York: Horizon Press, 1966) pp. 22–27 [on Baldwin].

James, H. *A Small Boy and Others* (New York: Scribner's Sons, 1913).

——. *Notes of a Son and Brother* (London: Macmillan, 1914).

Jones, LeRoi. "Brief Reflections on Two Hot Shots," *Home: Social Essays* (New York: William Morrow, 1966) [on Baldwin].

Kimbrough, R., ed. *Henry James, The Turn of the Screw: An Authoritative Text, Backgrounds and Sources, Essays in Criticism* (New York: Norton, 1966).

Leeds, B. *The Structured Vision of Norman Mailer* (New York: New York University Press, 1969).

Levin, H. *The Power of Blackness, Hawthorne, Poe, Melville* (New York: Alfred A. Knopf, 1964).

Le Vot, A. *"The Great Gatsby," Francis Scott Fitzgerald* (Paris: Armand Collin, U/U2, 1969) pp. 19–212.

*Lewis, R. W., Jr. *Hemingway on Love* (Austin: University of Texas Press, 1965).

London, Charmian. *The Book of Jack London* (London: Mills & Brown, 1921), 2 vols.

London, Jack, and Strunsky, A. *The Kempton-Wace Letters* (New York: Macmillan, 1903).

London, Jack. *John Barleycorn, or Alcoholic Memoirs*, 1913, *The Bodley Head Jack London*, vol. II (London: The Bodley Head, 1964), pp. 31–210.

London, Joan. *Jack London and His Times: An Unconventional Biography*, 1939 (Seattle: University of Washington Press, American Library, 1968).

Lowery, B. *Marcel Proust et Henry James, une confrontation* (Paris: Plon, 1964).

Lubbock, P., ed. *The Letters of Henry James* (New York: Doubleday, 1956), 2 vols.

McLaughlin, R. "Precarious Status," *Saturday Review of Literature*, XXXI, (Jan. 10, 1948), pp. 14–15 [on Vidal].

Mailer, N. *Advertisements for Myself* (New York: Rinehart, 1959).

——. *The Presidential Papers* (New York: G. P. Putnam's Sons, 1963).

——. *Cannibals and Christians* (New York: The Dial Press, 1966).

——. *The Armies of the Night* (New York: The New American Library, 1968).

——. *The Prisoner of Sex* (Boston: Little, Brown, 1971).

Marcus, S. "A Second Look at Sodom," *New York Herald Tribune Book Week*, June 20, 1965, p. 5 [on Vidal].

Mayoux, J. J. *Melville par lui-même* (Paris: Seuil, 1958).

Merle, R. *Oscar Wilde, ou la "destinée" de l'homosexual* (Paris: N. R. F., Gallimard, 1955).

Milford, N. *Zelda Fitzgerald: A Biography* (New York: Harper & Row, 1970).

Miller, E. H. *Melville: A Biography* (New York: George Braziller, 1975).

Mizener, A. *The Far Side of Paradise: A Biography of F. Scott Fitzgerald* (Boston: Houghton Mifflin, 1951).

Mumford, L. *Herman Melville: A Study of His Life and Vision*, 1929, revised edition (New York: Harcourt, Brace & World, 1962).

Murphy, George D. "The Theme of Sublimation in Anderson's *Winesburg, Ohio*," *Modern Fiction Studies*, Summer 1967.

Murray, H. A. "In Nomine Diaboli," *The New England Quarterly*, XXIV, (Dec. 1951), pp. 435–52 [on Melville].

Negriolli, C. *La Symbolique de D. H. Lawrence* (Paris: P.U.F., 1970).

Noel, J. *Footloose in Arcadia* (New York: Carrick & Evans, 1940).

*O'Connor, R. *Jack London: A Biography* (Boston: Little, Brown, & Co., 1964).

Odier, D. *The Job: Interviews with William Burroughs*, 1969 (New York: Grove Press, 1970).

Ozick, C. "Forster as Homosexual," *Commentary*, vol. 52, no. 66 (Dec. 1971), pp. 81–85.

Painter, G. D. *Marcel Proust: A Biography* (London: Chatto & Windus, 1959–65), 2 vols.

Peden, W. "On the Road to Self-Destruction," *New York Times Book Review*, Jan. 27, 1957, p. 33 [on Vidal].

Piper, H. Dan. *F. Scott Fitzgerald: A Critical Portrait* (New York: Holt, Rinehart & Winston, 1965).

Podhoretz, N. "In Defense of James Baldwin," in *Doings and Undoings: The Fifties and After in American Writing* (New York: The Noonday Press, 1964).

Reask, Ch. Russell. *John Knowles' "A Separate Peace"* (New York: Monarch Press, 1966).

Sartre, J. P. *Saint Genet: Actor and Martyr* (tr. Bernard Frechtunan, New York: George Braziller, 1963).

Schorer, M. *Sinclair Lewis: An American Life* (New York: McGraw-Hill, 1961).

Seng, P. J. "The Fallen Idol: The Immature World of Holden Caulfield," *J. D. Salinger and the Critics*, eds. E. F. Belcher and J. W. Lee (Belmont: Wadsworth, 1967) pp. 60–67.

Shrike, J. S. "Recent Phenomena," *Hudson Review*, I (Spring 1948), pp. 136–38, 140, 142, 144 [on Kinsey, Vidal and Capote].

Silhol, R. *Les Tyrans Tragiques, un témoin pathétique de notre temps: Sinclair Lewis* (Paris: P.U.F., 1969).

Spilka, M. "The Death of Love in *The Sun Also Rises*," *Twelve Original Essays in Great American Novels*, ed. Ch. Shapiro (Detroit: Wayne State University Press, 1958) pp. 238–56.

Stafford, W. T., ed. *Melville's "Billy Budd" and the Critics*, revised edition (Belmont, California: Wadsworth, 1968).

Stein, W. B. "Love and Lust in Hemingway's Short Stories," *Texas Studies in Literature and Language*, III (Summer 1961), pp. 234–42.

Stone, G. *Melville* (New York: Sheed & Ward, 1949).

Swann, M. "Henry James and the Heroic Young Master," *London Magazine*, May 1955.

Texas Quarterly, VI (Spring 1963), pp. 107–9.

Turnbull, A. *Scott Fitzgerald* (New York: Charles Scribner's Sons, 1962).

———. *Thomas Wolfe* (New York: Charles Scribner's Sons, 1967).

Vaid, K. Baldev. *Technique in the Tales of Henry James* (Cambridge: Harvard University Press, 1964).

Vidal, Gore. "Robert Graves and the Twelve Caesars," 1959, *Rocking the Boat* (Boston: Little, Brown, 1962), pp. 204–14.

———. "The Revelation of John Horne Burns," 1965, *Reflections Upon a Sinking Ship* (Boston: Little, Brown, 1969), pp. 58–62.

———. *"The City and the Pillar* After Twenty Years," *Reflections Upon a Sinking Ship* (Boston: Little, Brown, 1969), pp. 118–22 ["Afterword to *The City and the Pillar Revised,"* 1965].

Walter, E. "Conversations with Gore Vidal," *Transatlantic Review*, No. 4 (Summer 1960), pp. 5–17.

Watson, E. L. "Melville's Testament of Acceptance," *The New England Quarterly*, VI (June 1953), pp. 319–27.

Weiss, D. "Caliban on Prospero: A Psychoanalytic Study on the Novel *Seize the Day,* by Saul Bellow," *Saul Bellow and the Critics*, ed., I. Malin (New York: New York University Press, 1967), pp. 114–41.

*White, R. L. *Gore Vidal* (New York: Twayne Publishers, 1968).

Williams, T. "Gore Vidal," *McCall's*, (Oct. 1966), p. 107.

———. *Memoirs* (New York: Doubleday, 1975).

Wilson, E. *The Devils and Canon Barham: Ten Essays on Poets, Novelists and Monsters* (New York: Farrar & Giroux, 1973) [on *Bertram Cope's Year*, pp. 40–44].

Young, A. *Allen Ginsberg, Gay Sunshine Interview* (Balinas: Grey Fox Press, 1974).

*Young, Ph. *Ernest Hemingway* (New York: Rinehart, 1952).

———. *Ernest Hemingway: A Reconsideration* (University Park: Pennsylvania State University Press, 1966).

VI. BOOKS AND ARTICLES ON DRAMA

Asselineau, R. "Tennessee Williams ou la Nostalgie de la Pureté," *Etudes Anglaises*, X (Oct.–Dec. 1957), pp. 431–42.

Bigsby, C. W. E. *Albee* (Edinburgh: Oliver and Boyd, 1969).

Brustein, R. "The Men-Taming Women of William Inge," *Harper's Magazine*, CCXVII (Nov. 1958), pp. 52–57.

———. "Williams' Nebulous Nightmare," *The Hudson Review*, XII (Summer 1959), pp. 255–60.

———. "Krapp and a Little Claptrap," *The New Republic*, (Feb. 22, 1960), pp. 21–22 [on Albee].

——. "The Playwright as Impersonator," *Tulane Drama Review,* (Nov. 16, 1963), pp. 28–9.

Clurman, H. "Theatre: Tennessee Williams' Rose," *The New Republic,* CXXXIV (Feb. 19, 1951), p. 22.

Donahue, F. *The Dramatic World of Tennessee Williams* (New York: Frederick Ungar, 1964).

Driver, T. F. "The American Dream," *Christian Century,* March 1, p. 275 [on Albee].

*Falk, S. *Tennessee Williams* (New Haven: Twayne Publishers, 1961).

Franzblau, A. "A Psychiatrist Looks at *Tiny Alice*," *The Saturday Review,* Jan. 30, 1965, p. 39 [on Albee].

Gassner, J. *Theatre at the Crossroads: Plays and Playwrights of the Mid-century American Stage* (New York: Holt, Rinehart & Winston, 1960).

Goodan, H. "Edward Albee," *Drama Survey,* II (Spring 1962), pp. 72–79.

Hartweg, N. Letter to the Editors, *Tulane Drama Review,* (Fall 1965), pp. 208–11 [about D. Kaplan's article].

Hayes, R. "The Stage," *The Commonweal,* LXVIII (May 29, 1958), pp. 232–33 [on T. Williams].

Kaplan, D. "Homosexuality and American Theatre: A Psychoanalytic Comment," *Tulane Drama Review,* (Spring 1965), pp. 30–55.

Kaufmann, S. "Homosexual Drama and Its Disguises," *The New York Times,* Jan. 23, 1966, II, p. 1.

——. "On the Acceptability of the Homosexual," *ibid.,* Feb. 6, 1966, II, p.1.

Kerr, W. "Cat on a Hot Tin Roof," *New York Herald Tribune,* March 25, 1955.

Kostelanetz, R. "The Art of Total No," *Contact,* Oct.–Nov. 1963, pp. 62–70 [on Albee].

Krutch, J. W. *Modernism in Modern Drama: A Definition and an Estimate* (Ithaca: Cornell University, 1953).

McCarthy, M. "Streetcar Called Success," *Sights and Spectacles, 1937–1956* (New York: Farrar, Strauss & Cudahy, 1956), pp. 131–36 [on Williams].

Macdonald, D. "Truth and Illusion in *Who's Afraid of Virginia Woolf?*," *Renascence,* XVII (1964), pp. 63–69 [on Albee].

Nelson, B. *Tennessee Williams: His Life and Work* (London: Peter Owen, 1961).

Popkin, H. "The Plays of Tennessee Williams," *Tulane Drama Review,* IV (Spring 1960), pp. 45–64.

Rice, R. "A Man Named Tennessee," *New York Post,* April 21–25, April 27, May 4, 1958.

Roth, Ph. "The Play That Dare Not Speak Its Name," *The New York Review of Books,* Feb. 25, 1965, p. 4 [on Albee].

*Rutenberg, M. E. *Edward Albee: Playwright in Protest* (New York: D. B. S. Publications, 1969).

*Shuman, R. B. *William Inge* (New Haven: Twayne Publishers, 1965).

Tischler, N. M. *Tennessee Williams: Rebellious Puritan* (New York: The Citadel Press, 1961).

Waters, A. B. "Tennessee Williams: Ten Years Later," *Theatre Arts,* XXXIX (July 1955), pp. 72–77.

Wood, R. "Homosexuality on the Modern Stage," 1959, *The Third Sex,* ed. I. Rubin (New York: New Books, 1961).

VII. BOOKS AND ARTICLES IN PSYCHOSOCIOLOGY

Allen, C. "The Aging Homosexual," 1959, *The Third Sex,* pp. 91–95.

Altman, D. *Homosexual: Oppression and Liberation* (New York: Outerbridge & Lazard, 1971).

Anomaly, *The Invert* (London: Baillère, Trindall & Cox, 1948).

Arthur, G. *The Circle of Sex* (New York: University Books, 1966).

Bailey, D. S. *Homosexuality and the Western Christian Tradition* (London, New York, Toronto: Longmans, Green Co., 1955).

Bakan, D. *Sigmund Freud and the Jewish Mystical Tradition,* 1964 (Boston: The Beacon Press, 1975).

Baldwin, J. "The Male Prison," *Nobody Knows My Name* (New York: The Dial Press, 1961), pp. 155–62.

——. *The Fire Next Time* (New York: The Dial Press, 1963).

Becker, A. L. "A Third Sex? Some Speculations on a Sexuality Spectrum," *Medical Proceedings,* 13 (April 1967), pp. 67–74.

Becker, R. de. *L'Erotisme d'en Face* (Paris: J. J. Pauvert, 1964).

Berg, Ch., and Allen, C. *The Problem of Homosexuality* (New York: The Citadel Press, 1958).

Bergler, E. "Male Homosexuality," *Neurotic Counterfeit Sex* (New York: Grune & Stratton, 1951) pp. 184–207.

——. *Homosexuality: Disease or Way of Life?* (New York: Hill & Wang, 1957).

Bieber, I., and others. *Homosexuality: A Psychoanalytic Study of Male Homosexuals* (New York: Basic Books, 1962).

Brenton, M. *The American Male* (New York: Coward-McCann, 1966).

Brown, N. O. *Life Against Death: The Psychoanalytical Meaning of History* (Middletown, Conn.: Wesleyan University Press, 1959).

Cappon, D. *Toward an Understanding of Homosexuality* (Englewood Cliffs, N.J.: Prentice-Hall, 1965).

Caprio, F. S., and Brenner, D. R. *Sexual Behavior: Psycho-Legal Aspects* (New York: The Citadel Press, 1961).

Carpenter, E. *Homogenic Love and Its Place in a Free Society* (Manchester: The Labour Press Society Ltd., 1894).

——. *The Intermediate Sex: A Study of Some Transitional Types of Men and Women* (London: S. Sonnenscheim & Co., 1908).

Churchill, Wainwright. *Homosexual Behavior Among Males: A Cross-Cultural and Cross-Species Investigation* (New York: Hawthorn Books, 1967).

Cleaver, E. *Soul on Ice* (New York: McGraw-Hill, 1968).

Cleckley, H. *The Caricature of Love: A Discussion of Social, Psychiatric and Literary Manifestations of Pathologic Sexuality* (New York: The Ronald Press, 1957).

Commager, H. Steele. *The American Mind, an interpretation of the American thought and character since the 1880's* (New Haven: Yale University Press, 1950).

*Cory, D. W. *The Homosexual in America: A Subjective Approach* (New York: Greenberg, 1951).

*——. *Homosexuality: A Cross-Cultural Approach* (New York: The Julian Press, 1956).

*——, & LeRoy, J. P. *The Homosexual and His Society* (New York: The Citadel Press, 1963).

Ellis, A. *The American Sexual Tragedy* (New York: Twayne Publishers, 1954).

——. *Homosexuality: Its Causes and Cure* (New York: Lyle Stuart, 1965).

Ellis, H. *Sexual Inversion*, 1897 (Philadelphia: F. A. Davis Co., 1901).

——. *Psychology of Sex: A Manual for Students*, 1937 (New York: Emerson Books, 1946).

Erikson, E. *Identity, Youth and Crisis* (New York: Norton, 1968).

Fanon, F. *Black Skin, White Masks*, 1952 (tr. Ch. L. Markmann, New York: Grove Press).

Fisher, P. *The Gay Mystique* (New York: Stein & Day, 1972).

Flaceliere, R. *Love in Ancient Greece*, 1960 (tr. J. Cleugh, New York: Crown Publishers, 1962).

Ford, G. S., and Beach, F. A. *Patterns of Sexual Behavior* (New York: Harper, 1951).

Frank, W. *Our America* (New York: Boni & Liveright, 1919).

*Freud, S. *Three Contributions to the Theory of Sex* (tr. A. A. Brill, Nervous and Mental Disease Monographs, 1910).

*———. *A General Introduction to Psychoanalysis* (New York: Boni & Liveright, 1924).

Fromm, E. *The Art of Loving* (New York: Harper & Row, 1956).

Genauer, E. "Devilish Dilemma of the Devious Deviates," *New York Herald Tribune*, Feb. 6, 1966, p. 31.

Gerassi, J. *The Boys of Boise: Furor, Vice and Folly in an American City* (New York: Macmillan, 1966).

Gide, A. *Corydon*, 1925 (New York: Farrar, Strauss and Co., 1950).

Giese, H. *L'Homosexualité de l'Homme* (Paris: Payot, 1968).

Goldberg, I. *Havelock Ellis: A Biography and Critical Survey* (London: Constable and Co., 1926).

Goodman, P. *Growing Up Absurd: Problems of Youth in the Organized System* (New York: Random House, 1960).

Gorer, G. *The American People: A Study in National Character*, 1948, revised ed. (New York: Norton, 1964).

Gross, A. *Strangers in Our Midst: Problems of the Homosexual in American Society* (Washington, Public Affairs Press, 1962).

Hart, J. D. *The Popular Book: A History of America's Literary Taste* (New York: Oxford University Press, 1950).

Henry, G. W. *All the Sexes: A Study of Masculinity and Femininity* (New York: Rinehart & Co., 1955).

Heron, A., ed. *Towards a Quaker View of Sex: An Essay by a Group of Friends* (London: Friends Home Service Committee, 1963).

Hoffman, M. *The Gay World: Male Homosexuality and the Social Creation of Evil* (New York: Basic Books, 1968).

Hooker, E. "The Adjustment of the Male Overt Homosexual," *Journal of Projective Techniques*, 1957, 21, pp. 18–31.

———. "The Homosexual Community," 1961, *Sexual Deviance*, ed. J. H. Gagnon and W. Simon (New York: Harper & Row, 1967), pp. 167–84.

———. "Male Homosexuals and Their 'World,'" *Sexual Inversion: The Multiple Roots of Homosexuality*, ed. Judd Marmor (New York: Basic Books, 1965), pp. 83–107.

James, W. *Principles of Psychology* (New York: Henry Holt & Co., 1890) vol. II.

Jones, LeRoi. *Home: Social Essays* (New York: William Morrow, 1966).

Kinsey, A., et al. *Sexual Behavior in the Human Male* (Philadelphia: W. B. Saunders Co., 1948).

Krafft-Ebing, R. von. *Psychopathia Sexualis,* 1923 (Paris: Payot, 1969).

Krich, A. M., ed. *The Homosexuals: As Seen by Themselves and Thirty Authorities* (New York: The Citadel Press, 1954).

Kubie, L. "Psychiatric Implications of the Kinsey Report," *Journal of Psychomatic Medicine,* March–April 1948.

Lawrence, D. H. *Psychoanalysis and the Unconscious* (New York: Thomas Seltzer, 1921).

——. *Fantasia of the Unconscious* (New York: Thomas Seltzer, 1922).

Lerner, M. "'Scandal' in the State Department," *New York Post,* July 10–23, 1950.

——. *America as a Civilization: Life and Thought in the United States Today* (New York: Simon & Schuster, 1957), 1,036 pp.

Marcuse, H. *Eros and Civilisation: A Philosophical Inquiry into Freud,* 1966 (Boston: The Beacon Press, 1969).

Marrou, H. I. *The History of Education in Antiquity* (tr. George Lamb, New York: Sheed and Ward, 1956).

Masters, R. E. L. *The Homosexual Revolution: A Challenging Exposé of the Social and Political Directions of a Minority Group* (New York: The Julian Press, 1962).

Mead, M. *Male and Female: A Study of the Sexes in a Changing World* (London: Collancz, 1949).

Miller, M. *On Being Different: What It Means to be a Homosexual* (New York: Random House, 1971).

Mitchell, R. S. *The Homosexual and the Law* (New York: Arco, 1969).

Nacht, S. *Le Masochisme* (Paris: Payot, 1965).

Nathan, P. *The Psychology of Fascism* (London: Faber & Faber, 1943).

Newsweek "Special Report: The Militant Homosexual," *Newsweek,* (August 23, 1971), pp. 51–54.

Oliver, B. *Sexual Deviation in American Society* (New Haven, Conn.: College and University Press, 1967).

Ollendorf, R. *The Juvenile Homosexual Experience and its Effect on Adult Sexuality* (New York: The Julian Press, 1966).

Packard, V. O. *The Sexual Wilderness* (New York: David McKay, 1968).

Perry, Troy, Rev. *The Lord Is My Shepherd and He Knows I'm Gay* (Los Angeles: Nash Publishing, 1972).

"*Playboy* Panel on Homosexuality," *Playboy*, (April 1971), pp. 61–96, 108, 178–91 [I. Bieber, P. Goodman, J. Marmor, M. Ploscowe, D. Leitsch, W. Simon, K. Tynan . . .].

Ploscowe, M. *Sex and the Law*, revised edition (New York: Ace Books, 1962).

Reich, W. *The Sexual Revolution, towards a self-governing character structure*, 1930 (New York: Orgone Institute Press, 1945).

———. *The Mass Psychology of Fascism*, 1933 (tr. V. R. Carfagno, London, Souvenir Press, 1970).

———. *The Discovery of the Orgone*, vol. I: *The Function of the Orgasm* (New York: Orgone Institute Press, 1948).

Reik, Th. *Psychology of Sex Relations* (New York: Rinehart, 1945).

Reiss, A. J. "The Social Integration of Queers and Peers," in H. M. Ruitenbeek, ed., *The Problem of Homosexuality in Modern Society*, pp. 249–77.

Rogers, B. *The Queen's Vernacular: A Gay Lexicon* (San Francisco: Straight Arrow Books, 1972).

Rossi, A. S. "Equality Between the Sexes: An Immodest Proposal," *The Woman in America*, ed. R. J. Lifton (Boston: Houghton Mifflin, 1964) pp. 98–143.

Rougemont, D. de. *L'Amour et l'Occident* (Paris: Plon, 1939).

Ruitenbeek, H. M., ed. *The Problem of Homosexuality in Modern Society* (New York: Dutton, 1963).

———. *Freud and America* (New York: Macmillan, 1966).

Schelsky, H. *Sociologie de la Sexuality*, 1955, trad. M. Camhi (Paris: Gallimard, "Idées," 1966).

Sontag, S. "Notes on 'Camp,'" *Against Interpretation* (New York: Farrar, Strauss & Giroux, 1964) pp. 274–90.

Stern, J. *The Sixth Man* (New York: Doubleday, 1961).

Symonds, J. A. *A Problem of Modern Ethics* (London: 1896).

Teal, D. *The Gay Militants* (New York: Stein & Day, 1971).

Terman, L. M., and Miles, C. Cox. *Sex and Personality: Studies in Masculinity and Femininity* (New York: McGraw-Hill, 1936).

"Time Essay: Homosexuality," *Time*, Jan. 21, 1966, pp. 40–41.

Time, Sept. 8, 1975, "Gays on the March," pp. 32–43.

Towne, A. "The Sexual Gentleman's Agreement," *Neurotica*, VI (Spring 1950), pp. 23–28.

Trilling, D. "The Image of Women in Contemporary Literature," *The Woman in America*, pp. 52–71.

Tripp, C. A. *The Homosexual Matrix* (New York: McGraw-Hill, 1975).

Tyler, P. *Screening the Sexes: Homosexuality in the Movies* (New York: Holt, Rinehart & Winston, 1972).

Vidal, G. *Reflections Upon a Sinking Ship* (Boston: Little, Brown, 1969).

Wecter, D. *The Hero in America: A Chronicle of Hero Worship* (New York: Charles Scribner's Sons, 1941).

Weinberg, G. *Society and the Healthy Homosexual* (New York: St. Martin's Press, 1972).

*Weltge, R. W. *The Same Sex: An Appraisal of Homosexuality* (Philadelphia: United Church Press, 1969).

West, D. J. *Homosexuality* (Chicago: Aldine Publishing Co., 1968), 304 pp.

Westwood, G. *Society and the Homosexual* (New York: Dutton, 1953), 191 pp.

Wolfenden, Sir T., et al. *The Wolfenden Report* (New York: Stein and Day, 1963).

Wylie, Ph. *A Generation of Vipers,* 1942, new annotated edition (New York: Holt, Rinehart & Winston, 1955), 331 pp.

Index

Aaron's Rod (Lawrence), 21

Abrahams, Peter, 97

Absalom, Absalom! (Faulkner), 39–40, 61

Abysmal Brute, The (London), 241, 242, 269

Across the River and into the Trees (Hemingway), 268–69

Adventure (London), 246 248–50, 255, 257, 261, 276, 284

Advertisements for Myself (Mailer), 291

Advise and Consent (Drury), 162–63, 175, 176, 187, 190

Albee, Edward, 33, 134–49, 170, 185, 187, 190, 300, 301

Aldridge, John, 26

Ambassadors, The (James), 39, 200, 203–10, 304

American Dream, An (Mailer), 280, 283, 286–87, 289

American Dream, The (Albee), 137–38, 170, 187, 190

American Mind, The (Commager), 174

"American Sexual Reference, The Black Male" (Jones), 94

Andersen, Hendrik, v, xiv, 201–2, 206, 209

Anderson, Robert, 31, 174

Anderson, Sherwood, 14, 15, 20, 65–67, 153, 218

Another Country (Baldwin), 28–29, 58–59, 98–102, 170, 176, 177, 217, 294, 301

A Rebours (Huysmans), 304

Arthur, Gavin, 109

Art of Loving, The (Fromm), 43

Asselineau, Roger, xii

Astre, Georges-Albert, 263

Auden, W. H., 71–72

"Author of *Beltraffio*, The" (James), 199

Baby Doll (Williams), 110

Bailey, Derrick S., 9

Baker, Carlos, 214, 262, 269, 275, 290

Baldwin, James, xv, 21, 27–29, 44, 53, 54–60, 70, 95n, 96–103, 114, 168, 170–71, 172, 173, 177, 218, 277, 293, 294–96, 297, 298, 301–3, 304

Ballad of the Sad Café, The

(McCullers-Albee), 145–47, 187, 189

Baptism, The (Jones), 32

Barbary Shore (Mailer), 23

Barr, James, 31–32, 90–91, 162, 175, 298

"Basil Stories, The" (Fitzgerald), 38–39, 91–92, 212

"Battler, The" (Hemingway), 15, 16

Baudelaire, Charles Pierre, 13, 304

Beautiful and the Damned, The (Fitzgerald), 218–20

Beer for the Kitten (Pine), 19

Bellaman, Henry, 19, 46, 294

Bellow, Saul, xii, 104, 178, 230–39, 300

Bergler, Edmund, xi, 5–6, 16, 140, 179, 196

Bergman, Ingmar, 137

Bertram Cope's Year (Fuller), 14–15, 27, 67

Best Man, The (Vidal), 32, 162

Bieber, Irving, xi, 6, 140, 172, 229

Big, Money, The (Dos Passos), 18, 22, 165

Billy Budd, Sailor (Melville), xiv, 75, 78–85, 86, 91, 168, 242, 291, 296

Black Skin, White Masks (Fanon), 94

Bonaparte, Marie, 258, 259

Book of Jack London, The, 243

Bourjaily, Vance, 21, 62

Bowles, Paul, 50–51, 54, 158

Boy in the Basement, The (Inge), 132–33, 137, 147, 170

Boys in the Band, The (Crowley), 32–33, 166, 170, 174, 175, 177, 181, 182, 294, 301

Boys of Boise, The: Furor, Vice and Folly in an American City (Gerassi), 154, 162

"Brief Reflections on Two Hot Shots" (Jones), 97

Brill, A. A., 3

Bromfield, Louis, 44, 61

Brown, Norman O., 7

Bruccoli, Matthew T., 225

Brustein, Robert, 118, 126–27

Buechner, Frederick, 67–68, 297, 303

Burning Daylight (London), 241, 242, 244–46, 251, 257

Burns, John Horne, 18, 21, 25, 63, 174, 177, 293

Burroughs, William, 23, 179

Bus Stop (Inge), xiii, 123, 126, 129–30, 132, 133, 187, 204, 245

Cain, James M., 18, 22

Caine Mutiny, The (Wouk), 238

Cain's Book (Trocchi), 25

Calamus (Whitman), 1, 35, 105, 151, 193

Calder-Marshall, Arthur, 255, 259

"Caliban on Prospero: A Psychoanalytic Study of the Novel *Seize the Day*, by Saul Bellow" (Weiss), 232

Callaghan, Morley, 290–91

Call of the Wild, The (London), 259

Camino Real (Williams), 108, 110–11, 120, 177

Cannibals and Christians (Mailer), 290, 292

Cantor, Gilbert M., 10

Capote, Truman, 46–50, 51, 154

Cargill, Oscar, 200

Carpenter, Edward, 14, 18

"Casual Incident, A" (Farrell),
    16–17
Catcher in the Rye, The
    (Salinger), 62
Cat on a Hot Tin Roof
    (Williams), xiv, 33, 112–15,
    117, 176, 190, 196, 197, 301
Centaur, The (Updike), 173
Churchill, Wainwright, xi, 293
Circle of Sex, The (Arthur), 109
City and the Pillar, The (Vidal),
    xiv, 7, 22, 25–26, 28, 52, 58,
    120, 170, 171, 173, 177, 258,
    294, 302
City of Night, The (Rechy), 166,
    167, 169, 171, 179–80, 182,
    183, 258
Clayton, J. J., 234
Cleaver, Eldridge, 94–96, 99
Clock Without Hands
    (McCullers), 41, 58, 61
Cocteau, Jean, 37, 40
"Collaboration" (James), 12
Come Back, Little Sheba (Inge),
    121–123, 126, 128
Commager, Henry Steele, 174
Concert Pitch (Paul), 18, 118,
    169, 173
Confessional (Williams), 119
Confessions of Nat Turner, The
    (Styron), 103
Cooper, James Fenimore, 21, 62,
    92–93, 96, 103, 113, 186–88,
    295, 296
Cory, Donald Webster, 6, 8, 9,
    23, 164, 165–66, 167, 168, 175
Corydon (Gide), 6, 26
Crack-Up, The (Fitzgerald), 213
"Cross-Country Snow"
    (Hemingway), 270, 271
Crowley, Mart, 33, 165, 177,
    182, 303
Curzon, Daniel, x, 171, 172, 174,

177–78, 301

Dale, Allan, 13
Dana, Richard H., Jr., 73–74, 87,
    92, 103
Dark at the Top of the Stairs,
    The (Inge), 121, 123–24,
    126–27, 130, 137, 172
Dark Mother, The (Frank), 15,
    169, 303
Daughter of the Snows, A
    (London), 246
Death and Birth of David
    Markand, The (Frank), 15
Death in the Afternoon
    (Hemingway), 262
Death in Venice (Mann), 145
Death of Bessie Smith, The
    (Albee), 137, 138–39, 140,
    190
"Death of Love in The Sun Also
    Rises, The" (Spilka), 272
Deer Park, The (Mailer), 23, 24,
    283
"De Grey: A Romance" (James),
    200, 203–4
Delicate Balance, A (Albee),
    144–45
"Desire and the Black Masseur"
    (Williams), 103, 111, 119
Devils and Canon Barham, The
    (Wilson), 14–15
Disappearance, The (Wylie), 24
Dommergues, Pierre, 230
Donleavy, J. P., 24–25, 63
Dos Passos, John, 18, 22, 165,
    279, 294
Double Measure (Ford), 77
Down There on a Visit
    (Isherwood), 303
Dreiser, Theodore, 238
Drury, Allen, 162–63, 174
Dukore, Bernard, 144

Eastman, Max, 262
Edel, Leon, xii, 63, 198, 199, 200, 201, 206, 207, 209–10
Ellis, Havelock, 3, 175, 216
Enchafèd Flood, The (Auden), 71
End of My Life, The (Bourjaily), 21, 23, 62
"End of Something, The" (Hemingway), 271
Enfants Terribles, Les (Cocteau), 37
Europeans, The (James), 200, 203
Eustace Chisholm and the Works (Purdy), 87–88, 91

Fabre, Michel, 225
Falk, Signi, 109
Fall of Valor, The (Jackson), 20–21, 62, 70, 118, 176, 187, 190, 196
Fanon, Franz, 94
Farewell to Arms, A (Hemingway), 263–64, 267, 271, 272–73, 293
Farrell, James T., 16–17, 138, 173, 189, 279, 294
Faulkner, William, 38, 39–40, 51
Feminine Mystique, The (Friedan), 186
Ferenczi, Sandor, xiii
Fiedler, Leslie, xii, 93, 101, 103, 185–86, 187, 189, 203, 216, 219, 231, 238, 239, 270
Fifth Column, The (Hemingway), 268, 269–70, 271
Final Verdict (St. Johns), 252–53
Fire Next Time, The (Baldwin), 102
Fisher, Peter, xi, 8, 161

Fitzgerald, F. Scott, ix, 16, 38–40, 45, 61–62, 67, 177, 212–28, 238, 253, 262, 285, 290, 294, 299, 301
Fitzgerald, Zelda, 214, 216, 220, 223, 262, 276
Flanner, Janet, 275
Folded Leaf, The (Maxwell), 43–44, 52, 171, 214
Footloose in Arcadia (Noel), 72
Ford, G. H., 77
Ford, Gerald R., 305
Fortune and Men's Eyes (Herbert), 32, 145, 167, 170, 175
For Whom the Bell Tolls (Hemingway), 264, 265–68, 270–71, 273–75, 276, 282, 284
Frank, Waldo, 15, 169, 188, 302–3
Freud, Sigmund, 3–4, 37–38, 153, 173, 175, 186, 195, 231, 259–60, 261, 297
Freud and America (Ruitenbeck), 4
Freudianism and the Literary Mind (Hoffman), 4n
Friedan, Betty, 185–86
Friedman, Bruce Jay, 229–30, 238
From Here to Eternity (Jones), 23, 175, 196, 289
Fromm, Erich, 43, 255
Fuchs, Daniel, 238
Fuller, Henry Blake, 14–15, 174
"Fulvous Yellow" (Kaufmann), 157–58

Gallery, The (Burns), 21–22, 23, 89–90
Game, The (London), 241–44
Game of Fools (Barr), 31–32, 161, 170, 175

García Lorca, Federico, 133, 305
Gay Mystique, The (Fisher), 8
Geismar, Maxwell, xii, 218, 219, 228, 240, 245
Generation of Vipers, A (Wylie), 4–5, 185
Genet, Jean, 71–72, 87, 112, 124, 166–67, 183, 191, 211, 225, 258, 282, 297, 299–300, 303
Gerassi, John, 154
Gide, André, 6, 26, 27, 75, 77, 305
Ginger Man, The (Donleavy), 24–25, 63
Ginsberg, Allen, 8
Giovanni's Room (Baldwin), 21, 27–28, 57–59, 70, 97, 171, 176, 294
Glass Menagerie, The (Williams), 121
"God Rest You Merry, Gentlemen" (Hemingway), 263
Goodman, Paul, 8, 62–63, 64, 65, 175
Good Times / Bad Times (Kirkwood), 171
Gosse, Edmund, 202
Go Tell It on the Mountain (Baldwin), 54–57, 58, 97, 107, 171, 198–99
Goyen, William, 48–50, 51, 154
Great Gatsby, The (Fitzgerald), 220–24, 226–28
Green, Julien, 136
Gunnison, Foster, 18

Hair, 32
"Hands" (Anderson), 14, 15, 65–67, 176
"Hard Candy" (Williams), 180
Harris, Frank, 216
Hart, James D., 174

Hawthorne, Nathaniel, 278
Hayes, Richard, 118
Heart Is a Lonely Hunter, The (McCullers), 20, 155
Hemingway, Ernest, xiv, 15–17, 62, 89, 90, 92, 140, 164–65, 168, 173, 213, 214, 221, 225, 227, 262–80, 282–83, 284, 285, 289, 290–91, 293–94, 295, 301
Henderson the Rain King (Bellow), 104
Herbert, John, 32, 145, 165
Herlihy, James Leo, 182
Heroes and Orators (Phelps), 25, 176
Hero in America, The (Wecter), 161
Herzog (Bellow), 178, 233–38
"Hills Like White Elephants" (Hemingway), 270
History of Education in Antiquity, The (Marrou), 62
Hoffman, F. J., 4*n*
Holmes, Oliver Wendell, xiii
Homosexual and His Society, The (Cory and LeRoy), 164
Homosexual in America, The: A Subjective Approach (Cory), 6, 8, 23
Homosexuality (West), 9
Homosexuality: Disease or Way of Life? (Bergler), 5–6
Homosexuality and the Western Christian Tradition (Bailey), 9
Hooker, Evelyn, 8, 181
Hopper, James, 251
Hotchner, Aaron, 278
House of Bernardo Alba, The (Lorca), 133
House of Breath, The (Goyen), 48–50, 56, 59, 115, 173
Howe, Irving, 238

If Beale Street Could Talk (Baldwin), 102

Imre: a Memorandum (Mayne), 13–14

In a Yellow Wood (Vidal), 22

Inge, William, xiii, 33, 121–33, 136, 137–40, 141, 144, 146, 147–48, 168, 170, 172, 182, 185, 187, 190, 191, 204, 210, 218, 223, 298, 300–2

In Memoriam (Tennyson), 45

In Our Time (Hemingway), 269

Introduction to the Homophile Movement (Gunnison), 8

Invisible Glass, The (Wahl), 90–91, 169, 172

Isherwood, Christopher, 68, 169, 171, 176, 180–81, 233, 297, 303–4

It Can't Happen Here (Lewis), 18, 161, 175

Jackson, Charles, 18, 20–21, 25, 38, 41, 62, 70, 109, 169, 171, 187, 191, 196, 294, 303–4

James, Alice, 198, 199

James, Henry, v, ix, xii, xiv, 3, 12–13, 15, 47, 63–65, 108, 142, 170, 178, 197–211, 217, 218, 293, 294, 299, 300–1

James, Mary, 198, 199, 209

James, William, 3, 198, 199

Jeunes Filles, Les (Montherlant), 253

John Barleycorn (London), 251, 252, 259, 270, 290

"John Barleycorn Under Psychoanalysis" (Lay), 259

Johns, Cloudesley, 250, 253–54, 255, 296

Jones, James, 23, 98, 130, 174, 182

Jones, LeRoi, 32, 94–97, 99

Jung, Carl, 260

Kaufmann, Stanley, 157–58

Keats, John, 53

Kempton-Wace Letters, The (London), 252

Kings Row (Bellaman), 19–20, 21, 46, 55, 156–57, 169, 172

Kinsey, Alfred C., xi, 5, 18, 25, 26, 175

Kinsey Report, 5, 8, 22, 24, 41, 110

Kirkwood, James, 171

Kittredge, Charmian. *See* London, Charmian

Knock on Any Door (Motley), 22, 23, 179, 182, 190

Knowles, John, 44–46, 188, 295

Kostelanetz, Richard, 134–36

Krafft-Ebing, Baron Richard von, 76, 239, 297

Last Exit to Brooklyn (Selby), 166–68, 171, 295

Last of the Mohicans, The (Cooper), 92

Lawrence, D. H., xii, 21, 73n, 75–78, 79, 80, 82–84, 85, 88, 90, 92–93, 96, 103, 108, 109, 143, 187–88, 213, 228, 253, 258, 279, 282, 290, 294–95, 297, 299–300, 302

Lay, Wilfrid, 259

Leeds, Barry H., 290

Lehr, Wilson, 157

LeRoy, J. P., 164, 165, 166, 167, 168

Lesson of the Master, The (James), 64–65

"Letter to an American Mother" (Freud), 175

Le Vot, A., 220

Lewis, Ray, 26

Lewis, Robert W., 275
Lewis, Sinclair, 17–18, 20,
    155–56, 161, 196
Life Against Death (Brown), 7
"Light Man, A" (James), 12
"Light of the World, The"
    (Hemingway), 16, 164, 173
London, Charmian, 243, 251,
    253–55, 257, 260, 261
London, Jack, ix, xii, xiv, 62,
    72–74, 87, 90, 92, 103, 221,
    223, 228, 240–61, 263, 265,
    269, 270, 276–80, 282–83,
    284, 285, 289–92, 294,
    295–96, 297, 299, 302
London, Joan, 254, 259
Long Day's Dying, A
    (Buechner), 67–68, 176, 181,
    208
Longfellow, Henry Wadsworth,
    92
"Longstaff's Marriage" (James),
    200
Lorca. *See* García Lorca,
    Federico
*Lord Is My Shepherd and He
    Knows I'm Gay, The* (Perry),
    9
Lost Weekend, The (Jackson),
    41, 61, 118, 171, 175
*Love and Death in the American
    Novel* (Fiedler), 93, 185–86
Lucifer with a Book (Burns), 63

MacAlmon, Robert, 262
McCarthy, Joseph, 10, 154, 162
McCullers, Carson, 18, 20, 38,
    41, 58, 83–85, 87–88, 145–47,
    187, 245, 291, 294, 297
McIntosh, H. C., 165
McLaughlin, Richard, 26
Maddocks, Lewis I., 10
Mailer, Norman, xii, 23, 77–78,
    85–87, 99, 173, 221, 279–92,
    294, 295–97
Main Street (Lewis), 17–18,
    155–56, 173
Malcolm (Purdy-Albee), 145–46,
    148–49
Male and Female (Mead), 4, 44,
    185
Mammonart (Sinclair), 252
Mann, Thomas, 145
Marcuse, Herbert, 6–7, 79, 160
Marriage Below Zero, A (Dale),
    13, 15, 118
Marrou, Henri I., 62, 66, 72, 255
Martin Eden (London), 253
Marx, Karl, 256
Matlovitch, Leonard, 10
"Maude Evelyn" (James), 200
Maxwell, William, 43–44, 46, 52,
    55, 56, 188, 237, 296
Mayne, Xavier, 13–14
Mayoux, Jean-Jacques, xii
Mead, Margaret, 4, 44, 185–86,
    214, 304
Meeting by the River, A
    (Isherwood), 171, 303–4
Melville, Herman, xii, xv, 12, 13,
    42–43, 51, 52, 72–75, 78–85,
    87, 88, 90, 92–93, 96, 103,
    117, 168, 169, 182, 242, 278,
    289, 294, 297, 303
Memoirs (Williams), 107, 120n
Men Without Women (Woolf),
    162
Merle, Robert, 304
Michaud, Régis, 200
Miles, Catharine Cox, xn, 4, 174
Milford, Nancy, 216, 220
Miller, Arthur, 31, 238
Miller, Edwin Haviland, 278
Miller, Henry, 279
Miller, Merle, 22, 172, 173, 302
Millet, Kate, 185, 186, 288

Mineo, Sal, 32
Mr. Smith (Bromfield), 44
Mizener, Arthur, 38–39, 212–13, 214
Moby Dick (Melville), 82
Monahan, Michael, 72, 260
Montherlant, Henry de, 253, 305
Moore, H. T., 77
Mortal Antipathy, A (Holmes), xiii
"Mother of a Queen, The" (Hemingway), 16, 164–65, 262
Mother's Kisses, A (Friedman), 229–30
Motley, Willard, 22, 98, 130, 177, 179, 191
Moveable Feast, A (Hemingway), 214
Murphy, Dennis, 88–89
Murphy, Gerald, 225
Murray, Henry A., 42, 169
Myra Breckenridge (Vidal), 123*n*, 301–2
"Mysteries of the Joy Rio, The" (Williams), 180–81
"Myth of a New National Disease, The" (Bergler), 5

Naked and the Dead, The (Mailer), 23, 85–87, 91, 171
Nathan, Peter, 70, 257
Natural Affection (Inge), 121, 124, 130–31
Nephew, The (Purdy), 118, 140, 158–59, 176, 177
Newton, Huey, 97
Nietzsche, Friedrich, 256
Niles, Blair, 18, 20, 156, 165
Nixon, Richard M., 10
"No Competition" (Lehr), 156–57

Noel, Joseph, 72, 252
Notebooks (Fitzgerald), 16
Notes of a Son and Brother (James), 198, 199, 201
Notre-Dame des Fleurs (Genet), 297
Novels of Henry James, The (Cargill), 200
Numbers (Rechy), 178, 183

O'Connor, Richard, xiv, 251, 253, 257, 259
Of Mice and Men (Steinbeck), xiii
Of Time and the River (Wolfe), 17, 48, 65–68, 231
O'Hara, John, 212
Old Man and the Sea, The (Hemingway), 264, 268, 271, 275, 278
Omoo (Melville), 73
"One Arm" (Williams), 119, 183
One-Dimensional Man, The (Marcuse), 7
Opus 21 (Wylie), 24
Ordonez, Antonio, 278
Orpheus Descending (Williams), 108, 116–17
Other Voices, Other Rooms (Capote), 46–48, 49, 50, 56, 115, 170, 172–73, 187, 255
Our America (Frank), 188
"Outing, The" (Baldwin), 56–57, 59

Packard, Vance, 7
Pages from an Abandoned Journal (Vidal), 53
"Pages from Cold Point" (Bowles), 50–51, 54, 158, 171
Parents' Day (Goodman), 62–63
Partington, Blanche, 253
Paul, Elliott, 18, 169, 173

Perkins, Maxwell, 220–21
Perrein, Michèle, 305
Perry, Reverend Troy, 9
Petit Jules, Le (Perrein), 305
Phelps, Robert, 25, 176
Picnic (Inge), 122–23, 125, 126,
  128–29, 146, 187, 189, 190
Pierre; or, The Ambiguities
  (Melville), 42, 169, 171
Pine, Hester, 19
Piper, Henry Dan, 212, 214
Plato, 7
Ploscowe, Judge Morris, 10
Podhoretz, Norman, 101
Poe, Edgar Allan, 258, 259
Popular Book, The (Hart), 174
Portnoy's Complaint (Roth), 229
Presidential Papers, The
  (Mailer), 284, 285, 291
"Primeval Mitosis, The"
  (Cleaver), 95
Principles of Psychology, The
  (James), 3
Prisoner of Sex, The (Mailer),
  288
Problem of Modern Ethics, A
  (Symonds), 202
Proust, Marcel, 53, 99, 111, 191,
  204, 205, 207, 302, 303, 305
"Prussian Officer, The"
  (Lawrence), 75–78, 79, 80,
  82–84, 86, 87–88, 89, 91, 103,
  231, 274, 287, 294–95, 297
Psychology of Fascism, The
  (Nathan), 257
"Pupil, The" (James), 3, 12,
  63–65, 66, 170, 178, 197
Purdy, James, 87–88, 90, 118,
  140, 146, 148–49, 158–59,
  291, 294, 305

Quatrefoil (Barr), 90–91, 176
"Queen Is Dead, The" (Selby),
  166, 167
Querelle de Brest (Genet), 71,
  72, 87

Rabbit, Run (Updike), 173
Rahv, Philip, 238
Rechy, John, 137, 169, 174,
  178–79, 181, 182–83
Redburn (Melville), 73, 182
Reflections in a Golden Eye
  (McCullers), 20, 83–85, 91,
  170
Reich, Wilhelm, 6, 279
Reik, Theodore, 238
Remembrance of Things Past
  (Proust), 111
"Resemblance Between a Violin
  and a Coffin, The" (Williams),
  40, 61
Rimbaud, Arthur, 72
Road, The (London), 257, 260
Roman Spring of Mrs. Stone, The
  (Williams), 116
Rose Tattoo, The (Williams),
  113, 116
Roth, Philip, 137, 143, 144,
  229–30, 238
Ruitenbeek, H. M., 3
Rutenberg, Michael E., 136, 137,
  142–43, 145

St. Johns, Adela, 252, 255
Salinger, J. D., 62
Sandbox, The (Albee), 137, 138
Sartre, Jean-Paul, 125, 183, 200,
  211
"Saul Bellow" (Fiedler), 239
Season of Comfort, The (Vidal)
  52–53, 58, 70, 170, 172, 302
Sea-Wolf, The (London), 74,
  240–42, 246–48, 250, 255,
  257, 264, 300
Secor, Neal, 9

Seize the Day (Bellow), 232

Selby, Herbert, 166–68, 298

Separate Peace, A (Knowles), 44–46, 146, 208, 295

Serenade (Cain), 18, 22, 173, 176

Sergeant, The (Murphy), 88–89

Set This House on Fire (Styron), 231, 298

Sex and Personality: Studies in Masculinity and Femininity (Terman and Miles), x*n*, 4, 174

Sex and the Law (Ploscowe), 10

Sexual Behavior in the Human Male (Kinsey). *See* Kinsey Report

Sexual Inversion (Ellis), 3

Sexual Politics (Millet), 186

Sexual Revolution, The: Toward a Self-Governing Character Structure (Reich), 6

Sexual Wilderness, The (Packard), 7–8

Shakespeare, William, 218

Shaw, Irwin, 238

"Short Happy Life of Francis Macomber, The" (Hemingway), 264–65, 275, 276, 291

Shuman, R. Baird, 126

"Simple Enquiry, A" (Hemingway), 15, 89, 91

Sinclair, Upton, 252

Single Man, A (Isherwood), 68, 169, 177, 179, 181, 233, 303

Small Boy and Others, A (James), 198

Small Craft Warnings (Williams), 119–20

"Snows of Kilimanjaro, The" (Hemingway), 263, 270

Society and the Healthy

Homosexual (Weinberg), 302

"Soldier's Home" (Hemingway), 270

Something You Do in the Dark (Curzon), x, 167, 171, 172, 174–76, 178, 301

Sontag, Susan, 268

Soul on Ice (Cleaver), 94, 97

Spencer, Herbert, 256

Spilka, Mark, 272

Stein, William Bysshe, 263

Steinbeck, John, xiii

Sterling, George, 254, 255, 278, 296

Stern (Roth), 229–30

Strange Brother (Niles), 18, 156, 165, 175

Streetcar Named Desire, A (Williams), 108–10, 114, 117, 123, 176

"Strike" (Selby), 167–68

Strunsky, Anna, 250, 255

Studies in Classic American Literature (Lawrence), 73*n*

Studies in the Psychology of Sex (Ellis), 3

Studs Lonigan (Farrell), 16–17, 22, 161, 164, 165, 173

Styron, William, 103–4, 231, 293, 297, 298

Sud (Green), 136

Suddenly Last Summer (Williams), 118–19, 147, 170, 181

Summer Brave (Inge), 123, 129

Sun Also Rises, The (Hemingway), 263, 272, 275, 289

Sweet Bird of Youth (Williams), 107, 109, 116, 121

Symonds, J. A., 202, 300

Tea and Sympathy (Anderson),

31, 172, 174, 195, 295
Tell Me How Long the Train's Been Gone (Baldwin), 59–60, 100–1, 102, 171, 301
Tender Is the Night (Fitzgerald), 16, 164, 216, 223–28, 291
Tennyson, Alfred, 43, 45
Terman, Lewis M., x*n*, 4, 174
That Summer in Paris (Callaghan), 290
That Winter (Miller), 22, 173
Thielicke, Helmut, 9
Thirsty Evil, A (Vidal), 53, 172
This Day's Death (Rechy), 169, 174, 175, 183
This Finer Shadow (McIntosh), 165, 167
This Side of Paradise (Fitzgerald), 217–18
"Three-Day Blow, The" (Hemingway), 271
Three Essays on the Theory of Sexuality (Freud), 261
"Time of Her Time, The" (Mailer), 280, 283, 285, 289
Tiny Alice (Albee), 142–44, 300
To Have and Have Not (Hemingway), 15, 140, 176–77, 263, 270
Toilet, The (Jones), 32
Trilling, Diana, 86, 185
Tripp, C. A., xiii
Trocchi, Alexander, 25
Turnbull, Andrew, 213, 214, 215, 216, 223
Turn of the Screw, The (James), 12, 47, 170, 173, 197
Twenty-Seven Wagons Full of Cotton (Williams), 110
"Two on a Party" (Williams), 180
Two Years Before the Mast

(Dana), 73–74, 78, 93
Tynan, Kenneth, 262
Typee (Melville), 78

"Unexpected, The" (London), 241, 246
Updike, John, 173
"Up in Michigan" (Hemingway), 279
Uris, Leon, 238

Van Buren, Martin, 161
Verlaine, Paul, 304
Victim, The (Bellow), 230–31, 238
Vidal, Gore, xiv, 7, 22, 23, 25–27, 28–29, 32, 44, 51–54, 58, 61, 114, 123*n*, 162, 168, 172, 174–75, 177, 179, 238, 239, 294, 295, 297, 301–2
View from the Bridge, A (Miller), 31, 155
Visconti, Lucchino, 145

Wahl, Loren, 90–91, 92, 170, 177, 298
Watson, E. L. Grant, 78
Wecter, Dixon, 161
Weinberg, George, 293, 302
Weiss, Daniel, 232
Weltge, Ralph W., 9
West, D. J., 9
West, Nathanael, 238
Where's Daddy? (Inge), 124, 131, 190, 218
White Jacket (Melville), 12, 72–74
"White Negro, The" (Mailer), 290
Whitman, Walt, 1, 18, 35, 79, 105, 151, 193, 300, 305
Who's Afraid of Virginia Woolf? (Albee), 137–42, 190
Why Are We in Viet-Nam?

(Mailer), 280–82, 286, 288, 289

Wilde, Oscar, 199, 202, 218, 304

Williams, Tennessee, 33, 38, 40, 61, 103, 107–21, 125, 129, 131, 133–34, 136, 137–39, 141, 142, 144, 145, 147–48, 170, 172, 177, 180, 182–83, 185, 189, 190, 196, 210, 228, 262, 299, 300–1

Wilson, Edmund, 14–15

Winesburg, Ohio (Anderson), 14, 154–55

Withim, Phil, 78

Wolfe, Thomas, 17, 65–66, 297

Women in Love (Lawrence), 243, 282, 297

Woolf, Virginia, 262

World in the Evening, The (Isherwood), 169, 174, 176, 177, 179, 303

"World's Fair, The" (Fitzgerald), 16

Wouk, Herman, 238

Wright, Richard, 97

Wylie, Philip, 4–5, 24, 138, 168, 185, 195, 229

Young, Philip, 263, 264, 268

"Zenner Trophy, The" (Vidal), 53, 302

Zoo Story, The (Albee), 134–36, 300